Remember the Fifth of November

By

Michael Fitzalan

Faith, here's an equivocator, that could
Swear in both the scales against either scale;
Who committed treason enough for God's sake,
Yet could not equivocate to heaven.
Macbeth, Act Two, Scene Three

THIS IS A WORK OF FACTION

Copyright © 2014 by Michael Fitzalan

All rights reserved. No part of this book may be reproduced, stored, or transmitted by any means—whether auditory, graphic, mechanical, or electronic—without written permission of the author, except in the case of brief excerpts used in critical articles and reviews.

Chapter 1 – The Fire – i

The morning of the 8th November 1605, at Holbeche House, in Staffordshire, was peculiar for its lack of birdsong. The occupants had been tending to a man recently blinded and filling the time that they waited for their companions by talking.

The eerie silence outside went unnoticed.

"We have no news of Bates and Digby," Catesby admitted, "I was hoping we would meet them here by now. I cannot think why they have been delayed."

Catesby stood at six foot tall, so it was his preference to sit amongst friends. He positioned himself at the deal dining table on one of the matching chairs. He had dark hair, a thin face, which was handsome and aquiline, but he looked grave, as if he never smiled or took anything lightly. Despite his thin frame, he was one of the most dashing and courageous horsemen in the country. He was normally cheerful and brim-full of confidence, even early in the morning. Everyone knew he was concerned.

The house was cold on that misty morning but the sun had risen and the windows bathed the wainscoting and floorboards in light. Percy was a tall man, too, with a broad beard and a good-looking face but his beard and head had been sprinkled with white hairs; his head being whiter than his beard. He stooped slightly as he moved across the room to join Catesby at the table.

Normally, he was sprightly even though a decade older than his companion, but due to lack of sleep, he felt a great deal older than forty-two. He wondered how old age would treat him as he leant his hands on the table.

"Well, I do not pretend to understand events. We need to ship more *sack* from London, do we not?" he declared hesitantly, rubbing his ruddy face, he bowed his head after speaking, looking down at his big feet and short legs. Tiredness and despondency weighed heavily on his shoulders.

He could not understand what had gone wrong with their venture. They had planned to move their merchandise as quickly as possible and, yet, they had been prevented from delivering the goods by the absence of those organising the transport.

"We need to discuss our next move with the others," Catesby warned, his voice was soft; lack of sleep was fraying his nerves, too. "We wait."

"We have to arrange the transport of the *sack,*" Percy argued, stretching his long back as he leant on the tabletop. "We have customers waiting. Time and tide wait for no man."

"What say you Ambrose? We made good time to get here, but the others might not be as quick off the mark; there's no harm in waiting a few hours that's the truth, what do you think?" he asked, turning to Rookwood who was tending poor blinded John Grant.

"Fire, fire!" screamed Wintour running into the room, holding a copper bucket that he had intended to fill at the well in the courtyard. He was pointing at the outbuilding where the thatch was burning. Terror masked his handsome face; he was of short stature but very valiant and strong.

"The house will catch!" cried Catesby, sending his chair tumbling backwards as he rose in panic. "Fill that pail!"

Inside, the house there was the sound of breaking glass, followed by rumbling on the boards. Incandescent balls of fire rolled across the floor. The gunpowder spread on the ground sizzled and fizzed as sparks flew off the deadly bombs. When the glass had smashed, there was commotion amongst the occupants as they realised that they had been '*fire-bombed*'. They used the blankets they had slept under to smother the fireballs.

Behind the runners were several members of a pyrotechnic troop who had set fire to strips of clothing coated in tar, which they, in turn, tossed through the broken windows. The same happened at the front of the house. These rags smouldered, releasing thick smoke, and sparking the gunpowder making it crack like gunfire.

Soon three of the occupants appeared at the back door, Wintour, and the two Wright brothers, panicking wildly as they fled the infernos. As far as they were concerned, the house was, now, well and truly on fire. They carried copper coal buckets wanting to collect water from the well behind the house. They fully intended to put the fire out.

When the occupants dashed into the courtyard, the primed guns outside were fired. In each gun the lighted flax fuse, the match, was skillfully flicked onto the serpent lock, setting fire to the gunpowder in the pan. The flame from the pan entered the barrel of the gun and ignited the gunpowder that had been poured into it and the lead ball flew from the end of the barrel.

A furious fusillade of musket balls greeted the fugitives who had gone to fetch water.

Thomas Wintour, who had dashed into the courtyard to fetch water in his pail, heard a massive explosion and realised with horror that he had been shot in the shoulder.

At one moment, he was running towards the well, the next he threw the copper bucket down, as in a fit of temper, clasped his right shoulder and watched blood ooze into the linen cloth of his Belgian chemise. Looking up at the cause of his pain, Wintour saw a mass of men, some standing behind whiffs of smoke coming from the musket barrels. He tried to warn the others who were following with the same idea of extinguishing the fire.

The next shot struck the elder Wright, John, and after him the younger Wright, Kit, then, fourthly, a bullet found Ambrose Rookwood's head, sending him spiralling to the ground. Thomas Wintour, John Wright, Christopher Wright, and Ambrose Rookwood, had all been shot. Several more shots resounded around the courtyard, some struck their target others ricocheted off walls or struck the bricks and mortar. Thirty-six bullets had been fired; few had reached their intended target.

The Wright brothers had taken the brunt of the blasts and were moaning as they rolled around on the ground in agony. They had been hit at least six times.

John managed to stagger to his feet; he was too stunned to think straight. He was unsure where he had been hit or how many times.

Wintour reeled backwards at first, and, although wounded, he managed to make it to the house, cowering in the scullery, the smoke was too dense for him to enter the main residence, gritting his teeth with frustration. He could not understand what was going on. They were all unarmed and were being fired at for 'the devil knew' what reason.

John Wright, who had managed to scramble to his feet and stay upright, despite the pain, stepped backwards, clutching his stomach, where the wound oozed blood. He shuffled back to the wall and slid down it, determined not to pass out. Meanwhile, his younger brother had stopped moaning and writhing, he lay motionless. Groaning in pain, John sat against the wall, staring at his dead brother.

Ambrose Rookwood, whose handsome face was contorted in pain, tried to scramble back to the house but his short legs gave way under him. He was bleeding profusely from two wounds, one to his head, and one to his right hand.

"Dear Kit, my little brother, Christopher," John mumbled before becoming unconscious.

Ambrose was twenty-seven, Kit was thirty-five, John was thirty-seven, they were in their prime.

Before the blast - ii

It was the twilight before the dawn. Vaguely visible were the dark shapes of the rolling hills where wisps of ghostly mist snaked through the hoar frost. A gentle breeze full of icy air ruffled the bare branches of the copses lying scattered across the landscape.

On a flat piece of greensward, close to the river, stood Holbeche House, which had been built five years previously, was soon to be burnt down to the ground. The building consisted of a central block of three bays, with two storeys, an attic with windows, and projecting side wings with Dutch Gables at each end. The first floor and attic provided an ideal area to set up a deadly arc of fire. It was a handsome house with wainscoting and wood panelling inside, built in the new style, the talk of the Staffordshire countryside.

Hidden from view by the stark branches of a clump of trees in the copse, overlooking the courtyard at the back of the house, stood a man wrapped in a biscuit brown wool cape.

Striding stealthily towards him was another man, one hand on the hilt of his sword and the other holding the black knot that secured his crow-black cape. The figure crept carefully, on tip-toe, over the dewy grass, as he approached the bare branches, it was as if he were avoiding serpents on the ground. He was a man of soldierly bearing, wrapped in a thick, hooded cloak, looking like death but for the absence of scythe.

The man waiting by the tree turned and spoke first. He was a man with a large broad face, of pale complexion, a big nose, and one of his hands had been maimed by some shot from a bullet.

"Sir Richard Walsh, High Sheriff of Worcestershire, you come readily on the hour," whispered Griffin Markham jovially, turning from his excellent vantage point of the fugitive's house. He smiled as if their laying in ambush was all just a game.

Both men were tall and broad, fighting men, of equal stature and equal status, though Griffin Markham had fought at the siege of Rouen with the Earl of Essex and commanded the *Connaught Horse* in Ireland whereas Walsh commanded the local militia.

"Why if it isn't Sir Markham Griffin, you are a long way from Sherwood Forest, are you not? Yet I heard you were exiled, how is this so?" Walsh spoke softly but he could not hide the shock in his voice. His humour was not lost on Markham, he was from Nottingham, and Walsh was referring to the old outlaw of King John's reign, Robin Hood.

Walsh had met Markham at Derby when King James was making his procession through the kingdom as part of his coronation celebrations, riding through major towns on his way to London. He admired the man rumoured to be the finest swordsman in all of England.

Markham, in turn, liked Walsh's easy manner and admired his organisation; he had assembled a militia that would ensure no one survived the ambush that they were about to mount. Pulling the hood off his head and letting it fall to his shoulders, the sheriff removed his right glove, black like his cloak, to shake Markham's hand. The other knight shot a hand from under his dark beige cloak and did like wise. Their eyes locked briefly, both gave a firm, hard handshake, the sheriff serious, Markham still smiling slightly. Both men noticed how warm their hands were and how cold the damp air was, they were quick to return their hands to their leather gauntlets.

"I am incognito, you know, on the orders of Lord Salisbury, our master Robert Cecil, Secretary of State, officially I am in Flanders, and I have not been allowed to return to my beloved Nottingham."

"He mentioned he would be sending someone but I had never dreamt he would send such an illustrious warrior," the Sherriff replied, stunned by Cecil's ingenuity, "I thought all the old valiants had been executed or were in the Tower. It is very good to have you here."

"Thank you, Kingswinford is infinitely preferable to fields in Flanders and the Staffordshire hills remind me of my home in Ollerton. I feel welcome, but, I am here solely to observe the operation and act only should something goes wrong."

"So I have the responsibility, still" Walsh exclaimed smiling broadly.

"I know that you have rehearsed well and that you concealed the troops successfully, all to your credit. I shall let Cecil know that you have followed orders to the letter."

"I thank you for that, the Secretary of State is a hard man to please. We are glad to have you here in any role and I am very pleased to see you again."

"I look forward to breaking some bread with you after we have dealt with the business at hand. How many men have you gathered here?"

"More or less two hundred, I should reckon."

"Two hundred against six, maybe a dozen at most, I like your odds, let's cry '*havoc*' and release the dogs of war."

"As per our plan."

"Cecil has always said: 'Let us plan the work and work the plan'. You know how he likes to ensure there is no room for error."

"The gunpowder has been left in the house, we spread it over the floor before they arrived."

"Excellent, to look like coal dust, as instructed. That should have explosive consequences. Who is there?" Markham pointed needlessly but dramatically in the direction of Holbeche House.

"Six of them definitely, others have been coming and going, our intelligence says there are ten at most in the house. We have established from various reports that have come in from the south that we have the main body of those wanted. They include Robert Catesby, the two Wright brothers Christopher and John, Thomas Percy, Ambrose Rookwood and John Grant."

"Good, they have fallen into the trap laid, they were advised to gather here!"

"Were these half dozen men once friends of yours? Yet you attend their execution."

"In another life some of them were; now they are traitors condemned to death. My presence here is also a warning lest I forget to whom I owe my loyalty and life. Cecil convinced King James to spare the Trinity at the Tower and they have gone on to sin again, their punishment is overdue, they escaped execution once, as I did."

"You were to be beheaded?"

"Indeed, I was. Do I not appear like a haunted man?"

"A man who values his life, certainly. I have had orders to ensure that no one of the main body survives."

"I am aware, execute them, now, and save them the humiliation of watching their genitalia burnt in front of them."

"I agree, a bullet is a better bet than being hung and drawn, a horrible way to suffer, then quartered, it is a sight I have only seen once, the image of that man's face will stay with me forever; we are doing them a service."

"As I see it, they were condemned many months ago, they have had their stay of execution. Only the main culprits are knights, a beheading for them, worse for the others. I for one would prefer a clean kill; how long until we strike?"

Markham had breakfasted on the hard tack biscuits that had been handed out to the militiamen, he was already thinking of lunch.

"The sun is rising, not long, now, another hour two."

"Your men are getting ready?"

"They will be so at my signal."

"Good!"

The Sheriff waved a yellow silk handkerchief.

Three middle-aged Midlands men were chatting quietly, leaning on their matchlock stands, like farmers leaning on their rakes, by their feet were the stocks of the five foot weapons and the barrels they nurtured in the crook of their arms. At first, they did not see the sign for action but another soldier who was more alert ran up and pointed at the waving material. The men were galvanised into action by the signal. Following procedure that they practised endlessly in drill, and in battle, against the Spanish, the old hands went through the rigmarole of preparing their muskets.

They cleaned and primed their weapons in the time that followed. It was a lengthy and involved process, ensuring the musket was prepared and ready to fire efficiently. Misfires and problems with corrupt powder were commonplace and needed to be avoided. Gunpowder was notoriously unreliable if it got damp, so all the locks, pans and barrels had to be dried with wadding, either wool or linen cloths. The stock and barrels had to be similarly dry to stop them slipping and causing accidents. The powder had to be checked for efficacy. It was a lengthy and time-consuming business but their quarry was going nowhere and there were enough militiamen with swords and pikes to prevent an escape should one be attempted.

All the marksmen loaded their weapons in the same quick and efficient way; gunpowder was poured into the barrel and packed in hard with a thin ramrod. Then, almost in unison each marksman dug in his satchel for a lead ball, popped it carelessly into the muzzle of the gun and deftly returned to their bag to retrieve a piece of wool wadding to hold the ball in place. This they rammed home with their ramrod sticks. All this took only a minute and a half so skilled were they in the art of musketry.

Their weapons were, then, primed and ready to kill. All that was needed was to set the musket barrels on their supporting stands, empty gunpowder into the priming pan and cover it with one hand to protect it from blowing away, then press a lighted piece of flax into a metal trigger called the serpent. It was relatively simple compared to a crossbow.

The idea was to fire a volley of shots at the enemy and hope someone was hit at some stage. They were dangerous and clumsy to use but deadly in the right hands and that trinity of men were the right hands. All the final preparation would be done when they were in position.

Theirs was not the only group; their eagle-eyed companion was not the only one looking for the sheriff's signal. A wave of movement like a mistral blowing through a summer meadow, saw men hurrying to load weapons draw swords and get into their allotted positions. The original trio of marksmen would be joined by a dozen more, the group making thirty-six.

Their position was to be the courtyard at the back of the house. A similar group of men was preparing to pepper the front of the house once the fire was started.

The siege had been rehearsed, thoroughly, the day before the arrival of the fugitives at a similar location; Cecil wanted to eradicate the chance of any mistakes, his whole plot to discredit the Catholics relied on ensuring that Catesby and Percy were killed outright.

They were nobles and would be able to speak before their execution. They might even have a chance to tell the truth. The others were commoners who would be hung drawn and quartered, demoralised and keen to settle their affairs, they would be malleable.

As the sun painted the horizon white, stratus clouds scudded across the sky, the hoar frost at their feet glistened, feet slipped, slipshod steps jarred knees, everyone busied at their activities, fulfilling them to the best of their ability. Their religious zeal helped them ignore the cold and damp air. They were repaying all Catholics for all their treachery.

In silence, and with vengeance in their minds, the troops moved as quietly as their unwieldy equipment allowed. Already, they knew that they were dealing with Catholic conspirators who had tried to unseat James.

It was another *Main Plot* carried our by the followers of the old religion, perhaps? Again, more than likely, the Catholics planned to remove King James and replace him with his cousin Arbella, or like the later *Bye Plot*; they wanted to kidnap the King and replace him with a Catholic king. The Catholics were constantly plotting, so Cecil made it be known.

There was no surprise amongst the militiamen; after all, they expected nothing but treachery from the Catholics that they, now, besieged. The Catholics had always been painted as Papists, loyal to a foreign leader, not the King. Stories of the Armada survived, the telling improved by seventeen years of embellishment.

The Earl of Essex, a friend of these Catholics, had turned on the Queen; Raleigh was imprisoned; and Jesuits priests were invading from Douai. Trouble came 'not in single spies but in battalions'. These troops were all hand picked Puritans or Anglicans who wore their faith practically if not yet zealously. They shared a hatred of Catholics 'conspirators' and a common hunger for extra coins, which this adventure would provide.

Inside the house, the occupants were slowly coming around. Stephen Littleton and Thomas Wintour had left temporarily for 'Pepperhill', the Shropshire residence of Sir John Talbot, which lay ten miles away to get food. When they returned, the sheriff decided to launch the raid.

A group of thirty-six marksmen marched into the courtyard, taking care to make as little noise as possible, leather soles made only slight sound on cobblestone. Their lighted flax matches were held in their left hands along with the barrel rests, looking like tridents with their forks shrunk and the middle removed, or an old-fashioned, two prong, pitchfork with a shrunken head. In the cup of their hand they held the stocks of their muskets, slung over their left shoulders, the flax smoked ominously like some incense on a snaking, flaccid ribbon. Their leader signalled them to stop and in perfect unison, the troop stopped in a precise manner as if the signal froze their limbs and, as rehearsed with the minimum of rustling and other sounds, they unshouldered their arms.

Afterwards, they adopted the 'poise' position, which was holding the musket and its stand in separate hands, left for the musket, right for the stand, keeping gun and fuse as far apart as possible as the flax match was still smouldering in the right hand. Then, the noise broke out. With much rustling, clicks, and metallic ticks, they joined musket to rest; it was a loud cacophony of sound, echoing off the walls, which surrounded the courtyard.

Still no one came forth from the house or appeared in the windows, the fugitives, it occurred to many militiamen, were exhausted from their ride from London. Word of their arrival had been sent to the troops' camp last night before the explosion that has woken them. The gunpowder left for the morning raid had somehow picked up a spark from the fire and blown up prematurely. It had blinded John Grant.

The marksmen took forth their matches, those whose flax tapers had extinguished lit theirs from companions in their trios. They blew off any extra gunpowder that might cause the barrel to explode, put the base of the barrel-rest on the cobbled ground and together they cocked their matchlock, revealing the serpent 's' of the firing pan.

They were ready to kill.

By mid-morning Walsh's men had surrounded the house. The first part of the plan was to set fire to the thatch of the old outbuilding at the back of the house, drawing the occupants out of the house to extinguish the fire. This ploy had already resulted in one corpse, one mortally wounded, dying slowly, and unconscious, and one, further, rolling around in agony.

The Blast - iii

Coals from the morning camp fires had been wrapped in several layers of cloth, shirts stolen from the house, in fact, and, by the time the runners arrived, were burning with billowing smoke. These runners passed the musketeers and when close enough, threw the bundles through the broken windows at the back of the house, hoping to drive the remaining men through the front door and into a fresh fusillade.

Robert Catesby and Thomas Percy were busily extinguishing the fires burning on the floorboards when the flaming rags hit the floor. The smoke was becoming too much. There were so many small fires and the trail of gunpowder made them crackle and fizz producing more acrid smog.

Poor John Grant had been blinded by a spark from the fire on the previous evening. The ambushers had not expected the fugitives to light a fire on their arrival, after all they were meant to be hiding. The blast, which had seemed to ignite dust, had been the result of too liberal a scattering of powder. The gunpowder had been laid by the siege party the day before the fugitives arrived, in order to ensure that the fire started in the morning would force the occupants out.

The use of gunpowder explosions after the initial fire was Cecil's idea and it was hoped that would be enough to ensure the fugitives evacuated the building, running directly into the firing from the muskets. He did not necessarily want the house totally burnt down unless there was no alternative. Unfortunately, the militiamen had other ideas, smoke and fires were exciting sights; this was a bonfire, a hell on earth for the sinners hiding in the house.

Grant started choking, he could not see the incendiary bombs that had been thrown in through the windows but he heard the thud as they landed, and as each one smouldered, he breathed in more smoke.

The two able bodied men carried the poor man between them, even though they had both been injured by the explosion of the previous evening. Catesby and Percy were considered the main culprits. It was those two that Cecil wanted executed by musket ball.

"Do not fear, there is nothing to worry about, there are soldiers outside. Stand by me, Mister John," said Catesby, "and we will all surrender together."

The three men stood close inside the door of the house, poor John rested on Catesby and Percy's shoulders, one on either side as the blind man's guide. They ventured outside to surrender.

When the musketeers saw them, their guns were ready to be fired. On sight of their targets, the marksmen took the lighted flax, smouldering in the serpentine lock, lowered the 'serpent' down into the pan, allowing it to light the gunpowder. The flame from the pan entered the barrel of the gun and ignited the gunpowder that had been poured into it and the lead balls exploded from the muskets in a deafening volley of sound and smoke.

Thirty-six men were arranged in an arc around the doorway, twelve groups of three and they fired in turn one after another like clockwork. Catesby and Percy, standing side by side, fell, struck by the same lead ball. Grant blinded and having lost his tall escorts floundered in the front of the house, his hands outstretched, listening to the cannonade of discharging guns. The ninth group of musketeers managed to hit the moving target, and that was only because he was stumbling directly towards them.

A lead ball hit Grant in the thigh; another in the lung and the third smashed his collarbone. It was the bullet in the lung that felled him, he collapsed on his knees as if in prayer but his hands were limp by his side, his eyes were still closed but he gasped, he could have been pleading for help but no words came from his mouth. The lack of air, in his lungs, made him topple over sideways in a faint, and there he lay, listening to the gurgling sound coming from his chest and his last gasps.

Dear, loyal, Percy had been shot through the head, the bullet entering through his cheek before ricocheting off to top of his jawbone and passing out through his ear into the neck of Catesby and out the other side before feebly hitting a window frame, all its energy spent.

The percussion knocked him down and blood from ruptured arteries and veins seeped down his throat choking him to death before he could die from loss of blood.

Catesby, bleeding profusely, managed to crawl back inside the house, and clutched hold of the miniature of his wife, painted by Nicholas Hilliard, in one hand. His other covered the first hole in his neck, he could feel the blood ooze through his fingers and hear the blood dripping on the floorboards from the second wound caused by the bullet passing out of the other side.

He lay on his side, looking at his wife's beautiful face and waited to die. He prayed for his family and for his soul.

The marksman, John Streete, loudly claimed that it was his shot that had felled two with only one blow. The other two in his trio slapped his back and congratulated him. The other soldiers rushed into the house, the ones at the back capturing Wintour.

They were followed by further troops who had pails of water or brooms, standing by to extinguish the fire and sweep up the gunpowder from the floor. The operation had been a success, all the fugitives had been killed or been captured.

There were no injuries among the one hundred and ninety eight people involved in the siege and the house was only partially burnt and would be restored easily, which would please its owner.

Once all the commotion had died down, the fires had been extinguished, the floors cleaned, the bodies removed and put on a waiting cart, it was deemed safe for the bound Thomas Wintour to be returned to the house. Markham walked into the hall where Wintour sat on a stool and drawing his sword, he dismissed the guards who had bound poor Wintour.

"Do you intend to run me through, here and now as I sit shackled and defenceless?"

"You are the only one left of the main conspirators, there are too many witnesses, the others are dead or dying, and they will not survive."

"So, you will see me pardoned like you? I can become Cecil's puppy and betray my friends?" asked Wintour, almost spitting with disgust. "But, what crime have I committed? We merely followed Cecil's instructions. I knew we should not trust him, I tried to warn everyone. Why should we be condemned and why are you our judge?"

"I have stood on the gallows, you have not. Do not judge me as I do not judge you."

"My fine sword, ordered and paid for four months ago, though not drawn has been taken from me, please ensure it is returned to me."

Wintour stared at Markham impassively, Markham looked at Wintour with sympathy.

"The sheriff's men have already stripped the others of their valuables, their boots and silk stockings, but Thomas, I will ask the sheriff's assistant to find it for you. How is your shoulder?"

"The wound is but a scratch, the ball merely bruised the skin, the blood has been stemmed by my handkerchief, any worse and I would have been put on the cart with the dying."

"A dim view!"

"I heard the men talking, we are to be treated like carcasses; that is why I worry about my sword."

"You have more to worry about than that my old friend. Although, after the shocks you have had, it is better to think on a lost sword. I have my problems too, alas, I have lost Bates and Digby; they were meant to be here."

"What will happen to me?"

"You will be taken from here to Worcester and if well enough you will be taken to the Tower of London. Robert, your brother, and Stephen Litteton are still unaccounted for but Guido will confess in time."

"Guido, he is held, for what crime?"

"Surely, that is why you are here."

"Do not pretend to me that you do not know, you were there when Cecil made the arrangements for us to be here. We are here to move a consignment of *sack* while Guido guards the consignment in London."

"He has been seized by the guards at Westminster Palace."

"And why so seized?"

"He was plotting to blow-up the House of Parliament."

Wintour's face froze, the enormity of the charges filtered through his confusion.

"With thirty six barrels of *sack*?"

"A barrel of gunpowder was discovered, the rest of the barrels have been seized by Cecil's men and taken to the tower."

"I knew he would never pay."

"I fear it is you who will have to pay."

"I see how it plays out, we are considered conspirators and we will be tried as traitors. No doubt Cecil will give us our scripts like the witnesses at the trail of the Earl of Essex."

"There is nothing I can do."

"And if I do not comply, I will have a sword pushed through my innards?"

"This way you can put your affairs in order and with luck you might end up with Raleigh in the Tower or even working with me, spared execution and forever in Cecil's debt."

"What hell would that be?"

17

"A *living* hell over an eternity in heaven."

"I did not fear death until, today," Wintour remarked grimly.

"I would choose life, you are too young to be a martyr and the martyrs have all been created today, you would be a minor addition."

"Who survives from here?"

"Only Rookwood. I think he would advise you to stand trial, you have been pardoned once before."

"I think I have used up all my pardons, as you have, too. There is no hope for me but dear Ambrose, where is he?"

"He was almost loaded onto the cart, he had been knocked out by a ball grazing his head and bled profusely from a wound in his hand. He must have put it up to fend off the fusillade. He is being cleaned up now but you will be lead away separately."

"So it has come to this."

Foreword

In 1565, Mary, James VI's mother, married her cousin the Earl of Darnley. Their relationship quickly broke down and as the spoiled and petulant Darnley spent less time with Mary, she became increasingly close to her advisor, the Earl of Bothwell.

In March 1566, Darnley and a group of Protestant nobles murdered Mary's Italian secretary, David Rizzio. They claimed Rizzio was having an affair with Mary and was using this to gain influence in court. Darnley and the nobles burst in upon the heavily pregnant Mary as she was having supper with Rizzio and five close friends, including Bothwell. The group dragged Rizzio from the table into the next room and stabbed him 56 times.

After the birth of their son, James, in June 1566, Darnley and Mary's relationship continued to deteriorate. In February 1567, there was an explosion at the house where Darnley was staying just outside of Edinburgh. His body was found outside, giving rise to speculation that he had escaped the blast but had been subsequently murdered by the State.

By waiting a mere three months before marrying the Earl of Bothwell, Mary turned the Scottish nobility against her. Bothwell was exiled and Mary forced to abdicate in July 1567. Mary was imprisoned in Lochleven Castle and her infant son James was made king.

Having escaped from Lochleven in 1568, her army was defeated at the Battle of Langside near Glasgow, Mary fled to England to seek refuge from her cousin, Elizabeth I.

The exile of Mary Queen of Scots brought no peace to the turbulent affairs of Scotland. Catholic and Protestant parties quarrelled fiercely over Mary's infant son, King James VI, civil war threatened, and regents came and went.

By 1586, when Mary was being held at Chartley, there were real fears of a Catholic uprising in England and of a Spanish invasion.

The task of controlling the Catholic rebels was handed over to Sir Francis Walsingham, whose main goal was to destroy Mary Queen of Scots.

The young noblemen, Sir Anthony Babington, a double agent, managed to persuade Mary to give consent to backing a Catholic plot. Letters were duly intercepted, the plot was uncovered, and Babington was duly arrested and executed.

Mary was moved to Fotheringhay Castle in Northamptonshire and put on trial. At the trial, Mary was not allowed counsel or witnesses in her defence. She was duly found guilty and condemned to death.

The execution took place in the Great Hall on Wednesday 8th November 1587 at approximately nine o'clock in the morning. James was held prisoner, but in 1583, aged seventeen, he escaped, and declared that henceforth he would be king in fact as well as name.

Considering the poor state of matters in Scotland, James managed well. He did not make an impressive monarch because he dribbled when he talked and relied too much on court favourites, but he was clever by nature, well educated, and a sharp politician.

In 1586, James and Elizabeth I had become allies under the Treaty of Berwick. When Elizabeth executed his mother the following year, James did not protest too vociferously as he hoped to be named as Elizabeth's successor.

In 1589, James married Anne of Denmark. Three of their seven children survived into adulthood. James was careful to keep on good terms with Elizabeth's ministers, especially Robert Cecil, who planned to make sure of his own position by preparing the way for James to succeed.

In March 1603 Elizabeth died. At the end, when she could no longer speak, she made a sign agreeing that James should succeed her. As she breathed her last, Cecil signalled her agreement to Sir Robert Carey, who leapt on to his horse and galloped north.

In less than three days, he was in Edinburgh. He would have been even quicker, he claimed, but he fell on the way north and his horse kicked him in the head. James, now James I of England, had gone to bed, but he willingly got up when he heard the news. James's progress to London was a stately procession of triumph.

James was relieved to be king of England, believing it would be easier country to govern than Scotland. However, an English Government was not going to prove as easy to influence as he supposed.

James admired the organisation of the Church. It was a huge institution closely linked to the State, with elaborate customs and rituals and ruled by Bishops, appointed by the Crown. It was an effective way of keeping control, providing a legal framework and revenue for the Crown. However, not all English people liked the Church of England.

The Puritans favoured local presbyteries and like the Scottish Presbyterians, wanted to abolish bishops, which James recognised as a dangerous precedent. It would remove a tier of his governance. He found presbyteries disagreeable because they wanted to wrest control from the central government. He would not even countenance the removal of that echelon of the church and said so.

James asserted, "No bishop, no king!"

He did not favour local control of the church; it was counter to his belief in the 'Divine Right of Kings'. He wanted to have complete control of the church and appointing bishops as Supreme Head of the Church.

The Puritans wanted other reforms in the Church. Some wanted a Presbyterian system, while others wanted a looser organisation of independent local congregations.

One of James's great contributions to England's history was the 'Authorised King James's Version of the Bible', which was to become the standard text for more than 250 years. This cemented the translation of the Bible from Latin into English and guaranteed its accessibility. It was no longer an exclusive book.

However, James disappointed the Puritans, who hoped he would introduce some of the more radical religious ideas of the Scottish church, and the Catholics, who anticipated lenient treatment and an escape from fines for non-attendance at church, these fines were for recusancy, or the refusal to attend a Church of England service. Recusants were fined heavily.

The Puritans were well represented in the House of Commons, and they were not afraid to criticise the government. So strong was the opposition that Elizabeth had tried to ban all discussion of religion in Parliament. This just caused another row, over the rights of members.

The royal government, living largely on rents from royal estates, had suffered badly from inflation. The Crown needed extra subsidies in the form of taxes granted by Parliament. The House would refuse to vote taxes for the government if it disliked government policy. As far as possible, Elizabeth lived without subsidies, to avoid having to deal with Parliament. James, who could not hope to be as loved, or respected, as Elizabeth, so soon in his reign, found Parliament even more difficult.

James's firm belief in the *Divine Right of Kings*, and constant need for money, also brought him into repeated clashes and conflict with parliament.

In 1604, he ended the long-running war with Spain and tried to arrange a marriage between his son and the Spanish Infanta. He married his daughter, Elizabeth, to the Elector of the Palatinate, Frederick, who was the leader of the German Protestants

On 7th July 1604, James prorogued the parliament, having achieved his aims neither for the full union nor for the obtaining of funds sufficient to keep his expensive Court life buoyant.

He was not well pleased.

"I will not thank where I feel no thanks due," he remarked in his closing speech. "I am not of such a stock as to praise fools... You see how many things you did not well... I wish you would make use of your liberty with more modesty in time to come."

The parliament of 1604 helped to shape the attitudes of both sides for the rest of the reign. On the eve of the next parliamentary session, in 1605, Guy Fawkes was discovered. The Plot would have caused the destruction of the Stuart dynasty.

As James put it: "Not only...of my person, nor of my wife and posterity also, but of the whole body of the State in general."

James benefitted enormously from the discovery of 'the Plot'. It aroused relief at the delivery of the king and his sons and inspired in the ensuing parliament a mood of loyalty and goodwill, which Robert Cecil astutely exploited to extract higher subsidies for the king than most granted in Elizabeth's reign.

In his speech to both the Houses of Parliament, Commons, and Lords, on 9th November, James expounded the preoccupations of his monarchy: the Divine Right of Kings and the Catholic question. He insisted that the plot had been the work of a few Catholics and not of the English Catholics as a whole. He reminded the assembly to rejoice at his survival, since kings were gods and he owed his escape to a miracle.

In this book, you will see how Cecil could not only manipulate parliament but every player in this grisly immorality play. 'The Gunpowder Plot' was a subterfuge of breath-taking audacity, designed to remove the Catholic nobles from the Court and destroy any influence that they might have over the King, thus allowing Cecil to retain his influence on James, who at the Hampton Court Conference had removed the threat of Puritan influence. This allowed Cecil to maintain and develop his power.

Robert Cecil wanted James to be King; he was there when Elizabeth 'signalled' her approval of the Stuart king. Henceforth, he schemed to manipulate James like a marionette. Cecil had grown shrewd under the auspices of his father and Walsingham, the joint founders of the English secret service.

By removing the Catholic and Puritan threats to his power, he made James far more malleable. He could not remove the King's favourites but he could usurp their influence by saving the King's life and making him indebted to him and reliant on his advice.

James loathed the Puritans and their wish for autonomy, he dispatched them himself leaving Cecil to deal with the Catholics equally effectively.

– Breathing your last – iv

In the Parish Register of Mansfield, it is stated that Sir Griffin Markham was present on 31st March 1603, at the Market Cross at Mansfield to greet King James VI of Scotland on his progress through England to take up the crown in England. In July of the same year, Markham, with Sir Walter Raleigh, and some others were apprehended on a charge of conspiring to raise Arbella Stuart to the throne in place of James I. On 4th of November, in consequence of a plague that was especially severe in London, all the prisoners were sent under strong guard from the Tower to Winchester for trial.

They were all condemned, Markham by his own confession, possibly a bluff to ensure he would receive a pardon. Perhaps, Cecil had primed him, telling him that it was Raleigh that he wanted and if he admitted to being part of the plot, he would live. Great efforts were made by others to obtain his pardon and of course his confederates, which to the surprise of Markham were rejected, as he had been led to hope his life would be spared.

On 7th of December, the King signed the warrant for the execution to take place. Markham was the first led to the execution block and he complained that he had been deceived with false promises of his life being spared. When a kind friend offered him a napkin to cover his eyes, he thanked him, courteously, but refused it.

"I am still able to look death in the face without blushing," he announced bravely to the small crowd.

Just at the moment when he was preparing to lay his head upon the block, a Scottish gentleman of the King's household, John Ramsay, stepped forward and presented the Sheriff, Sir Benjamin Tichbourne, with a warrant. The sheriff told Markham that he was to have a respite of two hours and had him led down Winchester Castle Hill.

Next, Lord Grey was brought to the scaffold, and when all preparations were made and the prayers ended, the Sheriff, as before, ordered the execution to be stayed for a while, neither of the prisoners took any comfort from the delay.

Then, came Lord Cobham's turn, and when he was prepared to die, Sir Benjamin sent for the other two, and when they again mounted the scaffold, all the three were lost in amazement, for each thought his companions were dead.

The crowd was full of wonder, and the Sheriff solved the mystery by explaining that the King had been graciously pleased to spare the lives of all three.

Though Sir Griffin's life was spared, he was banished from the country. He survived for many years, though in a state of great indigence, or severe poverty, and it is said, he frequently visited his native land in disguise, and that he assisted in the attempted escape of Arbella Stuart.

Sir Griffin, the eldest son and heir of Thomas Markham, of Ollerton, commenced life with the brightest prospects, showing evidence of great ability, but he was ambitious and reckless, and he ended his days in poverty and exile.

He, with other young men of family, served under the Earl of Essex in an expedition to France sent by Queen Elizabeth to the assistance of Henry IV. In that war, he received the honour of knighthood for his valour during the siege of Rouen. He afterwards served with distinction in Ireland under the same general, by whom; he was made commander of all the Horse in Connaught.

But Sir Griffin had a restless spirit, and in addition to becoming a Papist, gave some further offence to the Queen, and was banished from Court nine or ten years before her death.

"Fealty to me or breathe your last, what is it to be?" she asked.

It was not, however, until the reign of James I. that he began to tamper with treasonable matters.

The official version does not tell the truth.

Sir Griffin Markham was supposed to be languishing in the Tower of London or some accounts say he was banished. In fact, he was Robert Cecil's right-hand man, a bodyguard, and emissary who would ensure that Cecil could be in two places at once.

Chapter 2 – The Cast – i

Robert Cecil stood under the gable of the cloister, his cape pulled around his body, accentuating his slim silhouette. It was dawn, he watched his breath cloud before his eyes as he surveyed the red-brick, the dozens of chimneys and the multitude of dark windows, searching for a candle light or some other sign of life, smoke from a chimney but nothing could be seen, the occupants were all abed. Only the palace guards, and he, were about and abroad that morning. Smoke rose from the kitchen chimneys but Cecil could not see them, the bakers and cooks were busy, the ladies and gentlemen of the Court were sleeping off their excesses.

The twilight journey to Hampton Court had been necessary though supremely uncomfortable. Two oarsmen as opposed to one had pulled their blades through the still water of the Thames; the timing of their journey was totally reliant on the tides. The rising tide meant their journey was much faster than usual; there was nothing worse than rowing against the tide. Cecil understood the difficulties of such a strategy since he had always rowed against the tides when statecraft had demanded it. He also tried to cement the sands that shifted under the castle of state, the currents that could potentially undermine the bedrock of the commonwealth. On this bedrock stood the mill of the Tudor and the Stuart state where treachery and intrigue threatened to dislodge the cogs of the machine. It was his machine and he had to secure its function; protect its foundations.

The Thames carried with it swift currents, flowing west, and therefore a journey to Hampton could, with the right tide and the right crew, sometimes, take only an hour and a half. An hour and a half of abject misery for all on board; the rowers had frozen extremities and their ceaseless endeavour was uncomfortably strenuous; the cocoon created for Cecil was just not warm enough. His very inactivity encouraged the chill to crawl around the hides he hid under and slip through chinks.

The cold chilled his very bones. Despite layers of sheepskin over his legs and around his body, two layers of gloves, one pair of thin pigskin and one pair of thick leather, the chill wind seemed to be able to find every gap and pierce every material. Cecil's velvet hat kept his head warm but he could feel his ears turning to ice.

Cecil dared not touch the red raw numb flesh of his earlobes and cursed his vanity, dressing to meet King James was important and demanded a fashionable hat but a muffler or a woollen shawl would have protected his ears. The rowers were swathed in scarves and mufflers made of cotton and wool.

Watching the oarsmen sweat; the steam rising off their bodies; vapour trailing from their open mouths; finding gaps in their swaddling like stew simmering in a covered pot; he marvelled at their industry. They moved like a pendulum, back and forth, their arms worked, rhythmically, they pulled the oars through the water in a reassuringly perfect synchronicity.

The oarsmen's hose were covered in horse-blankets and their doublets covered with a leather jerkin, which made him almost envious. They had the sense to wear caps that covered their ears and to cover their nose and mouth with a shawl, their breath trailed over the lips of their shawls, all that Cecil was able to see of the boatmen was their eyes staring at the bank behind him. Every so often, they would turn their heads to check their progress.

Cecil marvelled at their knowledge of the river as it meandered and twisted through the landscape, their ability to steer in the correct direction and use the currents to place their boat in order to speed its progress.

If only state and crown could work so closely or so effectively together, if only the bishops and lords could row so uniformly, he mused. If only the factions at court could make such swift progress together, admittedly, they all rowed together but it tended to be in different directions.

While the crew of the boat strived and sweated, he could feel his teeth chattering, the damp had penetrated his bones and it was difficult to keep warm, he had been convinced that he would catch a chill. The oarsmen's faces became redder and redder as his became bluer and bluer, it was as if he had cold blood running through his veins. As each minute passed, he wondered whether he would freeze to death. He wryly observed that fashioning a statue of him would perhaps be made unnecessary, as he would provide his own frozen monument.

Stiff with cold his body would only require gilding. Granted, he mused; his prone position would not be flattering for a statesman who should be seen standing up for justice not sitting at his ease. Instead, he was crouched in the bottom of the boat, under layers of animal skins, which would, surely, look less stately than he would wish. Thinking further, he decided that as he was the seat of power in England it was perhaps a fitting pose for him to adopt, after all. Little games and word play in his head kept him occupied; he also thought about the plots and schemes he had concocted.

All his recipes seemed to be producing the desired results: a pinch of piety, a spoonful of suspicion, all stirred in to the mix; plots peppered with the nutmeg and cinnamon of gossip and disinformation to spice them up; mistrust sprinkled liberally; stories and rumours, lies and half-truths were all added to the mix. A broth of most satisfying flavour was produced. The population was made too scared to think, too worried to become worrisome, too poor to be idle, that was the success of the State. The people were hard at work, all the time; there was no room for dissention. It was the bishops and the nobles that vexed Cecil. No gruel could be concocted or created to satisfy their desires.

In the court kitchen, things were baking, nicely. Fears and self-interest provided the base and all the ingredients, added together, combined to produce a cake of multi-layers and designed to suit all tastes.

'Time and tide wait for no man', he noted and 'needs must, the devil drives' he dutifully recited his Shakespeare in his head; he knew each quote by heart.

The need to be at Hampton Court for the forthcoming conference, the plague emptying London of its courtiers to the countryside and being at the mercy of tide had resulted in this miserable journey. He planned meticulously but he could not control some events. James was determined to have this conference and it could not be delayed. As he froze, he idly recited the lines of Brutus in Julius Caesar; he admired the sense and sentiments of the soliloquy:

'There is a tide in the affairs of men,
Which, taken at the flood, leads on to fortune;
Omitted, all the voyage of their life,
Is bound in shallows and in miseries.
On such a full sea are we now afloat,
And we must take the current when it serves,
Or lose our ventures.'

What wise words.

He had taken the tide at the flood and had overseen the successful succession of James to the throne, augmenting the earlier work Walsingham, his father, Lord Burghley, and he had achieved under 'Good Queen Bess', succeeding in securing the state.

The crown was safe for the time being. Nevertheless, there was constant danger of losing the advantage, there were different interest groups in the state and even his cousin, Francis Bacon, was vying for power, plotting to wrestle it from him.

Elizabeth had been unable to achieve all she could because of the wars that she had been forced to wage and the poor coffers her father had left through his grandiose lifestyle and costly warmongering. She tried to be careful but the cost of running a Court was expensive.

Henry had ignored the costs and benefitted form the windfall of selling property and land when he dissolved the monasteries. Elizabeth and James were not as fortunate.

James, with his extravagance and need for new palaces and entertainments, was likely to undo all that Queen Bess had achieved.

Late in her reign, Elizabeth's exchequer had become more bounteous, she had been thrifty throughout her reign and she was almost balancing the books by the end of her monarchy. James and his spendthrift ways were in danger of undoing all her hard work.

She had worked tirelessly to balance the Exchequer's books. The commonwealth needed to have peace and security in order for the country to prosper. It was an idea that had been muted long ago by Machiavelli but still it was not a policy that all wanted, especially hotheads like Drake and Raleigh. Cecil saw the sense, the gallants wanted glory and spoils.

He had succeeded in dispatching one such fool, Robert Devereux, Earl of Essex, and Sir Walter was, at present, languishing in the Tower of London despite his popularity. It was the safest place for him, inciting everyone to war was not conducive to Cecil's plans. Cecil had concocted a Catholic plot, put Raleigh at the head and persuaded several nobles including the fearless friend of Essex, Griffin Markham, to implicate Raleigh and be saved execution for a fabricated plot.

There was danger at every step. The Tudor state had seen much machination and persecution.

The Stuart state would perhaps fare no better. James's profligacy would have to be curbed. Cecil remembered the old farming adage: "After a gatherer, there comes a scatterer."

The previous evening he had travelled by *wherry* from London Bridge, past the Cathedrals of Saint Paul's and Southwark, past the Strand, past Westminster Palace, Edward VI's hospital, Saint Thomas's on the opposite bank, past Lambeth Palace, eventually mooring at Cheyne Walk at a house near Sir Thomas More's old home in Chelsea.

There he had dined with one of his spies in the House of Lords, Thomas Clinton, 3rd Earl of Lincoln and his wife, who was, by coincidence, sister to Thomas Knyvett, Elizabeth Knyvett, keeper of both Westminster and Whitehall palaces, a trusted servant of the Stuarts. They had a conversation into the night that revealed much.

Cecil had been woken as the tide rose for his trip to Hampton. As dawn broke, he broke his fast: a boiled egg, two Hampstead apples and some Camberwell artichoke hearts served with some Croydon saffron and Epping butter. Only the finest ingredients were offered to Robert Cecil, the Secretary of State, Baron Cecil of Essendon in the County of Rutland. He decided against the house beer and drank milk from Farringdon instead.

Once he had rubbed his gums with salt and combed his hair, he went downstairs thanked his host and hostess and walked down to the *wherry* where he stepped unassisted onto the long overhanging bow and into his seat. He greeted the two *wherry-men* with a jovial good morning. They sang 'good morrow' in reply, making sure they addressed him with a civil tongue; they, after all, wanted a tip for their good service and Cecil was well known for his generosity, if all went well. Equally, he had a reputation revenge on those who displeased him.

Distractedly, Cecil watched the scenery pass, ticking off each landmark in his mind, Chelsea Reach, Wandsworth, Fulham, Putney, Hammersmith and Barnes. All these places drifted by. Then, the boat sped onto Mortlake that he wryly noted might spell the death of him in the cold damp air. He truly believed he might catch his death of cold that day.

Further, the oarsmen rowed the boat, onto Ham, Twickenham and Richmond. Cecil spotted Queen Elizabeth's old palace there, Richmond Palace. He remembered how resplendent it had been, yet, now, it was barely visible between the trees, and, finally, they rowed past the village of Kingston.

Beyond all those villages, Cecil could clearly see, suddenly rising out of the mist, the mighty, redbrick walls of Hampton Court Palace, Cardinal Thomas Wolsey's magnificent edifice. He still marvelled at it scale, its truly awesome proportions, larger than any awe inspiring Cathedral Cecil had ever seen.

When the boat arrived at the palace's waterfront, the boatmen had to pull Cecil from his recumbent position; he was buried under skins of every type, deerskin, sheepskin and goatskin, so they had to remove these layers before they found him cocooned in his cape. The decision to avoid the beer at breakfast seemed like an error, the alcohol might have helped even if it had just dulled his perception of how cold he was.

The boatmen stepped up onto the wooden jetty where the frozen dew formed a white coating over the boards. Tying up the boat, bow and stern, they returned to haul Cecil out of the boat, taking an arm each, it was an operation completed with deference but without elegance. Cecil was small and thin, a light load for these strong men. The slippery boards that they trod on seemed to cause them few problems.

Gripping his arms, they shuffled along the slippery jetty and over the muddy hard until they reached the stone slabs that marked the route to the palace. It was with his cape wrapped round him that he stepped gingerly onto the stone path that led from the water's edge to the palace gates and it was there that the burly boatmen released him. It was a strange sight; Cecil was small and hunchbacked, flanked by two giants, a child escorted by two beefy bodyguards. He thanked them for escorting him and tipped them both generously while wondering why the palace guard had not rushed to greet him.

He watched the boatmen depart, stomping cautiously back to their vessel. He did no envy their return journey even if as he suspected, they moored in Kingston to drink some mulled ale or cider. They would be warm soon; Cecil wondered whether his cold bones would ever thaw.

The frost from dawn provided a slippery route that he found difficult to negotiate even in his leather boots with their soles scored with a knife, in a criss-cross pattern, to give them better grip. He slid several times. A shiver went up his spine as he almost toppled over; his usual purposeful stride was replaced by a hobble, which did not look very dignified in front of the guards.

Fortunately, it meant he prevented himself from slipping over, which would have robbed him of all his dignity. The King called him his 'little elf', Elizabeth called him her 'little beagle', and on that path, he felt more like a *Hobgoblin* than the most powerful man in England, after the King.

He had long grown immune to what people thought of him or his appearance. He had been trusted with the protection of the crown, trained by Sir Francis Walsingham and by his father William Cecil, Lord Burghley.

The affairs of state were like walking a tightrope or negotiating a slippery path, caution had to be balanced with progress. His caution accentuated his deformity whereas a determined gait did as much to disguise it.

"Hail, Watchman of the Guard, good morrow to you," Cecil cried haughtily, he was a consummate actor and could feign joviality even though inside he was a frozen ice block and was not in the best of moods either.

He stood, feet apart in front of the ornate iron gates, trying to imitate a valiant but managing only to look less crooked than he was. His breath came in clouds of impatience, he wanted to be inside and warm.

His good mood was an act; the gate should have been open and the waiting to welcome him.

If the guards had been doing their job properly, then, they should have seen the boat and come out to challenge or help the occupants.

It was admittedly early, Cecil conceded that, but he was expected and he could not forgive such an enormous oversight in security and courtesy. He would write a letter to the commander of the palace guard at a later date. He was too cold to tarry that day.

"Your Lordship, Baron Cecil of Essendon, good day to you; the King sleeps; 'you come readily on your hour', indeed you do," the guard joked. He hoped that by using a phrase Cecil often used, which they both recognised as Shakespearean, he would ingratiate himself to the Secretary of State.

His words sounded hollow in their false joviality and came out as gusts of steam. He too, like the rest of the guard, was chilled to the bone. The beer allowance eased the misery but there was a limit to how much alcohol you could drink and still perform your duty to an acceptable level. A slight drunken flush was all well and good; a staggering step was too much.

"You flatter me, using the expressions that I use, you flatter Shakespeare in knowing his quotation, and you know imitation is the greatest form of flattery, you do well in quoting the bard; I have arrived early, thanks, in part, to my oarsmen. I need to warm myself before my audience can warm to me; it is enough that I am expected."

"Expected and warmly appreciated," the guard continued obsequiously yet there was warmth there, too, it was clear he was fond of Cecil.

Years of experience had taught him how much ale was needed to lessen the cold without slurring the speech or affecting the gait, but he feared that he might have overdone the amount of beer that morning and Cecil might have noticed already.

He also hoped that Cecil would forgive the fact that, although the great man was expected, he was not awaited as befitted such an august personage.

If only he could have read Cecil's mind, he would know how irate Cecil really was at being kept waiting unnecessarily.

"I wish I were warm but I thank you for your sentiments," replied Cecil, trying to stop his teeth chattering and suppressing a shiver that threatened to rack his body.

At all costs, he would appear oblivious to the cold. Two Beefeaters armed with pikes stood behind the Watchman of the Guard as he fumbled clumsily with the keys hidden under two thick black wool cloaks. A pair of thick, tan, leather gloves, that he was reluctant to take off, did not help the struggle.

Eventually, he tore off his gauntlets and stuffed them in the wide leather belt around his waist. Cecil's face was impassive. The Watchman's face was flushed by alcohol and embarrassment.

"I won't keep you waiting Your Lordship," he promised rashly and he thought he heard a heavy sigh from Cecil.

With tremulous fingers, grasped the ice-cold ring of the keys from the hook on his belt. His fingers felt frozen already but he persevered. The cold was biting and he could feel his fingers becoming so numb that he could not remember when they were so cold and so difficult to manipulate.

He struggled with his dulled co-ordination and the multitude of keys that were on the ring that hooked onto his belt. Ice would have been warmer, but His Lordship should not be kept waiting, so he managed to push the largest key into the lock and, wrapping the key in one of his gloves, he turned the key to the left.

Gingerly grasping the cold vertical bar of the gate, he swung it open, pulling hard so that he should not have to hold on for too long. The momentum achieved and the design of the hinge brought the gate wide open to allow the baron through.

Cecil wasted no time in slipping through the gap, his countenance did not betray his fury at such incompetence, he had been clearly visible from the river and the fathead had waited until he was standing at the gate to open it.

"Thank you," he said slipping his slight frame through the gap as the gate swung back, and, for the first time that day he smiled with satisfaction, he would soon be warm, his penance was almost over, the ordeal by ice would be part of the history of the day, soon.

"Sorry to keep you waiting, Your Lordship; it is cold and bitter," the fumbling guard apologised profusely, again using one of Cecil's phrases that both knew he had borrowed from Shakespeare.

He hoped that the 'in-joke' would serve to lighten the tension in the air that lingered like tobacco smoke in a tavern.

It was not a very auspicious start to Cecil's visit. The Watchman of the Guard had noticed that his lordship had looked slightly displeased at having to wait so long and it did not do to upset one of the most powerful men in the kingdom.

It was difficult to know when Cecil might suddenly reappear so the guard decided, right there, to limit his intake of beer and redouble his vigilance just in case Cecil remembered his poor reception. He cursed his luck. Fortune's fickle wheel had turned.

He hoped that he had got away with not being at hand when Cecil arrived but he could not tell for sure and the beer was befuddling his thinking. All the guards had a generous allowance of beer and it helped to ease the boredom and the chill but it was easy to have one drop too many in cold weather or on long nights. While Cecil stayed at Hampton Court, and for the duration of the conference there, that would never be the case from thence.

The Watchman and Cecil had maintained a good relationship thus far but all knew what Robert Cecil had done to the Earl of Essex and Devereux had been the Queen's favourite and a charming man, he recalled.

Similarly, he was aware that even Sir Walter Raleigh, the people's hero, had been dispatched to the Tower while Cecil was Secretary of State.

"Indeed it is cold and bitter, especially for me, out on the Thames where the chill penetrates the very bones," Cecil explained casually as if he were describing the fate of someone he did not know rather than being the sufferer himself.

"You are most welcome to the palace and the warmth within," the guard mumbled, not knowing how to apologise properly.

"You are far too kind," Cecil breathed dramatically, leaving the Watchman of the Guard puzzled as to whether he was being genuine, or ironic in his remarks. The phrase had not sounded sarcastic and yet he was not sure.

Without glancing back or acknowledging the pikemen, who had appeared from who knew where and stood on either side of the gate as he passed through it, Cecil strode towards the archway that would lead to the Great Hall, willing himself not to slip or slide on the hoar frost. The grass on the lawn had ice crystals on every blade, the flowers in their beds had frozen fronds; he noted such, all nature was choked by the cold.

He did not feel so bad after all, on reflection, the movement was making him feel warmer and soon, he would be warmer still. As he passed through the main archway, he nodded at two further Beefeaters, who brought the shaft of their pikes to their right shoulders in salute. Instead of continuing straight on to the palace doors, he turned left and stopped under the third gable of the cloistered garden and there, Cecil stood under the arched stonework, waiting for his man, William Owen.

While he waited, he stomped his boots and flapped his arms inside his cape, looking like a raven at the Tower, trying to take off from a stationary position. Finally, Owen glided towards him in a cape, which had been hurriedly wrapped around his corpulent body, it was clear he was also concealing something he had tucked under his arm.

Cecil immediately recognised his greying black, curly hair, which was tousled. Evidently, there had been no time to brush it. Owen was grim-faced and his beard needed trimming; it was clear that he had overslept and, like the palace guards, he had mistimed the arrival of Cecil.

Both men knew that Owen should have been waiting for his chief not keeping him waiting.

Cecil was strict about punctuality and Owen knew that it did not do to antagonise him.

Owen cursed his misfortune, he was normally always on time, blaming his servant for oversleeping would not help the situation, though giving his servant a thorough kicking as he slept, before he left, would have done much to mollify Owen's mood.

"Apologies, Your Lordship," he hissed angrily, he had meant to sound apologetic but it sounded as if Cecil and not he was at fault. Remembering, at that very moment, the fact that he had forgotten to give his servant boy a round kicking for not waking him up made him feel even angrier. "Have you been here long?"

"A few miserable moments," Cecil responded casually, "but I am frozen inside and out so it makes little difference."

"What news of the Plague?" Owen asked, deciding a change of subject might improve both their moods.

"I think the plague will not be the death of me, the cold will."

"So it is spent?"

"Not yet, James was right to move his court here, even though it is a cold and desolate place, it is safer. I cannot see much smoke coming from the chimneys," Cecil said, seemingly depressed by all around him. He looked around the house for signs of light or life. "There are a few wisps of smoke from the direction of the kitchen."

Cecil's home in London was always warm. How he wished that he had stayed there, he would have done so but for urgent matters of state.

"The household stayed up late last night and the fires will be lit soon, when 'His Majesty' rises," Owen assured him, feeling relieved that Cecil's anger was directed at the slovenly members of the court and not at him.

"Only the kitchen fires are burning. You have the reports for me?"

"Indeed, Baron, I do," replied Owen, fumbling in the folds of the lining of his cape to extricate the satchel that he had managed to slip over his shoulder as he left his room.

Digging around inside it brought forth, three scrolls and a sealed envelope, which he handed to Cecil while stomping himself. He had not been out in the cold for long but dressed as he was it was long enough. Icy fingers of damp cold slipped under his cape and beneath his silk shirt. Cecil grasped the papers in his left hand before placing them carefully in a large leather purse he wore around his belly, hanging from a belt.

"Lead me to the kitchens where that fire will thaw me out!" Cecil demanded, having made his mind up as to the best course of action during this hiatus. Inwardly, he cursed the other members of the court who were still lying in bed at this hour. What had happened to: 'early to bed and early to rise'? The court seemed to have changed beyond recognition, in the time of Elizabeth, it was a time of hard work and inhibition; James's court avoided work and embraced hedonism. They preferred hunting to working for the common wealth.

Taking the circuitous route, to avoid being seen, Owen led Cecil down into the cavernous kitchen where logs burnt and two hogs twirled on a spit turned by two kitchen boys who bowed courteously at Cecil and rather fearfully at Owen; it was clear that they had been chastised by the big man.

Cecil placed himself firmly in front of the fire, staring into the flames as he stood. He could feel the heat from the roaring fire, felt the damp of the river evaporate from his body and could feel his blood becoming warmer.

"How was the 'Queen's Mask'?" Cecil asked passively as he gazed into the flames that warmed his nose and warmed his eyebrows. It was a polite remark showing indifference but at the same time fishing for any interesting information. He had already received intelligence from his spies and he would receive detailed written reports from his other *'spions'* in due course but a verbal summary was still Owen's responsibility. He would provide Cecil with the latest intelligence, the freshest details of James and Anne's antics. The Secretary of State often dismissed Anne as a token Queen, frivolous and self-indulgent, 'Anne of Denmark, too fond of a lark'.

A year earlier, James had fought with Anne over the proposed composition of her English household, sending her a message that 'his Majesty took her continued perversity very heinously', revealing his impatience with her and his wish to fill his court with his own favourites.

The King was also on record of saying that marriage was: 'the greatest earthly felicity of misery that can come to a man'. These reports filtered to Cecil. Yet, outwardly, they were seen as an entertaining royal couple, providing lavish parties.

Reports already delivered, by messenger, to London, informed Cecil that, during the weeks of New Year celebrations, Anne had taken exception to James's drinking. She had confided in the French envoy, telling him the following, rather indiscreetly: 'the King drinks so much, and conducts himself so ill in every respect, that I expect an early and evil result'.

Cecil was glad that there was strife in the house of Denmark and Stuart, they would both need respite, and he could offer it. Where there was disharmony, he could provide harmony, he was a skilled negotiator, charming and cunning. He was no stranger to scripture and where there was despair, he would sow hope. Where there was disunity, he would provide harmony.

"All the guests looked resplendent, the ambassadors and courtiers called it the best New Year celebration they had attended. The ladies were magnificently dressed," Owen reported stiffly.

"No doubt, since the Queen and her cousin were given permission to raid Queen Bess's collection of clothing stored at the Tower," Cecil announced curtly, rubbing his hands together behind his back before placing them before the heat of the fire.

"Queen Elizabeth's gowns, no wonder Arbella Stuart's dress looked so beautiful," Owen noted, smiling wanly.

"You are a diplomat or a wit; she looked like an angel, *nay*?" Cecil noted, giving a special emphasis to the last word.

He enjoyed word play, as it was a chance for him to reveal his cleverness; it was accepted at court that Arbella Stuart bore more of a fleeting resemblance to a horse.

"Neigh, like a horse, indeed, but in wonderful livery! There was even more horse play; the king had a new dais made and sat under the cloth of estate while the Queen played *Pallas* in Daniels' play. She danced before him to much applause."

The Queen, too, like her cousin Arbella, was not noted for her handsome looks but she did like to dance. Cecil was clearly not one to dance, you might think, but he enjoyed certain dances with certain people. He may have had a hunched back and a slight curvature of the spine but there was nothing wrong with his legs or his dance steps. Cecil was discerning, he enjoyed the '*Tinternell*' and the '*Maske of Queens*', he even, despite their animosity, enjoyed '*The Earl of Essex's Measure*', but he was especially fond of '*Lord Zouch's Maske*' and the '*Turkeylony*'.

He even enjoyed the '*Pavan*', though seldom admitted such. He was known to dance the Galliards and the Almain; though these were generally performed at baptisms, birthdays and weddings rather than more courtly events. Cecil could move about the dance floor with alacrity and grace despite his physical disadvantages.

Owen was not so discerning, he would dance with a goose, with or without music; he was a hedonist who would think nothing of bringing a 'doll-tear-sheet' home at the end of an evening. He enjoyed all the pleasures of life, wine, women and song.

He was not choosy, any wine, any woman and any song in the order they were delivered. He was one of the King's servants who embraced the looser feel to court life and the freedom to act beyond the penetrating eyes of the disapproving gaze of Elizabeth and the old men of her old court. There was no longer need for restraint. The old guard was gone and James enjoyed frivolity. Owen loyally followed his king's lead, ever the dutiful subject.

"*The Vision of the Twelve Goddesses*, I am familiar with the play and with Sam Daniels. Did not the King's Men and 'Will' appear?" asked Cecil.

He revealed at once that he adored the theatre, equally as much as dancing. He worked and schemed hard, he loved to forget all his burdens and challenges by dancing, playing tennis or by watching a play.

When winter came with a vengeance, he was also known to skate but only on ice when the ponds froze, not the hard at Hampton Court in unsuitable footwear.

"Not on New Year's Day, we had just the Daniel's play and poor Prince Harry was tossed between ambassadors and courtiers like a tennis ball."

"'Tis a hazard of that game!"

"Quite so, Your Lordship."

"That reminds me, I must have a game tennis while I am here but I will need to use a different ball, softer perhaps."

"I'll play a set with you."

"You have not seen my serve."

"We'll set the court roofs rumbling!"

"Indeed, we will."

It was best to agree with the Secretary of State at all times to avoid a visit to the Tower.

The heat from the fire had warmed Cecil so effectively; he almost felt he had never been cold. He was grateful for the heat and the blood that pumped to his extremities, warming them so rapidly. His mood had improved immeasurably now that his limbs were no longer ice blocks.

He watched dewy steam rise off his coat. Turning suddenly, he slipped the cloak off his shoulder, one boy gasped unable to disguise his shock at seeing the deformity on Cecil's back and shoulder but everyone ignored the sound. Even Cecil pretended not to hear the intake of breath.

It was best to pretend all was well with Cecil making a tour of inspection in the kitchen. He was expected, recognised and revered by the Hampton Court servants, at least. There was always a certain peril when dealing with Robert Cecil, all who knew him knew it. His fellow servant boy ran to one of the long chopping tables, slipped a small wooden stool from underneath, and ran to Cecil's side. Bowing low, he placed the stool at a distance that would allow Cecil to thaw out.

"A stool for your comfort and ease Your Lordship," announced the boy seriously and respectfully.

Cecil glanced over at him, he reminded him of his own son, William, in many ways, not as sickly but of a similar size and gait. The great man bowed his head in silent thanks, which the boy returned with an inclination of the head that made his chin point to his toes. The boys eyes then raised to look at his master and like an adoring Labrador puppy, he waited for the next command. Cecil sat down and laid the furled correspondence and the letter on his lap. Before he opened them, he met the boy's eye and smiled at him warmly. He certainly had the *common touch* when it was need. Indeed, he was grateful to be seated and warm.

"Thank you, boy," said Cecil kindly.

"A pleasure, sire," the boy replied, he was always eager to please. He bowed, very low, right arm in front of him, left arm behind him, just as he had been taught to treat those at Court.

"You are far too kind," Cecil breathed dramatically, leaving the boy puzzled as to whether he was being genuine or ironic in his remarks. The phrase had not sounded sarcastic and yet he was not sure.

"My Lord," he decided to say, bowing low a second time, still unsure but he was equally eager to escape Cecil's scrutiny.

There was no time to wonder. He had to return quickly to the spit and turn the hog or the skin would be burnt; there were plenty at court who liked the crackling crisp but not many of them wanted the skin blackened. An even, steady turn ensured the meat was cooked through, too. Cold pork for luncheon was one item on the menu at the palace.

Cecil opened the purse of correspondence, placing it on his knees. He unfurled the three scrolls one by one, before reading them and tossing them into the flames of the fire.

He saved the letter for last but gave away nothing of the correspondence's contents. Owen waited patiently while this was done. He watched Cecil scan the words expeditiously.

"Do you have anything to report from New Year? We can move elsewhere now my bones have warmed!"

"The usual masque and debauchery, followed by the race to the King's presence table for food, you would think these people had not eaten for a week. They stabbed each other's hands with forks as they tried to pile their plates; a few fingers were almost lost while they tried to carve off some meat. There was general confusion and scrambling about the plates. I met Sir John Harrington who complained that everyone was 'wallowing in beastly delight', he seemed to like that and said he was off to bed to write it down before he forgot it."

Both men chortled happily at the recount, it was amusing to hear of the court's bad behaviour. Cecil smiled all the more at the vision of the Lord scurrying to his bedchamber and sharpening his quill before scratching the comment on some scroll for prosperity. However, he knew the members of the kitchen staff were disturbed by such ribaldry.

They led comparatively sober lives, working hard and going home exhausted. Yes, they received a daily beer allowance and they drank, but the excesses of court were far worse. On Saint's Days, they may have drunk too much and said or did something they regretted but it was an occasional lapse, it was not a life of excess and debauchery, which seemed to be the habit of the James's Court.

The waste of good food alone horrified the kitchen staff who had laboured hard to produce the delicacies and would have followed a crow for the scraps off a rich man's table. They would have relished the plates of delicacies from which the Court took merely a bite before leaving it aside. The amount drunk at court also horrified the servants.

"I have seen the court at play; it is not a sight to see, ladies and gentlemen abandoning their sobriety and rolling about in intoxication!" cried Cecil chortling good-naturedly.

"The Danish ambassador commented on such. He thought that the court drank more than the Danes," Owen commented good-naturedly, his early bad mood had been completely forgotten; yet, it was Cecil who would have been justified in being in a dark mood.

"The man is almost a Viking and for Vikings to complain about the amount we drink would suggest that there is no longer something rotten in the State of Denmark but here," Cecil expanded, enjoying his reference to Hamlet. He always liked to show off his knowledge of the Bard, a very Elizabethan trait, but, lately, a very Stuart habit, too. The love of the spoken word and admiration for Shakespeare had continued to be fashionable, luckily for Cecil. Otherwise he may have seemed old-fashioned and out of touch not witty and blithe.

"His thoughts eloquently expressed," Owen replied, openly being obsequious to Cecil in order to make amends for his tardy arrival.

Cecil thought such behaviour becoming and because he was flattered, he forgave Owen whilst both men realised that such behaviour had won Owen a reprieve but only for the time being. There was nothing Cecil enjoyed more than a sycophant.

"Tell me of some good; anything at all; the play by the *'King's Men'*, which one was performed?" Cecil asked. His eyes became distant as he remembered, with relish, a scene from *Hamlet*, imagining its import on his thoughts and those of the rest of the audience who could be bothered to listen and were not chatting.

"*Othello*, my Lord," replied Owen. He knew that if there was anything that Cecil enjoyed it was a Shakespeare play.

"Ah the Moor of Venice, a true tragedy," sighed Cecil, reminiscing. "To mourn a mischief that is past and gone is the next way to draw new mischief on."

"As complex a play as *Hamlet*, I would venture to say," Owen whispered unsure of the reception the remark would receive. His knowledge of the play was gleaned from the *'King's Men'* themselves. Owen had been at pains to talk to them so he could share their views with Cecil.

"Not *Hamlet*? Surely that is his latest play? I read the folio, last year; I thought it would be the first play he would perform this year, there are so many perfect pieces of advice for the King, especially on caution; the sort of advice I could or would give were I his father. What a shame."

"They say it reflects our society and its impropriety," Owen added, trying to sound more knowledgeable than in fact he was and like so many did in the presence of Cecil, he overplayed his hand Cecil had already read the play, so he ignored the self-aggrandising remark.

Cecil needed to be aware of any censorship issues in plays so most were passed to him for his scrutiny; Shakespeare plays, however, were generally an enjoyable distraction. The others always had some overly obvious axe to grind or some political point to hammer home. They lacked the subtly and finesse of Shakespeare. Only he could master subtle subterfuge; plus he had the good sense to flatter those who gave him patronage and to support the queen or king not criticise the Crown or government like the others.

The whole thing was obnoxious and filled Cecil with a mixture of frustration and pity for the playwrights and their trite messages coupled with their clumsy and clunking attacks on the State. The irksome Philip Marlowe and Ben Jonson were particularly overt, trying to slip in some sedition or a criticism of the government on every folio.

Once Cecil was warm, he started to read his correspondence more fully, rising only to condemn the missives into the flames of the kitchen fires. As the kitchen became more frantic, and once he was satisfied that he had gleaned all that he could from the correspondence, he dismissed Owen by asking him to deliver a note to the King's chamber to let His Majesty know of his arrival.

Within the hour, he was summoned upstairs to the Great Hall for an audience. Striding into the room, the size of a chapel but much more richly furnished than a Cathedral, Cecil spotted James, his monarch, King James I of England, James VI of Scotland, the first Stuart sovereign, pacing one of the multitude of rugs spread over the dark, stained, bare floorboards.

Cecil collected his paperwork that had been sent overnight to his study in the palace. Clutching seven scrolls under his arm, he gambolled across the wool flooring, managing to look impressively busy and hiding his deformity through making haste. He lolloped like a clerk weighted down with paperwork to the table and chair that had been set for him.

There were a few chairs arranged around the walls almost touching the tapestries that lined them. The walls along the length of the room were covered in wall hangings. Along three walls, tables had been set up for the conference, the chairs were all facing the middle of the room where James would sit surrounded by Privy Councillors and their clerks. Two large stained glass windows at either end of the hall lighted the room.

The Monarch watched Cecil approach nervously. His beard of ginger hue marked him as a man and not a youth, his pale skin and red hair made him look unwell. His belly seemed bloated.

He had the limbs of a malnourished child. King James looked like a man whose head and legs were too small and thin for his body. It was unsettling to those unfamiliar with him. He had the appearance of a stick figure with a bee's body but with closer inspection, it could be seen that he was not after all a corpulent man with limbs that were not fully developed but he was in fact a bony figure dressed in a padded doublet to prevent being stabbed; he wore the doublet every day. The assassin's dagger was his greatest fear, he had heard of many nobles and kings who had been stabbed to death.

His second greatest fear was being blown-up; particularly, after being told about the explosions, in gruesome detail, that had killed many people in war added to the fact that his mother had suffered an attempt to blow her up at Kirk O'Field.

While Queen Mary, Queen of Scots was at Holyrood, attending the wedding celebration of Bastian Pagez, her court musician; a huge explosion destroyed the house where Darnley, her husband, was living. The incident had happened early in the morning of 10th February 1567, James was just a baby but he would have grown up on tales of that day.

The partially clothed bodies of Darnley and his servant were found in a nearby orchard, suggesting that they had dressed hurriedly. Apparently, they were either smothered or strangled but had been otherwise unharmed by the explosion. They were found with a cloak and dagger nearby, which was a strange combination of clothing; rumours circulated that this was a mark that indicated the assassination was an act of state.

James had grown up with this story and the story of the St. Bartholomew's Day massacre. Walsingham, later Elizabeth's chief spy master, claimed to have escaped death that day in Paris, but only just.

The slaughter of Huguenots had helped to add to the hierarchy's mistrust of Catholics. Beyond that, there was the assassination of the Duke of Guise where guardsmen of Henri III seized the duke and stabbed him in the heart during 1588, the year of the Armada.

Later, in July 1589, at the royal camp at Saint Cloud, Henri, himself, was fatally stabbed. A Dominican monk, of all people, Jacques Clement, gained an audience with the king and drove a long knife into his spleen. Clément was killed on the spot, taking with him the information of who had hired him.

In Europe, the '*Divine Right of Kings*' to rule as they saw fit was being challenged; this was the world James grew up in, and the history lessons he learnt. That was why he was determined to promote the '*Divine Right of Kings*'. His mother's husband murdered, a Catholic duke killed by a king, a Catholic king murdered by a monk, James felt that there was need for retrenchment in philosophy, theology and the role of the crown.

Cecil stood in front of the King who quickly sat down on a wooden chair with a plump, plum velvet cushion on the seat. He rested his elbows on the high arms but the chair had no back. Cecil would have called it a mere stool and James would have insisted on calling it a throne. One way in which the similarities and the differences of these powerful men could be summed up was through their respective description of the furniture.

James eyed Cecil with a mixture of awe and suspicion; he knew Cecil was such a consummate politician, he had engineered the succession and he was a master of espionage and intrigue. He was often left wondering what Cecil might do or say next, which he found exciting. The man fascinated the King, he was an ally but also someone to be feared. It was Cecil, amongst others, who had helped to put him on the throne. James liked the Earl of Essex, he had been a favourite of Elizabeth and he was also a favourite of King James but Cecil had destroyed him.

Cecil, however, was more trustworthy than his cousin, Francis Bacon, who had betrayed Essex and then once he realised that

Essex was also supporting the bid to make James the king, he had to apologise for his betrayal of his mentor. Unfortunately, the apology came too late to save Essex's life and also Bacon's reputation with King James. Francis Bacon could not be trusted, that was clear, such slight loyalty to his friends did not bode well, as far as the King was concerned.

Court life was fraught with traps, trials and tribulations; most of them were avoidable if you had common sense and integrity, both of which were in short supply at court at that time, even James realised. A pretty face and hunting aplenty were far easier to find.

Cecil was far more trustworthy than most of his compatriots. It was he who had protected Elizabeth's power, yet he was not to be totally trusted; he seemed such a Machiavellian character. Of course, the King had read *'The Prince'*. James was not sure in whose interests Cecil was working. He knew he would work in the Crown's interests. As King of Scotland and England, James worried that the Crown's interests might not serve James's interests. James wondered whether he would be allowed to get his way and fretted over, which issues Cecil would insist on tackling and which James might be allowed to decide for himself, it was a tightrope. Who had ultimate power, himself or 'His Elf'?

Furthermore, as Cecil took up position by his writing table, laid out his papers and stood before him, James was reminded of the figure of Richard III, he shared the same deformity of frame, the same courageousness and wit, so as Cecil cleared his throat, James was unsure of what to expect from his Secretary of State.

His contorted frame made him look like the deformed *King Richard*. The King expected the words: 'a horse, a horse, my kingdom for a horse' to be uttered in anguished tones, or even: 'now is the winter of our discontent'. Instead, he received a well-rehearsed and well-delivered speech, which epitomised the pragmatism of his best advisor. The frisson of feelings, safe in his role, yet having to impress this intelligent and competent state servant, made James feel alert and alive. James had to be on his mettle, there were few people he needed to impress, fewer still that he wanted to impress. Cecil was the exception.

James swayed between loving Cecil as a devoted servant, his little 'elf' who was as loyal as a 'beagle', he was aware of Elizabeth sobriquets; to fearing him and his powerful cadre.

"Our predecessors, my father William Burghley and his grace, Sir Francis Walsingham led the policy that prevented the Papists and their plots from overthrowing the state. I intend to continue that policy, so Your Majesty need fear no let-up in our efforts to keep the crown secure, above all your safety is paramount and that of the Crown is sacrosanct," Cecil boasted.
James knew that Cecil could prevaricate where necessary but, nonetheless, he listened attentively, waiting for a chance to make a witty remark or to detect any disloyalty.

His admiration of his chief advisor was obvious; consequently, he chose his words carefully in his reply, "A noble endeavour, the Tudor dynasty that our House of Stuart replaces was well known for being mainly peaceful at home, except during the reign of Mary, and I want my dominions to be the same!"

He nodded, awaiting Cecil's approval.

"You not only know your history but you are wise Your Majesty," replied Cecil.

He resisted the urge to look up at the stag's antlers that hung from the white washed walls at either end of the hall. They underlined Cecil's contention that his majesty preferred sport to serious thought.

James reassured by Cecil's remark, and the low bow accompanying it, continued his monologue, a sagacious soliloquy worthy of a Shakespearean character.

"I want Cornwall and Northumberland, Shropshire and Yorkshire to be as loyal as my court here in London. Though I know you cannot perform miracles, we need no Popish plots and no rebels, no processions down the Strand or dissension in our land. I want to see the bishops bring order in all things and for all my subjects to embrace the *'Divine Right of Kings'*," the King announced gravely. James's tongue tripped slightly over his words as if he spoke with a full mouth, though his wit shone through between the lines.

He had mentioned those counties where there had been either dissent, some form of uprising or had been scenes of open rebellion, he was well-informed, he had read his histories of both England and Scotland; he knew that history could repeat itself. Both men were aware how fraught diplomacy was.

James feared insurrection almost as much as being blown-up or being stabbed. It was a dangerous vocation being a king. He had been attacked already. James also knew, as everyone at court knew, that Walsingham and Robert Cecil's father William, Lord Burghley, had secured the throne for Queen Bess through their tireless work.

Cecil maintained that trust and perpetuated that consistency. James knew that Cecil would secure the throne for him if he could avoid being assassinated.

It was his turn to speak next and he did so loudly and clearly, setting out his arguments like an experienced and well- trained barrister of law.

"The Hampton Court Conference that you have called will provide ample opportunity to unite the different factions and provide security within the commonwealth and we have managed to secure peace abroad even if negotiations of final settlement take up much time."

"The Spanish are not easy to negotiate with but I cannot argue with you, Baron, please continue," insisted the King, rolling his wrist in encouragement.

"As Your Majesty has so often said the Lord Bishops provide a strong and loyal administrative framework and a brake to the nobles' power," Cecil announced this snippet officiously, his voice sounding as if he were addressing the Privy Council or in the courtroom at the Inner Temple summing up his case.

"Would you like to break the nobles or just put a brake on their influence?" James asked cunningly; he was trying to establish Cecil's desire and motive, he could not resist a bit of word play along the way.

"The nobles need controlling, as you know and the Lord Bishops help the State to do such, the Lord Bishops are supremely loyal and provide substantial money for the Exchequer."

"They aid us with both monies and influence, it is true, yet the Puritans oppose them," James observed wryly as if expecting Cecil to right the wrong.

"Indeed, Your Majesty, it is true," acknowledged Cecil sincerely.

"What do you propose to do about it?" asked James expectantly.

"The Puritans are opposed by the Lord Bishops who being men of influence and money are my natural allies. They provide the exchequer with their plate, the collection money all goes to the Crown, and they enforce and keep the country's laws. Therefore, I must support my good Lord Bishops and the Puritans must be opposed by the King!" Cecil warned dramatically, searching around the half circle of peers for approval. There was much nodding of heads and the odd murmur of 'hear, him'.

"These puritans are non-conformists, they refuse to attend our churches or sign the books there. We have the power to break them if need be," the King keenly offered. He despised the Presbyterians in Scotland and he thought that the Puritans were cut from the same cloth; they wore the same drab clothes at the very least.

"This seems your only course of action. However, the works of those who would undermine the commonwealth continue to form our main concern," continued Cecil soothingly.

"As always," agreed the King reflectively, "we are keen to stamp out sedition and trample on treason."

"The Puritans and Anabaptists provide the need for too much attention: avoiding attendance at services, costing plate and spreading sedition. Their pamphlets cause unrest and consternation within the Commonwealth. Their machinations cause much mischief and distress in a state that needs calm and conformity," Cecil asserted.

He knew his last sentence would hit home like a cross-bow bolt in a target. Cecil was managing to build up a strong case for attacking religions that might undermine the power afforded to the bishops whilst never betraying his mounting irritation at James's uncalled for and continuous interruptions. Cecil in full flow was impressive. Despite being irritated, he still managed to press his argument for curtailing the influence of the Puritans.

"There is much to be made of their desire for a presence and power at court," James agreed readily, not realising the torment that his interruptions caused in Cecil's mind. "Their support is growing in our parliament and their influence spreads throughout the land. These Puritans and their strict ways are worrying."

The King knew of the raids on Anabaptist homes, and the rumours of Puritan dissent, Cecil had provided him with the reports of all their activity, their pamphlets full of protestation and sedition were excellent evidence, the more fanatical the better for Cecil's needs. He had carefully constructed a picture of 'trouble-makers'. He was fully aware of James's detestation of the Scottish Presbyterians and their wish to undermine the authority of the monarchy. Cecil was able to build on that hatred. Everyone knew about their parsimony and their severe lifestyle, it did not want their influence, banning dancing and the theatre, frivolity and fun.

Cecil controlled the information James received in the hope that he would be more malleable. Elizabeth tended to procrastinate; James dithered but he was in fact more easily influenced. Even so, Cecil did not take this influence for granted.

Statecraft demanded a cool head and a firm grip on all subjects especially those who held sway at court. One whispered remark could win or lose the confidence of the King James. Therefore, constant vigilance was needed.

In his view, James, still, too readily favoured the opinion of favourites and he allowed them to influence him far too much. James was also well aware of the Puritans views on dance, drink, plays and parties. It was another reason to despise them.

"You embrace the Catholics as you should," Cecil continued, feeling for the first time that he might be making headway in his plans.

"Indeed, toleration is demanded," agreed James readily,

"They need to be reassured that they are safe and need not fear the Commonwealth. There has been too much persecution on both sides during the last dynasty and it does not bode well for security. However, I feel our leniency over recusancy needs to be reversed. All subjects should conform and attend church for their contribution to the Church and Crown and their observance of the laws of the land. Furthermore, my men report of much mischief making from both Jesuit priests smuggled into the country and from those nobles who have previously caused worry with their plots and plans. Recusancy is a crime against both the Church and the State, robbing the Church of England of respect and robbing the Crown of money collected from the plate passed around at services "

"Catholics, I do not fear; their peregrinating priests I do; they meddle and infiltrate and stir up hatred," James added for good measure.

Cecil ignored the interruption.

"Daily, we have news of such mendicant priests with their mendacious ways and their desire to stir up unrest!" complained Cecil.

James loathed any form of dissent and Jesuits seemed to ferment trouble. Again, Cecil's reports exaggerated the amount of priests who had landed in England, the threat they caused and omitted to mention the number who had been arrested or encouraged to return to their seminaries in France in return for their lives but as these reports were conversations and not recorded observations, it did not matter. He could fabricate or exaggerate the intensity of priests arriving on the shores.
No one could disprove these reports.

James was forced to take Cecil's word for it, the evidence he had provided for the Puritan unrest helped as did they arrest of enough priests to warrant concern. Cecil was quite capable of introducing a smidgeon of hyperbole. If James were suspicious of Catholics in his kingdom, he would be suspicious of those Catholics at Court, as well, Cecil reasoned.

"Keep me informed, I will act when necessary. As you well know the Queen left me with scant resources," moaned James.

He was unable to disguise his disappointment as he still had not recovered from the shock of taking over the English Crown and discovering how little money was available to him.

"Elizabeth struggled throughout her reign to save resources," Cecil replied, not willing to allow his Queen to be denigrated in any way, "She tried to match her expenditure to her income as far as it was possible."

"My court is costly to maintain. Therefore my main concern is to make more money for the Crown, and to achieve that, I need peace and prosperity not dissent and rebellion," the King confessed, ignoring Cecil's loaded comment about Elizabeth.

As a keen historian, James must have heard about the reputation Elizabeth had for her parsimony, perhaps he had heard stories of her constantly trying to save money but such noble actions did not move a spendthrift who wanted to indulge in hedonistic excesses.

She had tried to curb her spending, despite wars and huge demands on her exchequer; King Henry had left her with a legacy of ruined finances. Cecil had followed her 'progresses' about the country, staying at nobles' houses to save the Exchequer money. She knew it was better for her to progress through her kingdom and let her nobles, in their grand manors, feed and entertain the court entourage. Staying at one of her palaces was something she could not contemplate with her scant finances.

"Indeed, Your Majesty, the affairs of state weigh heavy," Cecil sighed dramatically, the King smiled, it was, in fact a slight grin of recognition, playing on his face, he knew the quote.

"These are troubled times," James replied, repeating Cecil's often used quotation from Shakespeare.

It succeeding in flattering him.

"Indeed so, Your Majesty, scarce a day goes by," he added, there was no need to finish the quote. "You are wise to fear the Catholics, they are always up to mischief, their loyalty is to the Pope and not to the king; they do not recognise the *Divine Right of Kings*' that you espouse. They would put the interest of a foreign ruler before those of their monarch."

"Indeed, I have heard such rumblings, not from the Catholics but their Puritan enemies," James replied, nodding his head sagely to show both concern and understanding.

James had warmed to Robert Cecil during this meeting, he remembered fondly, now, that, amongst others, Cecil had encouraged him to take the throne, but still he did not entirely trust him.

He was an efficient servant who put the interest of the King's estate to the forefront, state security was paramount for both men and that was not merely the extent of their bond, it was the cement of their bond.

"As you so rightly say, the commonwealth needs peace and trade, the state, security. No one should be above the law or behave counter to the State and its demands," Cecil argued, knowing that James's view on '*The Divine Right of Kings*' would not allow him to contradict what was said.

"So we need to bring back the recusant fines in order to bring the Catholics back in line," James surmised. "Your reports have insisted such since the fines were suspended at your request. You and I thought the move would be appreciated and that our trust would be reciprocated, but it was not and still the almost daily conspiracies and rumours of dissent filter through to the Court. "The Catholics need to be subjugated; I agree but what is to become of the Puritans?" James asked.

"Do not acquiesce to their demands concerning the bishops but give them a project and, as a sop, agree to one or two of their more simple demands, that would be my counsel."

"I will think on it."

"Your Majesty is wise and I have no doubt that he will reach the conclusion that will benefit us all."

"Have no fear, I will not treat them with kid gloves. Those Presbyterians are the same as these Puritan fellows and their demands caused me no end of trouble and consternation when I was in Scotland. They made my life a misery."

"Spare the rod and spoil the child, I agree. This religion is young and needs a firm hand and guidance as does any young thing, the young rose bush needs a trellis, a foal, a whip, a boy the birch on the bottom or a feral in the face, but ideal hands make much mischief, that we all know."

"Yes, a project might do. I have in mind a fulsome, wholesome and proper translation of the Bible from Latin to English as you well know, perhaps they could be involved in that!"

"Indeed, that would keep them busy, a wonderful idea, Your Majesty."

Cecil's interests were twofold, preservation of his place at the head of the Court and the continued survival and thriving of the Commonwealth. He wanted to see the thriving trade in London rival that of Antwerp in years gone by and to match the new rising star, Amsterdam, as it grew in influence.

Cecil wanted each city throughout the land to thrive as London had, and would continue to do so, if peace could be maintained abroad and at home. That was why he made peace with the Spanish after nineteen years of war. Then, each port would rival that great trading post, Amsterdam and England would have a greater share of the burgeoning shipping and the wealth created would secure the state.

The Catholics could be subjugated further by the reintroduction of fines for Recusants and that money would go some small way to help the exchequer with its finances. The Puritans would be kept under control and therefore bishops, appointed by the King, would continue to influence parliament on the King's behalf.

Cecil's thoughts of these great strategies, and even greater victories, were interrupted by the doors being opened by two Beefeaters. A cold draught that sneaked in behind the soldiers made him shudder. The King spun around in panic and watched nervously to see who appeared. If he had known who it was interrupting them, then he hid it well.

Cecil was equally surprised; he had not expected to be disturbed.

"Ah, here comes my friend to further advise me. Cecil, you know John Ramsay, first Earl of Holderness and Gentleman of the Bedchamber?" James announced. It was a rhetorical question, the men had met several times though never beyond being in the King's presence.

"Of course, always a pleasure," Cecil replied courteously; it was a testament to his skills in diplomacy that he sounded genuinely pleased to see Ramsay. There was no hint of animosity or clue to the contempt in which Cecil held him.

"A pleasure to see you my Lord Privy Councillor," Ramsay responded icily, unable to disguise his dislike of Cecil. Perhaps, he was just too little skilled at hiding his emotions or as Cecil suspected, he felt it was unnecessary to do so.

"The pleasure is all mine, Your Lordship," Cecil added unnecessarily but so sweetly that James felt that he bore nothing but admiration for Ramsay.

Cecil was a consummate actor, a diplomat and a deceiver. Cecil knew him to be the King's favourites and he also knew, from his spies, that Ramsay resented Cecil for his closeness to the King.

In an ideal world, Ramsay would have liked to get rid of the old guard, all the people like Cecil. He represented the 'established court'.

People like Ramsay knew their rise would rely on influence alone; they could not hope to rise while the old guard held control. Cecil, in turn, wondered how people who did nothing rose to be favourites where people like him who struggled and strived daily for the common good had to fight to maintain their position. Cecil bowed courteously, he had been expecting him, his spies had informed him that the King's bodyguard would appear at some point but not so soon, lunchtime he had surmised, but Cecil was alert and on his guard even so, and that was why he would not sit. He was smaller than Ramsay and to stand when he came in would merely accentuate the difference in height.

Cecil was older and wiser; it was well known at court that James had favourites and, generally, they were good looking. Cecil was determined that they would not disadvantage him in any way if he could help it. Cecil knew this favourite's story. Ramsay had been a page at the Scottish court when the Gowrie Conspiracy occurred in 1600. The young Ramsay had stabbed John Ruthven, Earl of Gowrie to death with his dagger, allegedly helping to frustrate a plot to kidnap or murder the King, then King James VI of Scotland. Rumours that the death of Gowrie might have been, in reality, a duel between the two rivals had also reached Cecil's ears and he felt sure that it was the latter case.

Many of those at the Scottish court felt it was a fight between two rivals for the King's favour and the story about kidnap and murder had been used to justify the death of the Earl but they dared not voice such concerns. Ramsay had been knighted in that year and his place at court had been cemented by his new role of the King's bodyguard. He had saved James's life as far as everyone else was concerned, but Cecil viewed him in the same way that Shakespeare viewed favourites, they were: 'made proud by princes'. James had made Ramsay his favourite; Cecil had to accept him. He was a fellow noble, after all.

"Your Lordship," said Ramsay bowing, to Lord Cecil. Everyone at the palace knew that Ramsay was a good looking, charismatic and well-educated Scotsman, no more than any other one of the 'pretty-boys' that the King surrounded himself with at Court.

Cecil decided that serious discussion was over. Education and charm did not make a statesman.

"Ensure you wear your protective vest, we'll do the rest, 'these are troubled times, scarce a day goes by when a king does not lose a crown'! Mark my words," warned Cecil.

He knew when to use drama and when to encourage fear in his king's breast, "however, I swear that it will not be this king and not this crown."

"Protective vest," Ramsay snorted dismissively. "I am here."

They continued their conversation in whispers. Meanwhile, James looked on indulgently, admiring his favourites face and noting it looked more handsome than ever compared to Cecil with his high forehead, widow's peak and pointy features. He did so love to have beautiful things around him.

"Yes, Henri of France was sure everyone loved him and then that mad monk stabbed him," Cecil explained quietly.

"I thought that was Walsingham causing trouble for our French cousins," chortled Ramsay dismissively. "I heard it was an assassin hired by Anthony Standen."

"I heard Gowrie wanted to assassinate you and not the King!" Cecil replied swiftly but equally softly.

"You cannot believe all you hear!" countered Ramsay.

"Be careful what you say without proof, no one would challenge the Divine Right of Kings to rule. Anyone who thinks otherwise had better watch out," Cecil warned.

"Hit a nerve, did I?" Ramsay mumbled so quietly that both men did not hear.

"Come, come, gentlemen, let us talk of more pleasant matters," soothed the King who had heard nothing of the hushed exchange but had merely recognised the change of tone in their voices.

"Your Majesty, your wish is my wish," Cecil breathed.

"I, too, apologise," Ramsay added. "I apologise to you Baron for my lack of decorum."

"You are far too kind," Cecil breathed dramatically, leaving Ramsay puzzled as to whether he was being genuine or ironic in his remarks. The phrase had not sounded sarcastic and yet he was not sure.

"Gentlemen, we have an agenda do we not?" asked the King, charmingly, demanding the men bury their hatchets for the time being. James actively encouraged rivalry; it made people try harder to please him.

"Indeed we do, Your Majesty, to the matter of Hampton Court and our conference here," Cecil answered respectfully. It seemed that all three men were determined to discuss the issues. Perhaps, he was wrong, Cecil reflected, despite Ramsay's presence or because of it; serious conversation would be had, after all. He reappraised his opinion of the Scot but only slightly.

"We have been impatient, the plague of last year robbed us of the opportunity to discuss matters of great importance," James testily complained.

He hated delay, he wanted to deal with problems immediately not leave them festering. The Stuart State took too much of his time in consideration, there was good hunting to be had around Hampton and at Richmond. Too much time was spent in administering laws and dealing with meetings with people who were paid to provide the answers rather than ask questions about solutions. They could be, they should be lie Cecil, checking that they understood what was required and then implementing the policy. He wanted less dancers and more minstrels.

"Yes, the plague in November robbed us of our chance to shore up support," Cecil agreed seriously. He had been frustrated by delays but he had a more sagacious view and greater patience.

"You make the project sound like a building, Lord Cecil, supported by buttresses," Ramsay complained.

He sounded naïve and ill prepared for talk on statecraft as indeed he was, that is compared to seasoned Cecil.

"I do, Your Lordship, the foundations of state provide the first course of bricks for any bastion."

"I expect you see the Puritans, Protestants, Catholics and Humanists as walls."

"How very astute you are!"

"And we Scots in all this?"

"The roof of course, which protects us all."

Cecil kept his true thoughts to himself but he felt that the Scottish roof would be too weak and would be full of leaks if in fact it did not collapse. He saw all the Scots as wet. James had surrounded himself with people who looked like him, pale, thin and sickly; it was like *Bedlam Hospital*. Yet most of them were pretty as well, he had to admit some looked more girl than man, and he resented their place at court, based not on merit but on favour, good looks and friendship, it was no way to run a commonwealth or practice statecraft in his opinion.

"A noble sentiment," Ramsay replied graciously, taking Cecil's comment at face value.

Cecil in turn made no sign that he was being ironic.

"We have the Millenary Petition," James explained. "It is claimed, but not yet proven, that this petition has garnered 1,000 signatures of Puritan ministers."

"Indeed, so, Your Majesty," Cecil said, feeling that perhaps it was his turn to interrupt.

The petition was the reason why they were all there, Cecil dragged away from his warm house and James and Ramsay torn away from their merriment and hunting. That was the whole point of Hampton and the conference. If the plague had not been raging, Cecil would be warming himself by a fire in Whitehall after a brief ride in a warm carriage from his house in the Strand.

"Ramsay," continued the King, oblivious to Cecil when addressing his favourite of all his favourites, "you may be aware that this so carefully worded document expresses Puritan distaste regarding the state of the church in this country."

"I have heard rumours," said Ramsay not fully privy to the detail of the petition, he was not a politician.

"Remind me of what you were talking about before John arrived. Pray, Robert, tell me what you feel about the matter of recusants' fines?" James asked. He wanted to remove the formality of the situation, addressing his subjects by their Christian names might help them relax.

Cecil paused before answering; he knew how much the Roman Catholics looked to James to allow toleration for their religion. Equally, he could not afford to let the Puritans gain an upper hand; otherwise, they might press for greater concessions. Cecil was sure that James wanted the topic repeated so that he could ask Ramsay his opinion.

Cecil had not been able to gauge whether Ramsay would support religious toleration or oppose it, he was rumoured to have Presbyterian leanings but Cecil thought this could be sour grapes and could find no foundation for the rumour, though it might be worth exploiting at a later date.

"We have no choice but to make the recusants pay their fines, in my view, the Puritans will see it as favouritism if we do not; the bishops will view our leniency as an affront to them if we allow any tolerance to the Catholics. Our duty is to support our allies the Lord Bishops, we have to stem the influence of the others. Recusancy is on the increase and Puritans are joining the Catholics in refusing to attend church. Recusants are an affront to Church of England and an affront to the State that demands attendance at mass on Sunday and finance demand a contribution to the State. This contribution in all churches by all subjects can be redistributed by the Crown and by the State to support and nurture the Commonwealth and provide the seed for our growth," argued Cecil convincingly.

"What do you think Ramsay?" asked the King casually, as though he were asking his opinion about the taste of a haunch of venison. It irked Cecil that Ramsay, who he considered a Scottish thug, should be asked for his opinion.

"I would defer to Cecil, Your Majesty, he knows the dangers the Catholics present," Ramsay diplomatically replied.

He was not so careless that he would make an enemy of Cecil.

Some harmless banter was acceptable, dangerous and exciting but allowable; challenging policy would have been madness. Ramsay was all too aware of Cecil's power. Rumours had abounded at the Tudor Court about the 'Trinity of Ruthlessness'; that trinity was Lord Burghley, Robert Cecil and Sir Francis Walsingham. Now, that Cecil was in charge, he was more feared than ever.

Cecil was implicated in three scandals: Christopher Marlowe was killed on the orders of father and son, Lord Burghley and Robert Cecil, who thought that his plays contained Catholic propaganda; the Earl of Essex had been executed at Cecil's bidding; and Sir Walter Raleigh had been implicated in the Main Plot and incarcerated in the Tower the previous year.

"Thank you, Good John," the King said, bowing to Cecil, signalling to him to speak, "Pray, continue Robert."

"It is the law of the land that all subjects are required to attend church on Sunday but the Puritans have started to copy the Recusant Catholics, calling themselves '*Non-Conformists*'. They should be paying plate every week. So the Catholics are encouraging and fermenting dissent. There are many thrones aboard who will exploit the Catholics in our midst; the Catholics, with their fealty to the Pope, are ripe for influence not least by the Jesuits," Cecil expounded, lecturing the King, knowing his audience would be listening intently. "There is the consideration that fines will yield a considerable sum for the Exchequer. The King needs more money and people contributing rather avoiding the plate will help and those not helping should be fined."

Recusancy had been exaggerated to make the Catholics appear in a bad light, the added advantage was that Cecil could pretend that it was a rife and therefore his reintroduction of Recusant fines would bring more money into the government coffers.

Pamphleteers and folklore kept the memories of St Bartholomew and Bloody Mary fresh; Cecil encouraged all of these methods of stirring up suspicion, and fear, of the Catholics. Tall tales further exaggerated details. It was the stabbing of Henri III that encouraged James to wear his padded doublet despite constant goading to desist from Ramsay. Although the event happened in 1589, fifteen years before; the story was retold repeatedly as a warning against religious fanaticism.

Jacques Clement, the assassin, was a Dominican Friar. James knew that fanatics and zealots had to be discouraged at every step. There was also a need to prevent the Puritans from disturbing the balance that kept the state on an even keel. Cecil had reasoned that by destabilising Catholics influence, he would be allowed to deal with the Puritans, next; they were only beginning to organise effectively.

"Have the fines yielded substantial sums of capital in the past?" asked the King. He was suddenly interested, he realised that he needed more money whether it was for securing his position or whether it was for throwing even more lavish parties. Despite wanting to support religious toleration, he had no compunction about raising funds through fines.

He did not mind whether parliament awarded him the money or it was raised in fines. James was desperate for money from any source. The Court was a hungry animal, with a wolf-hound's appetite, needing feeding constantly and that was without parties.

"Indeed, Your Majesty, it has made a contribution to our exchequer," replied Cecil artfully, staring hard at James in case his fib was discovered and carefully avoiding the word significant, he knew that the fines were few but he wanted to give the impression that Catholic dissension was rife, "sadly our expenses rise daily so their contribution needs to be increased still further."

"This is a Christian kingdom but it appears there are many Christians of different hues and persuasions. My Lord Bishops, for example, furnish me with support where I need it most, in parliament. They will help me to raise more money for the exchequer in exchange for my support in ecumenical matters." James decided.

He paused before continuing Cecil pressed home in the silence.

"However, their Christian brothers will not conform, the Catholics and Puritans refuse to attend services," Cecil insisted.

"The law is fair, we should demand that all Catholics attend mass, otherwise the Puritans will remove themselves even more from the mother Church and what will happen, then?" asked James.

"We will have to guard against these non-conformists and their damaging refusal to obey the law. I need the names of individuals in the parish books, I can see those who have not signed and single them out, we cannot afford to have disloyalty in the Stuart State," argued Cecil.

"My hands are tied or so it seems. I would like to debate with the Puritans but I cannot afford to displease the bishops that I need so desperately," warned James. Despite tripping over his over large tongue, making him sound almost unintelligible, what he said made perfect sense.

Any money raising 'Bills' would be passed as 'Acts' only with the votes of the Bishops. The one thing James needed more than anything was money. He had no choice diplomatically and financially speaking.

"There's the rub," Cecil agreed readily.

"I cannot please all my subjects, I wish to please only the useful ones."

"Your Majesty has seen to the nub of the problem as always," Cecil said. "You cannot afford to give the Puritans a say it would upset the Bishops and drive a wedge in our politics."

"Nor would I want to!" growled James aggressively.

"You cannot afford displeasing the Bishops either politically or financially. Your pragmatism impresses," Cecil acknowledged.

He enjoyed the word plays like these; he loved to use 'nub' and 'rub' in the same context, the 'nub' being the centre, the 'rub' being the problem. In writing he was keen to correct essai with the more modern essay, it was part of his bid to impress and surprise people, hoping to unsettle them.

"Thank you," responded the King genuinely, as he felt sure that Cecil had been sincere in his remark.

"Your Majesty," Cecil replied humbly, inclining his head slightly, moving his eyes from the King's face to the floor, to acknowledge his Highness and prove he was a loyal servant.

James was shrewd, clever enough to know the bishops could block the nobles' power in the House of Lords and astute enough to win them over; yet it was praise indeed to have the brightest man in all England validate your views even if you were a king of two countries.

No doubt, James realised that Cecil's own dissemination techniques, the machine that influenced opinion, insisted on proclaiming that Cecil was a genius, repeating it loudly throughout the land. The message had been relayed so often that it was becoming common currency in the court and beyond.

Cecil was always impressed by the words James used and the pragmatic approach he had to statecraft, although, he was less than impressed by James's profligate actions.

Admittedly, the King liked literature and, in particular, he enjoyed plays, but he also liked expensive entertainment far too much. That lavish lifestyle had to be paid for and Cecil knew it would be difficult to finance. James needed to fund his terrible extravagance and lavish lifestyle. He could not afford to live beyond his means without Parliament's consent as they awarded him the Civil List. He therefore needed the Lord Bishops who would award him finance as gratitude for their position.

The Puritan influence in parliament was not appreciated and their seditious vision of removing bishops horrified James. He felt they needed to be crushed and their dangerous ideas destroyed.

"Why have you called Richard Bancroft?" Ramsay timidly asked, he did not think that the Court needed an Elizabethan Churchman to offer advice. He was not yet adept at hiding his contempt for the 'old guard'. He and his contemporaries, the other pretty boys were the future, he felt the old people just clogged up the Court bumbling along and even their very presence was annoying.

"He is the leader of the church in all but name, he will argue on our behalf in all religious matters, I would not countenance anyone else. He will become the Archbishop of Canterbury very soon and as a result my ally in the House of Lords," James explained sighing as if addressing a small child who did not understand a simple concept.

The King spoke guardedly, because Cecil was there, but he was warning Ramsay that it was none of his business who he invited to his conference at Hampton and why. He despaired at Ramsay's inability to hide his contempt for ministers and administrators from Elizabeth's Court.

"Of course, Your Majesty," he replied.

"Remember, My Lord that, all I say is privy to us three alone, Lord Cecil will know if any of this information makes it beyond these walls," warned the King.

"Bancroft was John Whitgift's Chaplin; he will assure stability," Cecil continued supporting his King, "he shares our views, Bancroft believes that Puritanism has the potential to cause many ructions in both society and in the Houses of Parliament."

Ramsay swallowed hard, he had not expected to be treated in this way; he felt his ruff collar seem to grow a little tighter and he felt a cold sweat beading on his brow. No one knew if Ramsay was Presbyterian in views and therefore favoured the Puritan cause.

If any rumours did make it around the Court, it would be he who would lose favour with the King, even if those rumours were started by Cecil. For the first time, he truly realised how vulnerable he was and how Cecil maintained his power.

"We, Lord Cecil, Bishop Bancroft and myself are a trinity of agreement," James continued, "we have decided that Puritans need to be restrained."

"I understand," replied Ramsay nervously.

Cecil reckoned that perhaps this time, he did; both he and the King had been hammering the point home for much of their conversation. Cecil viewed Ramsay as a dullard and a bully he was armed and extremely dangerous in so many ways.

"Good, you will know, then, that much disturbance will come to the common wealth unless we have his support. Bancroft is a Lancastrian man, honest and true."

That addition made Ramsay raise an eyebrow, it seemed Cecil was suggesting that Englishmen were more loyal than Scots.

"Those Puritans would spoil our parties and other diversions, if we let them, my Lord Bishops are vital for my stability;

fortunately Bancroft supports Whitgift's views," added the King, he had been schooled by Cecil to think in such a way.

Ramsay and Cecil realised that the Puritans threat to James's enjoyment of hedonistic entertainment was the root cause of his detestation of these new non-conformists.

Later, Cecil was provided with a room between Ramsay and the Italian Ambassador. The accommodation was comfortable and his position along the corridor clearly displayed the wish of the King that Cecil should cement relationships with both of his neighbours. Above all, Cecil was to help with the conference and later that day, he established himself on one of the benches that, now, ringed the Great Hall. With ink, quill and parchment on a desk installed in front of him, he prepared to watch James at work; he had to admire the James's courage when dealing with potential dissenters and dissemblers.

Cecil wondered sometimes whether James's virtues outweighed his vices or whether his faults outweighed his virtues. 'Only time and tide would tell', he mused inwardly.

Sir John Harrington and several other nobles had tables arranged around the room. Cecil nodded at Sir Thomas Knyvett. Most of the Privy Councillors lounged on the wooden benches, trying to arrange the cushions into the most comfortable positions but some like Cecil, and Harrington, had a table set up in front of them, which they could use as a desk so they could make minutes or dash off a letter.

James had brought his son, Harry, to the meeting. Cecil imagined him as a tennis ball being thrown about by the Puritans and Protestant Bishops just like he had been tossed around by the courtiers at Christmas. He could, when he put his mind to it, picture Harry being thrown above the heads of some Catholic figures if they had been invited. Harry looked like his father but smaller and even more spindly. He sat on a cushioned stool next to his father's comfortable chair. His demeanour mirrored his father's; he seemed like a smaller version of the King, aware that he was being groomed for the throne, he sat patiently. James observed the room, his eyes rolling as they did when there was a stranger in his presence, the eyes were large and seemed too big for his head, similarly his tongue was too big for his mouth, which made him appear as if he was constantly chewing. His eyes darted from person to person and his mouth moved mechanically making him look like a startled cow surrounded by drovers.

The great double wooden doors of the Great Hall opened and a procession of bishops entered, all dressed in their finest vestments, their surplices marked them as high church. They were clearly not Puritans. The bishops were meant to be led by the Archbishop of Canterbury, John Whitgift, but he was too ill. Instead, the Archbishop of London Lord Richard Bancroft led the delegation. He ensured that they stood a good distance from the King, allowing him his ease, and allowing them to show off their ability to fill the hall with their voices.

Barely taking three strides into the room the row of bishops, with Bancroft at their head, bustled forward before stopping as a man and bowing their heads reverently. The doors closed with a reassuring click and James spoke.

"Good morning my Lord Bishops, I humbly welcome you all to our convening at Hampton Court. You are summoned to do great work. I am glad to be here, in England, *the Promised Land*, where religion is purely professed and where I sit among learned and reverend men who protect the Church of England and the law of the land," James announced graciously.

"Your Highness, you are the Supreme Leader of our church and we are your servants, we bow low and only ask how we may be of service," Bancroft responded respectfully, raising his head to speak before bowing low again like his fellow bishops. They remained supine until they were given permission to sit.

"We have called this conference to discuss the *divers* views of our people spiritual, our church theologians, and to examine the ecumenical and legal role of bishops in the realm and the ritual of worship, we humbly appeal to Your Lordships to assist in a expeditious and enlightened settling of matters spiritual and temporal, " James continued.

"Indeed, Your Majesty is wise and a holy man, ruling by the *Divine Right of Kings*," Bancroft added.

"I propose a new translation of the Bible to be named the *King James Bible*, an authoritarian translation, and a new prayer book, but with all these, I will need your tolerance and aid, we will reconvene in one hour."

"If it pleases Your Majesty, we will use the time to discuss how we might best assist you in these matters," announced the Bancroft loyally. He knew that they needed the King as much as he needed them. Their posts were part of his patronage; they knew, in return, James expected their vote in parliament. The Lord Bishops were all too aware of nobles wanting to flex their power, now Elizabeth was gone and the presence or Puritans pervading the House of Commons.

The King continued by reflecting bitterly on his time in Scotland and the struggle he had endured with the Presbyterian Kirk. He was a Calvinist, himself but the Scottish Protestants went too far for his liking.

"I am glad I am not going to be treated as before, elsewhere, a King without a state, without honour, without order, where beardless boys would brave him to his face," he complained, "You are welcome here as men of pragmatism and integrity, learning and sagacity. We will reconvene once I have given a welcome to our Puritan brethren "

With that the doors opened and the bishops faded into the background like water draining from a conduit.

All of them were unsure about who exactly James was referring to in the remark about 'beardless boys' being disrespectful but they assumed he was referring to the difficulty that he had appointing his bishops in Scotland against the wishes of both the Catholic Earls and the Presbyterian Kirk. James made a point of letting everyone know about how tiresome the whole process had been.

The door closed.

James nodded at Cecil who nodded back but the direction of the nod, and its intended recipient, was misunderstood by Prince Harry. He also nodded, necessitating Cecil to respond by nodding back to the prince. Whereby, the King nodded a second time, demanding a return nod from Cecil who received a nod from king and prince. He decided the pantomime had lasted long enough so he lowered his head to make minutes of what was said.

There was silence in the room for a short while, the monarchs staring ahead, Harry as still as statue apart from the swinging of his legs as his feet did not touch the ground; James seemed to be chewing the cud but was instead showing his son how to sit still while awaiting the Puritans. They both looked composed and calm. Cecil was impressed by Harry's deportment.

Cecil knew that James was determined to win over the bishops to keep control in the House of Lords. He would endeavour to do the same. The great double wooden doors of the Great Hall opened again, but this time all the figures were dressed only in black with no black skull caps on their heads; they did not wear the surplice favoured by the Lord Bishops, in the Puritan view, the white tunic was a hated Papist garment only worn to remind people of the Roman church. These Puritans wore pure black, sombre and dour, reflecting their seriousness. They were the antithesis of James's Court.

James knew they took a dim view of dancing, drinking, entertainments of all sorts and the theatre, he had thought he had escaped such Presbyterian 'spoil-sports' by moving south to London but it was not to be. He did not approve of the religious changes the wanted either quite apart from their wish to dismantle the bishoprics that provided much revenue and the rule of in England. Their religious demands included the banning of various garments as well as making the sign of the cross during Baptism, baptism by midwife; the sacrament of confirmation;

and the use of a ring as part of the marriage ceremony. They even seemed to have it in for goldsmiths.

Leading the Puritans was Laurence Chaderton, Master of Emanuel College at Cambridge.

"You have been summoned to this Privy Chamber to plead your case. Please, kneel before your King," James commanded haughtily. "Ad majoram gloriam Deum."

It was a device that Cecil had said would intimidate them and it did. The Privy Councillors spread about the benches of the room, in comfort, looked at the pitiful sight of men on their knees in supplication trying to argue for greater rights. Their faces were impossible to read. Led by Chaderton, the Puritans shuffled on their knees towards the throne to be better heard in their disputations. James found his eyes rolling uncontrollably in his head as these strangers approached; 'Which one of them could be holding a knife?' he wondered despite knowing they had been searched for weapons before being admitted to the hall.

It was another form of intimidation disguised as a precaution by order of Cecil, Secretary of State. He could make people dance on one leg if it contributed to the King's security. Cecil could see how tense the King was; he could feel the resentment and anger building up in James. He could almost read his thoughts: 'There is danger all around and worse than that, I find myself disgusted by the Puritan's petty demands. I might involve them in the translation of the bible to form the King James version of that good book but nought else.

When he felt that the throng had come close enough to be heard and yet not close enough to cause danger, he held up his hand to stop them. They halted. How men on their knees could launch themselves in attack across two yards of carpet before being cut down by a Privy Councillor's rapier or a Beefeater's pike was unclear, all James knew was: 'these are troubled times scarce a day goes by when a king does not lose a crown'. A glance to all his armed Privy Councillors, the beefeaters posted at all four corners and both doors of the hall coupled with the calm demeanour of Cecil reassured the King. The royal person was not under threat. These Puritans were passionate about their faith but, however zealous, they would not harm him. Of course, the Privy Council would cut down any attempt. After the greeting that James seemed to find tiresome, various spokesmen for the Puritans put forward their case, in reasonable terms.

Reynolds was last to make his point: "We object to the exchange of rings in the marriage ceremony and the words 'with my body I thee worship'," he complained loudly.

James replied: "Many a man speaks of Robin Hood who never shot in his bow. I give not a steaming turd for your preaching."

Sir John Harrington wrote what he heard, scribbling away with a quiver of quills and black ink that made spidery marks across parchment. He was using the finest black ink, iron gall nut ink, which had been made freshly that morning by the court scribes from iron sulphate and gallic acid that had been decanted into a pewter pots for the Privy Councillor's use.

He wrote the following: 'The King disregarded their arguments, seated on a chair, his son on a stool beside him. His Majesty talked much Latin and disputed with Dr. Reynolds but he rather used upbraiding more than arguments'.

The Puritans' demands were small but James found it hard to accept all of them, particularly as he planned to put his own practices into the new prayer book and canon. Finally, the King spoke harshly to dismiss them all.

"It seems you all want to strip Christ again! Away with you and all of your snivelling!"

"Your Majesty," Reynolds replied humbly.

The great double, wooden doors of the Great Hall opened, and still kneeling, the Puritans shuffled backwards out of the room, emptying the room of black like spiders crawling up a drainpipe. The door closed and silence reigned supreme for a few minutes while all digested what had just happened.

"That went well," James announced.

His voice broke the silence with a voice that sounded as if he had a mouth full of food and needed to be heard over some imaginary din. Spittle flew across the room and sprayed the floor but no one seemed to notice. The King stood and revealed himself to be a fairly young man. James had become king of England aged thirty-seven. He was tall and broad shouldered. Yet, he had thin spindly legs, which made him look odd with his padded doublet.

"My Lord Harrington, would you ask Lord Ramsay to join us for a glass of *sack* before proceeding with my Lords the Bishops?"

Ramsay as, 'Keeper of the King's Beds Chamber', had been excused attendance at the conference but James felt he now wanted to see a friendly face after having to deal with the Puritans; it took him straight back to his disputes in Scotland and the misery of it all.

"Of course, Your Majesty," he agreed, he could not refuse and so he bustled off to ask a clerk to send for Ramsay before returning.

"There'll be no hunting today, I fear," sighed the King when his messenger took his place at the table again to blot his ink and read his words over.

"Indeed, Your Majesty, the burdens of state weight heavy," replied Lord Harrington, bowing as he stood beside his work.

"We may yet get a new prayer book and a translated of a Bible fitting a king. Come Harry, we must drink and eat a little to keep our strength up for the day ahead; it will be long but we hope it will be profitable."

"You have indeed shown them the way forward, Your Majesty," Sir John Harrington agreed.

He was amenable to the King's arguments not least because the King's haste in dismissing the churlish churchmen meant that his hands had been saved much crawling over the page. Furthermore, his stomach told him it was lunchtime and the meeting's premature end would mean that the midday meal would be served on time. Frequently, under Elizabeth, food was served late or neglected completely. Harrington's servant had found out from the kitchen staff that there was cold pork and crackling on the menu and Harrington adored any meat from a pig.

James's appearance was a source of comment, though not criticism but his eating habits were questionable, to say the least. The formalities of the banquets held by Elizabeth were somewhat undermined in the era of James by his eating habits. Some English courtiers felt his clumsy eating bordered on the comical because his tongue was too large for his mouth. It was like watching an overenthusiastic puppy eating a bone.

His mouth with its over large tongue was described thus in a diary Cecil had read: his tongue 'made him speak full of mouth, and made him drink very uncomely, as if eating his drink, which came out into the cup of each side of his mouth'.

However, after the severity of court life in the latter years of Elizabeth's reign, there was a sense that James was a breath of fresh air.

At dinners in the evening, he could be vulgar or he could lead with jokes that suitably entertained those members of court who were present while shocking the clergy. It was a toss of a coin between the two. He entered into philosophical dialogue with church figures at these dinners though he usually ended his thoughts with some comment that bordered on blasphemous; James was apparently never drunk at these gatherings, it was just his way argumentative way so we are told.

"When will the bishops return?" James asked.

"You have twenty minutes," Harrington replied, "time enough to fortify your majestic frames."

"We have kept such a revel with the Puritans these two days as was never heard the like," James continued mischievously to his attentive audience.

"Indeed, sire," agreed Harrington.

"I was forced at last to say unto them that if any of their pupils had answered them in that way, they would have the rod plied upon the poor boy's bottom."

Two days of meetings had culminated in a humiliation for the Puritans, Cecil could concentrate on the Catholics, now; they were the next to be humiliated, humbled and, with luck, destroyed.

Chapter 2 – The Second Cast with Bait – ii - 15th November 1603

The alleyway was narrow; the light in the stable-yard was dim; the time of day was dusk; the man's stride was slow. He, of all people, knew danger. His hand was on the hilt of his sword as he made progress towards the low doorway of the *George Inn*. Wearing a cloak to keep out the chill of the November evening, he strained to listen for any unusual sound. He could feel his heartbeat. It was quiet outside the inn and, beyond the alley; the hustle and bustle of Borough High Street was barely audible, a dull mumble of indistinct noise that the buildings muffled with their thatch, plasterwork and brick. Robert Cecil, spymaster extraordinaire, listened for any sound of him being followed. There was no echo off the walls from footsteps behind.

Blue-green eyes moving from left to right in their sockets, he scoured the scene before him. Southwark was a dangerous place at any time, especially so at night, but he could see no one else in the gathering shadows of twilight that began to obscure the symmetry of the stable yard. Nobody was loitering in the stable yard; nobody was standing near the threshold of the inn; nobody was at the gutter where drinkers relieved themselves. Even the ostler was in the stables hoping to benefit from some of the warmth given off from the horses.

The chill of the evening penetrated the dark figure's clothes even though he had been out for less than an hour; he had left the tavern at Blackfriars without drinking mulled ale, which had been offered to him and would have brought a flush to his cold cheeks as he crossed in the *wherry* boat to the wicked side of the city. His spies had been informative, keeping an eye on his enemies in The Strand and in the Inns of Court. The figure moved towards the glow of candles inside, newly lit. He smiled to himself, this inn had been called *The Gorge* on old maps and was renowned for its food, it was the ideal place to have supper and gorge oneself and that was his intention.

Money was no object; a feast would be had by the spies. Cecil had a good appetite که night, he believed that the people he influenced should benefit from having the best and he knew how to spend money effectively. A good meal stayed in someone's memory far longer than the value of the purse that bought it.

As he stepped through the doorway, sound and heat rushed at him like a charging bull: the voices of market-traders and lightermen; the laughter of a group of city gentlemen, they had crossed the river, leaving the restrictions behind to visit the pleasures of the south-bank. The cock fighting, the bear baiting and the theatre were big draws to gentlemen and cutpurses as well as those who worked in the area. He had used a lighterman to ferry him from the north side to the south side of the Thames and the twelve-minute journey had chilled him to the marrow.

Crossing to the bar, people noticed the figure, dressed from head to toe in black: black leather boots, black hose, black doublet, black gloves, black Tudor hat and black cloak. This might have seemed ominous on anyone who was not as short as Cecil was; those who had taken too much drink might have thought this man with a forty-two year old face was a teenager wearing a mask but he was armed like a man and had the gait of a nobleman injured in battle.

Those who were particularly observant noticed that he had a hunch back, a deformity from birth, which made him look like a beggar stooping for alms despite his fine clothes. A tailor noticed the quality of the silk, wool, and leather that covered the man's hunched form.

Robert Cecil could feel the eyes upon him, the fleeting glances, the longer stares of the incredulous, the fixed gaze of the expert; all of them were surprised to see such a wealthy lone figure in their inn. They mattered less to Cecil than the mud stuck to the heel and sole of his boot, he would scrape off that dirt on the boot scraper outside his house later; his presence at the drinking house would not be remembered in a month or two.

Baron Cecil Essindene, Viscount Cranbourne, Privy Councillor to Queen Elizabeth the First, esteemed advisor and Secretary of State to James I, should never have been at an inn in the 'den of iniquity' that was Southwark but urgent secret state business needed to be attended to immediately. Even so, a spy must limit the outer appearance of their impatience in order to avoid raising suspicion; their mask must show calm even though they are boiling with frustration. Therefore, he waited patiently for the barman to finish working through the line of customers who had arrived, at the bar, before him, whilst inwardly cursing the lack of alacrity shown by the staff in serving the throng. He had preparations to make.

Robert Cecil was a slight, crooked, hump-backed middle-aged gentleman; dwarfish in stature, he possessed a face not irregular in feature; at times thoughtful and subtle in expression; thin, regularly brushed and combed, reddish hair; a thin tawny beard; and large, pathetic, bluish-greenish-coloured eyes; sometimes blue sometimes, green, sometimes grey. Despite his diminutive size and puny frame, he gave a withering look to a burly man who tried to press his way in front of him when both knew that the working man had arrived after the gentleman, Cecil.

He was short, not invisible. A quick glance at the hand resting casually on the hilt of his sword made the queue-barger think twice. The interloper bowed cordially and, when asked what he wanted, indicated with an open palm sweeping from his shoulder to waist that the gentleman was first.

"I am looking for the room booked by Monsieur Duende Sabueso Perrous," said the figure.

"Of course, sir," said the innkeeper obsequiously, before shouting over his shoulder for his daughter Mary.

"Thank you!" the charming Cecil replied cordially.

"Mary will show you to the room," continued the innkeeper formally, trying desperately to impress the stranger.

"You are far too kind," Cecil breathed dramatically, leaving the innkeeper puzzled as to whether he was being genuine or ironic in his remarks. The phrase had not sounded sarcastic and yet he was not sure.

The inn-keeper had wanted to show off his efficiency but he was not sure whether to beam with joy or steam with fury. Cecil had once been described as having a mind and manners that had been trained for courts and cabinets. Also, he had an almost ingenuous disposition to produce puzzles, convoluted conspiracies and massive dissimulation with which he controlled the opinion of some and produced fear in others.

This disposition was said to constitute a large portion of his character. He was much more complex and far cleverer than that. He was wilier than a fox. His strategies were more convoluted than a *Gordian* knot, and he was a better hunter than the *alpha-*

wolf using all those around him to bring down any prey that stood in his way.

Halfway up the stairs he dismissed Mary with a coin sufficient to reward her guidance but not too large to mark him as an over generous tipper. Discretion was what was needed at every turn, although when he walked into the room and firmly closed the door, he was assailed by indiscretion.

"A brilliant subterfuge," cried Griffin Markham. "Using your nicknames to book the room, my little beagle, my little elf. 'Queen Bes' used to call you by both epithets; I remember you told me that on our first meeting."

"How very careless of me, still I was trying to get you to like me," replied Cecil in a bored tone. He was being playful.

"Yes but then you translate them into Spanish, before finally; using a further trick to put Monsieur before and an 'ous' on the end so that people think it is a Frenchman's name. You are too cunning."

There was genuine admiration in Markham's voice; he thought his boss was a fox. Who else could have arranged for his release and allow him to roam freely around the city?

Markham had been tried and convicted of treason, yet he had been reprieved by Cecil and allowed to leave the Tower in secret; even his dearest friends imagined him still there and his correspondence likewise seemed to emanate from there. Later, rumours of his banishment to the Netherlands were circulated to stop the flow of correspondence to the Tower of London.

"You are far too kind," Cecil breathed dramatically, leaving Markham puzzled as to whether he was being genuine or ironic in his remarks. The phrase had not sounded sarcastic and yet he was not sure.

"The kindness is all yours," he replied swiftly, remembering as he always did that his freedom was a gift from Cecil himself.

"Yes it is," replied Cecil glancing around the room as though he had lost interest in the conversation.

"Your Lordship." Markham added sycophantically.

He was effectively a man in the shadows but it was infinitely preferable to execution. He should have been in the Tower of London serving his time in prison but Cecil allowed him discreet release as a bodyguard.

"I am glad you know your place," replied Cecil scathingly, he enjoyed praise and flattery but he hated the obsequiousness practised by sycophants even if they were from noble families and even if they were superb swordsmen. There was a fine line and Markham seemed to always cross it.

The room was sparsely furnished: a long, low dark stained bench in the corner, on which Markham had been sitting, an oak table, with heavy legs, was in front of the bench and on top of it were two carved thick wooden candle sticks. On the far wall, an identical bench and, by the door, a smaller rectangular table made of deal with four scrolled legs leading to bulbous feet and crossbeams slightly above the feet to give the table rigidity and strength. One table was designed for work and one for pleasure. The one by the bench was for dining; the one by the door was to be used as a worktop for deciphering.

Cecil had insisted on the layout, had seen to it himself, he knew the devil lay in the detail and he was a devil for detail himself. He seemed disappointed that this table was not laid with tableware, bread, cheese, cold meats and fresh fruit; he had not eaten well that day, too much correspondence had made him miss lunch and his breakfast had been rushed and small; a hunk of bread, less than a small handful and a small finger of hard cheese.

There was a second door in the opposite corner, hidden in the wooden panelling. On Cecil's silent signal, Markham approached the door and pressed a piece of panelling that released the latch. The door opened into the room, which was as large as the other but furnished with only two chairs and revealed the figures of Sir William Waad and Sir John Popham. Startled by the door opening, they broke off their conversation and gathering up the hats that they had laid on their laps, they rose from their chairs, slipped through the panels and so formed the congregation.

"Good of you to pop in Popham, Waad, you take a seat?" Cecil said without a trace of humour. Griffin Markham suppressed a smile, he was amused by the word play but he dared not show it in front of such esteemed nobles.

Waad had interrogated Markham in his investigation of the *Bye Plot*. He was fortunate to be spared; Sir Walter Raleigh and Sir Henry Brooke had been imprisoned in the tower for their alleged roles in these plots and there they remained. Sir John Popham was the Lord Chief Justice, the highest legal post in the country, his companion, Sir William Waad, had just been knighted for foiling the Bye Plot and the Main Plot and was lieutenant of the Tower. In the room were three of the most powerful men in England and Markham feared them all. They, in their turn, pretended not to have heard what Cecil had said.

Now, that they were all gathered together as co-conspirators, they could take off their swords; Cecil undid his belt buckle and placed the scabbard next to the fireplace. The other two leant theirs against the wall on the other side of the fireplace, which meant they were free to move around the room unencumbered; yet close enough to their weapons should they need it.
Markham still wore his sword only because he was the lookout and their main guard, actually Cecil's bodyguard. Markham was an excellent swordsman and he had proved his bravery and commitment in the Essex rebellion, albeit on the wrong side as far as Cecil was concerned. He supported Essex, Cecil's nemesis hence his time in the Tower.

"We have with us a coded letter," announced Waad pompously. He knew how important espionage was in securing the state and was puffed up by his own importance.

"I have the key with me," Cecil assured him.

Waad brought a scroll from behind the fold of his cloak and, with a flourish, untied the red ribbon, pulling on the bow and letting it drop to the floor where Markham would fetch it later.

Markham rushed to the door, opening it and looking down the stairs for anyone coming before closing it quietly and nodding reassuringly in the direction of the others.

"Who have you placed as look out in the other room?" Cecil asked sounding efficient.

"Smith and Parsons," Popham replied.

Smith had hair as white as snow; Parson's hair was as black as coal. They were two of Cecil's most trusted men.

"Ah, salt and pepper!" Cecil cried, smiling happily for the first time that evening, "very good! Markham, ask one of them to get us some ale, then take up your sentry post."

"They brought this letter from Tower Hill," Waad explained.

"Excellent, now, to work: we few, we happy few, we band of brothers," added Cecil. An admirer of William Shakespeare, he delighted in quoting from his plays.

"Ah, *Henry V*, my favourite," sighed Popham knowledgeably. He too enjoyed the playwright's work.

Cecil unhurriedly unfurled the letter on the table.

The three spies pounced on the corners; Popham and Waad, placed a candlestick on the top left and bottom right corner, before pressing their free hands on the free corners. Cecil took a book from the inside of his doublet; opened it at the centre page and unfolded a piece of paper that had been folded in four.

The unfolded folio had holes punched over it in order to highlight certain letters in the text. He waited for Markham to return to his position next to the door, heard footsteps cease, turned to assure himself that Markham was craning his head to listen at the door, nodded seriously and turned back again to the letter.

"Who's it from?" Waad whispered impatiently.

"What's it about?" Popham asked urgently.

"One of my finest operators," Cecil announced proudly, "one versed in Spanish and French, a trader recruited to Walsingham's spy school during the reign of Queen Bess. He sends outstanding intelligence from across the channel; we shall call him *the Man of La Manche*."

"What does he say?" Waad said, excitedly.

"Patience, My Lords, you must allow me to decipher the message with my key," Cecil warned menacingly.

Markham grinned from the doorway. He was on look out, listening for any sound on the stairwell. It was a pleasure working for one of the cleverest men if not in Europe, then, in England.

Markham had been saved from execution by Cecil and was now his most devoted ally. It was not just that he owed his life to Cecil; it was his realisation that the state survived thanks to him, the stunningly astute Secretary of State.

"Is it good news?" asked Waad, who was rolling up the message as Popham replaced the candlesticks. Cecil deliberately folded the folio in four and replaced it between the leaves of the book; page IV, his lucky number.

"My men at Katie's dock are working as efficiently as ever. The letter was dated five days ago. What do you think about that for an efficient messenger service?"

"Brilliant," Waad agreed. "Shall I destroy the message?"

Cecil nodded and watched Waad place one end of the scroll into the fire. He noticed the flame leap from fire to parchment before he continued, "That is the key to our success gentlemen, efficient communication of important knowledge."

"We have the finest network of informers in the known world," Popham exclaimed.

"Yes," agreed Cecil, "it is good news for us, but bad news for our Catholic friends. It is an ironic coincidence that it should be delivered to St. Catherine's dock for I fear the Catholics will yet be broken on this wheel."

"Is it some Popish plot, some fiendish Papal undertaking?" asked Popham, his indignation scarcely disguised, his face flushed, his hand trembled, he was physically excited almost jumping for joy, desperate to know the news, "what ghastly plot have they come up with, now?"

He, too, was fascinated by the pale blue, yellow and orange that crept up the scroll, the black ash fluttering around the fireplace. The men were all fascinated by fire and heat, Cecil because it could destroy everything, all evidence and trails; the others because it could grasp all their visual attention. The flames gave heat and a spectacularly colourful display.

"Better," teased Cecil, not wanting to reveal the truth. With barely four fingers width of parchment left, Waad tossed the rest into the fire before he had his fingers burned.

They knew the necessity of leaving no trace of their meeting. England was in danger of invasion and all manner of threats surrounded the state. They preserved it.

"What is it?" Waad wondered desperately, wishing that he and Popham had been sent to the spy school to learn the codes or had been quick enough to spot the message revealed by the alignment of the holed paper over the original. Cecil had barely placed the 'key sheet' on top for more than a minute; such was his practice in reading codes and his skill in deciphering his agent's words.

"The Jesuits are sending over three more priests; they will be landing at Polperro at the next full moon," Cecil revealed happily as self-satisfied as a cat after a mackerel snack. The information was just what he needed to ensure his spies followed the priests in their progress.

"But that is a disaster," Waad complained.

"Is it? Why pray?" Cecil asked.

"God knows what mischief they could get up to, especially down in the West Country, fermenting rebellion," Waad continued.

Waad was becoming more agitated; he began pacing the room anxiously. He strutted back and forth in front of the fire, getting more and more heated, physically and emotionally.

He was not known to be an anxious man but the idea of a Catholic revolt made him nervous, he had after all imprisoned several plotters and this note promised more trouble.

Cecil played on the fears of such men who saw Catholic insurrection as inevitable.

"You best explain, Popham," Cecil instructed smoothly and patiently. He carelessly examined his nails; the sight of which made Waad stop in his tracks and stare.

They were all aware of how much Waad despised the Catholic priests and plotters despite having friends who were recusants. He was a true patriot and devoted member of the state. Cecil's chief ability was to strike fear into the breast of normally overtly logical men throughout the court, throughout the City of London and throughout the land.

"Firstly, this is the Catholics playing into our hands. We want more priests being landed in secret. News of these clandestine landings stir up fear in the populace, just as you have expressed," Popham explained to Waad who was the newer recruit, having only recently been brought into the confidence of Cecil.

"With good reason!" argued Waad, stuck to the spot as if petrified, he was almost like a statue clothed in fine robes.

"Yes indeed," Cecil agreed, nodding sympathetically even though his face momentarily revealed his displeasure at Waad's constant interruption, Cecil hated his actors being interrupted when they were saying their lines. It had taken him careful rehearsal and its effectiveness was diluted if it was not delivered as one cold blast of fear.

"They are the greatest threat," Waad added, he could not be consoled so easily.

"Let us continue, though, nevertheless!" Cecil urged, more in frustration than in entreaty.

"Of course," apologised Waad humbly.

"We want the fear of Catholics to be paramount in everyone's breast, can you see?" argued Cecil, "That way, they cannot garner more favour with the King and, we in turn, become more powerful and more necessary. We are not the first state to use the fear of insurgency or rebellion to maintain a firm grip on power."

"But King James favours Catholics, he is tolerant of them, he has halted their fines," complained Waad, calming down slightly.

"We advised him to remove recusant fines," Popham announced, pausing to allow the momentous news to sink in.

"But why?" asked Waad, not seeing the reason.

"To make us seem reasonable, of course!" Popham exclaimed, a smile playing on his lips.
He did think this was one of Cecil's most brilliant moves

"I see," mumbled

"You see, good; we have been fair and just and still these Catholics try to undermine the state, to erode the Commonwealth, to threaten peace and trade."

"I agree trade is necessary for us, it is our life blood," Cecil added encouragingly, "we need unity in this isle as well!"

"As an island nation our common wealth relies heavily on the movement of goods in and out of the country," continued

Popham excitedly, following Cecil's train of thought, "look at Antwerp, they buy our wool, they sell cloth, they grow wealthy!"

"Should we not worry about those in the West Country? They have rebelled before, we should also be aware of danger elsewhere in the kingdom, remember the Pilgrimage of Grace from the north," Waad warned.

The room went silent for a moment and the group looked worried, revolution was a topic that no one wanted to discuss. They all feared the peasants revolting and seizing their property. They could not believe they had been able to maintain the status quo. They were all waiting for the nightmare that they believed inevitable. It never came.

Waad could not help feeling that all that he had achieved in his life might be snatched away from him; he saw the poor in the streets and wondered why they did not rebel and worried that they might give their allegiance to a Catholic cause. As a result, of his fear, he always gave alms to the poor.

"They very half-heartedly rose up; we pursue them not, they press us not," Popham pompously disputed, "we should not worry about them!"
He could only see the trade that came to London and the wealth it created, which made him rich and therefore more able to give alms to the poor. He did not shirk his responsibility to the poor unfortunates on the streets of London but he was secure in the knowledge that English Catholic's new Patron Saint was St. Jude, the patron saint of lost causes. The old influence over the Court and the parliament was being eroded.

If he considered matters carefully, he was not very concerned by the prospect of revolt on the streets. There was, he realised, little danger in rebellion with such a wonderful state infrastructure, which included such diverse elements as good communications, diamond-hard intelligence and a network of sheriffs and soldiers who would keep order.

"Those West Country Catholics look to their parish priests as village elders, dispensing advice and arbitrating over disputes in the locality; they don't want those haughty Jesuits spoiling their lives with their strict ideas and their instruction. The fishermen and farmers have no time for it. They want down to earth religion, simple rules and priestly advice, not lecturing from Jesuits about theology and theocracy," Cecil explained, managing to sound patient and knowledgeable.

No one could argue with his thesis, he, of all people, should possess the best information in the group.

"What's more," Popham continued, "the Jesuits know it; they cannot influence those people; so they provide services for the educated; they have no influence over the poor; so they try to bring their ideas to the rich."

"Precisely," interrupted Cecil, he liked to praise those who were perceptive. "Go on, tell us what that means."

"We have the ability to destroy the Catholic hierarchy," Popham continued gleefully, his face took on an almost ghoulish look.

"How so?" asked Waad, bewildered, no one had told him the last details for some reason; it irked him more, he hoped that he would have been included in the details of everything, he felt distinctly left out.

"We have already removed recusancy fines, thus allowing priests to settle in our land, we plan to reinstate the fines, they would be in place now, but the Hampton Court Conference has been delayed," explained Cecil.

"When will the conference take place?" Waad asked.

"Hopefully, it will take place in January, have no fear, 1604 will be the year that Catholics disappear. They will vanish from politics and in that they will lose their voice," Cecil replied.

"Soon enough," soothed Popham

"The conference will make it illegal to harbour the priests; we have them, don't you see? Outlawing the priests who come to these shores, and making it treason to help them, will allow us finally to dismantle the Catholic nobility."

"How?" asked Waad reddening in frustration.

"Only the rich can provide the Jesuits with hiding places, priest holes, food and transport or safe conduct from place to place, we are sending inspectors about the country even as we speak," Cecil continued, the listeners were spellbound and he drove home his message that he knew would be disseminated to the Privy Council in a few days. "We have years of intelligence, many of these Jesuits are trained to dress and talk like noblemen, to ride and hawk and hunt, to be adept at sword play, the Pope provides them with money, they are imposters who, in short, appear to be noblemen, with their gallantry and manners, even their swordsmanship and horsemanship, they are as natural as the real nobles, they seem to the manner born and like priests at prayers no one suspects any mischief."

"We have heard of such priests," Waad said, feeling that his voice had not been heard enough and that a wise word would not go amiss.

He was incensed by the behaviour if these mendicant priests and found himself incandescing that they should use subterfuge. Yet Cecil's *spions* acted in the same way, Waad did not realise, he was not able to make the connection. Even if he had, filthy Papists were underhand scoundrels who wished to undermine the state and turn the common wealth over to the Pope and his puppet, the King of Spain whereas Cecil's spies were brave *bravos*, defending the realm

"We cannot afford a standing army here to police all the Papist nobles. We cannot afford the luxury of waging open war, fighting other armies has drained our exchequer before. It is cheaper to fight our battles abroad, buying mercenaries to help our allies," Popham added needlessly.

"Your point is?" asked Waad imperiously. He had grown increasingly incensed by Popham's ability to talk merely in order to hear his own voice.

Cecil, too, wondered why he was discussing foreign policy when they were discussing the realm's security, at home not abroad. He suspected that Popham was trying to impress everyone in the room. It was not necessary nor was it clever, Cecil decided.

Waad, on the other hand, seemed to be quite reticent in his views and concerns, which was not at all like him; he was normally far more incisive and effusive. Markham watched warily from the door; he was not surprised by Popham's bluster and pompousness but he was shocked by the steeliness in Waad's voice. Something had clearly upset him in Popham's manner.

"I am aware of that," hissed Waad, anger seemed to be replacing his usual fear for the first time that evening, "You will remember my report on the matter, which I compiled while in the Low Countries, entitled, *'Volunteers, Mercenaries and Monies'*."

"A wonderful piece, I recall," Cecil said with such genuine honesty that Waad felt calmer immediately.

At least, Cecil appreciated his efforts and his experience, the buffoon Popham was just a self-aggrandising but Cecil had seen through him. Popham blushed, the heat rising through his head, in his pompous belief that everyone wanted to know how clever he was, he had treated Waad as inferior, having forgotten that he was the author of such a valuable and thoroughly researched report. He would have to be more careful, bide his time and bite his tongue. Trying to be erudite, he had shown himself to be ill informed, instead. He had to think less rashly if he were to command Cecil's respect and consider his actions more fully if he were to maintain toleration from the others.

Markham, opened the door quickly before shutting it again and whispering, "The maid, Mary approaches with our victuals."

"About time, too, I am famished; Popham, would you please get Salt and Pepper to bring up four tankards and a jug of ale? They'll not want; the landlord has a jug for them once they have made their delivery, they can drink it next door as they keep watch" Cecil announced thoughtfully.

Immediately, Popham left to order the beer, Cecil, ever the congenial host, stood while the two other noblemen moved from their corners of the room and sat at the bench complying with Cecil's request, communicated by a sweep of the hand.

He watched patiently as Mary approached the table. Was he examining her as a potential spy to add to his network or as a woman? Was he looking at the cloth and wondering which of the victuals he would choose to satisfy his hunger? She sensed his gaze and looked over to him. He smiled encouraging her and taking his cue, she spoke up.

"Good evening sirs, your supper fare has arrived," she announced, gently placing a large pewter salver on the table, which was covered in a muslin cloth. She was a pretty and comely wench, all the men could see that but only Markham would have admitted it. Once her hands were free to clutch the pleats of her dress, she performed a small curtsey and smiled sweetly at Cecil. He would not forget her in a hurry.
"Ah Mary, what do you have for us?" asked Cecil jovially. It was his order, he knew what was there, he wanted to entertain his guests with the items he had gathered. He watched as she deftly swiped away the cloth that covered their food. He noticed her elegant hands, which were raw from scrubbing and washing.

"Goat on the shank, sir," she replied respectfully, "mutton on the bone and pork trotters; oh and before I forget to tell you, that handkerchief, there on the side, was delivered and I was told to present it with the food. Pray gentlemen. If you require any other victuals, we have all manner of libations to quench a thirst or meats to fill a belly."

"Thank you Mary, but we have sent for some ale, we'll not want. Well-done, Mary, a veritable feast. *Crubeens*, are my favourite, the meat on a pig's feet can never be beat. Tell me, how do you manage to have goat in this season?"

"'Tis dried and scented with spices, Sir, coming from Spain," she explained smiling shyly and catching his eyes with hers to show the veracity of her claim.

Pretty and knowledgeable, Cecil noted as she spoke, a useful addition to his network were she a man, a useful spy even so. Popham returned and, causing as much commotion as possible, took his place opposite Waad and Markham, bowing at both. They bowed in turn. All eyes turned to Cecil.

"Not from Spain direct, Mary, surely, not so late in the year. Their gunwales are filled with sack. I'll wager this was traded in Galway for cod, the Spanish are mighty keen on those fish salted; *bacalao*, they call it. This, then, must have been sold on by an Irish trader, for what do you think Popham, not their ghastly cod that the Spanish salt and boil?"

"Perhaps the finished cloth, English wool is still the finest in the world," he guessed. "I am partial to the lamb that provides it too!"

It was well known that English trade with Antwerp benefitted the cloth-workers of the Spanish Netherlands as well as the sheep farmers in England. For decades English wool had been turned into finished cloth. Antwerp had been the centre of that trade. Until the Spanish had allowed the River Scheldt to become silted up, the trade between London and Antwerp had been huge, benefitting both nations. War had ruined that trade, the River Scheldt had been silted up and all of them, save Mary who was too young, were aware of the devastating effect such action had had on the sheep farmers, cloth-makers and tailors on both sides of the channel. They had sought other markets and the west coast of Ireland was good ground for sheep, a ready supply of wool.

"Absolutely, the cold climes make wool a weighty gift. You may leave Mary. We require nothing further at present," announced Cecil kindly.

He waved her away and joined the other three, he chose to sit next to Popham. Mary curtsied again and left, knowing that this was one of the most refined gentlemen she had ever served and that when she cleared away the plates after their repast, there would be a coin for her. She scurried to the door and skipped happily down the stairs. These were fine gentlemen and they would doubtless show their appreciation with a generosity she would remember.

"What's in the handkerchief, your grace?" asked Waad, his curiosity could not be contained. He enjoyed surprises and had done since he was young, it was shocks he did not favour.

"Something so rare," explained Cecil dramatically, warming to his audiences curiosity, "King James himself gave me a dozen today, which I have brought to share with you."

"What delicacies are they in such a small package, a dozen you say?" Markham asked, even his curiosity was piqued. Generally, he was a cool head who waited to learn.
He rarely demanded answers but the excitement of such a puzzling gift took control of his senses. They were suitably impressed by the gesture, as Cecil knew they would be. It was all part of the joy of working for Cecil. There were surprises all the time, some small, some great.

"Let me show you," Cecil exclaimed excitedly, he enjoyed the game as much as the other participants did. Undoing the knot that fastened the four ends, he spilled the contents of the silk handkerchief around the meat. All the men around the table gazed at the fruit that looked orange in the candlelight.

They were mystified and Cecil enjoyed the confusion. The New World provided much amusement with its unusual gifts and he enjoyed listening to his cadre vying for attention, a band of brothers, indeed. They all wanted to win his favour, the rivals all wanted to be the superior person and impress the Secretary of State like diligent school children who all knew the answer to an easy question.

"Are they cherries that have no stalk? They are not red enough, pale cherries but with a short stalk," suggested Popham who was closer to the light from the fire, which augmented the flame from the candle.

"Guess again?" Cecil smiled, stroking his ginger beard with enjoyment; he knew they would never guess.

"Are they small, smooth strawberries?" ventured Markham hopefully; they really were odd. The skin felt smooth like a grape and yet they were as red as pimentos.

"You can touch them," Cecil said encouragingly.

"They are a smooth as apples but as small as blackberries," noted Waad without committing himself. He, the master of hyperbole both verbally and in his report Cecil remembered squeezed one. "Do not press too hard," Cecil commanded, becoming concerned for the first time, "they will explode, treat them gently."
"What are they?" asked Waad not willing to guess.

"Love apples," Cecil announced proudly, picking one up gently and admiring the skin in the candlelight. "They have travelled far, yet see how delicate they are."

"Is it the token given to a sweetheart? I've never seen one, of course I have heard to talk of them but never laid eyes on this fabulous fruit," complained Markham.

They all murmured in agreement. They were a wondrous sight.

"That's the food that is given by a gentleman to a lady to show his interest in her," announced Waad gleefully.

"The same fruit, from the Americas. Only those in favour at court are given them as presents by our King, these are rare treats indeed, you spoil us, so," Popham sighed gratefully. It was an honour to have such rare fruit bestowed upon them.

"Some people call them tomatoes!" Waad said.

He was a very knowledgeable individual despite his anxieties. His knowledge of law was legendary. It was a surprise he knew of the tomato.

"You mean potatoes," Popham corrected firmly. "I am sure of it!"

There was no end to Popham's bluster; he was convinced that he was always in the right.

"No, no," Cecil interrupted before the two men could start to argue, he did not want a dispute. "Potatoes are white and must be boiled or baked or they are as hard as a devil's toenail."

"Really!" marvelled Markham, "Potatoes are hard and tomatoes are soft, incredible."

"The New World is full of wonders," Waad added obsequiously, not wanting to be left out of the conversation. "We are blessed to receive them."

"If only we could swap all the rotten Papists for all this sweet fare," Popham said his voice full of menace. He truly loathed the Catholics; he had been brought up on tales of the cruelty that had been attributed to Queen Mary by Elizabethan historians and the gall and temerity of Thomas More attributed to him by Henrician scholars.

"I have an even better plan, and those Catholics left in England after my plot will wish they were anywhere else but here. The die is cast," Cecil countered with malice in his voice.

His blue-green eyes blazed in the reflection of the fire.

All the men in the room knew that his words would become true, not one of them doubted it. They were aware of all his manoeuvring behind the scenes, in Queen Elizabeth's reign, removing Essex and Raleigh who were trying to influence her; his work to put James on the throne and his plans to limit the power of Catholics and Puritan.

"So when you have finished, the Catholics will be finished too, we will be chartering boats for them to take them across the ocean; those Recusants will become potato and tomato merchants. They will take their Virgin to Virginia and there they will establish their Promised Land," added Waad, trying to mimic Cecil's malicious tone; it just sounded as if he had something caught in his throat, as if he were choking.

"I like your imagery, white potatoes our purity and red tomatoes for the blood spilled," said Popham. He, too, was trying to impress, unfortunately, he only succeeded in demonstrating his ability to make connections.

He thought that his words were impressive; the others did not. Like shadows, *Salt and Pepper* appeared in the panelling as the partition popped noisily open. *Salt* coughed to announce their arrival; not so much a cough, no one would want his tankards, more of a closed mouth, ahem.
Then, carefully carrying two tankards each, they deftly delivered the receptacles, placed them on the table and silently withdrew.

"Gentlemen, may I ask you to stand and toast the King whose reign is safe in our hands. A toast to the King James I of England, God save the king," Cecil cried heartily.

They all rose; raised their tankards to their chins; and after toasting King James with loud grunts and growls, repeating precisely Cecil's last sentence, they drank a draught of ale.

"And before we eat; one more toast; confusion to our enemies," he added, raising his tankard another time.

"Confusion to our enemies," the other three chorused in perfect unison, before raising them again in toast and quaffing more ale.

This toast was much more to their liking as was the hearty meal that awaited them after they had quaffed back more ale. Beer was wonderful stuff for heightening the appetite, they all agreed on that. They had not noticed that Cecil had merely raised the tankard to his lips and had not drunk a drop, nor would they later notice that as their tankards were filled through the night, with jugs delivered by Mary.

Cecil would merely bring the brim to his lips before returning his to the table. He was a small man and only a little beer could make him tipsy. He might drink at home to help him sleep, but abroad, out and about, he kept sober and let others sing and shout. His success also lay in his ability to listen to others when alcohol helped their tongues loosen. When he thought of loose tongues, the image of his King drinking and eating immediately appeared in his mind's eye. He dismissed the thought and satisfied his hunger with the feasts, his favourite foods would help him forget all beasts.

Chapter 3 – Getting the Sack – 4th November 1605

"Captain of the Guard," cried a sentry, his voice echoing off the vaulted cellar ceiling.

The sound of footsteps filled the brief silence that the sentinel's voice had created. Even the rats scurrying about the dust searching for spiders stopped as his voice boomed, bouncing off the brickwork. A stout soldier, with a grey beard, led a troop of four men each armed with a sword and carrying a pike. His hand rested on his sword and it was clear that although beautifully polished, his breastplate was old. He smiles benignly to the sentry on duty.

The protective plate was fashioned to fit a thin young man and the leather straps had only just managed to contain the expanded frame lashed on the final notch. On his head, he wore a helmet with a wool cap underneath to soften the feel of the metal and to keep his head and ears warm. His legs were clad in grey wool hose; they looked strong and slender, like those of a young man. His girth showed a love of taverns, ale and food, food and ale and perhaps a little more food with the ale.

"Well, Tom, soldier of mine, any news this November night?" the captain asked warmly.

"I have none, only that I'd like to go home uncle, 'tis cold and bitter," replied the sentry shivering slightly, his teeth chattered almost imperceptibly.

These cellars were cold; the Thames nearby was almost frozen, chilling rather than warming the structures on the banks of the river. Furthermore, the November evening had no cloud cover to trap any heat from the day and there was a bitter north wind blowing, cold and damp, an uncomfortable atmosphere for those abed, more so for those abroad on such a night. Remaining still in cold weather was not a comfortable experience particularly with the cold Thames running by and a chill wind blowing.
He might have got as cold, anyway, in the market. He knew, though, that on a stall, outside, he would have been moving about and working, piling crates and moving stock about, rummaging about around the place. All he could do on guard duty was wriggle his toes and pace back and forth between the walls, occasionally he put his pike against the wall and flapped his arms to get some feeling back into his frozen fingers. His gloves helped little.

"Hear men, he calls me uncle, there is not a better loved officer in the Palace of Westminster, I'll wager, nor London itself. I would have been proud to serve with you all in the Low Countries had you been old enough, I've often told you," continued the captain, "I told you to wear your warmest clothing, November 4th 1605 promises to be the coldest night we have felt and I've felt a few in my time abroad; there was once...."

"Captain, good uncle, can I be relieved, I have been here a long time, my bladder is almost full and I need hot soup to bring life back to my cold bones," Tom whined, not caring that he was interrupting and revealing to all that he was not a man but a boy of fourteen.

"Be in good humour, Tom. You, Petigrew, your turn on duty at this door," the Captain commanded using his voice of authority to end the matter.

"Why can't it be Benjamin, isn't it his turn to do it?" Petigrew asked petulantly.

He stopped himself from stamping his foot in frustration but could barely hide the resentment in his voice. He had, in his opinion, done more than his fair share of standing around.

"All right, Ben, you take position," the captain growled more sternly.

"What about Jon? He hasn't done guard duty all week, he was ill and you let him off," whined Ben like a young child. He was young enough to have a strong sense of fairness, but not old enough to sound assertive.
"What say you?" asked the Captain of the Guard

"We all had to take on his duties when he had the plague."

"I did my fair share, I stood-in for you when you were ill, we all did, we had to do a fourth more work all week, thanks to you, what about Hal?" Jon complained.

"Hal, come up here this instant and take over guard," cried the captain almost as loudly as he had been announced.

"Sir, captain, uncle, father of mine for I have none, have pity on me I have just recovered from the ague. My fever was such my mother poached an egg on my forehead," pleaded Hal, he was sweating still; beads were on his upper lip and were breaking out beneath the helmet.

His face, even in the light of the sentries' lanterns and the flaming torches on the walls, looked pale and pasty. His uniform looked too big for him, his tiny frame sticking out from under the breastplate; the gloves were far too big, suede gauntlets that made his arms look even thinner and more pathetic than they were.

"Very well, I love you like my sons and I am old enough to be your father, we are a family. Therefore, the oldest will do the duty, I have no lots to draw and that is the fairness of a family the eldest takes responsibility. Ben, tell me, when were you born?"

"The year of our lord fifteen-ninety-one," he replied proudly.

"What day?"

"Dunno."

"Month"

"Dunno. All I know is that I'm fourteen and, come the New Year, I will be a year older," he explained.

"I see; and the rest of you?"

The captain of the guard would not be diverted a second time.

"1592, spring," Petigrew replied.

"Winter; it was the winter of 1591," said Jon.

"Are you sure?" asked the captain.

Jon nodded but not convincingly.

"Summer, 1590, worst luck," said Hal, sweating even more with the tension and the knowledge that the cold cellar was not the best place to recover with its stale air and smell of rat excrement, cat urine and dust.

"That's settled my boys, let's go a searching the cellar; come Tom, a march around these cellars will warm you up and make you less stiff."

With that remark Corporal Falsdart marched ahead of his troop of teenagers, holding his lantern aloft, reassured by his resounding footsteps and the echoes of those formidably armed and well trained sentries as they tramped loudly behind him. The exchequer had deemed that boys should be used, it cost less but that did not mean that his guard would not be the best that it could be, he ensured they were drilled in using the pike and in swordsmanship.

They practised marching and military craft as if they were real soldiers. He was proud of his boys even if they were sick a lot, but not as sick as his friends who had been crippled by disease, dysentery and fever when he fought abroad. He had met and lost many a true friend on that adventure. He was also proud of his service in the Low Countries and his lineage, which stretched back to the Housecarls of King Harold Godwinson. His ancestor had been the King's personal bodyguard and had tried to save Harold from arrows and swords. They had been the Housecarls of old. These favoured men would die in order to save the King's life.

They were the ancestors of the Beefeaters and of his small guard. Members of his family were still protecting the monarchy. He reckoned that they had been bodyguards since 1066. That was five-hundred-and-thirty-nine-years of tradition, at least. 1605 was a year away from 1606, so he calculated that next year his family would have been guards for five hundred and forty years, if not more, a record he could be justly proud of and he was, all humility aside.

Guido had rolled the barrels around, as instructed, to keep the sediment moving; he upended a small firkin and sat on the face where the tap would go. Using his mallet, he knocked the keystone in further so that it was flush with the barrel and provided a more comfortable seat. Sitting down on the small barrel, he could feel the cold stone of cellar floor through his shoes and his hose.

The chill of the cellar had penetrated his very bones. Wrapping his cloak around him, made him feel only slightly less cold; his hat with a fine leather crown, was covered in felt, that had kept him warm on many a voyage and did so again that night. He had, next to him, a hessian sack that had once held corn. The sack had been cut in half and each portion had been half-filled with spiles for the top of the barrel.

One bag carried identical-sized, soft wood cone-shaped pieces of wood, the other bag identical-sized, hard-wood, cylindrical pieces; the cones were soft spiles put in the bung-hole at the top of the barrel once it had been tapped and put on a settle; soft spiles were used for serving, they were porous to allow any fermentation gases to escape.

These allowed the barrel to be poured once they were eased out and were left nestling over the bunghole. They were made of porous wood they allowed gas out of the barrel and prevented air from entering and spoiling the sherry while the settling process continued. The cellar-man's art was knowing when to use a soft spile and when to use a hard spile. It was confusing for Guido. The hard spile cylinders were put in once the barrel had settled and also when the sherry was not being served, they were more or less stoppers, preventing air from getting into the barrel through the bung hole and making pouring almost impossible, reducing the flow from the tap to a mere trickle.

The vintners and innkeepers treated the sherry like beer because it had sediment; the *flor* produced by the sherry formed a blanket over the liquid so such precautions were superfluous but they were not to know that, sherry was a virtually unknown drink in

England, only available to the wealthiest. Being a cellarman for such a large amount of *Jerez sack* was a huge responsibility.

This was *Jerez* from the Sandeman family and therefore of finest quality. He felt the responsibility of guarding the shipment weigh heavily. Before he dozed off again, he heard the echo of footsteps approaching. He knew the drill; he had been told what to do by that charming esquire, Thomas Percy: 'Pretend to be John Johnson, let the soldiers roll the barrels to show it is indeed fine *sack*, give them a drink from the jug and guard the barrels until they are collected'. They were simple instructions.

"Hail, keeper of the *sack*," cried Captain Falsdart using his loudest and warmest voice while raising his sword hand in salute; his exaggerated annunciation bounced off the walls; he deliberately made his movements theatrical and if the room had not been full of barrels, his booming voice may well have echoed.

"Captain Falsdart, a welcome sight and sound," replied Guido happily, not even attempting to match the volume of the other's voice.

"John Johnson, alone in the dark, alas, alack," replied Falsdart smiling, "poor keeper of the *sack*!"

"Would you care for a mug of sack to ward off the cold once you have checked the cellar here?" asked Guido, quite used to his pseudonym by now.

"By all means, bless you, kind sir, my boys and I would love a warming mug on our way back from patrol, thank you."

Captain Falsdart gratefully accepted the offer; they had of course had some small beer for breakfast and a mug of ale at luncheon time but the warming effects of the alcohol had worn off. Most servants of the Crown were given a beer allowance, as part of their wages. However, a little extra drink would be a bonus, the alcohol would warm the blood and the bones; chase the chill from their cores.

"I would appreciate the company; this work wants for entertainment as surely your work does!" Guido acknowledged cheerily. He was very lonely indeed; it was a long night without diversions.

Thoughts of sleep and warmth preyed heavily on the mind. The chill of the cellar insidiously crept over flesh and between cloth, seeping into blood and bone. Guido dismissed them as he busied himself with sloshing sherry into six small tankards.

"Fortune's fickle wheel turns too slowly for the poor; our time is full of drudgery and pain; we must take comfort in each other's company at every opportunity, for our work is hard and dull, lacking any entertainment, providing only the satisfaction of a job well done," Falsdart replied.

"Well said, your Saxon ancestors furnished you with a keen mind!" Guido noted smiling; he knew the Captain of the Guard had a warm heart and a wise man's outlook. Derek Falsdart was a good man. Guido knew instinctively that he would make a loyal friend and one day Guido might tell him about Rosa if they were able to maintain the friendship that they had built up over the past few months.

"You are a kind man and good company, John," Falsdart replied, for he knew Guido only as John Johnson and he liked the man. He was a man like himself, an old soldier and survivor with no family to look after him in his dotage. They had talked enough to know that they had both suffered in the Lowlands conflicts.

"Patrol these precincts for a while longer," Guido suggested trying to keep any hint of a plea out of his voice.

He was glad it was the last night he would have to be on guard and that he had occasionally helped out at the docks during the daytime so that he would have work when this job was done.

"We will return, have no fear," the captain assured him confidently, which assuaged Guido's feeling of mounting loneliness.

He did not want them to leave, he basked in Falsdart's warmth, marvelled at the open faces of the young men, watching and listening to the older men's conversation, just in case they could pick up a quip or a quote to show others how clever they were. As they left, with their lanterns carried aloft, the cellar became darker and seemed suddenly colder. Guido wrapped himself in his cape and stamped his feet, desperately trying to get warm and waiting for his relief. Of all the jobs he had performed, night watchman was the most tiresome by far. The boredom and the loneliness were almost too much to bear. The palace guard had become his only respite. He was a man of action, moving stores, hauling ropes, manhandling barrels and boxes, moving cargo from hold to hard, from warehouse to yard.

He had experience of tapping and spile-ing ale and wines, fortified and otherwise. If you were not a master of one trade, you had to be Jack-of-all trades. Flexibility had kept him in work whether fighting or hefting, he survived, he did not expect to prosper in these troubled times. The monotony of sitting around did not suit his personality. If he had been able to sleep, he would have been happy, but the cellar was too cold, the floor too hard and he dare not risk being discovered asleep, he would lose his night's pay and the role that he had been generously given would no longer be a harbinger of further rewards to come. In the morning, he would sleep at his digs off Fleet Street, work the docks on the evening tide and, then, find some other as well work and another bride. He was too poor to keep his previous pride; he would take what work he could.

Perhaps his drinking friends from the pub would give him more commissions, he might be able to find an old spinster who would enjoy his company, and they could grow old in contented penury. That would be his dream come true, he was very lonely, all alone, but he would settle for maintaining his strength and being able to work for whatever wages that he could get. At the moment, he had no choice but to work from day to day. His lonely job made him feel more vulnerable and he wondered whether it might be time to move up to the north and find his family as he had not found his fortune. He had too much time to think and this thinking time made him wonder if he had left everything too late.

He prayed for his relief, the hours dragged, the minutes passed slowly; Guido said a decade of the rosary to occupy his mind and bring him from his physical discomfort to a spiritual plane, to move his mind from temporal to godly matters. His relief would come when the King's servants arrived early in the morning to roll the barrels into the room where King James would hold his reception. There, they would tap and soft spile the sherry so that it would undergo a secondary fermentation, it would ferment again, and in a few hours any remaining sediment would be settled at the bottom of the barrel and the *flor* would have already risen up through the liquid and formed on the top. All would be right for the reception by noon.

Even so, as an added precaution, the tapped *sack* would be poured through a muslin cloth to ensure total clarity and that none of the dregs made it into the glasses. Real glass, Venetian, the best, would be used; the light would reflect off the stem and bowl in a rainbow. Guido had been told all this but he no longer wanted to witness such a sight, he merely dreamed of release, impatiently waiting his relief.

The prayers were said and time weighed so heavily.

"For this relief, I would, indeed, give much thanks," he mumbled, echoing Rosa's favourite phrase, "'tis cold and bitter!"

How he missed her.

He stepped up onto the upturned barrel and tried to get comfortable on its round face, the opposite end of its circular base, drew his frozen feet up off the cold floor, furling his cloak around him, looking like the top of a candle snuffer, a cone shaped figure, then, he allowed himself to doze off. He would be relieved to be enveloped in the arms of Morpheus; it would extinguish his feelings of loneliness. Yet, he dared not sleep.

Chapter 4 – The Missing Items – 4th November 1605

On the first floor, in a room connected to the Palace of Westminster, a roaring fire danced in the grate, a basket of large logs promised a warm night for the occupants. The fireplace took up one fifth of the brick wall; the other three walls of the space were plastered, the finest plaster, of course, with goat hair in the mix to stop the screed from cracking from expansion in the heat and contraction in the cold.

The walls were bare and plain, painted white, the joist and beams were made of seasoned timber. It was late and the small leaded windows, opposite the fire, looked like an ink spot on parchment paper. Most rooms in the building had wall hangings on at least one wall but Mr John Whyneard, member of the Privy Chamber and keeper of the King's Wardrobe, preferred unadorned simplicity. Two high-back, low-seat armchairs were arranged near the fire. Behind them was a table where the occupants of the chairs had sat and supped on leek soup, cold mutton and pickled onions. A quantity of *sack* sufficient to induce a feeling of fatigue had been consumed, each man matching glass for glass.

The pewter decanter had remained on the table but they had filled their glasses before they had risen and they had taken them to the fire to warm the spirit and to warm their spirits. The dining table suffered from a draught blowing through the leaded windows, which chilled the room. The whole palace was cold away from the fire and Whyneard worried that Knyvett might want to go on patrol of the precincts.

Sir Thomas Knyvett had been the other diner at Westminster Palace that night; Whyneard wondered why he should have visited on such a cold night, his house was opposite Whitehall, a stone's throw away from where they sat. Knyvett could have invited Whyneard there, it would have been warmer, the food better and a messenger could easily be dispatched, it was five minutes at most, by foot, to where the house was to be found.

It was most disturbing to have a surprise visit.

He would not have minded if he had been invited there. The draughty palace was only good for a snooze by the fire away from doors and windows. Knyvett House was modern in comparison. The stone walls of the Palace seemed to breathe in the cold, whereas Knyvett's house was built of brick, Flemish qualle and timber, and the roof was tiled. It was warm and welcoming, a spacious house that had first been leased from Queen Elizabeth. Whyneard had visited and had noted that it was wainscoted inside from ceiling to floor in the main hall and two parlours, which had brick floors. In the buttery, kitchen and cellar there were jointed dresser boards instead of wainscoting, and stone was on the floor. The first storey had a wainscoted dining room, with a fireplace and painted tile surround, along with six more rooms and three closets. There were four garrets along the roof.

It was a fitting house for a loyal servant of the Crown, an ideal place to have a pleasant dinner and Whyneard felt the food would have been better cooked, he had found his mutton tougher than normal, and the dishes would have been more varied and plentiful, he was becoming sick of leek soup. The Westminster Palace chef was an old Beefeater whose cooking skills had been honed serving the Earl of Essex's soldiers in Ireland, he favoured bland and plentiful. Knyvett House was renowned for its architecture and its cook who as widely regarded as one of the finest in the kingdom. It was not time to wonder about what might have been had the venues been reversed, but to reflect on their previous conversation.

"I think you may be correct in your assumption that I have mislaid some of the King's properties, a French hunting scene embroidered on a wall hanging and some other trifles," wearily Whyneard complained. He sounded somewhat pompous. "You gave me the list a few days ago; I checked this morning and they were there, all items, every single one of the King's props for the opening of parliament; it was a wonderful piece of tapestry work that hunting scene."

"Well it is missing, now!" complained his guest, Sir Thomas Knyvett, irked at having mentioned the situation three times already and chastising himself inwardly for allowing the conversation to veer on to lighter subjects. He was not willing to let the matter rest despite Whyneard's attitude of 'away dull care'.

"Oh, dear me," declared Whyneard, showing real concern for the first time, he had managed to dismiss Knyvett's remarks previously.

He had been hungry, after all, and that had taken precedent at the time, but the importance of the situation finally hit him as he ruminated after his supper, his belly full. Whyneard was preoccupied; sleep would be most welcome but rest was not possible with all the thoughts swimming in his head. There was nothing like the taste of dry *sack* and mutton, he had to admit, it induced sleep, too, experience told him, but the responsibility given him by King James weighed heavily on his mind. It had been a huge shock to be told that certain items belonging to the King himself were missing; in truth he had not noticed.

"I can search for those props," volunteered Sir Thomas Knyvett.

Whyneard's surprise dinner guest, a man of equal importance at court, a fellow member of the Privy Chamber, had been only slightly less than that shock; it was not a good thing, he felt sure, to be thus disturbed at his age. He wondered nervously whether Cecil was checking up on him, it would not be the first time. Sir Thomas was known as not only High Sherriff of Norfolk but also Member of Parliament for Thetford and had been Master of Arms to Queen Elizabeth. His knighthood had been bestowed in 1604, showing how respected he was by the King.

"I would not countenance that," Whyneard almost whined, just managing to keep his voice steady.

"Say no more, it is a trifle."

"I cannot allow it."

"But, I insist."

"It is not necessary."

This offer to personally hunt over all the rooms of the palace was even more of a shock. First, this privy councillor arrived unannounced and unexpected, then, he had spotted that various wall hangings and trifles that James had specifically requested were missing. These items were to furnish the chamber where

James would wait before summoning parliament. Not only had he lost these items, Whyneard knew that he was not going to be trusted to find them. He felt sure that they were not lost, but merely mislaid, but he was powerless against Knyvett and his masked accusations and insistence.

"It is really no trouble and I would do anything to avoid the displeasure of the King," replied Knyvett, sounding as if it were a rebuke rather than an offer of assistance.

"But you are part of the Privy Chamber, you cannot leave the warmth of the fire for such a mean task," argued Whyneard. Anyone listening would have detected the half-heartedness of his plea for Knyvett to desist. The whole situation was getting out of hand; it was not right to have the King's finest men patrolling the precincts of the palace at such a late hour.

"I am a Justice of the Peace, so perfectly suited to search for these things, capable even of punishing the thief, if these items have been stolen. We might even find the culprit. I have served both Her Majesty and His Majesty, allow me to search," Knyvett insisted, rising from his chair with determination.

"I cannot argue!" demurred Whyneard; he was exasperated; the events of the evening were in danger of spoiling a good dinner. "It is a mean task and I cannot allow you to go alone, I must accompany around the grounds."

Whyneard rose from the comfort of his chair by the fire; his seat, stuffed with horsehair and the cushions crammed with goose down, had been a comfortable place.

It was particularly irksome to leave his nesting place with the fire giving off a most delicious, soporific heat.

"I will go alone, I do not wish to trouble you."

Knyvett was insistent so he bowed graciously to the knight, relieved to let him go. He had searched the cellar earlier with Lord Thomas Howard, Earl of Suffolk and all they had found were *sack* barrels and brushwood. He had not expected a visit from Suffolk's brother-in-law, Sir Thomas Knyvett; he did not like either of them, but had no choice but to offer the latter supper. They were part of Cecil's cultural circle and so they need to be treated with the utmost respect.

"My cloak!" demanded Knyvett putting as much force and drama into the request as he could muster, he might have been an old soldier but he was still a soldier and, as such, he possessed a soldier's lion heart.

Whyneard winced, he did so abhor such boorish behaviour, a 'please' would not have gone amiss he felt, after all, he noted, 'manners maketh man'. Knyvett was not one to worry about such trifles. That was why so few warmed to him. A pageboy, dressed in a doublet of the knight's colours, and green hose, materialised from the corner of the room. He had taken one of the dining chairs and sat on it, fidgeting and waiting for his master's command. His position close to the far corner of the room meant he hardly benefitted from the fire but despite that, he had dozed. It was vital that he rested when he could. His days were long and hard, waking before his master to prepare the breakfast and sleeping when his master bade him leave, which could be in the morning; he had no daily nap, in the afternoon, like his master.

Fortunately, he had woken moments before with cramp in his thigh, stirring to shift position. At his master's command, he had leapt up. Like many important men, Knyvett was impatient; it was fashionable to be so.

"But it is near midnight," remonstrated Whyneard, not looking forward to leaving the fire.

He rang the bell for his servant while shuddering at the thought of having to brave the cold.

"No matter, I cannot sleep. I will take my valet and rouse the Captain of the guard." The page had collected his master's cloak and sword from the table by the door in the time that it had taken for this exchange to take place.

"I should accompany you," Whyneard half-heartedly suggested, feeling that he had to show willing, he even walked a little way towards the door, waiting, as Knyvett put his sword belt around his waist. The heavy leather belt and it scabbard hung slightly below the more elegant and thinner belt of his doublet. He looked every inch a man of action. Whyneard was not and wished Knyvett would act alone. Once fastened, the visitor held out his hands for his cloak, which his page laid on his forearm.

"No need to do that; why who would be here to answer a call should there be another crisis?" Knyvett said. Whyneard had to admit that he liked the way the fellow thought; there was no need to be rash when Knyvett's reasoning seemed so sensible. He could settle back into the fire and await news. If this knight wanted to go out on such a night, he would not fight.

"Your Lordship, your wishes cannot be denied, if you wish to search the precincts for the properties, then, you have my blessing and I hope you have more luck than I" said Whyneard, admitting defeat, this was no time to argue.

Knyvett was determined and Whyneard realised that he was partially to blame for losing the items being sought. It was not a very auspicious end to a rather long day. Instead of arguing, he smiled graciously, watching as, in one deft movement, the knight's cloak was suddenly held aloft before him, the collar forming a veil for Knyvett's face, his arms were crossed, his hands held the wings of the collar. The beautiful green silk lining shimmered in the firelight. In one graceful movement, the knight raised his hands above his head, flipped the cloak by uncrossing his hands and brought his arms down to his collarbone, instantly turning the coat from inside out to right ways.

Just like a conjuror, he made the green silk disappear and revealed the drab brown colour of the thick wool cloak, a mantle on his shoulders. The fire roared in its grate when he swept his cloak onto his back, creating a gust of wind up the chimney, embers glowed, visually signalling action as clearly as a cannon blast would sound it, and he was off to do his duty. Within a blink of an eye, he had tied a bow at his neck, then, he bowed to his host, thanked him for the meal and marched through the room.

Master and page strode over towards the exit and their exeunt. Neither spoke until they had negotiated the narrow stairwell, a stone spiral staircase, which was not conducive to men in cloaks, carrying swords, making swift progress. As they slipped down the steps, Knyvett took a pair of buckskin gloves from his doublet-belt and eased them over his fingers. At the bottom of the stairs, the page collected his cloak from Whyneard's servant who had been sitting in the pantry waiting for the bell to ring so he could clear away the plates and pottery, cutlery and crockery and go to bed.

He loathed long nights, he had to be up early the next day, he had been relieved by hearing the sound of them leaving. On hearing, footsteps on the stairs Whyneard's boy had guessed his guests were leaving and had snatched up the page's flimsy black, wool cloak whilst running for the door. He had been in a similar situation himself and he was determined to show some kindness to Knyvett's boy, he did not like the knight and his high-handed ways. He was not sure whether he liked his pageboy either, he seemed sullen; he sensed the boy was judging him and the rest of Whyneard's household as just not good enough and was sure that that came from living in a house opposite Whitehall. Still, a kindness was a kindness and he was glad to dry a fellow servant's meagre mantle.

Rich people took their cloaks to the room to show their expense and thickness; the servants took off their protective layer at the door, rolled it up and handed it to their equal to stuff somewhere, preferably by the oven or near the cooking fire.

Servants who had the heart and time to do so would try and hang the cloak by a fire. Whyneard's servant, Ben, stood by the door, only opening it as the knight's foot hit the last step. As he passed, he took out the bundle from under his arm, handing it to the page before nimbly stepping forward to open the door for the knight.

"Thank you," the page whispered, his cloak felt warm. Jerome was genuinely grateful and smiled at Ben.

Whyneard's boy was a thoughtful one, many a time the page had worn his cloak as wet or as cold as it had been when he had entered a premises. On this visit, the cloak had been aired by the fire and felt warm to the touch. The drizzle that had coated its fibres had disappeared, steamed out by the heat of the fire. They both thanked him and wished him good night and the boy closed the door behind them, shivering at the cold outside, the draught of which had almost numbed him before he managed to scamper towards the dying embers of the cooking fire to wram himself before having to traipse upstairs to clear the room as Whyneard dozed by the fire waiting for Knyvett's return.

Barely had the door closed, when the knight slowed his pace to allow the page to come level with him and with a swoop of his cloak, rested his arm on his shoulder. The page recognised this signal, matched his pace to his master's, and inclined his head towards the head that now moved towards his ear to whisper. It was cold but his cape was warm, the drizzle, that had fallen when they arrived, had finally stopped after starting at dawn and lasting the day. The chill wind that had brought the Arctic to the Palace of Westminster still blew icy draughts.

Within a few miserable minutes both knight and servant were chilled to the bone, it was not a night to be abroad. Both page and master wished to abed or it to be St Crispin's Day, October had been a milder month. Had not King Henry blessed the day himself on the eve of Agincourt? Many more would know of the events of that November night. Jerome was unaware that he was stepping into history; he was doing his duty, yet he would be a forgotten piece of the puzzle.
"Come, Jerome, we have official business to perform. Are you armed as I instructed?"

"I have a small stiletto dagger hidden in my tunic," he replied, wanting to pat the front of his doublet to make sure it was still there, the cold metal had warmed next to his skin and he barely perceived its existence. He decided against such an outward sign of doubt.

"Good, Cecil says we will find him in the cellars."

"Under what pretext?"

"Whyneard is missing some articles for tomorrow's opening."

"What pray?"

"The hanging and trinkets I told you to store for me."

"I have them hidden!"
"Good."

"Ha, I wondered why you gave those to me," he admitted. "I dared not ask why you had given me that task but knew that it must be a part of a greater plan than I was privy to."

The page admired his master and hated all Papists. After all, they were a threat to him directly, if they took over what would happen to those associated with the previous power brokers. He would be without work. They would almost certainly seize property, lands, and shun those of the protestant faith.

He had heard enough horror stories of the 'Bloody' Mary Tudor. His childhood had been filled with the ghastly and gruesome acts of that Catholic queen. He had been baptised in the Church of England but his parents had been swayed by the convincing rhetoric of the Puritans, joining their cause. They had instilled the persuasive non-conformist ideology in his mind and in his heart. He knew where his loyalty lay; he was knowledgeable enough to know that those people who surrounded Cecil, and did his bidding, when asked, often gained promotion. Thankfully, his master had been given many tasks and had been richly rewarded for carrying them out. That was why he would follow his master's rising star. He kept pace as Knyvett made his way to the guardhouse.

"The fool," hissed his master, "first he had not realised anything was missing until I noted it this evening, just before supper. I suppose that is understandable with all the activity and changes but then he tried to talk me out of searching for them!"

"It is a little strange looking for them at midnight don't you think?" the page ventured meekly. His opinion was rarely sought but he hoped that such insight would reveal his ability. He was at an age where he wanted to show how clever he was.

"We need a little incredulity to make the story more credible! Even the most credible lie has some fault in it; people are suspicious of perfection. We have to dissemble when giving information for public consumption. That is his maxim, his *maxima propositio*. You know his ways; we have, as our chief, the most brilliant mind in Christendom."

"So where is the Papist? Is he armed?"

"He is waiting in the wine cellars as instructed, armed with a lantern and that's all! We will take the captain of the guard as a witness to corroborate our story!"

"Did you want him dispensed with?" the page offered with the bravado that had secured him his post. He had been thoroughly indoctrinated. He was keen to take out the stiletto and intimidate people with it.

Even when he was first questioned over his religious beliefs during his apprenticeship, he had shown his Puritan nature. He was a product of those who believed in double-predestination, *'I am saved and the rest are damned'*. Anne Boleyn would have been proud of his Calvinist leanings.

He was an ideal agent, passionate and committed; Cecil could use people like that extremely easily to further his ends but they would have to be disposed of or deposed afterwards. Puritanism might be a threat to the state but its adherents had their uses in his book. They were pawns, the foot soldiers on his chess board. Cecil would use anyone of any religious persuasion in order to execute his plans.

"I want him alive unless he makes too much noise, he is part of a group of plotters; we would like him to tell us about them all, if it is possible."

Hastily, the knight broke away and marched hurriedly to the guardhouse where he rapped violently on the door three times with his gloved hand. He stood legs part, feet firmly planted, hands on hips, demanding a response from those inside, it looked as if he could break the door down if need be.

Inside there was the sound of chairs scraping and candle light shifting as someone rose and took a lantern from the window ledge to better light their way in order to answer the door, the page, catching up with Knyvett, could see the candlelight and the glow of the guardhouse fire through the windows, shadows leaping on the walls, and he wished he could step inside and not have to visit the dark, cold cellars underground. He awaited the door being answered with bated breath, his chest felt tight; his heart beat hard and fast with anticipation.

Jerome was not sure whether it was because he suspected that this would be a momentous occasion or whether it was the apprehension at what he had to do; he realised that rather than merely use his stiletto to threaten the conspirator, he might have to kill him. The thought filled the boy with dread but his Puritan determination meant that he was fully prepared to do so if it was necessary.

As a committed Protestant and a volunteer, in Cecil's service, he was prepared to die to protect his country. He had been told the story they would tell to the authorities if anything went wrong.

"I am Sir Thomas Knyvett, Master of Arms, member of the Privy Chamber; I command that you open the door," he demanded in a booming voice that made Jerome shudder in terror, momentarily.

Ben opened the door sheepishly.

"Yes, Your Lordship."

"Send a messenger, to Edmund Doubleday to meet me here, you'll find him at the *Saracen's Head* in King's Street, he owns the place. Then, summon the Captain of the Guard."

"I am here your Lordship," Falsdart announced rushing to the door. "Can I help in any way, sire, we are at your service, what is it you need?"

"Good, I am glad you are here, it will save time. Have word sent to Doubleday, double quick."

"Why I know him and where, he lives, I will send our boy immediately. He is a scrivener and vintner. He used to be High Constable of Westminster. He is a fine gentleman and an honest and upright man."

"That's the man, send your boy to fetch him without delay; we will need a man of great stature, valour, gravity and activity!"

The plot was thickening and Knyvett did not want to take any chances. Doubleday was a loyal ally and would help intimidate the man they meant to catch. He would also provide a well-respected witness to events. If Guy Fawkes said anything at all that night that might jeopardise their story, Jerome was to thrust his stiletto into his neck or chest to silence him forever and so seal the fate of Catholics throughout the land.

Chapter 5 – Midnight – 4th November 1605

Guido woke to the sound of marching feet. Slowly he looked around him, he had fallen asleep on the firkin on which he sat; his cloak was draped around him and covered the barrel, his head poked out from a black cone of material. He still looked like the end of a candle extinguisher. His hat was over his eyes and he could not imagine how that had occurred. Through his sleepiness, panic gripped him and suddenly he was wide-awake. If it were the soldiers of the guard, he could not be found sleeping; he should not have taken that last mug of *sack* after they had left. Drinking and talking often led to that 'one too many' he had found.

It would not do for a night-watch-man to be caught sleeping on the job. Otherwise, it might be his employer, in which case he must look lively despite the cloudiness of his head. Admonishing himself for being lazy, he willed himself awake. In one fluid movement, he launched himself from his squatting position and up off the barrel. Quickly, he turned the barrel onto its side and rolled it towards the others. The steps were louder but he was alerted to their presence in the room by the walls becoming suddenly lighter, from black to grey and then to a dirty cream.

They must have an inordinate amount of lanterns, he thought to himself. He guessed it was a final search before dawn; he had no idea of the time or how long he had slept. Turning slowly, he was just about to say he was rolling the barrels, as good an excuse as any, when ahead of Falsdart he spied a tall stranger in a heavy cloak that he had drawn back to reveal fine clothes and an ornate sword hilt. The stranger stopped and stood in front of him; barely a yard separated them.

Guido took in the new scene. His candle, sitting on a pricket saucer, was spluttering on the floor in the corner; the third or fourth that he had brought with him that night, he was not quite sure.

He had not realised that the cheap candles, that he had bought, burnt so rapidly; beeswax candles would have kept alight longer; he would make sure he did not visit the same tallow merchants in the market at Borough again.

Still, with four lanterns in his vicinity, he had no need of its light. To the stranger's left stood a pageboy who raised his lantern high as he fiddled with the buttons of his doublet. Guido assumed that the page had dressed hurriedly, although when he looked again there were more buttons undone than fastened. Perhaps, this was Sandeman checking on his shipment, he idly thought. Certainly, the man looked important. Maybe it was his relief, the sombre, distinguished gentleman could be the King's steward of wine ; perhaps the others were there to shift the barrels upstairs to tap and spile them so the sediment would be settled by evening. That was why the strange youth's doublet was undone, in preparation for the work of shifting the barrels. With that in mind, he moved to collect the bag for them.

"Halt!" cried the stranger, "I am Sir Thomas Knyvett, member of the Privy Council. You are Thomas Percy's man?"

"Yes, John Johnson commanded to guard these barrels by the same person, Sir Thomas Percy. He engaged me to move these barrels from the dock to here and preserve them," replied Guido, sweeping off his hat and bowing gracefully as he doffed it.

"Without a weapon?" challenged Knyvett. He stood with his hands on his hips, his sword hand behind the hilt and his legs spread apart, there was no doubt that he was in command of the situation.

"Being within the vicinity of the palace and knowing the guards patrol around here, there was thought to be no need, it was to protect the prize from a sneak thief who might be daring enough to roll away a barrel once the guard was gone."

"Why was this not left for a soldier?"

Guido remained silent for a moment, all ears awaited his answer, he had not challenged his role, he had accepted it readily as any itinerant gentleman would. He had not questioned its sagacity.

"I suppose a soldier could have been on guard, but the King, Sir Thomas told me, was not in favour of armed men in his precincts, save for those who form his guard. I am merely a night-watchman whose challenge would see off a magpie."

"Sir Thomas Percy is more of a fool than I think he is, we have no need for a *bellman* here!" spat Knyvett venomously.

"What do you mean?" asked Guido nervously.

"Guards put down your lanterns; I will need to question him further."

This command was designed to intimidate Guido, leaving him in the dark and allowing the guards the freedom to use their weapons. It worked. All he could see was strange figures bathed in lantern light while he was left in the shadows, a silhouette that made an unnervingly large target. A sudden fear gripped him. The cellar became shrouded in darkness, making Guido feel more vulnerable. In the shadows, unfriendly faces surrounded him. The situation was desperate; he could see that. He had no way of escape or denying the accusations.

The Captain of the Guard, Falsdart, rested his hands on his hips mimicking Knyvett's stance, the boys of the guard held their pikes stiffly at their sides as they did at inspection before starting any duty; they dared not fold their arms in Knyvett's presence. The guards, who had been his friends earlier in the evening, were now his enemies. They seemed twice as wide and much more threatening, all of them suddenly older and more dangerous. Where there had been warm, conversation and merriment, there was coldness, silence and seriousness. This stranger meant danger and Guido would have to treat him with kid gloves.

"Your grace let me see you better; I shall light the lantern to see your face and be able to read your meaning more fully," Guido suggested amicably.

He had no idea why the man before him was being so aggressive.

"Observe he has matches, he is clothed in boots and cape at this late hour, the dead of night. Corporal Falsdart, you will ensure that is noted in the report you dictate to the scribe, is that clear?"

"Of course your grace," Falsdart agreed meekly. His family had served the crown for almost five-hundred-and-thirty-nine-years, he was not going to let Crown down, now.

He had every intention of carrying out each and every order. It would not be a good political move to upset such an important person and he was unclear why the kindly John was being interrogated in this way. However, he needed to obey every command that he received as soldiers always should, he knew the Privy Councillors well; John Johnson was a relative stranger.

"Indeed, you are right your grace," Guido acquiesced, "I am dressed for my duties and the matches are to light my lantern. I am to guard the barrels of *sack* there, all thirty six of them, kilderkin, barrel and firkin for the Members of Parliament on the express orders of Sir Thomas Percy."

"Do you know who Percy is?" asked Knyvett testily. His had wrapped tighter around the hilt of his sword.

"The kind gentleman who gave me employ, only that," replied Guido simply, he really did not want to rouse the overexcited stranger any further.

"He is only, the most notorious ringleader of a Catholic plot to overthrow the king!" Knyvett screeched

"That cannot be true, I saw him talk to the King!" objected Guido, for indeed he had seen Cecil talk to the King and Cecil had told him that he was Sir Thomas Percy, why would anyone doubt a servant of the King? Why would he lie about his name?

"Search the cellar!" cried Knyvett impatiently, pacing up and down in an agitated fashion. It was what he assumed he should do to show his concern at the situation. He knew what would be discovered, he wanted to ensure that it was not missed by these fools. Whyneard had failed to spot the evidence, they might.

"There is nothing here but the *sack* and a pile of winter fuel," countered the captain of the guard, Corporal Falsdart. "We have searched once already on the command of Mr. Whyneard, you have dined with him tonight have you not?"

"Yes," replied the knight unsure why the guards were siding with Guido. He had not expected to be challenged; normally his commands were followed forthwith and if not then, immediately, or soon after. It irked him that he should be defied in this way.

"My men let you in and I reported that a thorough search of the cellar had been undertaken to both you and Mr. Whyneard, the Keeper of the King's Wardrobe. No one has left or entered the precincts since your arrival. Otherwise I would have been notified by the other guards."

"I am aware of that, but we need to find some items and without delay."

"Of course we will search but it would help to know what we need to look for," objected Falsdart, he was a soldier but he saw no reason to have his men needlessly diverted.

However, he knew from experience that the nobility were most unforgiving if they were agitated.

"Indeed, it is his Lordship that bade me commit another search for he has found some wall hangings, belonging to the King, and other items, missing, all of which are needed for tomorrow; it is time for a more thorough search with a narrower purpose."

"Your Lordship, I had no idea, accept my apology and I beg your pardon for challenging your command, I had no idea such items were missing," replied Falsdart humbly, he realised there were mysterious circumstances surrounding the disappearance of the King's items, "This intelligence was not shared with us.

"Typical, Knyvett replied, spitting the words dismissively through his teeth.

Whyneard would not and could not admit the loss. He had searched for them himself without the assistance of the guards. No wonder the items had not been discovered, Knyvett seemed to be insinuating.

"Sincere apologies."

"They have only recently gone missing and their absence was only revealed tonight, I know you would rather be by the warmth of the guard house fire and I would, willingly, be a-bed and asleep myself."

"Indeed, Your Lordship is correct. We must find the missing items."

"We are all agreed in our purpose; all of us will be vexed if we fail; we must find those items if we are to avoid the King's wrath and upset the proceedings."

"I am at your command, Your Lordship!" Falsdart replied bowing low as he spoke.

"Good!" snapped Knyvett. "Watch the prisoner, John Johnson, make sure he only speaks when spoken, too, better still keep him quiet until we councillors can speak freely to him."

Jerome drew the stiletto from his unbuttoned doublet, the blade caught the light from the lanterns and it flashed in the dark like a struck match. Despite wondering why anyone would hide any items in such a filthy place, Falsdart decided he had to acquiesce. He did not particularly like Knyvett and his ways but he did not want a fuss to be made so he decided to do precisely as he was told.

"What is it that you require?" he asked, sounding like a good soldier awaiting a command.

"Search those logs, the coal, upturn even the faggots, clear that brushwood," growled Knyvett.

Falsdart motioned his men to action, Petigrew and Ben to clear the coals, Hal and John to clear away the faggots and brushwood. While Jerome threatened Guido with his stiletto, the guards rested their pikestaffs on the floor against the wall behind him, oblivious to the mortal danger Guido was in at that time. Guido looked on mystified, Knyvett seemed satisfied, looking on indignant, almost incandescent with rage, or so it seemed. In fact, like any liar trying to pull off a subterfuge, his embarrassment showed on his flushed face. All of the guards suspected that Knyvett saw Guido as the thief of the properties for the ceremony and nothing would convince him otherwise, whereas they, to a man, felt Guido was innocent, even though they were so young. They could see truth; they could sense Guido's integrity.

Reluctantly, they picked up their lanterns; the job would be dirty work. Once at the pile, they took it in turns to move the coal and logs. Falsdart joined them, standing between the pile of coal and the pile of wood. They worked for a few moments before they were able to discover something. Cecil had laid his trap and ensured that the concealment would seem plausible; he did not want things to look too contrived.

"What have we here?" Hal asked askance, stepping back from the cleared faggots.

"Captain, what have your men found?" asked Knyvett seemingly mystified, as if he did not know.

"Why three small barrels," Falsdart responded with admiration.

It was not clear as to whom he admired more, Knyvett for guessing something would be revealed or Guido for pilfering some of the King's own tipple. "I never would have looked amongst the winter fuel, your Lordship!"

"I have never seen those," protested Guido vehemently. He knew well enough the sentence for theft and he had no wish to be in the Clink. Added to which he was telling the truth since Cecil himself had arranged for them to be placed there

"Really," Knyvett sounded surprised. "Open them!"

Guido stood his ground; he knew nothing about Knyvett.

"I have not stolen anything; the thirty six are on this bill," Guido argued.

"Give me that bill!" ordered Knyvett, steel in his voice.

"It is written there," complained Guido triumphantly, "thirty-six barrels of Spanish *sack* from Senor Sandeman."

"We will use it as evidence. Watch out men; we have intelligence of a misdemeanour here tonight."

In fact, he intended to take it home and burn it. A waybill for *sack* would not sit well on a charge of blowing up the houses of parliament with gunpowder. He knew the gunpowder in the cellar was corrupt. It was so old and spent that it would only splutter like a candle. That was not the point though; those three barrels were evidence of a plot to blow up parliament.

"This barrel seems lighter than the rest," noted Petigrew. He shook the barrel violently, which made Knyvett start. It was difficult to know if he was acting or whether being an old soldier he was wary of gunpowder even if it was corrupt.

His reflexes overruled his logic, perhaps.

"Be careful, keep your lanterns covered, put out all the naked flames anywhere around. Watch this man and his matches. The King himself has been told there is a plot to blow these great houses to kingdom come."

"Have no fear," said Falsdart reassuringly, "we have only these covered lanterns; we extinguished the torches at ten, as part of our husbandry here."

"Very well proceed; breach the barrel but watch that man, he is clearly dangerous," Knyvett warned.

He contemplated drawing his sword but felt it might seem to be slightly overdramatic. Jerome's stiletto was sufficient.

"What with, we have no tools?" replied Petigrew who, on hearing he might be carrying a bomb, had placed the barrel gently on the floor in front of his feet, taking a few steps towards the others.

Secretly, he wanted to put himself at the back of the group so that the others would protect him from any blast. The two other barrels remained untouched; it was assumed that they, too, would be lighter than the barrels that the guard had checked earlier.

"You, John Johnson, you have nothing?" asked Falsdart kindly, he was still not clear about what was going on.

At first he had thought his cellar drinking-partner had been caught stealing barrels of drink, and then he suspected there was more and now it appeared these mystery barrels contained gunpowder to blow up the cellars.

He was shocked, there was no doubt in his mind that the rest of the building would have caved in once the walls were breached, he had seen mines under siege towns work spectacularly well and gunpowder could do the work of a dozen men digging at the foundations of a fortification.

He could not believe that his newfound friend intended to blow his guard and him to kingdom come.

"Only taps and spiles," replied Guido, equally mystified at the appearance of the barrels of gunpowder. "There is mallet in the bottom of the bag, for tapping the barrels."

"Use the end of your pike, but do it gently," commanded Knyvett. There was trepidation in his voice; it was the fear that they might try to open the other thirty-six barrels and discover *sack* not gunpowder. He had been assured that the gunpowder could no longer explode, being corrupted, but he did not want to take any chances.

"A better idea would be to use the tap to knock the bung out of the keystone, but do it very gently," suggested Guido.

He was feeling nervous, now. Gunpowder was dangerous, he knew from his time in the Low Countries. There had been many accidents and incidents with the dangerous compounds that blew bridges and dykes, fired weapons of all kinds and exploded in transit. Gunpowder was a wickedly unpredictable substance.

Many sappers had lost their lives.

"Very well," Knyvett agreed after a short pause, it was difficult to argue with the logic, the tap was wieldier than a pikestaff.

Knyvett signalled to Petigrew to collect a wooden tap and the mallet from the bag next to Guido.

He had seen innkeepers tap and spile barrels of beer and copied their action, up-ending the barrel and placing the wooden tap above the keystone.

One tap of the mallet and the bung was pushed through; the tap rammed home; Petigrew teased and wiggled the tap from the keystone, before tipping the barrel over and spilling out what looked like coal dust onto the floor.

"Why there is black powder here," cried Falsdart, in surprise. He was shocked, though in the light it was difficult to tell whether it was gunpowder or coal dust or just dust from the cellar.

"Gunpowder, I will wager. I am sure of it; search him!" cried Knyvett excitedly, drawing his sword.

The others dared not doubt him. He nodded at his pageboy, Jerome, who pulled out his stiletto from the fold of his clothes, its clean Toledo steel shard glistened in the lantern light.

There was no possible way for the unfortunate watchman to escape Cecil's trap. Ben strode over, his hands blackened with coal dust, which he inadvertently smeared on Guido's clothes as he searched the folds, adding further to the appearance that

Guido had been handling gunpowder. He produced only three matches, there were no weapons on Guido, he possessed nothing else not even a purse.

"I have but three matches on my person to keep my candles alive, nothing more," protested Guido.

"To take the life of King James you mean and the lives of the parliamentarians! Three matches to light your fuses! A trinity of terror!"

Knyvett had accused him loudly; there was anger in his voice. His acting was appalling but in the heightened atmosphere of the cellar that did not matter. He stepped back and put his hand on his sword hilt, Guido's eyes followed him and that was when he noticed the glinting blade of the stiletto and saw Jerome step forward a pace.

"Why would I want to harm the King?" asked Guido nervously eyeing both armed men. His words came out as an incredulous mumble, heard only by those close by.

"Hear that men, he said that he wanted to harm the King!" cried Knyvett.

Guido had only his cloak, his doublet, hose and shoes to keep out the cold; he was not armed; Guido posed no threat to the guard or to the nobles who were due in parliament that very day. Guido said nothing; he was a mere scarecrow to scare any chance thief who might want to help himself to a barrel of *sack* not knowing that it had been supplied for the King's party. He was in no position to protest, he could not fight his way out; he would have to wait until Catesby explained everything.

"What else has he on him?"

"Some rope is coiled by the barrels," Ben said.

"For the fuse, no doubt!" cried Knyvett. "We have discovered a dastardly plot, gunpowder fuses, what do you say about the rope? Were you about to set the match?"

"No," argued Guido, "the rope is for lowering the barrels onto the boat and hauling them up on the other side. They will be needed tomorrow to hoist the barrels up onto the first floor, that's why I have them here still."

"Balderdash and poppycock," Knyvett countered.

"I am John Johnson, a night-watchman," he said calmly, that was what he had been told to say.

"Ha, that is the alias that the Secretary of State uses all the time, he is also the leader of our espion network. How very witty and clever; was that one of Percy's jokes? He has run into our friend, Lord Cecil, many times, with his Papist plots."

"That is not true," complained Guido vociferously. "I am not part of any plot, I swear."

"Silence, clearly, this is one more plot, only more audacious and more dastardly. So you planned to blow up this house and the King, his kinsmen and his children with it. How do you plead?" spat Knyvett venomously.

The two continued their dialogue as the others looked on with mounting disbelief as the man they had shared a drink with was accused of treason and of attempting to commit mass murder. Their shock was clear; they were all astounded, such a charming companion, had been revealed as an assassin. It was truly incredible.

Knyvett manoeuvred Guido away from the others, ensured that they were in the corner, so that the page and the sentries could barely hear their words. That way he could interpret them, as he felt best. He could select details to omit and those to shout over his shoulder as words that actually came from the mouth of the man who planned to explode the cellars. It was an excellent piece of deception; manipulating words expertly. Whatever Guido mentioned could be twisted to entrap him.

"To guarding the *sack*, I plead guilty. I would never blow up the houses with that," mumbled Guido perplexed, pointing to the small, breached barrel that had spewed out the incriminating powder. He could not believe that anyone would think he a capable of blowing up himself and others.

"Hear that men, he pleads guilty."

"To guarding the barrels, how could I cause an explosion with '*sack*'?"

"But with thirty six barrels of gunpowder you could, these would be the catalyst! You could blow this place apart," cried Knyvett.

"No doubt myself too, but I like life too much," argued Guido forcibly, he had no desire to die.

"Hear that he was going to light the match!" Knyvett shouted. He had deliberately misconstrued much for match, he was twisting all Guido's words and shouting his misinterpretations so all the witnesses could hear, the more Guido replied, the more he became entangled in the web. The web Knyvett weaved, when he practised how to deceive.

"Why would I blow up the house above my head and all those persons therein?" Guido replied weakly; it was a damning accusation. He was almost paralysed with fear.

"Mark these words guards; he was to blow up the house above our heads and everyone therein. Record that remark in your report, men. Ensure the scribe writes it exactly as he said it. Do you wish to say anymore?"

"I see, you will twist my words," he whispered, realising that it was no use saying anything.

He was guilty as far as this man was concerned and even if he uttered the simplest thing, his words would be twisted horribly.

His role as a night-watch-man had suddenly turned to the role of traitor. Guido's thick accent and soft voice helped in the deception, match, sounded like much, life and like, sounded similar, no matter what he said or how he said it, the skilful Knyvett would twist his words, misconstrue his meaning and contort his intention, the stranger was danger and every utterance he made would be used in evidence against him. Silence was the best defence for the time being until he could get a message to his friends. They would make Knyvett understand; they would clear up this mess. Cecil had sent them away deliberately.

His friends were organising the delivery of the rest of the *sack* to the Midlands. Their order to the Crown had been delivered and a watchman employed to protect it. The remainder of the shipment was to be distributed at Cecil's request, personally, to various customers he had won them throughout the Midlands. These non-existent customers had wanted to toast the opening of parliament and so it was vital the barrels were delivered and escorted by a nobleman who could pass on Cecil's compliments to the recipient. They could not help Guido so far from London.

"Securely bind this man, use those ropes to tie his hands and guard him, tie this scarf about his mouth, he is to speak to no one and no one is to speak to him, is that understood," commanded Knyvett sternly. He tugged at the scarf that had been loosely draped around his neck, held it out for the gag to be administered.

"Yes, your Lordship," the captain of the guard replied, stepping forward to do his duty as none of his subordinates dared.

Even though following orders to bind a plotter, Falsdart was gentle with Guido who met his eyes as he meekly opened his mouth to allow the cotton gag to be placed in his mouth and wound around his head. Falsdart had no choice but to securely bind the scarf at the back, using a simple knot, left over right, right over left, the type favoured by seamen to secure two ropes.

"I must return to the King's palace to tell him about the danger that has been prevented. You have done well guards, but we must make sure that he confesses to the right people!"

At that moment, Doubleday arrived and that was when Guido realised the whole drama had been orchestrated, he recognised the man who had been in partnership with Catesby to buy the *sack*. When the whole horror of the situation sunk in, he realised that any hope of justice was gone. His heart sank. That was when it dawned on him that he was lost and it was then that he decided to make a run for it, feeling it was his only choice. The others were so surprised by this sudden action; they did not react at first. He had been so compliant that resistance was totally unexpected.

Unfortunately, Doubleday's bulk stood in the way of his exit. He ran towards him hoping to side step at the last minute but his adversary was light on his feet and held his arms up to block him. Guido gripped Doubleday's fingers on his left hand in order to push them away and the next thing he knew he was lying on his back, Doubleday had stepped behind him and moved his left leg swiftly behind Guido's while slipping his fingers from Guido's grasp. He pushed hard against the poor Guido's chest. Guido toppled backwards and fell hard on the stone floor. His cry of pain was muffled by the gag and escaped as a tortured moan.

Dazed, he tried to struggle up but the big man's hands rolled him onto his stomach and in no time were around his legs and undoing the garters from around his hose. With his improvised bindings, Doubleday proceeded to secure poor Guido's hands together behind his back. He ensured he pulled the strands tight. Then lay his bulk on top of him in a beastly revenge that knocked the wind out of Guido who gasped pitifully. Doubleday was no stranger to scraps and had a reputation as a cruel adversary.

"Bring him along to the King when I send for him, you can keep him at my house until then," Knyvett ordered.

"Will we be expected at Knyvett House?" Doubleday asked, looking up, his large bulk crushing Guido's comparatively slight frame.

"Of course," replied Knyvett impatiently, "my man servant awaits my return even at this hour."

Chapter 6 - The Eve

Knyvett made haste to the King's palace, at Whitehall and told the news both to the Earl of Salisbury, Lord Robert Cecil, and the Lord Chamberlain, the Earl of Suffolk, Thomas Howard. Howard was genuinely shocked; Cecil appeared so. The two men would see that Guido never saw his friends again.

Howard immediately woke the rest of the council who were staying at the Palace. Guido was taken to a house opposite Whitehall, Knyvett House, but Doubleday did not take him inside at first, instead he watched from the corner to see the candlelight flickering across the rooms in Whitehall. The palace guards that surrounded Guido wished that Doubleday would open the door and give them access to a fire.

As the Lord Chamberlain, Thomas Howard, Earl of Suffolk, interviewed Whyneard and, as Cecil hoped, discovered Thomas Percy had rented a house in Westminster from Whyneard himself; he went with Whyneard to the next room to interview Knyvett, leaving Cecil free to put the rest of his plan into action, which he did with skill and alacrity. Knyvett sat on a stool, warming himself by the fire and immediately stood in deference to the Lord Chamberlain; the other two men pulled up the chairs that had been, up until then, decoratively lined on either side of the chimneybreast. Howard signalled to Knyvett that he should sit and indicated the same to Whyneard.

"You may report to me," Howard breathed reassuringly as he made himself comfortable.

"I found Thomas Percy's man, standing abroad, his clothes and boots on; at so dead of the night, I decided to arrest him. I went and searched the house, where I made the guards open a small barrel that had been buried under some of the billets and coals, which was added to the thirty-six there. I demanded the fellow be searched and on him was found three matches. He was clearly in the process of preparing gunpowder to blow up the palace. "

The audience listened, riveted by the tale as Kynvett explained excitedly, he had rehearsed his speech several times so he knew chapter and verse. Cecil had made sure it would be dramatic and had drilled Knyvett.

"Then, you came directly to me, is that correct?" Howard asked.

"At first to the guardroom and thence to collect the keeper of the King's wardrobe, John Whyneard," Kynvett replied.

"We must await Lord Salisbury, the Secretary of State, Cecil will need a full report, and from thence we can go to the King and give him the good news," cried Howard. "You have done well."

Knyvett and Whyneard had done a very good job, but more so, Cecil had done extremely well; the fiction was holding up to the further scrutiny. Meanwhile, Cecil would tell his network the good news that Guy Fawkes had been captured, which would spread rapidly. If the witnesses could be persuaded of what they had seen, all other details could be changed.

As Howard escorted Whyneard to the King who was staying at Whitehall, Cecil was encouraging Catesby and his sherry consortium to flee London. By four in the morning, the Privy Councillors and witnesses had gathered in the King's bedchamber, including Cecil, and as soon as the King's

Chamberlain entered, the Lord Chamberlain, Lord Thomas Howard, Earl of Suffolk, told them all Knyvett's news.

"All is well," he announced, assuring King James that the traitor was bound and that Edmund Doubleday had custody of the villain. James considered the news, knowing that Guido alone would not have been able to pull off such a plan. It was clear he had accomplices and they had to be found.

"Thank you, Lord Knyvett, for discovering this plot, particularly as its existence had been missed by so many. Undoubtedly, your actions have saved many lives, not the least mine, and you will be rewarded. You did not find the props I had missing? I"

"Indeed not, I am sorry for that," replied Knyvett.

He thought this would be the least of James's concerns but he did not know James as well as he thought. A house opposite the King's favourite palace of Whitehall did not guarantee understanding of this monarch.

"It is of little consequence now, I will arrange for similar items held here at Whitehall to be transported to the Palace of Westminster. Are Waad and Popham here yet?"

The two men walked forward and bowed, greeting James with the pomp a king deserved, they wished him a long and peaceful reign for good measure.

"My Lords, it is your duty to find out who helped this man in his endeavours is that not so?" James asked.

"Indeed, Your Majesty," Popham agreed.

"That is the least of our duties, Your Majesty," Waad added. "a Mr. Doubleday has him im the house in the street opposite this very window. Beefeaters have been dispatched from the Tower to collect him and take him directly to the dungeons there."

"Very, well," the King announced in a loud voice so all in the room could hear his fine words, "you must make him speak and if he will not otherwise confess, the gentler tortures are to be used first, and then the utmost pain must follow."

"Your Majesty's wishes will be followed," Waad said.

"We will make him sing like a canary bird," Popham added.

"Very well, I will not detain you; there is an escort for your carriage waiting for you downstairs, ensure they make great speed to conduct you to your destination."

The two men bowed and left immediately. The rest of the inner circle gathered around James and started talking animatedly to the King, registering shock and indignation. Only Cecil held back waiting for his messenger to call him away so that he could oversee the rest of his true plot, which was to wipe out the vestiges of the Catholic courtiers. His plan was working even more smoothly than he had envisaged.
He would arrange for the arrest of those who had escaped from London, those in the far off corners of the land whose movements had been watched constantly by the Justices of the Peace, as well as those who might compromise the subterfuge of the Gunpowder Plot. As for the conspirators themselves, he had sent them himself to Holbeche House and Markham, helped by the sheriff, would ensure no one would survive.

Chapter 7 - i - The Hampton Court Conference – Bilson

Cecil and Markham sat in the small chamber next to Markham's bedroom, it was a goodly size with a large window looking over the lawn of the garden at the back of the palace and it had two doors one to the landing outside the room and the other to the Markham's chamber next door. However, unlike the chambers adjoining, this had several writing desks between the window and the fireplace, arranged opposite each other, standing on a beautiful rug from France depicting a hunting scene. There was something of a theme in James's furnishing. Markham had been studying the beautifully drawn yet vicious dogs between the table legs; he could not see clearly but they appeared to be devouring the hind legs of a stag.

Arranged around the roaring fire, burning since dawn to ward off February frosts, on the specific orders of Cecil, there were three tall chairs of the latest design, scrolled carving on the high back, cane in the centre, the seats had soft cushions filled with horsehair and duck down and were covered in tanned suede.

Markham wondered whether it might have come from one of the royal deer or the stag on the rug. Whilst he was contemplating matters to relieve the boredom of waiting, he noticed a large rectangular table had been brought in and pushed against the panelling of the wainscot to form a sideboard. Plates of cold meat were arranged over the surface, sliced beef, chicken and pork, as well as chicken legs and a large veal and ham pie.

"Is Bilson here yet?" Cecil asked the clerk peevishly, "Markham, would you check for me, please?"

"You do not like my Bishop Bilson; remember he gave the sermon at my coronation," replied King James indulgently, the remark had not been addressed to him, however, he felt he should make a comment.

"The 25th July, 1603, was happy day," replied Cecil smoothly; he paused before continuing to allow the King to speak.

He had realised over his time at Hampton that it was inevitable that he would be interrupted so he had decided to make sure he allowed for such.

"Yes, a joyous occasion," the King agreed.

"However, I am here to protect you and the Crown, I need not remind you of all the trouble in Europe, there is much dissent amongst the religions here too, we need unity to ensure that there is peace in England; I do not need Bilson reheating his dish of dissent."

"But he supports the *Divine Right of Kings*; he said so in his sermon!" argued the King. "I remember the words he used."

"He added a caveat about resistance to the Crown being acceptable, the fool!" Cecil spat venomously; he did not want church leaders encouraging defiance to the Crown.

"I did not hear that part, I must have drifted off!" admitted James shyly; it was difficult to deny that he had missed one of the salient parts of his Archbishop's speech.

"The theme from Bilson's book of 1585, you do not remember it?" continued Cecil calmly, he was secretly aghast at the King's lack of knowledge or poor memory.

"Those bishops, I need them but do not heed them," replied James, he had read the book, indeed it had been a gift, but he had found it dull and uninteresting and had never finished it.

The subject matter had not appealed and the argument had not been gripping. James would become totally immersed and involved in subjects that interested him, tobacco smoking, the Divine Right of Kings and Puritanism to name but three.

"And Bilson, what has he asked Your Majesty to do here at Hampton?" asked Cecil warily.

He knew the answer and was prepared but he needed to know the King was equally forewarned and forearmed. There was much preparation to be done so that the king would ready.

"He arrives with Bancroft to plead for me to maintain the status quo; the church never likes change, which is good. Dick and Tom want me to keep things the same," said James feeling confident of the bishops' support.

"You are saying Richard Bancroft and Thomas Bilson demand nothing? Is that what you are stating Your Majesty?"

Cecil, a consummate lawyer and liar always liked to check his facts carefully. He was a martinet and liked to control his marionettes.

"Indeed," the King said.

"We should set them to work on your new prayer book," suggested Cecil, wanting to give the bishops a purpose at the conference.

"A splendid idea, we need not worry, therefore!" cried the King.

"The Puritans want change!" argued Cecil, "Your Majesty has friends in the bishops but many enemies amongst the Puritan ministers; they want reform."

"They will not have it!" exclaimed the King.

"They are a growing band," warned Cecil.

"They will be crushed," insisted James vehemently. "Bilson and Bancroft offer no threat; the Puritans offer annoyance, they are the fly in my ointment, a bee in a closed closet. I consider them not. Bilson advised me last year not to hold the Conference, and to leave religious matters to the church, and yet I am its Supreme Leader; theology more than common sense rules his mind, I am afraid. Patrick Galloway came to my rescue in the matter and his advice prevailed."

"The Moderator of the Scottish Assembly moderated your assembly!" Cecil quipped. James smiled at Cecil's remark; he appreciated wordplay, whether it was the words of Shakespeare or of the elfin Cecil. The *Beagle* was shrewd; James knew what he was trying to do.

"Galloway is a good man with an iron will and common sense. We need to ensure the Puritans do not upset the balance of our State with their demands. He understands this well and has helped me; he realises the importance of the bishops."

"Wise words, Your Majesty, we do indeed have to keep the Puritans in check, they would sweep away all vestiges of the common weal's power," Cecil added appreciatively.

"I need the Lord Bishops, I do not need these upstarts undermining their authority; I do not need these Puritans trying to come up with their own way of governing the church."

"You are wily, Your Majesty."

"It will undermine me and it will affect the state," complained the King, taking a swig of sherry.

"Indeed, sage words, Your Majesty."

Miles Smith arrived, opening the door noisily so everyone turned around, announcing the arrival of the two bishops. It was a dramatic entrance as was the intention; these were the chief bishops in the country. It was these two that James and Cecil relied on for support influence and information. Equally, the bishops realised that their influence relied on the King's indulgence. He could support the Puritans and sweep their power away, should he so desire.

"My Lord, Richard Bancroft, Archbishop of London and my Lord Thomas Bilson, Archbishop of Winchester," he exclaimed *basso forte* as the two Bishops swathed in layers, swept into the hall through the stone, arched doorway.

Their outer cloaks were thick wool, dyed a rich russet, with ermine collars and skirts that trailed over the flagstones of the hall. The tedious pleasantries were exchanged, the King welcoming them; they wished him a long and successful reign. Cecil greeted them and the four men continued bowing and expressing delight at meeting again. They were allies against a growing menace, a threat to the status quo and were thus friends.

Necessity made strange bedfellows.

"Your Majesty," Bancroft announced grandly in his soft Lancashire accent, "You can rely on my full support! My Lord, Archbishop Whitgift, apologises for his late arrival."

The bishop bowed humbly.

"I am sorry Whitgift has been delayed, he was so gracious at my coronation; as for your loyalty, I never doubted it; you have acted loyally as Bishop of London and will do so as Archbishop of Canterbury."

"Thank you, Your Majesty," the bishop breathed gratefully.

"I have chosen you as Whitgift's successor and I can think of no worthier a candidate. We need steadiness; there should be no change without the need for change. Our church needs no reform."

James stood with his hands on his hips and with his spindly legs spread in a tribute to the stance of Sir Walter Raleigh, a warrior's gait; everyone in the room wondered if he might fall or stumble.

"Your Majesty confirms my appointment and rewards my loyalty; I thank you for the honour. I will continue to serve both Your Majesty and the Archbishop of Canterbury," Bancroft agreed a little too readily and a little too smugly.

"Congratulations my Lord Archbishop!" Cecil cried. "You have been de facto head of the church for some time and now it is official in the eyes of the government. Whitgift has discussed your appointment and it will take place when he feels he can no longer complete his tasks, the succession is now secure and we need worry about it no longer."

"I thank you Lord Cecil," said the King, bowing slightly to his Secretary of State, before turning his head to Bilson and looking at him imploringly.

"Your Majesty, may I make a brief petition," breathed Bilson breathlessly.
He was determined to show his loyalty to the King, he was conservative and against all change that might undermine his power and wealth.

"My Lord Bishop, pray continue."

"I was commanded by your predecessor, Elizabeth I, of England, to counter Puritan doctrine, she bid me: 'neither to desert the doctrine, nor let the calling, which I bear in the Church of God, be trampled underfoot, by such 'unquiet refusers of truth and authority'; I know you agree, we cannot have change."

"I have a copy of your book: *The Perpetual Government of Christ's Church* and although written a decade ago, it still has verve and veracity today, a sage work that supports our Episcopal views, an excellent work."

"Splendid," he ejaculated proudly, unable to contain his pride; the King had read his writings. What flattery was that? " I am pleased Your Majesty finds approval in my humble musings."

"Having read it, I would like to repeat my offer that you help in the new translation of the Bible and with our new prayer book," James decided; he felt that Bilson's loyalty should be rewarded with a royal undertaking as well as promotion.

"The King James version, I have heard of the undertaking, I would be delighted!" replied Bilson, genuinely pleased and not a little flattered to be chosen. As a theologian first, he would be able to influence the content of these important books. It was a great opportunity.

"First we must counter these bleating Puritans who want to make my church less pure," explained the King testily.

"You have led the Scottish Church, Your Majesty, since your mother's abdication with John Knox's counsel and I know the Puritans would like a church like the Scottish Reformed Church, no bishops, only church elders, picked by the community," Bilson replied knowledgeably.

"It is not something I wish!" James exclaimed testily.

"I am glad to hear!" Bilson replied.

"As you bandy your book, I bandy mine of 1599, *Basilikon Doron* chided every Puritan!" James continued.

He would not be outdone; he was the King after all.

"Yet many feel that you will agree to reform in moderation," Bilson pressed despite feeling apprehensive.

He had been given a glass of sherry but would not drink it until King James took a sip; instead he put the glass on the dining room table where food was spread, looking at the rainbow reflections in the Venetian glass.

"I will disabuse them, read the 1,000 signatures on the Millenary Petition and their petty requests!" James barked angrily, spittle spraying from his mouth.

He drank thirstily and messily from his glass, there was a mark where he had eaten but not wiped his mouth with a napkin before drinking, leaving a spittle smear and lip print around the rim. Bilson hid his disgust at this display.

"All Puritan ministers who signed this must have been coerced," Bilson suggested sycophantically. Everyone there knew that it was unlikely that a thousand people could be thus influenced. The petition was a genuine document of dissent and reflected the feelings of a significant number of influential people.

"Look at their pathetic demands! Cecil what do you think?" asked James.

"The petition is careful not to challenge the royal supremacy, Your Majesty," noted Cecil.

"It recognises me as the Head of the Church of England. That is all it does!" complained the King, beckoning to the servant with the sherry decanter to approach. "Otherwise it tells me how to change the church, bend it to the form favoured by those perfidious Puritans."

"Your Majesty has right and might on his side," Bilson added obsequiously and unnecessarily.

"I want to forge a new church but gently with smooth tapping with the blacksmith's ball-peen hand-hammer, tapped against the forge, not the violent blows that are used to twist the horseshoe," James asserted mildly.

"The petition has called for a number of moderate church reforms to remove ceremonies which are perceived as popish," Cecil added for the sake of clarity.

The king hesitated before replying, allowing his glass to be filled.

"They delivered this to me on my progress through the county of Leicestershire; it spoilt my time there reading their nonsense. Read it, please, good Bishop Bilson and give me your opinion."

Bilson read, although he had already seen a copy.

He glossed over the Puritan's wish to remove making the sign of the cross over a baptised baby, many of his friends did not bother with the old fashioned gesture, and he saw that the older ones could not break the habit. Bilson was convinced that the success of the Church of England was due to the toleration of slight differences, celebrating the spirit of the canon laws and turning a blind-eye to small discrepancies in their execution. Old habits from the Reformation were hard to break especially in rural communities where priests resolutely refused to pass away and never retired.

Furthermore, he read that the Puritans argued that as the sacrament of Confirmation was not mentioned in the Bible; it should be abolished. Bilson knew that many plain folk enjoyed the coming of age party for their family; the children were treated as adults from thence. He felt it was an ideal time for children to reconfirm their faith, taking communion at the age of twelve or thirteen; it was when most started work properly even if they had not already been contributing in small ways by doing odd jobs and errands for others. It seemed a sensible rite of passage, yet the Puritans were opposed to any *'Catholic ceremony'*.

The richer people saw it as an excuse to celebrate; Bilson saw it as the chance for the commitment to Christ to be taken seriously. Because the poor saw it as a 'rite of passage', a tradition as well as an excuse for a party, he felt it should be left in place, after all the church had adapted to the community under Edward, it made allowances not demands. Christ, Bilson realised, was tolerant, he forgave; it was difficult for his people to behave in the same way. On the other hand, the Catholics went too far with their claims of transubstantiation, in his opinion, communion was a celebration, a remembrance, nothing more; he found the Catholics assertion that the bread and wine were in fact transformed into the body and blood of Jesus quite laughable, but again harmless.

It was not the typical view of a Calvinist and his rise through the ranks of the Church relied on him keeping such thoughts to himself. The Puritans also wanted to disallow baptism by midwifes, yet as far as he was concerned, even if the child was baptised by a midwife, most children were christened later in the church. He saw no harm in it; he even felt it should be encouraged if it gave the mother peace of mind and reassured her. Typically, in these cases, he knew from experience, the family would come to the church for a proper Christening even if the child had been baptised the midwife if she felt the child's life was in peril. The Puritans however felt that the practice reinforced the Catholic idea of purgatory, the idea that once the child arrived, its soul had to be saved and it allowed a lay-person the opportunity to dispense a sacrament that many felt should be reserved solely for the Church to administer.

The Catholics argued that an un-baptised child would go straight to purgatory. Most clerics opposed the practice as it allowed a layperson to perform the administration of a sacrament. Bilson was ambivalent; there was no harm in a double baptism but much harm, in double-predestination and, equally so, in the idea of purgatory that could be paid away with Indulgences. He realised it was divisive and he was also a true Calvinist who believed in predestination. He felt that he was indeed saved due his religion but he could not agree with the Puritan view that everyone else, as a result, was damned.

The Puritans said they wanted to expunge all Catholic practices, popish rituals, superstitious nonsense; Bilson had grown up with these rituals. The Puritans were further prepared to upset the traditions practised through generations by banning the exchange of rings in marriage. The Puritans argued that wearing wedding rings was not in scripture and seemed to be another Catholic superstitious ritual.

Bilson was also ambivalent to the wearing of rings, as he wore his rings of office and his signet ring, they were part of his garb of a bishop; he also knew that the matrimonial ceremonies were steeped in ritual and this was a pivotal point of that service. The eternity symbolised by the rings, and the exchange of them, allowed the bride and groom to pledge their troth. The rings were a powerful symbol of the unbroken circle of eternal love, which had nothing to do with religion but everything to do with the couple's endless commitment to each other, but the Puritans, Bilson realised, were not interested in people's feelings but in destroying superstition and ritual in any form that it occurred in the Church.

He wondered where the distinction lay between superstition and tradition, perhaps only the Puritans knew. The Puritans did not want people to bow at the name of Jesus in services yet bowing for the blessings through the service were to remain unchanged; it seemed strange that bowing was not dispensed of altogether. The reformers seemed to lack the zeal to fully reform. They seemed to be accepting many popish rituals whilst trying to ban some; it seemed the wrong way around. He wondered why the Puritans could not dispense with bowing all together. It seemed to Bilson that the Puritans were being very selective in the main and ridiculous in certain aspects.

The Puritans wanted the clergy to wear clothes other than vestments, which looked too much like Catholic clothing and they wanted to remove the custom of the clergy living in the church building. These habits were dying out or being ignored in the urban areas where the merchants embraced Puritanism, rituals were dispensed with and simple services remained.

Bilson felt time would see these changes through and there was no need to order change or create a fuss. He could not change the fact that the rural brethren favoured a service that had changed little since the reign of Henry VIII and that those in cities and especially ports were adopting more continental ways f worship, some involving just a bible and a table. Bilson assumed that the Puritans wanted praise for setting these rules in stone or at least getting them in writing while they were at Hampton and pushing them through parliament at a later stage. If they were going to make their '*Bills*' into 'Acts of Parliament', the removal of the Bishops in the House of Lords would go a long way to ensure the '*Bills*' were not blocked by the Lords.

Apart from being in opposition to Archbishop John Whitgift's policy that clergy must subscribe to the Book of Common Prayer and use vestments in services, the Puritans also wanted a Presbyterian and not an Episcopal system. In other words, these iconoclasts wanted groups of local churches to be governed by a higher assembly of elders known as the presbytery or classis; presbyteries could, then, be grouped into a synod, and presbyteries, along with synods nationwide would join together in a general assembly to administer the Church. Responsibility for conduct of church services would be held by the ordained minister or 'pastor' who would be known either as a 'teaching elder', or a 'minister of the word and sacrament'.

This Presbyterian polity was to be developed as a rejection of governance by hierarchies of single bishops; this would undermine the whole structure of the present church and wrest power from the bishops; Bilson obviously did not like this section and showed his displeasure, his face flushed and he tutted loudly. With this gesture, that he knew Robert Cecil and King James would hear, he aligned himself fully to the view of both State and Crown. He paused before looking up, he caught Cecil's eye and nodded sagely before returning to the writing to see if there was any more bad news to be read.

"As you know your King has studied theology and enjoys debating theological points," warned Cecil when he saw that Bilson had finished reading.

"Indeed the whole of Christendom knows," re-joined the bishop, bowing in the direction of King James. "He has written tracts and taken part in many debates, I am aware of this."

"I know you are."

"The thrust of your comment is?"

"He has graciously agreed to hold this conference at Hampton Court Palace where supporters and opponents of the Millenary

Petition can debate the merits of reforms to the church," Cecil continued, "We rely on you to help, in fact, not to put too fine a point on it, we put our faith in your hands!"

Bilson translated Cecil's rhetoric, James is displeased with your stand on the 'Divine Right of Kings'; I have organised this charade in order to crush the Puritan dissenters once and for all; are you on our side or do you want to risk losing the lucrative lease on Southwark?

Bilson had rehearsed what he was to say to the King months before he was to appear at Hampton Court, he was above all a politician who wanted to retain his lucrative diocese. He would appear to King James as the King wanted him to appear. His views had been expressed in print and no one had expressed an interest, it was therefore sensible to play the politician. The conference had been delayed due to a small outbreak of plague in London. Wisely, he had used the extra time before the conference to gain support and to seek advice from the best minds in his church as well as researching what was definitely known about James's views on the church. There was no sense in upsetting the King.

"I was disappointed when this conference was postponed due to an outbreak of the plague, but it allowed me to reflect on my position and I fully support the King in having no changes to the mass and I would be grateful if the King condescended to have me assist in the new translation of the good book!"

Cecil looked relieved and Bilson looked as smug as ever, Cecil found that most irritating. Cecil wondered whether he should get Markham to wipe the supercilious smile off his face by asking him to stamp on the bishop's foot. Politics did not allow for such an assault but just imagining it, in his mind's eye, brought Cecil immense pleasure and diffused mounting ire. He felt calm again.

The King spoke: "I have chosen four Puritans to represent the Puritan cause: John Rainolds, the president of Corpus Christi

College, Oxford; Laurence Chaderton, the Master of Emanuel College, Cambridge, along with the esteemed Thomas Sparke; and John Knewstubs."

The King paused to gauge the reaction of those present. No one dared speak; it was the King's wish. Cecil continued, "His Lordship, the Archbishop Whitgift leads a delegation of eight bishops including his protégé, Richard Bancroft, Bishop of London and seven deans and two other clergymen, all of them are opposed to the Puritans and their reforms. Eight on our side and four on their side."

All the men in the room smiled, the Puritans would have little say; it would appear that they were involved but their influence would be slight. It was another masterstroke from the master manipulator, Cecil. He had created his twelve marionettes and he would pull their puppet strings.

At the first meeting of the Conference, held January on 14th, James met only with Archbishop Whitgift's party, Bancroft and Bilson were amongst that group of eight. The 15th was a day of reflection. On the second day of the conference, 16th January, he met with the Puritans. Rainolds mentioned the Puritan proposal for creating presbyteries in England.

"Your Majesty has seen how well presbyteries have worked in your native Scotland and therefore we propose that here in England we should replace the Lord Bishops. Each local group of churches would be governed by a classis, you call them Presbyteries in Scotland," asserted Rainolds calmly.

"Presbyterianism is a Scottish religion, fit for Scotland, but I am the Supreme Leader of the Church in England, I need the Lord Bishops to protect the Church of England and all of its Canon Laws," interrupted the King, dismissing Rainolds argument for removal of the bishops in one fell swoop.

"Indeed, Your Majesty but these assemblies of elders could form synods," continued Rainolds unabashed, "perhaps they could perform the role of the Lord Bishops in canon matters and in parliament."

"Classis, non plus ultra," James replied furiously, "or in English, presbyteries, go no further; Synods, synods, you speak of synods. From the Synod of Whitby, the synods have produced no good but a lot of hot air like tobacco smoke, fetid and unclean, along with garbled and unclear arguments. Let me make it clear: no classis, no synods, no elders, no general assemblies, I have my bishops, I have no need for plebeian presbyteries while I have my Praetorian Guard."

"Your Majesty, has graciously agreed to hear our suggestions for how the church in England could be shaped," interjected Laurence Chaderton mildly. James viewed the proposal to replace bishops with presbyteries as an attempt to diminish his power in the church. James did not want the bishops removed they were his ally in parliament against the other Lords. They were the difference between victory and defeat in any battle against the House of Lords.

"No, bishop no King," the King cried disdainfully, "How dare you challenge my authority; question my divine authority as supreme leader of the church; undermine my authority as the king of this country! You are dismissed and the business of the day is ended."

"It is fearfully early," complained Chaderton, elected the leader and spokesman for the Puritans on that day.

"And I am fearfully upset!" replied the King impatiently.

"As Your Majesty wishes," said Chaderton meekly. He had been puzzled by the King's reaction but he could not argue with his dismissal.

"Good day to you!" cried the King, spitting wildly barely masking his annoyance.

On 18th January, the king initially met with Whitgift's party and an assemblage of ecclesiastical lawyers before calling in the Puritans to hear his verdict. James declared that the use of the

Book of Common Prayer was to continue, and made no provisions for a preaching ministry. James addressed the Puritan representatives, there assembled in a cold and haughty manner:

"I will however allow a few changes to the *Book of Common Prayer*; the mention of baptism by midwives is to be eliminated; the term absolution, which you perceive as too closely associated to the sacrament of penance and popish ways, I can understand. It will henceforth be referred to as the 'remission of sins'; as for the Confirmation, it will be renamed 'laying on of hands' to divorce it from its Catholic sacramental meaning; we will also make one or two minor changes that some of you have suggested. Other than that, I offer you nothing else."

"Thank you Your Majesty," Chaderton replied gratefully. He had won more concessions than had been hoped for after the previous meetings; he had to be grateful for any of the King's offerings.

"Finally," James announced, "I have agreed to lend my support for a new, authorised translation of the Bible, and thus the King James Version will live on in churches for generations to come. I will call on some of you to assist with this and the revised prayer book."

Chapter 7- ii – Hampton Court - Cecil and Bancroft

"Richard Bancroft, my good Archbishop of London, you are the Privy Council's main choice as Whitgift's replacement as Archbishop of Canterbury. You have argued well against the Puritans at this Hampton Court Conference," surmised Cecil.

"Lord Robert Cecil, Privy Seal, you flatter me; I know that my appointment will help you to block any other reforms by the Puritans."

"Precisely."

"I am your man!"

"We will therefore commission you to produce a book of canons so we can call convocation of the clergy and set everything in stone."

"I am flattered that you would choose me and accept your commission."

"You are far too kind," Cecil breathed dramatically, leaving Bancroft puzzled as to whether he was being genuine or ironic in his remarks. The phrase had not sounded sarcastic and yet he was not sure.

"Most seriously, I cannot tell if you are toying with me," Bancroft announced without embarrassment and with a smile playing on his lips. He had risen through the echelons of the church by guile and intelligence, integrity and honesty. He admired Cecil and was acutely aware of the politics of court, as he was keenly aware of the politics of the church. He was not going to let Cecil intimidate him.

"Friends can tease but you know how we value each other, in all seriousness, so have no concern with my intentions," Cecil assured him warmly. "Be careful our parliament passed the Act of Uniformity but that was under Elizabeth, you will find the Puritans allying with all sorts of politicians, therefore you must ensure all your bishops attend the House so we can defeat the reformers. We cannot allow for any slipshod horses in this race."

"They will surely approve the *Book of Common Prayer*. It is in their interests to do so, surely?"

"Undoubtedly!" Cecil exclaimed, after all, he had planned the whole thing, he was more Puritan than popish in his views but, politically, he could not admit that.

Politics dictated a more pragmatic stance, he was fully aware and, he could not allow the old order to be disturbed at the present juncture.

Having everything set out in writing was an important step in retaining order and James's book of prayer and bible would provide a template. The Puritans could not win too much too soon. It would unsettle the King.

"You are worried about what else they might do as well; pray tell me your concerns," Bancroft eagerly inquired; he tried to balance obsequiousness with concern. He knew that if Cecil was worried, then, he should be alarmed. Nervously, he adjusted the cuffs of his cassock.

"I have been informed that they might claim that Parliament, not Convocation, should be the body authorised to pass new canon law," explained Cecil carefully, he held Bancroft's gaze with his own; steely and determined. "Puritans will argue that you bishops are attempting to aggrandise yourself at the expense of everyone else."

"They will endorse my book of canons; surely they have no choice with James supporting me?"

"I sincerely hope so and wish that I could reassure you but my informers do not have the skill of prophecy, observation yes, soothsaying no! Only time will tell," Cecil replied, not wanting to give the prelate false hopes.

"Beyond the canon law what other role do I have in your schemes?" asked Bancroft starting to fret about his situation for the first time. He wondered what Cecil actually wanted. He wanted a straight answer and Cecil replies were coded and cloaked in secrecy.

"Your role is to tell me everything that I might need to know and to block any and all the reform proposals put forward by the Puritans. Then, we can give them a few concessions and they will feel less aggrieved. Beyond that, hold up the example of how poorly treated the Catholics are by the Estate and the Puritans will be grateful for any gains that they may make. "

"I will do my best Lord Cecil."

"I know you will my Lord Bishop."

"My duty is to the Church and the State, I serve them tirelessly."

"Indeed, I know that is so. With further regard to the Catholics, I believe that it is important to separate those who are loyal to the crown from those who are allied to the Spanish and influenced by Jesuits."

"The Catholics are slowly being erased from English soil, they will disappear, soon," Bancroft replied.

"They are few and far between I admit; even Catesby has converted his children," admitted Cecil. "Those who remain, though, have too much influence as far as I am concerned. Ironically, your Bishop Bilson's writing encourages those loyal to the Pope to oppose the Crown, but you know that. Bilson has allowed that if anyone perceives the King to be unjust, he can oppose the 'Divine Right of Kings'."

"I have read the inflammatory piece," replied Bancroft.

"So you see how '*The Church*', and specifically Bilson, have inadvertently given the Catholics just cause to rebel now that James has not given them the rights they had hoped for."

He paused to draw breath. For the listener, it was really quite impressive to hear him speak and to realise, as he did so, how supremely intelligent he was. It was an effort to keep up with the alacrity of his mind. This bishop knew how Cecil worked; he was building a case, checking its plausibility on a willing pair of ears.

"Fortunately for you, many are happy to maintain their positions rather than forfeit them by association with the Pope or Catholic monarchies. Many, like Catesby have become lapsed or Crypto Catholics, even more have converted to the Church of England and denied the Pope."

Bancroft was feeling considerably uncomfortable with Cecil's emphasis on the bungling Bilson's theories on the 'Divine Right of Kings' and mention of the stance he had taken on it, in his writings, so he welcomed the opportunity to mention something of a positive nature.

Bilson's idea that the King's authority could be challenged was an annoyance to James and Cecil and an embarrassment to the bishops.

"So, we have reconciliation there!" cried Bancroft happily. "At least that is something."

"Perhaps, but the State only pays lip service to toleration; I have lobbied hard to reinstate the 'Recusant Fines'; we would benefit from the revenue raised and the Catholics need to be kept in their place. We cannot have them muddying the waters further with their demands. They need to be in retreat at all times or they will attack."

Cecil was ever the masterful chess player.

"I suppose the fines are necessary and I can see that it is vital we keep the Catholics out of politics, they could challenge the authority of the King himself. They need to be reined-in, even if harshly so."
"At this Hampton Court Conference, you have taken a path of conciliation and cooperation, ever the diplomat, I thank you for that." Cecil said and it seemed that he meant it. He needed the Puritans kept in check.

"It is kind of you to say so," Bancroft sighed with relief.

"Once this conference has broken up, I will put the Puritans back into the *'Pandora's Box'* that they crawled out of and shut the lid and hopefully that will be the end of it for the time being. I can devise ways of dealing with that box later"

"I look forward to watching you at work," Bancroft simpered.

"They will have won some concessions that will keep them satisfied for the moment and that is all we can wish for at this time. We understand each other perfectly; I could not have planned it better."

Cecil delivered this with a hint of pride in his voice; they both knew he had indeed considered every eventuality.

"Tell me about Galloway, is he a threat?" asked Bancroft, knowing that time in reconnaissance was never wasted.

"There is nothing to fear, I assure you."

"I am assured, go on."

"He is a moderate and the King's favourite. He has shown his loyalty but refused to enforce fealty amongst his preachers, he has allowed members of the General Assembly freedom to speak as they wish and act so, too, within reason. He is seen as a fair Moderator and spoke well after the Gowrie Conspiracy. Thus endeth the history lesson," Cecil reported, proud of his network of espions and the intelligence it could gather. His informers and reporters were at the very heart of Court and there were few conversations that escaped scrutiny.

"And what is he doing here at Hampton if he is Moderator in Scotland?"

Bancroft knew the questions to ask.

"Advising King James unofficially but ostensibly, acting for the Edinburgh presbytery, that is his official role but he knows the King from old and understands that there is little hope of influencing him in church or kirk matters."

"Does he favour any of the parts of the Millenary Petition? Would you happen to know?"

"I have had access to his diary of 12th January! He notes James spoke with *'great fervency'* about corruptions in the Church and about bishops allowing plural parishes. That is something for you to deal with and quickly."

"Clearly, what else?" asked Bancroft eagerly.

"Further, he notes how the bishops argued that to make any alterations in the prayer-book would be like admitting the 'Recusants' and the 'Puritans' had suffered for refusing submission to that very book and that would make a mockery of Canon Law."

"And so we did!" cried Bancroft.

"And so you should have done; Galloway is on our side, or rather not opposed to us and our endeavours," explained Cecil more patiently than he normally would have, he thought Bancroft a good man and made allowances for him. He also knew that the bishop had a spy network as good as his and that any further information that he needed could always be found at Bancroft's door. They were equals, one worked for the Church, the other for the State. Their goals were shared: security of the realm and security of their positions. "he was merely reporting to the King."

"Praise the Lord!" Bancroft sang happily.

"Here comes Bilson!" Cecil warned.

"I haven't seen you alone since the 'Dejesus affaire'! Do you still say Christ went to hell, not to suffer, but to wrest the keys of hell out of the Devil's hands?" asked Bancroft playfully.

"Yes, I do unlike our Puritans who say he went there in spirit!" Bilson replied light-heartedly, the two bishops were old friends and past sparring partners.

"I thought it was metaphorical, myself!" mocked Bancroft. They loved their little metaphysical and theological jokes; it bound them.

"Stop it you perfidious, Puritan!" squealed Bilson, enjoying the deliciousness of the friendly joshing.

"Serious faces, John Rainolds approaches!" Cecil announced in mock horror.

"Hail Aristotle!" teased Bancroft unmercifully. It was a double barb as Aristotle was not as spiritual as Plato.

"Rhetoric is what I teach not name calling!" complained Rainolds seriously

"Should we call you Rhetoric Rainolds?" Bilson suggested, encouraged by Bancroft's banter.

"Cecil, you young pup, I still remember Sir Francis's support when the Queen took away my Regius Chair, he was a wonderful mentor and a father figure to you, I hope you are following his counsel still." remonstrated Rainolds good-naturedly; he smiled unconsciously revealing his worn teeth.

"Walsingham made sure you had somewhere to sit your largess!" teased Cecil in an equal vein.

"The Lord giveth and it would take a miracle for him to take my girth away," continued Rainolds, he was impervious to insult and his corpulence was not a concern to him. In his view, it showed his affluence, to him largesse meant success and, if that were the case, he had proved himself to be extremely successful. He also detested the popish ways of the Catholic church; all their popish pomp and ceremony, the magic of transubstantiation performed behind the rood screen and their selling of Indulgences, "If you gentleman need any anti-Catholic polemical theology, let me know!"

"You have a considerable reputation as a disputant on the Puritan side; we are surrounded by our opponents all in one man," parried Cecil artfully.

Rainolds smiled slyly; Cecil was correct in his summation.

"I know you secretly support our cause, why not go the whole hog and set down the Puritan laws?" suggested Rainolds cunningly.

"Remember at university in 1592 when Queen Bess scolded you for your 'obstinate preciseness', telling you to follow her laws, and not run before them," Cecil reminded him gently.

"Obstinate and omnipotent, how kind you are in your description of me. I modestly suggest that I am the most prominent representative of the Puritans," he boasted.

"Carry on," Cecil urged, feigning fascination.

"I have received a good deal of favour from King James," responded Rainolds, unwilling to allow Cecil to get away with too much.

These were two powerful men and their pride was evident. Cecil was the most dangerous man in the kingdom but the people whom he tried to mould to his design were not without influence themselves and they were not afraid to stand up to him. He had the state on his side and they had God on theirs. The struggle for temporal and spiritual dominance was an equal one. They had to reach a compromise.

"Stop bragging, the State must pander to more disparate demands than that of one part of the church, we have many more diverse demands and requirements to fulfil," warned Cecil kindly, he had the tone of a gentle father admonishing an overambitious son, "Here comes Laurence, master of Emanuel College on the river Camb."

Cecil had noticed the arrival of a lean figure, dressed in simple black Puritan church garb, standing at the doorway.

The man entered fully into the room, bowing slightly to all those gathered and received a reciprocal gesture from them all. He was very big.

"I have been appointed one of the four divines for managing the cause of the Puritans at this conference," Laurence complained loudly, "yet, if I could be sent home, it would please me."

"Go, Puritan pestilence!" Bancroft demanded dramatically before he chortled.

"And leave you to translate the bible; I would not countenance such buffoonery!" exclaimed Laurence, seeming to forget his previous despondency. There was little theological love lost between the Edwardian church and the Puritans but Laurence was determined to stand his ground and assert that he had a contribution to make. "I have much to offer the book and much to do in order to check your ideas that if left free rein would see more *popish-ness* than any man could bear."

"Is Thomas with you?" asked Cecil casually, he always wanted to know where his friends and where his enemies were to be found.

"Thomas Sparke? Have you seen what he is wearing?" asked Rainolds in mock horror.

"He lights up the room with his garb, it must have been a shooting star that I saw; both are blinding to the eyes and upsetting to the spirits," Bancroft added.

"Sparke, more like sparkle with his bright garb, we know him as troublemaker, he and Travers spoilt the conference at Lambeth in '84, protesting against lay baptism, it seems he objects to midwives!" Rainolds complained.

"That was not all, he bleated about the reading of apocryphal scriptures in churches!" Bancroft continued. "He opposed any apocryphal liturgy."

"Only Apocryphal?" Cecil wondered.

In his view, Sparke and his ilk tended to complain about everything, baptisms, blessings and blasphemy, bibles, testaments and all other tracts or texts.

"In this case, only the hidden gospels came under his attack," Bancroft explained, "fortunately his ire does not stretch to the canonical gospels; I think he favours the Old Testament. In truth he likes its simplicity of message and purpose. "

"I see, it is an 'Old Testament' God that we can all fear."

"But, presently, he only disputes any gospels that were not written by Matthew, Mark Luke and John."

"That does not seem unreasonable," Cecil decided.

Cecil was hoping the group might move on to what they had in common rather than their differences.

"They are against private communions, too!" added Bancroft, stirring further division, he really was not helping Cecil to find some common ground.

He awaited a shocked response from those gathered but none came, it seemed private communion was not a topic to be disputed, ill people had to receive a private communion, no one seriously thought the Puritans would ban that.

There was much to do in agreeing between themselves what was needed in the service and in the bible and what was popery and what was superstitious ritual that could be left out.

"Who summoned Sparke hence?" asked Rainolds.

"He was summoned by the King; he has appeared as a token member of the non-conformist church; he has made an impression being unconventionally dressed, but he has said little. The King, however, has been most gracious towards him, he shows him great understanding and respect," explained Laurence calmly, trying to hide his anger at his fellow Puritan being so roundly disabused. "We cannot judge a book by its cover nor can we judge Sparke by his bright garb."

"What of John Knewstubs?" Cecil asked, feeling that the situation should be diffused.

"Since the year eighty-two and the incident at Cockfield, he has stirred up the East Anglian Puritans, for over twenty years, they have argued about prayer books, clerical dress and other customs," Laurence explained.

He did not have much patience for these people who caused trouble, they damaged the image of the religion but that was not to say that he did not agree with what they wanted, it was just the way they went about it.

"What would you expect of a follower of Thomas Cartwright; really we have enough problems elsewhere, stirring up the good people of Cambridge, Norfolk and Suffolk is not helpful," Bancroft argued.

"What has he said to offend?" asked Laurence.

"He has appeared as one of the four ministers deputed to oppose conformity. He has taken especial exception to the use of the sign of the cross in baptism and also to the wearing of the surplice," complained Bancroft.

"With what Sparkes is wearing, I think a surplice, would be infinitely preferable," Cecil noted dryly.

"I agree!" cried Bancroft. "If he is to represent nonconformity in the country dressed like that, give me conformity any day!"

They all guffawed. The tension was taken out of the situation, it was important that those gathered let off steam and said their piece before the real work started.

These men had the serious job of trying to balance and match all the demands and needs of both the Church and State.

"What of the Catholics?" asked Laurence, he was forever asking questions, so that he had a clear understanding of all matters to be discussed and so that he knew the key issues; he was highly intelligent and he argued well, clearly and succinctly.

"They are broken, reduced to priests in priest holes!" Bancroft announced happily.

The Catholics were a common enemy; they had been against the reformation let alone further reform. No Catholics had been invited to the conference.

"I have heard the new rhyme, do you know it?" asked Laurence.

"Of course!" they all chorused.

"Shall we?" asked Cecil devilishly.

There was much coughing and clearing of throats, all of them had sung in choirs when they were younger, they knew how it was done but their voices were no longer young. However, it did not stop them from reciting the rhyme about Catholics hiding Jesuits in priest holes in unison:

"Goosie, goosie, gander where shall I wander, Upstairs, downstairs and in my lady's chamber There I met an old man who wouldn't say his prayers, I took him by the left leg and threw him down the stairs."

There followed much guffawing and backslapping at their performance. If they could sing in unison, perhaps, they could solve all their problems in chorus.

Chapter 7- iii – Hampton Court – Markham and Bancroft

Markham found Bancroft sitting at a table on a high-back chair, an extra, red velvet, cushion had been put on the seat to make it more comfortable over the long periods of time he was due to sit on it. Markham chose a chair form the corner of the room and moved it deftly to the table. He placed it not opposite the Bishop but beside him so they sat next to each other. The Bishop would therefore be forced to turn his chair around to face his guest, which is what he wanted. They had not spoken except to acknowledge each other. Bancroft was preoccupied with the prayer book and bible and besides he seemed to be with Cecil in the need for destroying the Catholic hierarchy.

However, Cecil had sent Markham to double check he was complicit and that they could rely on his loyalty. Bancroft finished working on his paragraph while Markham waited; he was early for their interview. With an accentuated flourish, Bancroft placed his quill on a large piece of blotting paper next to his folio and turned his chair to face Markham as he had intended; it was a trick taught to him by Cecil to put people ill at ease. The orientation of the chair was not quite right, not quite positioned for work and not quite angled enough for social discourse.

"You come most readily on the hour," Bancroft said by way of a greeting.

"My Lord Bishop is a busy man and I know he is engaged in the King's business so, therefore, I wish to take up as little time as I possibly can, this interview will be short."

"I know only that you work for Cecil and that I was to expect you, might I have a name."

"John Johnson," replied Markham, "at your command and ready to do Your Lordship any service. I am, indeed, sent on Cecil's orders and with his instructions."

It sounded to Bancroft as if all of what this stranger said had a hollow ring to it.

"Then, I know you have the command of the King's estate and that business must be more pressing if it is to interrupt the making of Canon Law."

"Shall I come quickly to the rub?"

"It will save both me and you time and you are aware, are you not that tide and time wait for no man'?"

"Kindly tell me, Lord Bishop, what you know of the Puritans and their petty plotting," demanded Markham conspiratorially.

Markham did not need to give much encouragement for the old bishop to share his extensive knowledge. Bancroft imagined that if he did not talk he would be given an incentive to do so and that would be a stiletto blade held at the nape of the neck, the point resting on the carotid artery. Markham had such a blade strapped to his belt. He had given his cape and sword to the servant at the door, Bancroft only knew that Cecil had sent this man as an emissary; he had been told to expect him but he could not help feeling that he dangerous. Only the most trusted of Cecil's men or the King's most favoured were allowed to go armed at Hampton Court Palace.

"Their first conspiracy was hatched by the Roman Catholic and Puritan nobles, hoping to bring religious toleration for all religions. Anthony Copley was one of the Catholics involved," explained Bancroft wearily.

"We know of him. He had been marked as a *'bravo'* and when he returned from the France and the Lowlands to England, without permission, he was put in the Tower," confirmed Markham.

"A *'bravo'*?" asked Bancroft, never one to bother with colloquialisms.

"A *'bravo'* is someone who is considered under suspicion by the state," replied Markham. "He was an exile returning illegally, he was someone to watch."

"I, now, remember who you are. I recognise the hand of your captain, Cecil; you must be the Sir Griffin Markham, plotter supreme, pardoned and imprisoned," declared Bancroft feeling satisfaction at finally fitting the last piece into the puzzle. "John Johnson is your master's pseudonym! He uses it too readily, you must be the reformed Markham."

"I have only been reformed in my frame, a little bit larger than I used to be. When you knew me I was different; I was thin and athletic in my youth, but my heart is pure and beats for England above all else. My reformation is physical and spiritual, I have allowed practical matters to rule my thoughts; my heart beats, my head thinks and that is what keeps me alive," Markham admitted.

"Shouldn't you be in the '*Tower*'?" whispered Bancroft uneasily, scanning the room for further battalions of spies. He feared being found guilty by association even though Cecil had sanctioned the meeting. "Shouldn't you still be there for your sins? Your contrition is surely not complete,"

Bancroft could not resist a jab at Markham's Catholic past, yet, Markham knew better than to rise to such a bait, especially, knowing that their new honesty allowed them to discuss matters more openly. Markham had worked with Cecil for long enough to know how to handle Bancroft.

"Cecil uses me when he sees fit, I am after all a man who has disappeared. In return, I have a more than comfortable room, far more comfortable than the usual London dungeon and, as you can see, I have a good diet of Beefeater's food; a cape and a hat and I can pass through London freely," answered Markham good-naturedly.

It was inevitable that Bancroft would recognise him sooner or later; he knew that.

"Cecil is far too clever, who has ever heard of a bodyguard who all men think is in the Tower.

"He is the wisest of men; he used me during my exile when Queen Elizabeth wore the crown. I spied abroad when I was an outcast, then I was brought back to spy on people in high office like Your Lordship."

"And what an excellent spy you must make; you wear the cloak and the dagger, you are a loyal one, too, one false move and you'll be sent to those rooms near the Watergate. Cecil has your loyalty."

"Indeed, Cecil took away my liberty when I floundered too often, but he granted me my freedom and, as you say, he can remove it at his will."

"You are his tame dog," he teased.

"I may be tame, now, but I am not lame so watch your tongue, Cecil keeps me by his side because of my fighting skills," he warned.

He smiled mischievously to show he was only mildly serious

"Murder would send you back to the Tower!" he laughed, wagging his finger. Bancroft could not be so easily intimidated, now that he knew the situation.

"I have become accustomed to fresh air and I do not miss the White Tower or the ravens there or the view of the Watergate. I am loyal to the State and the Crown without such incentives; that I can assure you," he continued more seriously.

"We may not be united in religion but we are united in that, what can I do for you and the Crown?"

"My friend Cecil and I need some help to destroy the threat of Catholic invasion."

"And what can a poor Lord Bishop do in order to help you achieve your aim; as you know, I wield little power, I am charged with the management of ecclesiastical affairs."

"Francis Bacon says knowledge is power and you know those influential people who we need to topple."

"How will that be achieved, Spain and France are greater powers than ours?"

"We have managed using our guile."

"So how will we remove the threat of invasion by a Catholic usurper?"

"Why, by destroying the Catholic nobles, once and for all. Spain or France will need support for an invasion. Without that, they will be like the sailors and soldiers of the Armada, alone at sea, floundering as an invasion force, heading for Galway and thence home to Coruna," suggested Markham cleverly, appealing to Bancroft's recollection of the last serious invasion threat.

"The 'Cod Line'?"

"Indeed."

"I have heard the Irish had a great trade in salted fish for Spain and olives and all manner of cured meats were returned to Ireland in exchange," replied Bancroft, suddenly remembering a rumour he had heard.

"Indeed, a great number of ships and a great deal of men were helped by the Irish navigators and merchant ships," Markham agreed, he had soldiered for many years in Ireland.

"I was told the Irish ate them all! Rumours reached London and spread, saying the ships were all wrecked and the Irish ate the soldiers and sailors became the dispappeared. I must admit, it sounded more like a danger that Thomas More would dream up in Utopia!"

"The image of the Irish savages must be maintained, we cannot have these savages eating olives and *jamon*, no doubt the rumour was started by someone working to discredit the Irish further! It could have been an English trader who wanted to take over the trade of an Irishman. Discredit him and his ilk and take over."

"Perhaps."

"Perhaps, Walsingham himself, hoping to justify a further invasion of Ireland, I was not privy to such matters in those long gone days."

"I had no idea they had room to take the Armada sailors. Is that really how they disappeared?" Bancroft asked incredulously.

"According to Walsingham's reports," replied Markham.

"He was a thorough individual," agreed Bancroft.

"As is his successor," noted Markham quickly, "he, too, has eyes everywhere."

"You are right, Walsingham was clever and it is true, Cecil is cleverer still, Lord Burghley made sure of that," added Bancroft.

"Cecil is more Machiavellian than the 'Prince'; he has certainly made even King-making an art form," Markham agreed admiringly.

"I would rather be with him than against him."

"My thoughts precisely."

"I will give you all the information you need before you take your leave."

"We are agreed, then." Markham breathed, feeling relieved.

Bancroft repositioned his chair, picked up the quill and dipped it in the ink, taking a fresh piece of parchment paper. He started to write. This was not Canon Law but a report for Markham to take to his master, Robert Cecil.

Chapter 7 – iv – Hampton Court – The King and Markham

James disliked crowds, but he remembered his subjects' welcome and often dwelt on the celebration of his coronation, living off the memory of its glory. His subjects had adored him then, before he began to let them down. Many saw James as the new hope for England after Elizabeth's long reign.

"I dislike the throng but I shall never forget how people ran to meet me on my progress from my Scottish home to take the crown of England, they cheered me and greeted me in droves," James bragged as he paraded around the long room in the palace of Whitehall.

"Your Majesty, I have read your books on witchcraft and tobacco," a courtier, Phillip Herbert mentioned as the King passed, his remark was ignored.

James felt that everyone should have read his books. Herbert had told the King to impress him; the Court knew Phillip more for hawking and hunting than for reading and writing. At twenty, he was one of the youngest gentlemen in the Privy Chamber and he was a Knight of the Bath.

"Here comes Robert Carey, he rode to Edinburgh from London in two days," announced Ramsay jovially.

"I did, indeed, from London to Holyrood House," Carey readily admitted.

"I heard you had a fall on the way and the horse hit your head with its heels," added Herbert, keen to show he was privy to every detail of court stories.

He was a mere youth but being noticed for his hunting skills had won him the King's favour, he hoped he would continue to be noticed at court and his rise would be rapid. As long as the King appreciated his good looks and good humour, his place was safe.

"Indeed, but I had an important journey to make so it did not stop me; I arrived so late that the King was abed; I kneeled by him and saluted him by his title of King of England and Scotland," Carey added.

"It took me three weeks to make the journey to London with Sir Robert such were the crowds who wanted to see us," James responded before continuing his progress around the room.

Wine and food was dispensed to him as he paraded around, the courtiers indulged freely in the food and drink that was provided by a series of servants in a constant stream. Robert Cecil was in the corner, talking to the Venetian Ambassador, knowing that their conversation would be repeated to the Pope. It would take time though; Cecil was a patient man, he had learnt to be. Once the letters reached Venice, the reports would be read and transcribed before being taken by messenger to Rome. The Pope paid for this information, the Venetian State and Papal States were in conflict, trying to carve up and take control of the countryside around them.

The Pope needed to have intelligence about England, France and Spain in order to direct the priests in those countries; he was a politician and a priest. He was willing to buy the information off the Venetians as much as the Venetians were willing to sell any information, just like any other commodity that they traded. Cecil was a master at spreading rumours that reached the European courts and informed their monarchs, much of which he had manufactured specifically for their consumption.

"The King's excessive kindness has ended in this; Catholic priests go openly about the country saying Mass. This gives great offence to others," Cecil whispered conspiratorially.

They both kept a weather eye on the King as he progressed around the room, eating noisily and messily, slurping his wine and talking with his mouth full. He cared not a jot, he knew he would spray his words rather than say them, if there were bits of food in his spittle; it bothered him not. He seemed oblivious to the consternation he caused.

"I'm sure it does," said the ambassador not really believing this, who would be offended he wondered, the peasants shunned the priests, and the nobles housed them, 'who actually ever saw them?' he wondered.

Who but the strictest Puritan could take offence at a subtle celebration of faith that went on behind closed doors? The Catholics wanted to avoid the 'Recusant Fines', the Jesuits disguised themselves; there was nothing open about their behaviour. In Stuart England, Catholicism was an underground religion just as much as some of the more bizarre non-conformist religions were forced to be. The Stuart State demanded conformity. Many ships in London housed different preachers preaching their brand of Protestantism.

"We cannot hope for good government while we have a large number of people who obey foreign rulers as the Catholics do," Cecil warned.

"Again, I agree," the ambassador said; he was a spy after all; he could not make it clear that he did not agree, no matter how much he wanted to.

Throughout the Tudor period, and even before that dynasty had brought stability to England, English Catholics had been loyal to the crown. An awful lot of unrest had been blamed on them. In actual fact, the ambassador wondered how many Catholics had priests and how many ever defied the government with Cecil's tight rein on the country and his eyes and ears everywhere.

"The priests preach that Catholics must even kill the King to help their religion," Cecil complained, feigning shock. He knew that it was not the Catholics who challenged the 'Divine Right of Kings' but his own bishops.

"Is that so? How terrible," sighed the ambassador, trying to sound sympathetic.

In reality, he wanted to shout: 'what nonsense' He was used to Cecil's machinations; he would report the conversation and add his opinion on the words spoken as he usually did.

Cecil wanted everyone to know that he would be turning his attention to the Catholics in order to appease the Puritans and to deflect them from their demands for the abolition of the bishops and their lucrative bishoprics. The ambassador was aware that James needed to pack the House of Lords with bishops, the Lords Spiritual to dilute the influence of his Lords Temporal. They watched as James left the room, both wondered where he was going and with whom he was going to talk. In fact, he was going to relieve himself and it was easier to urinate in the garden than to locate the Keeper of the King's Stool and have him accompany the King to the next floor and walk along the corridor to the King's chamber.

"I must ensure there are more piss-pots in Whitehall and Hampton next time I have a party," James thought to himself, the wine had made him feel happy.

He was surrounded by those who brought him to power, the Puritans had gone to bed and would leave the next day or had already left returning to their synods or back to their small congregations; it was just wonderful, James mused, to gaze up at the huge house, the windows lantern lit casting their light onto the lawn in the night. The crowd outside stood a few yards away from the bay windows, opposite a turret, looking up at the polygonal shafts of the chimney on either side of the lantern tower, a flag, decorated with the lion and the unicorn fluttered from the ogee turret roof but few could see the monarchy's imagery.

The stone pressings of the doorway were lit by moonlight, white like a swan's neck against the russet brick, an amazingly clear, ink blue sky above was filled with stars. It reminded Markham of an ermine collar flecked resplendently. James walked through the doorway of the cloister catching Markham standing outside, slightly removed from the group, smoking a clay pipe. Some of the crowd were smoking but desisted as soon as the King was seen; only Markham continued. Although Markham was aware of the King's hatred of smoking, he could not hide the pipe in time so he decided to smoke on.

The King had approached from behind. Before he could apologies, James launched into one of his customary tirades.

"Have you not reason to be ashamed, and to forbear this filthy novelty, so basely grounded, so foolishly received and so grossly mistaken in the right use thereof?" asked the King indignantly.

"Apologies Your Majesty, I have been told by a well-respected herbalist that the smoke clears hot humours," explained Markham.

"Do you realise that in your abuse of tobacco you are sinning against God?" James asked, probing further.

"I had no idea, Your Majesty," gasped Markham, incredulously.

"Not only that but you are harming yourself in person and all your goods reek of horrible smoke like the bottomless pit of hell."

"I beg forgiveness, Your Majesty."

Unimpressed by the apology James continued.

"You smokers are an abomination, making yourselves to be wondered at by all foreign civil nations, and by all strangers that come among you; you are scorned and condemned for your filthy ways," complained James in disgust, warming to his favourite theme.

He was always keen to point out his knowledge; and to decry the evils of smoking.

"I had not thought about it in such a way," whispered Markham, growing even more embarrassed.

Markham had suspected the King objected to smoking but had not realised with what passion he despised the practice. He had not read any of the King's tracts being hidden away from society.

"Well perhaps you should, it is a custom loathsome to the eye, hateful to the nose, harmful to the brain, dangerous to the lungs and that black stinking fume that follows you around upsets me," continued the King, waving his arms; his eyes sparkled with genuine anger.

"I apologise, Your Majesty," Markham spluttered nervously.

"Put it out, and then hold my glass, will you?" commanded the King, sounding as if here were drunk and tripping over his tongue, which perhaps he was, "I need to go for a piss and I want to see if I can get a good shot at the drain."

"Of course, Your Majesty, with pleasure." Markham heard the King shuffle over the lawn towards the drain pipe, a rustling of garments and a very loud fart, were followed by a childish chortle and a rush of water down the drain.

Markham decided to finish his smoke later, moving away, just as he heard a cascade of water, royal urine, hitting the clay surround of the drain. Not bad from that distance, he mused, as he wandered off in search of any fellow smokers and failing that a good long drink. He left the King's glass on the window ledge.

In the distance, he heard a troop of guards reciting the old rhyme about Cardinal Wolsey, the man who built Hampton Court, as they marched about the precincts impressing the guests with their presence. The rhyme told of the Cardinal's failure to get Henry his divorce and led to his downfall, the bone was the divorce, the doggie was the Henry VIII but the rhyme was so old it caused no offence to the incumbent king:

"Old Mother Hubbard,

Went to the cupboard,

To get her poor doggie a bone,

When she got there,

The cupboard was bare,

So the poor little doggie had none".

Chapter 7 – v – Hampton Court - The Main Plot explained.

The Story of the Bye Plot of 1603

Three men, Markham, Owen and Ramsay sat by the fire, their bellies full, they had dined on roasted hog, parsnip and turnips, which Ramsay ate with relish, calling them '*neeps*', their glasses were filled with sweet wine from southern France, the Gironde and its surroundings, perhaps.

It was difficult to discern their expressions given the poor light, they had let the candles burn down, dismissing servants who tried to replace them and the light from the fire cast shadows that obliterated rather than defined the men's countenances.

"We must work together," Markham warned, "we cannot have the division of the Church, our venture is to unite all the people and here we are, English, Scottish and Welsh, showing the men of God that unity is possible."

"Indeed," agreed Owen looking into the fire, letting the warmth lull him into sleep, too soon, it would be time for him to brave the cold corridors and find his cold bed.

"We all have the King's interest at heart," Ramsay added. As chief bodyguard and keeper of the keys, he was senior to them all.

"We have drunk his health many times tonight but there are dangers all around," Markham warned menacingly.

"Plots?" cried Ramsay, sitting up in his chair; he felt the handle of his sgian-dubh secreted in the upper sleeve of his jacket.

The knife blade was sheathed but within seconds, the small knife would be in his hand.

"Yes, you are aware of the '*Bye Plot*'?" Markham asked.

"Aye," Ramsay replied, the wine had made him more Scottish, "I know of it, tell me more details. I never did hear the full story."

"Markham knows more than me," Owen suggested mischievously.

"Well go ahead, then, if Owen doesn't mind hearing it again," Ramsay replied encouragingly his accent thickened and his expressions were more highland than Sassenach.

"Not at all," Owen laughed.

"The plot was known also as Watson's Plot, the Catholic Plot, the Surprising Treason or Treason of the Priests, I believe," said Markham casually on being asked to elucidate. "Shortly afterwards, though, not everyone knows, King James ordered by edict all Roman Catholic clergy, 'Jesuits', 'Seminarians and other 'Priests' to leave his kingdom."

"This edict had been drafted in July 1603 on the discovery of the '*Main* and *Bye Plot*' but has not come into force as yet!" Owen added. "Rumour has it, the edict will be passed into law after this conference; and then all the popish priests will be banished."

"Poor Anthony Copley was condemned to death, he languishes in the Tower," explained Markham before taking a large swig of wine.

The mention of that place made him wonder why he had been given the freedom to roam and whether Cecil might one day swap Copley for him.

Markham had been drinking copious amounts of wine, smoking more tobacco than was fashionable and as a result, he was extremely happy, enjoying his freedom to the full.

"Tell me more, a man condemned pardoned, I had not heard of this, I was in Scotland for a wee while."

Ramsay helped himself to some more '*sack*', pouring from a Venetian glass water jug, into his Venetian glass and at the same time, he took the glass from Markham and Owen and filled them.

"As you know when good Queen Bess died in March," Markham continued stopping himself just in time before he made the sign of the cross and prayed silently, saying 'may the souls of the faithful departed rest in peace', which would have been an embarrassing confession of his faith.
He continued nonetheless.

"The Catholics wanted the 'Recusant Fines' removed and the constraints on their worship relaxed," Owen added.

"Of course," Ramsay said for the sake of being heard. It came out as *'orf curse'*.

"A divisive quarrel and pamphlet war among English Catholics, the Archpriest Controversy, meant a scion in the plotters."

"William Watson took the 'appellant' side in the Archpriest Controversy, hostile to George Blackwell who had been appointed by the Holy See. Watson was under the protection of Bancroft, Bishop of London," Owen elucidated further.

"In September 1601, Watson was resident at Fulham Palace but by 1602 he was confined in *The Clink*. He did manage to keep in close touch with Bancroft," Markham said. "The plot was initially exposed by the archpriest Blackwell and two Jesuits, John Gerard and Henry Garnet who were on the other side of the dispute."

"Fine men by all accounts," added Owen.

"Indeed," Markham agreed.

"Continue," demanded Ramsay.

"These three passed on information that they had relating to the conspiracy. So much for Catholic conspirators, these papists were protecting the Crown. They had other reasons besides the on-going controversy: they feared retribution against Catholics if the plan failed; and entertained suspicions regarding the political motivations of the secular priests."

Owen took up the narrative.

"Those involved were not in fact exclusively Catholic priests: Thomas Grey, 15th Baron Grey de Wilton was a Puritan layman who became drawn in, though the plot never went further than farfetched discussion. Another lay conspirator was Sir Griffin Markham," he said waiting for Ramsay to gasp.

Ramsay looked blank, and then, the importance of what was being said to him suddenly dawned on him. Markham had been instrumental in a plot against the King.

"I was in fact working for Cecil, to undermine the plot," Markham said. "Watson wished to have no more fines for recusants and the removal of certain ministers of the King."

"As you know," Owen added, "King James moved south at a leisurely pace, having reached Theobald's House in Hertfordshire by May 3rd. The scheme depended on Markham's view in May that there was a 'Scottish precedent' for seizing the person of the King for political advantage."

"It was in late May when I tried to recruit the Jesuit John Gerard, Cecil wanted all the Catholics to implicate themselves. Gerard must have been told that I worked for Cecil because he refused to join the plot. In haste, he wrote to Henry Garnet and George Blackwell asking them to put a spoke in the wheels of the plot."

Owen again took over for Markham: "The date set by Watson for the plot to be carried out was June 24th. This was St. John Baptist's Day and a collar day; the courtiers would be at court and regaled in ceremonial clothes."

"I remember now," Ramsay interrupted, "I have heard of this tale, as the date approached, Gerard had contacted a Scottish courtier asking that he make the King aware, meanwhile Blackwell revealed something of the plot to the government through an intermediary, the recusant John Gage, who had married Margaret, the daughter of Sir Thomas Copley."

"Exactly," agreed Markham. "When Gage wrote to him on June 28th, Cecil was already aware of the plotting."

"Cecil knows everything," Ramsay added.

"The Catholic former exile, and conspirator, Anthony Copley, had also written to Blackwell about the Bye Plot," continued Markham, "he was Sir Thomas Copley's son and therefore Gage's brother-in-law. Blackwell had written to Gage and Cecil assumed there was something more behind these exchanges, so, he asked Gage to produce Blackwell before the Council."

"It has been suggested that Copley consciously played the double agent, only Cecil would know the answer to that and he would not tell us!" Owen added.

"In the event, Lord Grey withdrew from the plot ahead of the day, and the plotters scattered," elucidated Markham. "Sir George Brooke wanted to replace members of the Privy Council. Henry Brooke, 11th Baron Cobham was his brother and a conspirator in the more serious *'Main Plot'*. Sir George was arraigned, on 15th July, and in his eagerness to clear himself, made various confessions. Speedily, on 16th July, a proclamation was issued for Watson's arrest."

"Bancroft, at around this time, had good reason to distance himself from Watson, not least the fact that he could be hung for treason and so Bancroft claimed he had not seen him since before the Queen died," Owen continued.

There was a pregnant silence, Court talk was to be light and entertaining, and these thoughts were too dark, too real. Bancroft had narrowly missed being implicated in the plot, no wonder he favoured Cecil. Ramsay was reeling, first Markham, now Bancroft, both associated with plots against the Crown and both of them staying with the King at Hampton Court.

"Bancroft managed to escape unscathed," Markham announced to break the silence.

"King James's coronation went ahead on July 25th, his name day, as planned but his entry into London was delayed because of an outbreak of the plague in London, similar to the one which keeps us here at Hampton Court," interrupted Ramsay again.

"Watson was arrested around the fifth of August, last year, in a field by the River Wye," Markham confessed.

"In Kent?" asked Ramsay; he had been to an abbey nearby with King James.

"No, Hay-on-Wye, on the border of England and Wales, by Welshmen, of course," Owen replied, beating Markham, wanting to mention the involvement of his countrymen in the arrest. "He made a confession on the tenth."

"William Clark another priest who had been an active organiser, was arrested in Worcester on the thirteenth of August," Markham added. "Further details of the Bye Plot were revealed by the Catholic priest Father Francis Barnaby who was in prison. He was another appellant contact of Bancroft."

"He communicated for him with Christopher Bagshaw and had worked with the plotter William Clark against English Jesuits. The Court had moved to Wilton House in Wiltshire where it was decided that trials could be held at the bishop's palace. The trials took place between fifteenth and eighteenth November," Owen continued barely drawing breath, his mouth was quite dry and he craved a drink, any drink to slake his thirst: "On the fifteenth the two Catholic priests involved, as well as Sir George Brooke and Sir Griffin Markham, and others, were tried. On the seventeenth, Sir Walter Raleigh was tried, and the prosecution managed to make a case that he had been involved in the Bye Plot. Lord Grey as a baron was tried and found guilty by thirty-one peers, on the eighteenth November with Lord Cobham who was implicated in the Main Plot."

"Dudley Carleton who witnessed the proceedings, took it to be a well-scripted drama of the King's mercy, staged for the benefit of Raleigh, who had been caught up in the Bye Plot," revealed Markham conspiratorially, he enjoyed passing on the gossip surrounding an event. "Guilty verdicts on the conspirators were reached; the only acquittal on charges of high treason was for Sir Edward Parham."

"And he was not involved?" Ramsay asked.

"Not as far as we know, I think we can trust him," said Owen.

"Sir Edward Coke had a flimsy case for Raleigh's involvement in the Bye Plot but Raleigh's role in the Main Plot left him with much to explain," said Markham. "The two priests, Watson and Clark, were executed for their parts in the scheme, on the twenty-ninth November."

"George Brooke was executed on the fifth December and on the tenth Lord Grey and our esteemed Lord, Sir Griffin Markham were taken to the scaffold, pardoned, and spent the rest of their lives in the Tower," said Owen.

"As you can see," said Markham rashly.

"You were working for Cecil?" Ramsay asked incredulously, taking a sip of *sack*.

"Of course, ever since the Essex Rebellion, he recruited me, then," revealed Markham. He was revelling in the deliciousness of this announcement that he was a secret servant of the State.

"I see," whispered Ramsay, still shocked.

"I assume Lord Grey was also working for the Commonwealth, in some way," Markham revealed, "otherwise Cecil would not bother to feed him in the Tower; he could execute him whenever he liked!"

"And you Owen?" asked Ramsay, taking a gulp of *sack*. He seemed to be surrounded by spions and he suddenly felt less special and less favoured at court.

"I have always been in Cecil's service and his father, Lord Burghley before him, since I was a cook's apprentice here. I was chosen to serve at this place and my promotion came swiftly, therefore I love Hampton Court but love Robert Cecil more warmly," Owen replied.

The fortified wine and his good mood led to him to quite forget that he had kept his master waiting when he had first arrived at Hampton.

"How may I help you?" Ramsay asked, knowing he would be helping himself more, no matter what poisons or tortures these men could administer or make him endure. He drained his glass in one draught.

Chapter 8- i - The Vole – October 1604

That autumn in London provided chill winds and clear skies. The sky above the river was a pale blue, a smattering of wispy clouds hung there looking like boats in an ocean, the Thames was as smooth and shiny like melted lead except where the currents and eddies swirled near the bridge, the leaden water crumpled like discarded cloaks draped around tree trunks, as the water wildly played around the bottom of the buttresses that held up the bridge. The sun was high in the sky; the light was bright; the time of day was noon; the man's stride was purposeful.

Guido Forcanessi was looking for work on the busy dockside. It was a wonderful autumn day, and despite the north wind, he was in good spirits. He was tall for an Italian and muscular, a fit man as befitted a docker in London, or a fighter, ready for action, as mercenaries should be. He was bold enough to brave the chill wind that swept across his face on every corner.

He wore a fashionable hat that covered his brown hair that the sun had flecked with a marmalade tinge. This gingery colour was more pronounced in the marvellous moustache, and well-trimmed beard that he wore. He blended in with the other itinerant gentlemen on the dock; impoverished individuals whose only wealth was the clothing that they stood in.

Once busy with waging wars, the peace meant no wages for making war, they had been the traders of choice in conflict, traders in weapons and fighting skills. Basically, they were mercenaries or merchants, they did not fight for causes but coins; they might have traded in supplies of food or clothing to the multitude of soldiers. All of them had made a lot of money during the war years, but years of peace and lack of work had brought penury to many. Peace had certain dividends but they had no shares in that company.

Guido had left the lowlands to seek his fortune in London.

Where war was waged, there had always been work for a strong man, but in London things had not gone as he had hoped. When he had originally arrived in Antwerp from Italy, it was easy to find work; you simply went to the church and asked. Even if times were tough, a stroll around the Cathedral grounds would be enough for most able people to find work.

In London, the church was not the same. You had to know the pastor well for him to recommend you for work, no one trusted strangers in London, especially foreign ones. There was too much suspicion and with so many returned from the war looking for work there was no need to trust them. There were almost one hundred ocean craft in the safe harbours north and south of the riverbank.

London was teaming with people and the docks provided work for so many but Guido had only had a few days piecemeal work since his arrival from the Low Countries, his money was running out. It seemed as if there was one large ship after another over the whole city's length, from St. Catherine's suburb in the east to the Bridge. This was where those looking for work started their search. The masts towered over the streets like church spires; the docks were full of boats riding high on the flood tide. Merchants from all over the world came to the city: the moneychangers and bankers on the north bank, in the city, were joined by guilds of Lightermen and others, from apothecaries to wheelwrights.

Whereas on the other side of the Thames there were wool merchants, sellers of all manner of expensive luxuries and purveyors of wholesale goods plus the diversions of drinking dens, doll-tear-sheets and gambling. Apart from bear baiting, cockfighting, whoring and watching plays, there was work and trade to be had as well as play; warehouses and foreign goods dominated the south bank.

More importantly, ships from all over the known world docked at London, foreign ships from Spain, the United Provinces, France, the Holy Roman Empire, Ireland, Italy, and Scotland and beyond. You could step aboard most ships from Catholic countries and hear mass being said.

It was not safe and it was not wise but it showed how devout you were.

Some Londoners attended mass under the pretext of inspecting a shipment; it proved their devotion if not their common sense. Cecil's men were looking out for such people. They were tolerated for the moment but they were also 'marked men' and it was not healthy to be at Cecil's call, at any moment they could be taken in by his men for not signing the parish book.

On that day, there were Dutch, French vessels, and those from the Holy Roman Empire, tied to the wooden docks. Guido had been past so many, waiting for his opportunity and he suddenly found himself wandering past two boats tied up alongside a wooden dock, a Dutch *dogger,* and an English merchantman. Seagulls circled the Dutch fishing boat, hoping to swoop down and steal a fish. Guido had never seen such crowds milling around the water's edge and beyond. There must have been thousands, he reckoned. The boat that he was passing had just come in on the rising tide and docked at the quayside, if you could call it that, it was more of a wooden companionway. The surroundings were swamped with people.

Figures swarmed on the deck out of the holds, down the gangplanks and over terra firma, into the side streets and main thoroughfares. The crew delivered items to various warehouses and bills of lading and bills of exchange were swapped for bags of coins and promissory notes. The quartermaster would be too busy finding a home for the ship's cargo and buying new stores for the next voyage; he would not get a job there.

However, he did notice a maiden who was selling apples, so all his effort was not wasted in his perambulation along the hard. Her beauty was obvious despite her simple clothes, a brown wool skirt and a black bodice and a brown wool shawl, a vision in black and tan. She sold the fruit from a basket hanging from her shawl. It was a neat trick to free her hands; the ends of her shawl were tied around the handles of the basket, so she looked like she was wearing a yoke.

Her hair was black and her eyes brown; she was from a foreign land; most of the Anglo-Saxons in the city were blonde or brown haired; their faces were pale, not dark like hers. Guido wondered how her face looked so brown in this poor weather. Her skin needed only to enter the sunlight to become the colour of tanned leather, he supposed.

Those Latin looks and that look of confidence made Guido stare at her in disbelief, she reminded him of the pretty girls from Italy. She had to be from the Mediterranean, he was sure. Maybe, he reasoned further, she would know where to go to find work; Guido was forever feeling that fortune's fickle wheel would turn in his favour.

His luck had run out since he had quit the lowlands and decided to find his fortune in London, it was much harder, and work had to be found on the streets. Perhaps, he thought, it was time for the '*optim*a' to takes its place. Either way, the rent had to be paid and food needed to be bought.

Still, he reasoned, charm had got him thus far, even if the pretty girl with the lovely apples could not find him a job, it would be nice to flirt with her for a while before he continued his search. He pushed through the people to get to her. By the time he reached her, she had just repositioned herself near a quiet corner and was doing a brisk trade.

"*Ola chica!*" he cried and was rewarded when she looked up but sadly she stared at him as if he were mad and then turned away to serve someone else.

He was sure she was Mediterranean, after all, he was Italian, what else could you be, with a name like Guido? In Antwerp, he had met Italian mercenaries fighting against the Spanish in the Netherlands; they had offered him work and he had lived alongside these Italians, although, he did not actually fight; he had a shared faith, and had shared their hardship. He had been a porter then, a good strong pair of hands; then he became a sapper, good with a spade; he had been a quartermaster, too, good with foraging for food.

His work was building fortifications and destroying dykes. He had seen their easy ways with women, the flattery, and word play, he had seen their sweethearts and wives when they had followed the camp, and he knew how even in cold climes the glow of the skin was unmistakable.

"*Ciao bella,*" he tried again; he knew all the greetings, in all the European languages, that would win the attention of English, Dutch, Saxon or Latin speakers.

She smiled and replied, "Ciao."

A burly Cornishman stepped in his path, looming over them both like the masts of the boats, "Hello Rosie Rosa, I'll help myself to two of your firm apples, let me give them a squeeze before I nibble them."

"Harry, you old devil, I sell apples, you cannot try before you buy; I'm not a punk!"

"I can have a punk and pay her handsomely; I'd like to think you'd do it for free."

"Have hold of my apples for free?"

The two bantered on.

"Why not?" asked Harry.

"You'll pay like any other," Rosa replied, smiling sheepishly.

"I'd pay to have hold of your apples."

"You'll need a bigger purse than that to impress me."

"A rose by any other name would smell as sweet."

"Come on Harry, you know you're no Shakespeare, I'm not a stupid crow and you're no steer, if you can't come back tomorrow, I won't shed a tear, If you can't buy an apple from me then have no fear, an apple a day's not as good as a draught of beer."

Guido almost fainted with admiration at her word play.

A passer-by smiled and Harry laughed.

"Poetry and apples," Harry chuckled happily, each day Rosa had a different role to play, she was good at selling and performed, sometimes sweetly and sometimes sourly. "Give me four; I've got the lad working with us today."

The two of them stood close and it was clear that the man would love to stand closer, fortunately her basket protected her and she ensured she placed it firmly between the two of them. She was used to the men who would like to press more than her apples.

"Four it is, fresh Kent apples, straight off the branch," she told him truthfully. The apples were fresh off the tree; she could vouch for that.

They had been picked the day before and brought up in a cart, at dawn, the following morning; she had to wait until ten before they arrived and she could collect them to sell. By mid-morning she was roaming the hard, selling her wares, some of the freshest apples in London. By noon she was almost sold out, down to her last load, a dozen left in the basket.

"Thank you Rosa, they look lovely," he said, looking not at the fruit that she pushed into the open doublet that belted, doubled as a bag. Harry paid her and they bade each other farewell, and that was when Guido stepped forward.

"Finest Kent apples," she cried.

There were few people around and he sensed that Rosa would be moving off to another busier pitch almost immediately. He had to act quickly.

"Where can an honest man get a job?" he asked in Italian.

"In London there are no honest men," she replied in their shared mother tongue.

They conversed from thence in Italian, as Guido's English was not up to such sophisticated conversation. He could understand more than he could speak but even that was limited.

"Then where can a simple man get a job?"

"Is that why you came to see me? Everyone else comes by to buy my fruit. Cosa fachamo?"

"I need work to get money to buy the fruit."

"Can you read?"

"Not English, a little Latin, a priest once taught me. Can you read?"

"A little."

"Que cosa, voluo jocare."

"You want to play, where?"

"Questro, anywhere with you!"

"You need to buy an apple if you want to tarry with me!"

"Can't a man talk with a beautiful maiden on a cold day to warm his heart?"

"You'll have to get in line," she replied saucily. "You haven't even bought an apple yet."

"Will you be here tomorrow?"

"Hereabouts, I pay for this patch, why?"

"I'll have money for apples tomorrow."

"I've heard that one before."

"Not from me!"

"I'll believe it when I see it."

"You are a doubting Tomasina!"

"My name is Rosa Zucchiatti!"

"And I am Guido Forcanessi!"

"Where is your family, in Italy?" she asked. Her smile was so warm, Guido found himself under her spell already.

"Mostly, they are in the Stato de Presidi between Ansedonia and Porto Longone; a wonderful part of the country but it is an area occupied by Spain, and you?"

"I come from Sicily, the 'Kingdom in the Sun', from the north of the island if you know it."

"I know of it, the Norman Crusaders settled there, many speak of its beauty, wine, olives and lemon groves! Many say that the most beautiful girls come from there."

"That's the one and many blonde bastards, have been sired there, too! Have you nobody here in England?"

She enjoyed ignoring his clumsy attempts at flirting.

"I have a few cousins in York but I have to work to get there before I can work with them; I must tarry in London for a while as a result, I need money to pay for my rent, firstly, and then, perhaps, a journey to see my relatives in the north!"

"And you need Italian company while you are here? Or are you just looking for a girl to stay with?"

"Either or both," replied Guido cleverly.

"You can have both if you take me to Petticoat Lane and I'll be your, not so plain, Jane!" promised the girl emphatically.

Guido smiled back at her and waved, he watched as she turned to serve another customer.

Guido smiled to himself before turning on his heel and heading for the docks with renewed zeal. She had provided him with a new incentive to find work. He would find work, take her to Petticoat Lane and buy her something there; she would look like a lady in a good quality second-hand skirt bought with his coin, he decided.

Chapter 8 – ii - The Snare

The room was small and narrow, up in the eaves; the light from the moon was dim; the time of day was dead of night, in winter, darkness prevailed; the woman's stride was slow, shortened by stupor brought on by lack of sleep, slowed by caution; the steps were steep and ill-lit. She of all people knew danger. The last tenant had fallen back down the stairs and that was how she got the room. She had help with the rent, it wasn't a bad spot and not too far from where she collected her apples each day.

She shared her room with an actress, Mary, who was out all night, they shared the same bed, a collection of blankets with straw stuffed between the layers; there was no pillow. Sometimes Rosa would get into bed and feel the heat from Mary's body still on the material. It worked well, they shared the rent, Rosa was up at dawn and that was when Mary would return to sleep. Rosa would return after nightfall and Mary was at rehearsal or on stage or being taken out.

She said she was an actress but Rosa suspected that she was a pert part-time punk or one of the stews employed by the Bishop of Winchester; they called them his 'geese'. They could often be seen at the theatre on the top tier with the rich gentlemen. Rumour had it that the Bishop had paid towards work on the cathedral and his palace down in Winchester with proceeds from his pimping.

Exhaustion was setting in as she pushed open the door of her shared room; there was laundry to be done, a fire to be made. Her breath on the stairs condensed in front of her face, reminding her of how cold it was. September had been unusually and cruelly cold and October was proving just as harsh with a north wind cutting through the layers of her clothing. All she wanted to do was lie on her bed for half an hour before contemplating her chores. There was one wooden chair, fragile and old, and on it sat the slightly deformed figure of Cecil.

"What have you got to report to me, Rosie?" he said without bothering to greet her or enquire after her health. He paid her rent so politeness and niceties were not necessary. She was a chattel, he was a martinet, she knew but at least he could wait until she flung herself on the bed. Out of deference for such an esteemed visitor, she stood in the doorway. He was not sure if it was deference or distrust, she waited, knowing that if he made a grab for her she could flee.

"Ah, it is you, just when I need to sleep."

Cecil sat and recited: "Pussycat, pussycat, where have you been, I've been up to London to visit the Queen, Pussycat, pussycat, what did you dare? I frightened a little mouse under her chair, Meow!"

"Your pussycat has been keeping her eyes open," she assured him, lulled almost to sleep by his rhyme.

"Which is what you are paid for," he responded coldly, letting her know it was what she knew that Cecil was interested in and not her infinite charms.

"I may have someone for your task," she admitted.

"Close the door," he commanded, it was gentle request but with no politeness. It was a firm instruction. She did as he bid.

"I have a possible Italian," she declared, necessity forcing her to lean against the doorjamb.

"Italian, a foreigner, that's no good, I need someone from England, and you know that. How can we destroy the English Catholic hierarchy without an English Catholic uprising?"

"His cousins moved to York," she feebly mentioned, knowing it would displease him.

"I wanted someone English and Catholic, you must try harder!"

"He will not protest when you catch him, his English is not very good at all."

She hesitated, waiting for him to encourage her further.

"Go on."

"He could pass for an Englishman in the way he dresses."

"That is something, what is his name?"

"Guido Forcanesi," she replied cautiously.

"Guido we can change, 'Gui', or Guy, yes Guy, is a good name, like Guy of Gisborne, I do so enjoy the tales of Robin Hood. What was the last name?"

"Forcanessi."

"Fork, Guy Fork, no, where did you say his family went?"

"York."

"Guy Fork of York, easy for the masses to remember, this gets better. Wait, there is an old family name up north, Vaux, Guy Vaux, that sounds better, let us call him Guy Vaux, better still Guy Fawkes, sounds like Hawks, a vicious bird. Clever, Rosa. The more I think, the more I like the link."

"If he is not suitable, I will try for an Englishman, but Catholics keep their faith a secret these days; it will take more time and a more patient stalking. I have seen some men boarding ships for confession or a mass but I know not whether they are gentlemen or knaves, they go about at night cloaked in dark garb."

"We do not have time. I think, upon reflection, you have done well, the ideal name, I shall see if he is the ideal man. Yes, congratulations you have found our patsy. We can alter the records in York, copy a whole page or book, it can be done, inserting his name; we can give him a heritage even, a family, a school. If necessary, provenance can be created; we can devise his life before coming to London, when did he arrive here?"

"He has been here only a few days; he was working in the Lowlands; helping soldiers to move their goods, he is trying to find portering work down at the dockside."

"Even better, we can turn him into a soldier, fighting for Spain."

"He hates the Spanish; they invaded his homeland and his family were forced to flee."

"These are details, I will change them as I see fit."

"Of course, Your Lordship."

"Yes, you have succeeded; I am pleased with your work."

"Thank you my Lord."

"We could forge a birth certificate, create a family for him, I suppose that would do, the records could be altered quite simply. Does he read, can he write?"

"Not in English, is it necessary?"

"He will be required to read his confession and sign it, we'll send him to a school for an education so he can read his confession; I was hoping for a slightly more educated patsy but he will have to do; we have much to do."

"As always!"

"We can make up his education, send him to any school we want to, we could even make him a gentleman. The main thing is that he is Catholic, however lapsed, or a devout churchgoer, which he will be when I am finished with him. "

"That will have to do, then. A *pazzo* is not so easy to find these days! Everyone knows everyone and everyone's business."

"It's the best we can do, under the circumstances, we can work wonders," he decided thinking with the alacrity that had made him famous. "When will he meet you again?"

"Tomorrow!"

"Ah, only a woman as beautiful as you could be so sure. I envy you."

"A humble fruit seller and the most powerful man in England, really, you make jests where jests are not called for."

"Truly, I would trade all my power for your good looks."

"And I would trade all my good looks for a quarter of your wealth and an eighth of your power."

"There's the rub, we are who we are, we play the role we should play and we would trade our lives for others in our minds but not in reality, you would not want the heavy responsibility that I carry, believe me."

His father's faith in his mind was rewarded every day. The king was fortunate to have one of the ablest minds in the known world working for him. The relief was palpable and could be felt in the room as Rosa relaxed, moved across the room and collapsed on the bed. She gathered up the skirts of her dress and sat demurely on the bed, her legs firmly closed, heels together, she did not need an old man making a pass at her. She had been in enough trouble already. Her debts had been greater than her income when she had some apples go bad. Cecil had saved her from prison and then he had taken on her share of the rent; she was in debt to him, she admitted, but she did not want her indebtedness to encompass old flesh crawling all over her. Just because she paid her rent, it did not allow him the rights to her body.

"I believe it, I'm so tired just selling apples and spying for you. That is enough statecraft for me. Do not look so sad, you see, we have someone, he is as open hearted and as artless as a baby, he would be as malleable as copper in our hands, he will make a perfect patsy, which is what you wanted," she announced proudly despite her tiredness. She was used to fighting her corner with him whether she was sitting on a bed, below him or standing above him, in a muddle, feeling foggy, while he sat with his mind as clear as day.

"Let me think about his usefulness, I may well use him yet. Everyone seems to know everyone in the city, is it not so?"

"Indeed my Lord, but you seem to know everyone of little or great significance, their whereabouts and their intentions, it is late and I have to rise early."

"I have an appointment myself; let me know if you have any other information for me won't you."

"Of course my Lord," Rosa promised bowing her head, her brown eyes watched as Cecil struggled to his feet and shuffled quietly to the door, cautious in the ill-lit room.

"God be with you," he said as he stepped through the doorway.

"Goodbye to you!" Rosa replied, trying to hide her relief.

The door closed behind him and as she undressed, deliberately and carefully, folding her clothes and draping them on the chair; it was then that she noticed that he had left a small copper coin on the table next to the bed where she kept her candle. It was enough for a place at the theatre as a groundling, a promise of more to come. Her rent paid, it was a gift from him to show his pleasure at her work. It was a generous tip, a promise of more to come; in the past she had used it to see a play, she had the same admiration for *the Bard* as Cecil if not the depth of understanding.

Chapter 8 – iii - The Southern Side.

Guido Fawkes would have been able to work harder and be more successful if he had found the Italian community, to which he belonged, the dealers in Veronese leather and dried horsemeat, the Venetian glass merchants with their wonderful wares and the salami sellers form Sorrento. It never occurred to him that his best route was with his kinsmen. His attitude was that he had arrived in England and he would have to learn English, just as he had originally wanted to blend in with the Flemish. He had gradually learnt some of that difficult language.

Admittedly, he had met very few of Italian artists who were working in Antwerp but it was only when the war brought him in contact with Spanish troops that it was no longer necessary to speak the local language fluently. He could be understood in Italian and could understand most of the Spanish words. With gestures and filling in spaces, he was able to learn enough phrases to make himself understood by most people he came across and to understand their replies. This knowledge allowed him to survive and thrive in areas where Spanish was the *lingua franca*.

His cousins had moved up to Yorkshire but he considered it too far from the opportunities that London offered with its European connections. He hankered after the Continent with its easier ways and he felt sure that one day he would amass a small fortune, which would be enough for him to return to Italy, he might even settle in Sienna even though the Spanish occupied the town. There he could buy a small olive grove close to the town and die in the area in which he was born. The cousins were devout Catholics and knew that their religion would be easier to practice far away from the centre of administration, Guido was ambivalent, he was happy to be a lapsed Catholic. He was almost Protestant in his belief that he had direct access to God, without the need of intercession by a priest.

He felt guilty about not taking communion, but he was in a foreign land. It had been difficult to practice as a Catholic in England for many years and he welcomed the excuse not to attend church but he still prayed every night.

On the continent, he had attended the Latin masses where he could but he soon lapsed into the life of a soldier. The temptations of camp women, punks most of them, had also been at odds with his Catholicism but driven by others, he had sinned on lonely nights fuelled by cheap wine and the need to be close to another human being, to feel the comfort of a woman's embrace. Once he had fallen from the straight and narrow, it was difficult to get back onto the path of Righteousness. He could not confess his whoring and therefore could not take communion until he was absolved of that sin.

It had been a hard time for him, physically demanding, but he had enjoyed the daytime companionship of men with Latin blood in their veins; the Spanish soldiers or the Italian mercenaries. One day, he hoped, Spain's power would be broken and he could return to Italy. He would be a *pazzo* if he kept with his own kind, particularly as Rosa had entered his life and he was sure that, in no time, they would be making a life for themselves in England, or attempting to forge one. She was successful, her pitch was busy and she dealt with an honest Kentish apple farmer who gave her the best of his crop, the rest going to apple sauce makers, compote with pork never went out of fashion.

Guido was less fortunate in his search for work. In the Netherlands, his Italian was helpful; he had worked for and against the Spanish, he undertook orders from rich merchants or noblemen in the administration in peace, understanding their language with its similarity to his; he interrogated Spanish soldiers in war and helped the Italian sappers destroy the paths the soldiers took or their fortifications. On other occasions, he helped the Spanish invaders with their transport, happy in the knowledge that one day they would be defeated by flooded dykes, and the rebels, who had help from England.

He was a pair of hands for hire; poverty necessitated taking coins from wherever they could be found. Guido was Italian first and hated the Spanish who had invaded his country: he was a Catholic second. Yet, his ability to communicate with Spanish people helped him to find work in Antwerp and Ghent.
When the devil drove, needs must, he worked for them and against them depending on the wages he could negotiate and the work that was available.

In London, his Italian accent was a hindrance; no one could understand him and most mistook his Italian accent for a Spanish one. Stories of the Armada still circulated, the English despised the Spanish though they still traded with them either directly or through the Irish or Flemish. Guido despised the Spanish because of their occupation of his lands, nothing more and nothing less, yet he had been forced by his location and his poverty to work with the Spanish troops on occasions, though mainly he worked with other mercenaries against them whenever he possibly could.

That was the past and he was determined to find some sort of work now that he was in London and therefore he helped out unpaid on occasions; he kept going back to the same places where he had heard the pay was reasonable and the foreman was fair. He was persistent in his approach, he noticed the faces looking for work changed from day to day but he was a constant apparition, a recognisable figure on the docksides. The *dockers* got to know him, sitting with his cape wrapped around him in the early hours of the morning next to the same bollard, looking like the top of a candlesnuffer.

His route around the quay would be the same almost to the minute. Once he became known, he was offered a few hours here and a few hours there. He took whatever he was given; he was greedy for pennies, not for himself but for what he could buy his sweet, darling, Rosa. Already, she was the only woman that he always thought about. There was not one woman in London who, no matter how stunningly beautiful, incredibly attractive or remarkably striking, would merit a second glance from him. He would not consider looking at another woman.

Guido trawled from St Olave's Church to the east of London Bridge with little luck; he traipsed through the Thames-side streets of the *Banck Side*. He applied to the men of the Bishop of Rochester for some work in his Borough properties; he applied to the estate manager of the Bishop of Winchester for work on his farm to the south. He knew little about cows and sheep but he was willing to learn, he was not even offered work at the pike gardens feeding or netting fish, no work grinding or malting in the granary, nor carrying flour bags in the mill. These were good jobs with regular work and were jealously guarded by the families that had obtained employment from previous Bishops. Guido was told that he could get work if he was a woman, entertaining visitors to the theatres.

These ladies were paid for their time and the money given to the Bishop in return for food, accommodation and a little money. They were known as the *Bishop of Winchester's Angels*. Guido would often see the Bishop climbing into a *werry-boat* at the end of Stoney Street in order to be rowed to Westminster for an audience with the King. If only he could work for such a powerful man, he was aware that the bishop had his own court in Southwark and even his own prison, the Clink. Whenever they spoke of his estate in the country, they talked of large houses and hundreds of acres, a rural paradise where work was plentiful.

The Bishop should have had work for a tall strong man like Guido but, like all men of influence, he was surrounded by a retinue that would ensure that 'their people', their relatives and friends, got the job. Nepotism was rife. Family members who had worked for the Church for decades had precedent over anyone else and it was therefore a closed shop.

Along the bankside, there were twenty inns built on walls put up to stop the bishop's estate from flooding, but there was no work there either. Again, the jobs were passed from brother to sister or sister to nephew, niece to uncle, cousin to aunt. A boy apprenticed as a pot boy would work his way up through the inn management, looking to family for reliable employees, their honesty would be beyond question or they would be out on their ear.

The George, the Swan, the Tabard, and the *White Hart* promised strong ale and cooked food, which Guido could never afford. He ate stale bread and hard cheese, the occasional apple and he drank *small beer*, ale that had been diluted with well water. He eked out his little money and waited to take his first day's wages before he would eat properly, he lost weight as a result. The rent on his room was reasonable, he shared some empty warehouse space with four other dockers, sleeping on a straw mattress, covered in old sail-cloth, which they shared between them but it was money going out and he had none to replace it, he had seriously underestimated the difficulty of getting work. He planned to move to York when he had earned enough money.

The wherries ploughed between St Mary Overie's Stairs, Bank End Stairs and further west at Paris Garden stairs but he could not afford them. He dreamed of taking Rosa across to the city when he had work to see the order and calm that he had heard about but never seen; there was no need to cross the river the only bridge would do but it was frenetically busy. Compared to his life among the beggars, cutpurses, punks and vagabonds, lining the streets, the city was all 'sweetness and light'.

At the end of Clink Street was a dock where Guido eventually found work. Edward Alleyn was not yet 'Master of the Royal Bears, Bulls and Mastiff Dogs' but he was well known in the area and it was for his men that Guido found work. It was just simple portering to start with and then checking stock with the stock-taker. Finally, Guido was establishing himself in London after many trials and he knew that his perseverance had paid off; not only that, but he had found a kindred spirit and a fellow Italian who he now considered his sweetheart even if he was not sure how she felt. Rosa was always so frivolous and carefree; it was difficult to know her feelings. He had to be careful still, his Catholic roots and foreign looks might yet put him in any of the three prisons in Southwark, *the Marshalsea, the King's Bench or the Clink*. On odd occasions, he would accompany her to pick up apples or escort her, at the end of the day, carrying her empty baskets to the warehouse where she left them for the night.

It was an excuse to speak to her and spend time with her. They had known each other for such a brief space of time but as this was Guido's first time in love, his first 'true love', he thought little of time.

There were people from around Europe, Humanists, Lutherans, Calvinists and all manner of religions but they kept to themselves and operated on a strictly business basis, religion was never discussed; pamphlets were wasted on all but the educated and those who could read. Those interested in Puritan tracts devoured them, of course. If Guido had wanted to, he could have attended solemn mass on any number of ships in the port of London; Portuguese barques or French traders. Many merchants brought their priests with them, although they would also make up part of the crew.

He had become a lapsed Catholic over the years and seldom felt the need to board a foreign vessel to take communion. It was not dangerous; he just wanted to spend his free time with Rosa and as she was not practising, they were at least sinning together. He saw no problem in attending the Anglican services at *St Mary Overie*, it cemented his place in the community and it meant that, in time, he might be accepted, he was in his thirties and wise enough to know that good things came to those who waited, in the right place. Recusancy was the luxury of others; everyone knew that if you did not sign the book you risked a visit from Cecil's men and you would never get work unless you had registered at your parish church and an entry had been made in your name by the scribe there. Like many of his contemporaries, in a fast changing world, economically and politically, he was a pragmatist.

Adapting to the ways of the English was all part of survival in London and he was a survivor. At his work, friendships developed over time but it was rare for a foreigner to get work as there were so many people coming up from the country to the fringes of the city. These migrants swelled the street, having no work at home in the fields. Cecil feared them most, the poor were suffering hardship as prices rose and they could well rebel.

A revolt was not his greatest fear. His greater fear was that the Catholic nobles might harness the malcontents and sweep away the Government.

Fortunately, Southwark was safe because it was London's playground and a relatively rich neighbourhood but there were other areas where poverty reeked and there was a chance of sedition and rebellion. Cecil made it his business to know what was happening in these areas and to ensure that his intelligence would warn of any dissent. The Bishop of Winchester profited from the inns, bear and bull baiting rings, the Stews and the theatres. He was the largest landlord in town; proceeds from various activities had made him wealthy. He could afford to ignore Cecil's fears. He did not worry about the State's security just that all the money was coming his way. Many people profited along the way but the bishop's coffers swelled all the same.

Guido and his dockers paid a night watchman for their dormitory amongst the bags, barrels and sacks in a warehouse; the watchman paid the owner of the warehouse. The warehouse owner paid rent to the Bishop, in fact through various intermediaries the Bishop was Guido's landlord. Everyone took their cut, their commission for passing the money on but they just skimmed a little from the top, they made sure the Bishop got his fair share. That was how the system worked. All of the innkeepers, baiters and brothels leased their land from the Bishop and he was therefore pleased to fulfil his role as decreed by Elizabeth and her Government that every Parish should care for its poor.

The Bishop of Winchester ensured that the Poor Rate was collected from these merchants of 'pleasure and of misery' and from the genuine merchants who plied their trade in his fiefdom. The *Helpless Poor*, the young, the old and the sick, were helped and his Parish paid for apprenticeships. Some elderly and disabled, especially those injured during the war in the Netherlands were given a licence to beg.

The Able Bodied Poor were given work in a workhouse until they could find work; Guido was a week away from finding himself in that position. Thanks to his savings, he was spared the longer road out of poverty. He still had to watch out for the Rogues and Vagabonds. They might escape a flogging and their begging was illegal, but they knew many ways to cheat a man from his hard-won coins. Even though they knew that they would suffer from any of a list of punishments from having their tongue branded, to being kept as slave for two years, to even being hung, necessity drove them on, and Guido was determined not to fall for their tricks, only the money he had earned could be trusted.

Guido was very much taken by the expression: '*In deo fidemus, aurum omnibus allis*'. He kept his leather purse on a string tied about his neck rather than risk it being cut from his belt.
They would have to murder him to get the money and as that was not beyond some, he avoided the more dangerous streets and always travelled on the main thoroughfares wherever possible. He avoided walking alone in areas he had been warned were unsafe and, whenever possible, attached himself to a group whenever he could.

Although, he was fairly new in the town, he kept his ears open for the canting of the *cut-purses* offering *lifts* or stolen goods and he would make sure he was aware of his surroundings and crowds where a *draw* could be made. He had no desire to buy stolen goods or to be pick-pocketed, and these thieves, who were so skilled, had even taken purses hidden inside a doublet or jerkin. There had been many *cronies* and Guido was determined not to be one of the victims; he may be a patsy in some people's eyes but he would never be a *crony* to *cut -purses* and *nippers,* around town, if he could help it.

Guido and Rosa met that evening; Cecil sat watching their reunion for half an hour, remembering Fawkes's features, wondering what he could do to make his villain more villainous. He wondered about his story and where he might come from.

He let the two of them leave before him and watched as they walked briskly along the *Banck Side*. The weather was particularly cruel that night and he wanted to be back by the fire. Rosa allowed Guido to take her hand, his was warm and large, his fingers wrapped around her cold palm and the back of her hand, she grasped his hand in return. They scurried along past all the crowds that mingled in the streets along the Southwark shore, past the Clink, beyond the church, the Minster of St. Mary Overy, past London Bridge to the drinking dens of Bermondsey close to St Mary Magdalene of Bermondsey Street, which dated back to the thirteenth century.

"Joris Hoefnagel lives in that house," Rosa declared as they hurried along.

They had been walking for twenty minutes, and both felt hot despite the cold after ten minutes of moving as such a quick pace.

"A friend of yours?" asked Guido, his voice rising, as he tried to disguise his jealousy.

"Ha, he is far too grand for the likes of me and I am too good for him, he is an artist, someone told me about that being his house."

"If I had enough money, I would get him to paint you."

"Would you do that for me?"

"Of course!"

"Even though you do not know me."

"I feel I know you and," he paused before admitting, "I have asked about you."

"Have you?"

"Of course."

"What did they tell you?"

"That I should marry you."

"You have not wooed many women have you?"

"Not women like you."

"Slow down Guido or you'll scare me off."

They walked along the rough track that led to the hog roast. A pig of goodly size was turning on a spit above a clay-pit that had a fire of wood and charcoal piled up below it.

Leaning on his warebench, next-door was a man with a pan, he cried out, "Amulet, fresh omelette, makes a lovely rear-banquet or nunchion, it's a long way to breakfast. Get your argent out of your bung and have yourself a kickshaw."

Rosa explained that the man at the counter was offering an omelette as a late night snack, asking everyone to take their money out of their purses and have a little something. Guido rolled his eyes, it was hard enough to learn English, let alone slang.

"Are you hungry?" Guido asked.

"Not yet, we'll get some cullis from the ordinary anon!" A blank look greeted her remark. "We'll get some meat broth from an eating house later!"

"I'd prefer some Poor John," replied Guido.

"Ah so you know that much, you sound like a sailor, I don't like salted hake, it is far too much like the bacalao, you spent too much time with the Spanish, they love that dish!"

"It is delicious if cooked well," asserted Guido.

"If you say so!"

"So what brought you here?" he pressed.

"Your invitation to spend the evening with you."

"No, what brought you to England?" he asked, becoming increasingly exasperated by her humour.

"We moved from Sicily to Milan, my father was a tailor and he had little work on the island. I grew up in the city, but in 1597, the Spanish conquerors expelled nine hundred Jews from Milan."

"I have heard of the barbarity."

"My family had to flee north away from the Spanish. My father worked in the 'Hanseatic League' towns until he could raise the money for the passage. We arrived here the next year."

"That is terrible; the Spanish army is a terrible monster."

"And the Inquisition too!"

"I remember Italy was tolerant of the Jews," Guido continued.

"It is, only last year Leone Modena started services with a choir in Ferrara."

"Really?" Guido pretended to be impressed but, in actual fact, had never heard the name.

"I have heard that the harpsichord accompanies services on weekdays and the Simchat Torah in Sephardic synagogues in Venice," continued Rosa.

"You are well informed; you could have moved to Leghorn, the Medici welcomed Jews."

"Italy is not safe from the Spanish and from the Medici family. My father wanted to come here, he had heard of Thomas More and his deeds, his uncle had come here in the reign of Mary before I was born, before he met my mother. He knew he could find work as a tailor."

"And I am glad you came here though it seems you have missed your family. You look lonely. Do you have no one here?"

"My father and mother were old when they met and disease took them away, my uncle died before we came here. I am an orphan, but luckily, I had established my apple trade before then. I now share a room and work all hours of the day. I have food in my belly and good health, too. I am very lucky indeed, many are worse off."

"Lucky indeed."

"And you Guido?"

"My family moved to York, a haven for *Romans*," he replied.

"Not for a Jew like me. There was slaughter there many years ago, it was the first thing my father told me when we arrived."

"Both faiths can still be practised there, but then my parents moved to West Riding, they both worked wool."

"And you a soldier?"

"I never went to war, I have no training with a pike, staff or sword and I cannot ride either."

"What, then?"

"I have little strength compared to others but I make my living by moving things from one place to another, off ships, on fields of battle. When there is war, I follow the soldiers as they have many stores and munitions to move, battlements and embrasures to build; tunnels to dig; there is always work for willing hands such as mine."

He was boasting quite shamelessly about his strength and potential to earn, to impress her.

"They are very large hands."

"Better for holding you."

Rosa stared at him and he blushed, she smiled before quickly changing the subject.

"War is hard."

"In peace I follow trade."

"A follower, we cannot all be leaders!"

"I have no education and little English despite the time I have spent here. I speak with foreigners in a foreign land. I have been in the Low Countries and Italy more than I have been here. I took work where I could."

"We will practise your English, now!"

"Very well but not bare with me, please."

"Very well. Your parents fled the Spanish?"

"All those who fled, were full of dread, for the Spanish are fearsome in their conquest, all men and women subjugated and distressed," Guido rhymed in England, using words he had heard and hoping that Rosa would understand the gist .

"Indeed that is true, a common view, the Inquisitor and the conquistador, the Ejercito de Tierra, spread fear and terror," she replied, satisfying him that she understood. By a combination of complicated words, that were similar in English and Italian, they were able to communicate with each other. It was a language that had a semblance of English. Rosa wanted him to practise his English but he was not confident enough. Later on, Rosa suggested that they started to speak in English using simple rhymes.

"You are too clever for me, your rhyme is." Guido struggled for a word to rhyme with 'me'.

"Rhapsody," she suggested.

"Rhapsody?" asked Guido.

He could not understand.

"Come on voluo jocare, let's forget our woes, I'm hungry let's eat," she replied, falling back into Italian.

"Eat, drink and be merry!"

Guido repeated the phrase he had heard often spoken on the streets, he knew it came from a play but had never been to one while he had been in London. He was too busy working to pay his rent to enjoy the plays around town that would have allowed him to understand more words and enjoy the language. He spoke only to his workmates and that was not conversation but instruction or commands.

"Sounds sweet to me," Rosa cried, playing along.

"Sweets to my sweet," Guido responded playfully.

He had heard the expression on the dockside when some dockworker wanted to attract the attention of passing pretty girls. His English consisted of overheard phrases, which were not always used in the right context. They moved through the stalls of oyster barrels and cold mutton laid out on wooden plates, a cauldron of boiling chicken at one stall and a table laid-out with wooden bowls and stew pot of pottage, the smell of ginger wafting from its steam.

"What will you eat Rosa?"

"Some hog, I have not eaten meat all week."

"Roasted hog should do the job, shall we shog?"

It was another overheard expression, used by Guido to impress her. They moved back down the stalls towards the hog-roast.

"Three rhymes, good times, protected by Saint Valentine's."

They held hands and smiled at each other.

"Again, I bow to your superior wit, mine can never match it!"

Guido's strong accent and diction did not make it easy for Rosa to follow, so she decided to return to Italian. She told him honestly what she thought.

"Your rhymes are crimes against the English tongue. I hope it's not contagious I might catch it! Let us return to our mother tongue."

They spoke from that point in Italian.

"I want you to be infected by me not my rhymes, but your word play I cannot compete with," Guido complained good-naturedly.

"You would have to be a good player to catch my quick returns."

"You will make me a better player," he suggested cheekily.

"You might do the same for me, too!"

Drizzle swept in from the east as they moved around the market, most ignored the rain, pulling up the hoods on their jerkins or pulling scarves over their heads; others without scarves hurried for shelter under the awnings which would soon start to sag under the weight of water. There were voices of good natured chatter, laughter, rhymes recited and songs sang; they heard the rhyme that celebrated the defeat of the Armada: Rain, rain, go away, Come again another day, Little Johnny wants to play; Rain, rain, go to Spain, Never show your face again!

It made them feel more alien than before and Guido gripped her right hand with his left and they smiled at one another. They had felt part of the city but the words reminded them that they were foreigners. Rosa had decided that Lord Robert Cecil and his machinations would no longer include her. She would fail to signal him by leaving an apple at The George Inn, Guido was far too good a soul to be mixed up in his schemes, she liked him more than Cecil's money and he would keep her warmer come winter.

Chapter 9 - Escape to Amsterdam

Plague had arrived again in London, it was not a great plague, a few of the villages on the roads out of London had small outbreaks, the London situation was not dire, two deaths in the city and a dozen in Southwark, but the effect of such news had a dreadful outcome for the people of London.

All those wealthy people who milled around the town, attended plays, ate fruit, dined in inns and shopped in town, suddenly disappeared. They left for relatives in the country or stayed at home to avoid the bad humours. To start with, Guido was busy, ships still arrived and needed unloading or their cargoes would spoil. Goods that would have been mopped up by the London hoards found their way further afield in a desperate attempt to sell them before they spoiled. The shrinking market drove down prices. It was a quick fall, too quick for many, apples, fortunately, took a to while spoil. Meat sellers were not so fortunate despite the cold spell.

Some cargoes from infected areas ended up in the Midlands and meant there was a plague in that area. The disease wiped out a dozen cloth-workers. The bad news spread quickly and orders were reduced until better times arrived, the first few shipments kept Guido busy but within a fortnight, many of the men were threatened with being laid off. Rosa's trade halved immediately plague was announced; then, dropped further and further as more and more people fled town or stayed in their homes.

Warning rhymes could be heard from the street: 'Hark, hark! The dogs did bark', 'The beggars are coming to town', 'Some in rags and some in jags', 'And one in a velvet gown'.

Sometimes the old rhyme about Bloody Mary's persecution of the Protestants, which prophesised the pain that plague brought, which was a type of torture, were heard as well. People were keen to learn different songs or new rhymes about the State or the landed gentry and their crimes but they loved the old rhymes.

They loved the old ones more: 'Mary, Mary, quite contrary', 'How does your garden grow'? 'With silver bells and cockleshells', 'And pretty maids all in a row'.

The silver bells and cockleshells and maids were instruments of torture. Mary was Mary I, the garden referred to her estates in Spain, she not only tortured Protestants but she made herself rich by her association with a foreign Catholic power. The pain of plague was meant to feel like being tortured by these terrible implements of pain.

A few days after visiting the fair Rosa felt pains in her shoulders, legs and back. She felt tired and weak as she sold her apples that day, it was raining throughout the day, business was bad and all her clothes were soaked through. She thought she was going down with a chill and went to bed without anything to eat. It was a common enough occurrence in the wet winters.

Guido woke her when he called on her that evening; the landlady let him up to the room. When she explained, he went out into the evening rain to try to fetch an orange or a lemon to squeeze into some water. He managed to get his mug filled with fresh water from the water carrier in Bermondsey but he failed to find any citrus fruit.

The next day, she felt tired and weak, the following day she could not sleep, and her body temperature rose and her head throbbed. Her brain and nerves were being attacked by the bubonic plague. She staggered to use her chamber pot and drunkenly she returned to bed, feeling giddy, it was worse than being drunk; the same feeling of helplessness, but the mind was not numbed, as it was when she drank alcohol. She was unable to speak properly to Guido when he returned. He thought she was dazed or that she had been drinking but she had a fever and there was no aroma of beer or wine. Rosa lay still in her bed, she had a fever; she had no appetite, and abdominal pain. Every so often, she vomited and there was blood in her vomit.

She looked over at Guido apologetically as she sat up and her shoulders heaved as she retched into the empty water jug. He looked for signs of blood. Tiny broken blood vessels, called petechiae, had ruptured, the blood from these appeared in her vomit, which all those who had come across the plague, recognised as a bad sign.

"How do you feel?" he asked, trying to hide the fear he felt for her and her condition.

"My armpits are tender and swollen and so are those in my nether regions. My sore throat is still here and my glands around my neck are swollen," she whispered hoarsely, she was still hot and her throat was dry.

"I'll look after you," he promised and he meant it, he would protect and love her.

"Thank you," she sighed.

"You'll get better soon," he assured her confidently.

"I hope so," she replied weakly without smiling.

Her fever had been a worry, she had started by complaining of a headache on her way to work, by evening, on her return, she was feeling giddy and Guido had checked her for any delirium or shivering. He had seen plagues in the Lowlands and remembered fearing them when he was young in Italy.

"I'm going to ask advice from the *plague pilots*."

"Please stay with me, I have been starved of company all day" she begged, her voice was feeble and her breathing shallow.

"I will not be long," he said firmly.

"Do you promise?" she begged.

"I promise that I won't be long but I need to know how to treat what ails you," Guido said firmly but inside his heart was heavy; he almost agreed to her request for him to stay.

He gave her a drink of water from a leathern drinking pouch, which he had filled from the well nearby on his way back from work. Then, he tucked her in and smiled reassuringly, kissing her hot forehead before turning and walking slowly to the door. As he opened it, he smiled back at her. He ran down the stairs in order to make the meeting. The pilots started their talk promptly at eight and as he did not have a watch, he had to get there as quickly as possible. The meeting took place in an empty storeroom in a warehouse on Bankside, the floor had been swept and the roof above with it beams made it feel like an abandoned village church. At one end, sat three people who had lost their loved ones to the plague. They sat on simple wooden stools, there was no other furniture in the room; a crowd huddled around them. The one on the left, a grey haired, short, thin, stooped tanner spoke first.

"Watch out for signs of the plague before you have to pay for the doctor to call. In men and women alike, it first betrays itself by the emergence of certain tumours in the groin or armpits, some of which grow as large as a common apple. In others, the size of an egg," he warned gravely, "I lost my Miriam and that was the sign of the plague in her, lumps that grew and caused her pain."

Guido remembered that Rosa was complaining of such an affliction; the second man then spoke; he was a barber surgeon, not yet grey, well fed but not fat, who favoured letting blood as a cure all to everything. He justified such action by accentuating the fact that the body was covered in swellings, swellings, which would be relieved by his bloodletting. The man spoke with authority and seemed to have great knowledge.

"From the groin and under the arms the deadly gavocciolo soon began to propagate and spread themselves in all directions, without rhyme or reason and indifferently," he continued.

There were murmurs from the crowd standing in small groups like groundlings, at a theatre, each group avoiding being too close to another.

They were families or friends but they did not want to become infected by others, especially those in the barber surgeon's survivors. They had seen these markers on friends and relatives who had the plague. He explained how the swellings spread from the armpits and groin to the rest of the body. He had saved one or two plague victims it was true, they skulked at the other end of the storeroom not wanting to be re-infected by the mob that included Guido. The barber surgeon had persuaded them to appear to show his efficacy, as they owed their lives to him, they had agreed even though they had paid handsomely for his services. The promise of some small beer afterwards had persuaded them further, of course, but the barber had reckoned they would drum up enough business for him to look upon such largesse as a mere trifle.

Finally, the local apothecary spoke up. He was lean and young and tall, behind his back, he was called *'Master Grave'* because many thought he would be there shortly, he was so scrawny, but he was good at his job; many people came to his shop for advice, potions, lotions, honey syrups and herbs.

"We call the plague the 'Black Death', because if the unfortunate survives the time of swelling they might recover and thrive but look out because after these swellings, these gavazzara, the form of the malady can change."

Guido listened even more closely.

"Watch out for any changes in the following way: black spots or livid spots make their appearance in many cases on the arm or the thigh or elsewhere. Some are few and large, some small and numerous."

The barber added, "These swellings are an infallible token of approaching death; such also were the small red spots on whomsoever they showed themselves."

It was not strictly his place to speak but he knew of the apothecary's reputation and he did not want everyone to forget him and his successes.

However, he could not risk undermining the youngster too much. It was enough to remind people of his presence, there were always some people who would go to the apothecary but the rest, who could not afford such an expense could line his pockets with coins.

"There is a chance that the plague victim will pull through. In more than half the cases, the victim has survived," the apothecary concluded, trying to calm the crowd who had been shocked into silence by the details.

There was a physician there too, at the front of the crowd, who hoped to drum up some business and once all the others had spoken, he too took his place on the stage though he had not been invited. Those gathered we far too poor to afford the fees of a plague doctor.

"The four humours need to be brought back into balance," he claimed confidently, "the victims have too much yellow bile, too much fire. I can cure them for a good price."

He believed, as many doctors did at that time, that it was melancholy being revealed by the black bile and that had to be in balance with the choleric yellow bile, and, in turn, in balance with blood, or the sanguine humour, and the phlegm, or the phlegmatic humour.

All four elements, earth, fire, air and water needed to be in balance for a healthy life, needed to be in harmony, perfect harmony, for perfect health. It was a doctor's role to balance all the humours. Guido did not understand this, nor did he trust doctors, besides which he could not afford their fees. The money, he knew, would be better spent on their escape from the plague area. The meeting broke down as panicked people begged the three experts to let them know which was better; poultices for the swelling, or bloodletting, laxatives to loosen the bowels or emetics to induce vomiting, caring little that all three men had lost loved ones to the plague or that the fourth speaker was an unwelcome interloper, taking advantage of the situation. All they wanted were answers, solutions to save their situations.

There was no questioning of the speakers' knowledge; they had survived being in plague areas after all.

Guido slipped out of storeroom as the crowd pressed forward on the four experts. He did not consider them experts; he knew that in the kingdom of the blind, the one eyed man is king. He had gathered the information he required, all his impulses told him that London was a dangerous place and should be abandoned. The plague was spreading fast, despite, barber surgeons, apothecaries and the rest.

The Court had abandoned London and moved to the palace at Hampton; all the richest people had left for their country estates including the Bishop of Winchester. Those who had no estates stayed with relatives outside town. Otherwise, they closed up their windows and doors, surviving on what they had in the larder. Merchant ships left the harbour as soon as they could unload or load their cargoes. The inns and theatres were deserted. Few people roamed the streets.

He realised that Rosa needed to be taken from where the plague was in danger of becoming rife and the chance of another infection, whilst she recovered, would be greater. She was weak, now; a second bout would carry her off without doubt. They had enough money to leave, just. That, he decided was what they should do. He raced back to their room, he knew her swollen glands were a bad sign, those 'buboes' or swellings of the lymph glands, might be caused by any infection but their presence in all areas, in the groin, in the armpits and on the neck, suggested a very bad infection. He knew that much. He had seen many soldiers die through infection but their inflammation of the glands was more noticeable than Rosa's.

He was not even completely sure she had the plague; he had to wait and see if her belly became covered in small, red, round spots. That meant rolling back her covers unless the spots had spread elsewhere, he might be able to see them on the arms. It was dark when he returned and she slept, he did not want to disturb her sleep, the fever might pass.

Many suspected plague victims awoke with no symptoms the day after, suffering from no more than a chill. Guido, now, knew that he had to be wary of the aches and pains she might feel in her stomach, back, arms and legs. Again, these could be part of any fever or any number of maladies, so he needed to look out for the spots and the blue, black patches on her thighs, which would confirm if she really had the plague.

Guido suspected she needed to be away from the crowded streets of London with their festering effluent and dirt and dust. The speed with which the plague swept through the city was incredible; literally, it was difficult to believe how rapidly it had spread. That night it was settled; not because Rosa was keen but because Guido knew it was their only chance, they had to get away from England and already the price of passage to the Continent was doubled, only by offering to help load and unload had Guido managed to afford the fare. No one was safe and then the chanting on the streets had began. Odd individuals patrolled the empty streets, ranting at any of the few people who were forced to be abroad. Even those not affected were harangued.

"See the punishment for your sins, harlots and thieves, a painful death; the fires of hell burning inside you!" cried a Puritan as he passed groups of people; he was swathed in scarves and capes, there was not a chink in his clothing.

He had faith in God but he wanted to ensure he did not breather in the humours that could give him the plague. It seemed that everybody's mouths were covered in case they breathed the plague air too deeply and succumbed. Sometimes it was difficult to hear the insults they hurled through muffled mouths. In those times, the bad air of London was blamed for the plague not the rats and their fleas. The foul fetid air smelt unpleasant enough, there was every reason to believe it was so.

"The Dutch plague is upon us," wailed another sitting on a barrel, everyone recognised him as '*Mad Bill*', whose trade in Portuguese pottery had been ruined by Dutch porcelain.

He spent his days drinking Dutch *Juniper* whilst haranguing passers-by. He had convinced himself by that time that the Catholics brought the Portuguese pots while the Protestants bought the Dutch wares.

He told anyone who would listen that his trade had been affected by the wars of religion on the Continent whereas people preferred the Dutch pottery to the Portuguese and the price was more competitive. Many Protestant and Puritans preferred the patterns of their co-religionists and so Dutch Delftware was fashionable, Portuguese porcelain was passé.

"The Jews are carrying the plague!" cried another stranger; any minority could be held responsible for any disaster.

Many dismissed him as a bitter competitor of a Jewish merchant, some became wary of Jewish areas. Guido knew it would not be long before the Roman Catholics were blamed and anyone who looked Spanish or Italian would be pilloried and shunned, the plague would be named 'The Dutch Plague'; 'The Italian Plague'; 'The Spanish Plague' or the French Plague'.

Once the plague developed fully, Guido would get no work on the docks, as a foreigner, it would be taken for granted that he would have the plague and would be spreading it to all the English dockers. Before that happened, they paid the rest of their rent, pooled their money and wrapped it in the bundle of clothes they possessed and left their lodgings as quickly as possible. It was not quite the dead of night but close enough

They walked down to the Thames where Guido had negotiated a good price for a passage to Europe. Guido and Rosa took the next available ship that was heading for Amsterdam. They were part of the cargo and slept in the dark hold amongst the goods that were stored in barrels and packages until the morning high tide allowed them to slip out of London. Guido had helped load the cargo and would help unload it, saving the captain from employing too many people; the more dock crew you used the greater the chance of employing someone with the plague. Guido looked healthy and strong, it saved their skins.

Even Cecil was unaware of their departure.

"We will be safe there," he assured her while they made their bed of packaging straw among the stores on board. "We'll be away from the plague."

"Why Amsterdam?" she asked perplexed, she hoped that she would be going back to Italy when she left London.

"It is a great city, second only to London in size, there will be a lot of work for me there, and you cannot hope to work with your illness. I will get work enough to keep the two of us. We need to get away from what ails you; you have been weakened by past plagues, the one that carried your father off. Once we have saved enough money, we can move on."

"I see, we cannot stay even a bit longer in London?"

"I was advised to take you away from the Plague."

"Could we not go somewhere warmer? I am so cold," she complained.

Guido had known her for only a matter of months but he had never heard her complain before; she never moaned. He needed to get her away from the fetid air that hung around the plague areas and move her to the clear crisp air on the Lowland shore. It was too dreadful to think that he had just met the love of his life and he might lose her. He had never loved another woman the way he loved Rosa. His heart ached when he thought about her being ill.

"You cannot travel too far, yet. Amsterdam is close and the docks are busy, I will earn money for us to start a life in Italy, down south away from the Spanish, I will get work unloading pepper and cinnamon and sugar, and you shall have all three for your larder!"

"I can earn my keep then, you have been so good to me, looking after me when I could not work," Rosa said, smiling at him weakly, but her eyes lit up a little.

"What else could I have done?"

"Left me to rot like apples after their fall. Why didn't you?"

"Because I love you, you are the apple of my eye and my love for you will never, ever die!"

They both began to cry, Guido leant over and hugged her, clasping her shoulders. He could feel her thick hair that brushed against his cheek, and not caring about any danger he might be in, hugged her even closer still. They loved each other, recognising in each other a good heart and kindness.

Guido had worked in Antwerp before arriving in London but the failing economy, due to years of war, had forced him to leave the Lowlands and seek work, but once Rosa became sick with the plague, Guido had reluctantly decided to return to the Lowlands. Earlier in the autumn, a chance conversation with a dockworker led him to consider the move to Amsterdam; Guido had been told that the port was flourishing even more than London.

He had considered Amsterdam before but was unsure of the wars that might break out between the Dutch and Spanish. It seemed that peace had reigned, at least in the port itself, he was told, and therefore it was a safe place to take Rosa; she would get better there and all would be well.

Amsterdam was fast becoming the wealthiest city in the world, its ships sailed from the city itself to the Baltic Sea, North America, and Africa, as well as Indonesia, India, Sri Lanka, and Brazil, forming the basis of a worldwide trading network by latching on to the Spanish, Portuguese and fledgling English trade networks.

Once Guido had heard the news of its success and understanding their change in circumstances, he became convinced that the port was their refuge in stormy times. If they could establish themselves there, they might be able to move back to Italy together. Amsterdam's merchants had the largest share in both the Dutch East India Company and the Dutch West India Company.

These companies acquired overseas possessions.

Amsterdam had become Europe's most important point for the shipment of goods and was the leading Financial Centre in the world. In 1602, the Amsterdam office of the Dutch East India Company had become the world's first stock exchange, trading in its own shares. Guido hoped to ride high on the tide of its success.

Antwerp was their first port of call, the boat took them to Europe from Dover; Rosa was wrapped up in a shawl against the cold but also to hide her condition in case the captain refused her passage. They managed to get to Antwerp with a wool merchant and his fleeces London to Flushing and then by cart to the city. All the rumours about the city crumbling were true; the Scheldt was silted up and trade in Antwerp had dwindled even more than it had in London during the height of the plague.

Finally, they made it along the trade routes, from Antwerp to the English Garrison at Bergen-Op-Zoom, by boat to Brill and from thence by sea to the teeming city of Amsterdam where they found a room at the top of a narrow house by the canal, directions to which had been provided by the second stranger that they had asked in faltering Flemish. By immense good fortune, Guido got work immediately.

It was spitting with rain, the clouds chilled by their passage across the North Sea brought cold rain, frontal rain, which fell in large blobs that fell with a splat on the tiled roofs of the old town. Guido wore his canvas gloves and a leather jerkin, the rope held firm in his grip. He had learnt the Flemish for 'heave' and 'stop' when he was there previously.

Guido was learning all the time, on the first day he had added to his vocabulary and was surprised at how much Flemish he remembered. His days fighting the Spanish troops, in the Lowlands, flooding dykes to drown them or cut off their advance were but a dim memory. This was peacetime and the work was not as onerous as digging ramparts and fortifications or digging away at the foundations of a dyke before the troops arrived.

He was able to eat regular meals and change out of his wet clothes when he wanted, he had seen war and its misery; he had never enjoyed being cold, wet and hungry. Much of warmongering was waiting around or digging feverishly, nothing else, there were few battles, and he had never been in one. Peacetime was infinitely preferable. There was less dirt and deprivation.

Guido genuinely hoped that there would be better work for him later but at the moment he was providing for Rosa and himself so he was happy to be learning the ropes, quite literally. He was also getting to know his team better than he might have done, thanks to his knowledge of their language gleaned from his previous time in the Lowlands. There were six of them who hauled the cargo from the hold; loaded the goods onto a barrow, unless the cargo was barrels, which could be rolled, wheeled them to the warehouses on the quayside, great terraces of buildings with no sunlight visible between them.

From there, the 'warehouse teams' hauled the goods up into the lofts for storage or distribution using hooks and cranes. It was like looking at an ants' hill in summertime gathering up the crumbs from a kitchen table. Some cargoes were light enough to be carried in the arms or on the shoulders; some could be put on your head and steadied by your hands, but it was more efficient to load the cart and wheel it around the hard with several cargoes aboard.

Once loaded it only took one trip to the warehouses whereas by hand it might take several trips. The engine of importation was in full swing and goods had to be unloaded quickly on the quayside because on the opposite side, the backs of the warehouses, the goods were being made ready for distribution throughout Europe and beyond.

The backs of these warehouses were as busy as the fronts were; they, too, were filled with people rushing over the cobbled yards to load a cart or inside packaging goods to protect them in crates or boxes lined with straw.

Carts and wagons were waiting to take goods to the cities of Europe as far away as Hungary.

At lunchtime, they took their break, it was noon but the grey skies gave no clue to the hour, it was clocks and not the sun that ruled their lives. For the workers, Guido and his workmate, they knew it was time to break because of the dull ache of hunger in the pit of their stomach and the tiredness that crept over their bodies. Their rumblings stomach, and the dull ache of exhaustion, acted as their timepieces. They worked and ate together adjourning to a tavern a stone's throw from the docks to drink and eat.

Their lunch consisted of a beer that was strong; a slice of meat or cheese and some boiled seasonal vegetable. These were always on offer or there was fish, of course, herring in particular. All were made into local specialities, pickled or brined. The dishes varied little, perhaps soup or stew was offered, but they were all served with bread and washed down with *Juniper*, at the end of the meal, designed to keep the chill out and numb the monotony of the afternoon. Alcohol fuelled their afternoon, their aching limbs felt less heavy after fortification with food and gin; it gave them the ability to continue their work in less pain. Guido had not told them of Rosa's terrible illness. He had to work; if not they would both starve; he could not stop to look after her otherwise all their rent monies and savings would be spent within a month, their revenue would dry up and they would both be destitute. His job would be filled within hours, daily more people thronged into the city to find work.

He had found work by sheer fluke. He would never have believed it would be possible to find work so quickly and so easily, it was a miracle. He was almost tempted to renew his faith. Of course he still prayed, more so for Rosa and her recovery. After finding Rosa and he a room, in a garret, in a tall house, he had wandered the streets looking for work before buying them some food. An injured man sat near a ship that was unloading, a heavy box of spices had fallen on his left foot.

Without thinking, Guido had offered to help him away from the throng and tend to his injuries. Another team member took up his offer of help and together, Guido, the injured man, and the team worker walked away from the busy dockside. Limping between the two men who propped him up, it became clear that his foot was seriously injured; he hopped slowly supported by the shoulders of the two men on either side of him.

Once they had walked to the injured man's home, they sat and drank a glass of juniper to warm their bones. In conversation, they spoke of what was the best course of action. It was clear the foot needed rest, his wife worked in the flower market and would be home to look after him; he would be well cared for.

However, it was clear that he would be off work for at least a week. The member of the dock team suggested that Guido should join their group of workers until their friend was back up to strength and there might be a chance of making him part of the team. Guido was thrilled; it could have taken days to find work and he readily agreed. On the strength of starting work in the docks the next day, he bought vegetables and chopped mutton to make a stew. He was in good spirits when he returned to tell Rosa, but once he saw her lying there, he felt sick in the stomach and his heart sank.

Rosa was not getting better, they had been fortunate in finding lodgings in the port, she benefited from the fresh north wind that blew through the city and she slept in the bed all day. While he cooked their celebratory meal, he made plans to lift her spirits and force her to think of the future, their future together. If love conquered all as she so often said, it might defeat the plague, too.

"We'll go to Middleburg, it used to be a busy town during the old days when it was trading with Bruges and Ghent; the wool merchants are doing well in these days of peace, dealing directly with England. A fellow worker tells me that the spices and goods from the Indies travel through there. We can move when you are better."

"But I feel so weak," she groaned.

"You will be stronger soon, we will move away from the coast, they will have work for us both there, I have been told, and it won't be so cold and damp."

"I so want to escape the damp. What about Italy?" she asked hopefully, she had made money in London, but she longed for the south and the way of life there and she was sure that Guido would get work, she was young still and they would marry and have lots of children who would bring them joy and look after them when they were old and grey.

"All in good time."

"Why Middleburg?"

"My friend told me that in winter, like here, the days are short with the sun rising above the horizon for only eight hours. Yet, they have mild winters, though like here, they can be gloomy, with barely any sun but there is not so much wind and rain. We will wear our gabardines and wrap up well."

"I hate being cold!"

" I know you are a fair weather flower that hates the frosts and cold winds. Though, they do say that where we are headed even when there is a cold winter, it tends to be snowy, freezing but also dry and sunny. You can find people skating near the city. It is not cold and damp like it was in London."

"And what of the summer?" she asked longingly, "I need sun to make me well!"

"He tells me from May until July the sun does not dip below the horizon, so it seems it is day all the time, like living in a twilight, sometimes when the sun is brighter it never gets dark and the horizon is always lit up by the sun just behind it. There you will have more sun than here and longer days. We'll save money and move south for the winter like the birds," Guido told her reassuringly, smiling at her willing for her to understand and agree to his plan.

"That sounds more like the place, I need, my mother called me Rose because I need sun like other flowers, I need to have sun, I need to have fun," she said happily.

"The climate is good for agriculture surrounding the city. Grain, sugar beet, potatoes, corn, and grassland for horses and cows are the most common sight. In addition, apple and pear trees are cultivated there. You can sell fruit like you used to do; you were so good at that!"

She was paler than ever and seemed so terribly weak. He just hoped that she would fight on. He knew that evening, as the coming of twilight necessitated the lighting of candles, that Rosa might not survive long. The realisation saddened him; it was inevitable but no easier to bear; he loved her so much.

She had not made the recovery that he had expected, her skin was still as bad as it had ever been and she was a bony shadow of her vital self, only a miracle would save her now, or her maybe her own determination or her inner strength, or perhaps his love alone.

His only fear was that she would die while he was at work and they would not be able to say goodbye.

After a week in their new home, he had slowly lost hope; he had expected to see a slow but noticeable recovery after keeping her warm with a good fire and plenty of cloaks on her straw bed. He had tried to build her up with vegetable soups and good salted pork sliced from the bone; a hock brought cooked from a reputable butcher, recommended highly by his landlord. She was getting weaker not stronger. She could not retain her food and her skin was getting worse.

While Guido worked on the dockside hefting heavy cargoes, barrels of different victuals, bales of wool and sacks of barley or rye. It was young men's work but Guido was the right side of 40 and able bodied, strong and hard working so he did not mind although by nightfall he was exhausted and by the time he got home, he just wanted to sleep. He would not show this to Rosa, she was his patient and he pretended to be full of energy.

Each evening he made her as comfortable as possible on her straw bed, tucked the folds of cloaks around her emaciated body, and wondered whether she would survive the night. Each night and every morning, he would empty her chamber pot, walking down into the street before returning to see her, night and day, staring up at the ceiling or sleeping, her head never moved, just her eyelids opened or closed.

They communicated with weak smiles, he watched her face contort in pain, and then he watched her sleep in the darkness. Another worry was whether she might pass on the plague to him. Listening for her breath as she slept, he would doze off only to be woken by her cries of pain, he lay on his back with his hands on his chest in the far corner of the room on his pile of straw, his eyes would grow heavy, and he would drift off again. The nights became an endurance for them both. The pain she was suffering was clear; she tried to suppress her screams of pain but she was too weak to do so. She felt so worn out that she welcomed sleep and dreamed of the long sleep she would soon have.

Praying helped, it focused her mind, and she repeated the Ave Maria, until each decade of the rosary became a comforting chant, helping her to drift off to sleep after spasms of pain. He could only look on helplessly, only able to comfort her by stroking her forehead as she sweated in fever, mopping her brow with a sponge dipped in vinegar, which was meant to heal the sores but seemed to achieve little. It seemed to stop them weeping so much, he had tried everything, beer, lemon, water and wine; the vinegar worked best.

It was six in the evening when her strength deserted her, the next day was Sunday, and Guido had promised himself that he would look after her the next day. They could spend time talking, her throat at least seemed better and perhaps she would take a walk in the fresh air and the air would restore her. He would not give up hope, he reasoned that she had not got better and apart from having lost so much weight, she had not become any worse; he had seen many worse cases recover.

Guido had worked on the docks all that day and had brought back some slices of roasted duck and *juniper* that he had bought from the gin shop; some stale bread he had bought cheaply from the baker, which he intended to fry for her. Over previous nights, he had collected lard in a dish for their special meal. He planned to use the pan in which they cooked all their food to fry some bread to eat with the cold roasted duck, heating the pan over the coals of the fire.

His intention was to give her the largest slice of duck despite the fact that he had been working all day and was famished. He knew she was equally hungry; even though her appetite was like that of a sparrow, she could hardly eat. Using a wooden spoon to scoop out the lard and move it about the base of the pan that sat on the red coals, he spoke to her about his day, trying to make her laugh by exaggerating trivial events. She would smile weakly or give a weak laugh that was all her strength allowed. She enjoyed the stories he told her, she felt like a child being told tales by a nurse.

She remembered her mother's stories, which she told before bed. He had been home an hour, building up the fire to keep her warm and to cook for them; he thought she might actually be getting better, finally.

Rosa could not move to stoke the fire, so each morning, before he left the house where they rented the top floor room, he built up the fire as high as he dared; he did not want to cause a fire in the chimney and set fire to their home.

After taking coals from the bucket, which he filled every other day when he returned from work, he pumped hard with the billows so that the fire roared at him. Once the coals were glowing, he would set the fireguard, a metal sheet on legs that radiated heat into the room, site-ing it firmly on the tiled floor that surrounded the fireplace. The Dutch might have built their houses higher than in England but they knew how to keep rooms in their houses warm, all the paraphernalia had been provided by the Landlord. He had given them kindling, wood and coal, billows and pokers and shovels and rakes for the ashes.

Before leaving, he would kiss Rosa's forehead, stooping down to her, necessitated kneeling down on the floor, and bending down. Rising, he would hope that the heat would be sufficient to ward off the chill as Rosa lay-a-bed. She never moved from her prone position if she could avoid it.

On his return, Guido would rebuild the fire, ensuring he put enough coal on and that he used the billows effectively to make the coals glow, while he told her about all the commodities he had unloaded or seen on the dockside from far off lands, sounding astonished to find such a diversity of goods beyond anything that he had seen in London. Sometimes he described them without knowing what they were called; it really was a cornucopia of goods. In turn, she was fascinated by these commodities and oddities.

He told her stories about the far off lands that they came from, stories told when they stopped for lunch or went for a drink, to quench their thirst, after work. That evening he told her that they had unloaded bananas from Brazil. There was always some sailor willing to tell of far off lands if there was someone like him who was willing to learn about them; Rosa enjoyed his tales, she dreamed of being better. She dreamed often, once dreaming that, as orphans, they should go to new places on their travels, perhaps the Americas; she could cook on board the ship and sell fruit at their destination.

Maybe they would take the *Spanish Road,* what the French called: 'le chemin des Espagnols', travelling from Flanders, to Cologne, Mainz, Worms, Altbreisach, Besançon, through the Alps and then moving on to Milan, Parma, and Florence, picking up work here and there if need be. From there they could move further south beyond the reach of the Spanish into the territories in the south of Italy, although even that drew risks with the Ottoman Empire expanding. Once she was well, they could decide together what they should do, head west or even east, better still south to her old home.

She wanted to move to warmer climes and he, now, dreamed of her getting better and of them travelling south to a part of their homeland not occupied by the Spanish; maybe the far south where the dialect was difficult to learn but where the language could be understood. There, they could pick olives or lemons and never worry about the biting wind nipping at their clothes and their hands and lips drying out and chapping with the cold.

Frost Fairs and long winters still promised to be a feature of life for them in the Lowlands, if they remained there. Guido dreamed, too: once Rosa was better, they could go where they pleased, Rosa could work when she was better, and all he needed to do was earn enough money to get them to the south. Once there, they would work on a farm and have food and lodgings and perhaps Rosa would be blessed with children.

Guido had already told her of several South American countries but he felt his stories fell on deaf ears; Rosa wanted to go home to Italy.

The billows gasped loudly as he squeezed them for the last time, he heard a sigh from Rosa that was heavy, heavier than he had ever heard before.

In the light of the fire, he turned and saw her still form, her head turned away from him as if she could not cope with having to tell him that she had left him.

Chapter 10 – The Plot Thickens - 15ᵗʰ November 1603

Markham and Cecil decided to walk together across London Bridge, the tide was too high to take a boat across; the currents between the bridge's piers were too strong. It would only be safe to take a ferry across from Tower Hill to the east or the Globe at Southwark to the west but both were a good ten-minute walk away, then there were the queues to wait in once there. It would take the same time it would take to cross the bridge, there were queues on to and off the bridge and crowds milling on it as well as drovers and merchants using it as a thoroughfare but Cecil preferred being on *terra firma* and Markham had such poor sea legs, he threatened to sink any wherry they took. They would mingle with the traffic on the approach road, cross the bridge, and still be in Guildhall within the half hour.

As they walked, they talked, both keeping a weather eye out for anyone who might hear more than a snippet of their hushed conversation, the Bishop's spies were everywhere. Cecil was annoyed to hear an old song about his old enemy, the Earl of Essex, being sung by minstrels close to the bridge. Equally annoying was the amount of coins they had collected from singing. The song lamenting Cecil's deposition of the popular earl had become even more popular in the years after his execution.

" 'All you that cry, 'Oh, hone', 'oh hone', 'Come now and sing oh Lord with me', 'For why our jewel is from us gone', 'The valiant knight of chivalry', 'Little Cecil trips up and down', 'He rules both Court and Crown', 'With his brother Burghley clown', 'In his great fox-furred gown', 'With the long proclamation', 'He swore he saved the town', 'Is it not likely?' "

Cecil pushed Markham on in case he should be recognised by the minstrels, it was bad enough being sung about, he did not want to be sneered at. Ever since Essex had been ousted from the Elizabethan Court and hung for treason, the song had been sung.

For years, Cecil had been forced to listen to the song about him and his elder brother, Thomas, who had inherited the family title. It was a hateful song and Cecil was irked by it, Essex had been vain, foolish, and above all wrong. His brother, Lord Burghley, was no clown, not as bright as he, but then he, Robert, did rule over the Court, the Crown and a good deal of other places and he had saved the Crown on many occasions and there was no mistake about it. Thomas his brother was a politician, a brave soldier, President of the Council of the North and Lord Lieutenant of Yorkshire, as well as being made 'Knight of the Garter' during the reign of Elizabeth.

"I did save the town and my proclamation was shorter than it should have been," complained Cecil, trying to illicit sympathy from his companion, quite forgetting, or, perhaps more accurately, caring that Markham and Essex were firm friends who had fought together in Ireland. "Why do they still worship that fool? He was a dullard, he only succeeded in getting in my way; his only other success was to let Tyrone take over Ireland," hissed Cecil angrily pulling Markham closer to him so he could be heard by his confidant but not overheard, Markham almost toppled over contorting himself in order to stoop to Cecil's level.

"Never mind Essex, we cannot bring back the Queen and we cannot bring back her favourite, all that matters now is that you are now James's trusted lieutenant," whispered Markham reassuringly in his ear, walking slowly and wanting to straighten up, it looked like he was drunk and his smaller friend was supporting him.

"Drake and Essex cost the crown over £100,000, I cannot afford those figures under James; I must fight the influence of his favourites, those Scots who mistrust me and whom I mistrust. Yet, they are too close to him. We need a calamity to underpin our court society. If I deliver the King from disaster, he will have to favour me over all his other favourites!" Cecil cried, suddenly releasing Markham and forging ahead through the crowd, seeing a gap opening up and filling the space. The surge of people on the road approaching the bridge was quite staggering and Cecil did not intend to be victim to the crush.

He wondered how so many people could fit into such a narrow space and how there was a flow of people north and south, he felt sure that a concerted effort by one of the tidal streams would force the other stream of people back across the bridge from whence they came.

"What disaster?" cried Markham unembarrassed, it was a time of disaster and strife, his cry was unremarkable in London where all manner of dangers lurked.

There were disasters all the time: goods spilt from a wagon; a baker dropping his bread basket; a werry-man drowning; theft by footpads and cut-purses, the odd fight between friends, or between punks and customers, verbal and physical.

"A truly dangerous event!" Cecil said to the back of the group of French pilgrims who seemed to inexplicably crossing London Bridge without paying due respect to the Christian Martyrs who dangled from the bridge.

There was no recognition of Thomas More or any of the other numerous Catholic martyrs. They just added to the milling throng that oozed over the bridge, Cecil marvelled at how shops did any trade with the mass of people rushing by. He wondered why these pilgrims were in London; there were plenty of shrines in their own lands, Conques for one, or Mont Saint Michel.

In Spain where the weather was better, there was Santiago de Compostela, in England, Bishop's Waltham was on the other side of the city to the southwest, if they had come in at Dover and had been to Canterbury it would have been better to avoid the city but then there were many shrines and churches in the capital, they must have been tempted. They seemed to be unable to walk and talk, milling about in the road approaching the bridge over the Thames, chatting excitedly, not a care in the world, especially for others, not very Christian, thought Cecil wryly. Whatever their origin, whatever their destination, they were in the way; Cecil wished he had taken the wherry boat, then looked up at Markham and remembered why he had not, the last time they had crossed Markham had almost sunk the boat.

"Who will be your patsy?" asked Markham in awe at Cecil's audacious plan, he has heard the raised French voices and had felt the breath from a horse behind. A drover called for his horse to slow. It was unnecessary, as Markham rushed to Cecil's side to hear the answer.

"I have the perfect patsy, Percy, his family is back under the grill after I persuaded Henry Carey to commission a history of Henry IV," Cecil replied. He was often stirring up mischief, old plays were brought back, or new plays commissioned, in order to irritate, infuriate or undermine influential people. He could not help smiling at the thought of his masterstroke, he really did remind himself of Machiavelli, at times, he felt.

Cecil had considered many means to win James fealty but only a direct threat to his life would win his undying friendship. He had seen that with the dullard, Ramsay, who had saved the King from an assassin's knife. Cecil heard another rhyme as they finally were swept on to the bridge approach; he reflected what a terrible idea it had been to walk but the rhyme he heard from people working below the bridge heartened him.

"'The lion and the unicorn were fighting for the Crown', 'The lion beat the unicorn all around the town'; 'Some gave them white bread, and some gave them brown'; 'Some gave them plum cake and drummed them out of town'."

Cecil smiled with satisfaction when he heard them chanting.

"You see the king is popular, we just need to keep him so!" Cecil cried happily.

Markham knew the King was not very popular amongst many of his people. They walked to the bridge with the unwritten agreement that only two sentences would be spoken in twenty paces as they passed through the street towards London Bridge.

They both looked up instinctively at the tower of the southern gatehouse on top of which, mounted on pikes, were the severed and tarred heads of over thirty traitors and those executed by the Tudor kings and Queens. Markham could not see Thomas Cromwell, John Fisher or Thomas More but he knew they were there, a reminder of the King's power. The bridge was built of stone and at eight hundred feet long, it took time to cross, which allowed them to continue their conversation as they jostled with the carts, barrows and hawkers returning home to villages beyond the city walls. There were twenty stone piers, thirty foot wide and sixty feet high. Cecil did not like heights. Looking out of the window at Whitehall made him feel quite queasy. So he was glad all the shops, stalls and dwellings blocked out the view over the side of the bridge.

"Henry the Fourth?" wondered Markham; he had heard how the play had upset everyone and been the downfall of Essex.

"Indeed, why not? It talks of revolt."

"I was told that Shakespeare presented the play to the Lord Chamberlain not that it was requested by him," Markham argued.

"But that is indeed what I wanted. We have encouraged everyone to believe that the Papists endanger the Commonwealth while Percy and the Dukes in the disloyal north get hotter and hotter in the flames of scrutiny."

"Not more torture?"

"Perhaps, rebels then, perhaps, rebels now! Now, they are Catholic rebels. Sometimes this is all too easy. History repeats itself, fear breeds fear," Cecil noted proudly. He had stirred up a wasps' nest, the basis of division, creating a climate of fear; 'divide and conquer, provide a bulwark against danger and you will prosper' might well have been his motto, if it had not been so long and complicated.

Cecil was entitled to be proud, Walsingham had taught him well, but he had been groomed by his father and his natural cunning and intelligence had been thoroughly nurtured. James had allowed himself to be surrounded by flattering fools, who he had to indulge like children. Cecil, on the other hand, was a sharp politician much more useful than a disparate group of good looking nobles gathered together through nepotism.

The nobles had been kept in check by maintaining the power of the church, in particular the bishops in the House of Lords. As the richest and largest landowners in the country, they provided a powerful influence over what laws were passed by the Upper House. Besides his confidence in the support he had from the bishops, he also knew that he was one of the most experienced and loyal members of King James's inner circle. He was the giant of the Privy Council and that fact had reassured the King, allowing Cecil to maintain his influence. There was no brighter talent than Cecil in the whole kingdom.

"Will only Percy and his family be accused?" Markham wondered aloud.

"We have the names. Those involved in the Essex Rebellion," replied Cecil, his voice seemed detached.

Markham was one such rebel and he almost stopped dead in his tracks but for an egg seller, a huge lady with a chicken in a cage, prodded him in the back and told him to get a move on. He fell in behind a cart with empty wicker cages on its bed, goose and duck feathers were scattered all over the boarded floor.

"But, that was another reign," Markham argued.

"1601 was only three years ago, their treachery against the Crown may have grown," warned Cecil menacingly, Markham felt a chill run up his spine.

"You know that I am loyal to the Crown, loyal to the State!" Markham insisted passionately.

"Your freedom rests on my favour alone. We have been aware, for some time, of the names of many of those who are at the forefront of the Catholic cause."

"Surely, they have all sworn allegiance to James. We are still hoping he will yet suspend Recusants' fines, most Catholics are loyal to the king; they are acutely aware that his mother was a *Roman*."

"I insisted that they should be maintained, he ignored me; at Hampton Court."

"But the fines do not work," complained Markham, "very few people pay them."

"I will persuade the King that he needs the money from the fines and he needs to keep the Catholics in check."

"So we are still to be treated poorly?" asked Markham softly. His face was flushed with anger; he hated the injustice of intolerance yet if he wanted his family to be left alone, he could do nothing about it.

"It is the way life is," Cecil explained gently. He was not a religious man but he had been bought up in a religion.

"Second to the Church of England, come the Puritans and last come the Catholics and the Jews! Why are we the lowest of the low? The Jews are not persecuted, yet we are. Catholics are treated as dirt on the State's shoes."

"I will protect you and ensure that you are safe!" Cecil assured him kindly. "Just do exactly as I bid."

"Who will lead the Catholics?"

"Robert Catesby, the handsome young gentleman, will become the leader of the gunpowder plan."

Markham looked at Cecil in disbelief.

"You know he is a friend of mine?"

"I do!"

"This to ensure that Essex's friends and supporters cannot unseat you from power?"

"Those very friends and supporters, and the infuriating Francis Bacon, who would like to usurp my power if he were given the chance."

"But the Catholics are easier to remove from your path, is that why you chose us?"

"Precisely, why do you think that I released you and pardoned some of the others? Essex, the fool, tried to defy me but he was executed for treason; that was my doing."

"My God, you are heartless."

"The fact that so many of you survived any purge was no mistake. My purpose was to ensnare even more of you and cut out the canker from our common weal."

"We were used as part of your greater plan?" Markham was incredulous.

He knew that Cecil was cunning but he had not realised with what precision and planning he had set up the Catholic nobles. First, he engineered that all Catholics should side with Essex in a political plot. Then, the Main and Bye plots, were used to discredit the Catholics, in general. All three were used as proof of the Catholics disloyalty, whereas their involvement had, in fact, been incidental or actively encouraged by Cecil and his people. Markham decided that Cecil's Machiavellian ways were truly stunning.

"You fools fell into my trap and now I have you where I want you. Did you think your amateurish attempts at gaining power would not be thwarted by my father's and Walsingham's efforts and then the efforts of myself. Did you think the Catholics would ever be allowed back in to share power after Mary Tudor's behaviour to those Calvinists loyal to Henry?"

As Cecil stopped and held Markham's arm, the crowd passed around them as if they were cataracts in a fast moving stream.

"Now, I see it all! Of course there is more, let me think," he paused as he gathered his thoughts. "The Catholics were so relieved when James came to the throne. We believed that the son of a Catholic monarch would surely provide a promise of greater toleration and yet you have always encouraged him to institute even harsher 'Recusant' fines. Was it to bait the Catholic nobility or for the money raised?"

"The money was a consideration of course; remember I am still negotiating a peace treaty with Spain, the components of which were trade deals."

That made him think, the war had been expensive and had not helped the lot of the Catholics in England; peace with Spain would improve everyone's life, it would improve trade, which had reduced considerably between the two countries during the conflict.

"I had not realised."

"All the merchants care about is money, politics is not something they are paid to care about. Our friends across the water in the City of London did not and do not care about the politics in the City of Westminster."

"Surely, they do!"

"They only care about trade, they are tolerant, they deal with Calvinists, Jews, Lutherans, Moors and Orientals with all their different faiths."

"What a wonderful situation that would be if the State behaved in that way."

"I have heard it repeated that they even deal with Catholics. That is the future not you and your pathetic factions."

"So you intend to fabricate a plot to stop the Spanish allying with the Catholics."

"The wheels are in motion."

252

"You must stop them!"

"You should know, as a soldier, a nation needs peace and not civil war; the merchants need trade abroad, to make friends, not enemies. The State comes first, all other matters are nought."

"Why the Catholics?"

"What do you think?"

"You perceive them as a danger? They are a threat? That is truly ridiculous."

"Why not choose the Catholics? Papists have caused enough problems for the State, haven't you; Thomas More, blocking the divorce; rebellion in all sorts of places, causing trouble alongside the Puritans, the list is endless."

"Catholics have been persecuted and yet we have been loyal to the Crown, Essex only wanted his monopoly returned to him. He wasn't even Catholic, only some of his friends were, like myself, Percy and Catesby."

"Stop baulking; your friends did nothing to save you from execution. Not one of them petitioned for your release or for you to be granted clemency. I saved you from hanging, remember that, you are my man first, a Catholic second. I will be sending you back abroad to Flanders so you will not be involved. We still have a military presence in the Lowlands. There is still much to be settled abroad by soldiers like you."

"You want me to continue monitoring the activities of the Jesuits and the Spanish in the Netherlands, so be it. Let me see, your spies are everywhere; I take it, they are abroad, too. I will be sent with one of your servants, Tom Thompson, I suppose, to keep me in check."

"Exactly; first, however, I expect you to get this plot going. I want you to light the spark of interest; my men will do the rest. We'll recruit '*Kate's Bee*' and he'll produce a hive of activity."

"Then, I can disappear abroad."

"I am saving your life; otherwise you will hang with the others. It is your choice."

"Who will be your patsy?"

"My people have already found a drifter down at the dock that will help us."

"What ss he a drunken sailor or a fervent Humanist?"

It was Markham's attempt at a joke. Tudor Humanism was still all the rage in the city and had been ever since the wider dissemination of the printed works of Erasmus and Thomas More my secret presses spreading the word. It had been a slow process.

"Now, now, no need for flimb, flamb, he is a soldier like you; a man called Guido Forcanessi. He's an Italian."

"And what are you going to get him to do?"

"Why, he will blow up the palace of Westminster, of course."

Markham stopped walking and stared at Cecil's back.

Cecil continued his progress before realising he was no longer accompanied. He turned back to face the petrified Markham; he was frozen to the spot. The two men faced each other, standing in the thoroughfare that led north from the bridge. People passed them as if they were water moving around a stone in a fast moving river.

Cecil waited for the silence to be filled by Markham, it seemed like an eternity; the more time that elapsed the greater, the distance seemed to grow between them, a very uncivil servant of the Crown and a good man who had been in the wrong place at the wrong time, too often. Markham wondered if he would ever claw himself out of the hole that had been created for him. It seemed unlikely.

"That means killing members of the government," he whispered, delivering the words like a punch, a long powerful ejaculation of sound.

He felt as if someone had just told him calamitous news; he felt as if someone had struck him. There was a dull ache in the pit of his stomach.

"And the king when he enters parliament to open it," Cecil noted with alarming callousness.

"But the King will have to recall parliament for that to happen," Markham said, still stunned.

"I will advise him to do so," Cecil said cunningly.

"What will that gain?" Markham asked, still trying to fathom the enormity of what he had been told.

"Absolutely nothing if it succeeds, panic and mayhem, but plenty if the plot is discovered," Cecil admitted casually.

"I cannot go along with this; it will result in the persecution of every Catholic in the land," Markham remonstrated with resolve, his strength returning as a fighter recovers from an almost debilitating blow.

"Keep quiet or I will carry out that deferred execution, now," warned Cecil menacingly.

"What if I were to run you through, instead, right here, right now?" asked Markham, half convinced that it was the only sane course left to him.

"You know I keep diaries, you know my men would pursue you until they found you and killed you; you love life too much. Do you think I would be doing this if there was another option?" Cecil replied, fury in his voice and his bluish-green eyes. He had expected a similar reaction; he had been prepared; he had chastised Markham as if he were a strict father.

Cecil continued on their journey through the crowd; Markham had no choice but to follow Cecil, sidling up to his shoulder in order to speak to him.

"Of course not but the Puritans are the troublemakers!" replied Markham like a scolded wilful child.

"The Puritans are causing all the trouble at the moment," explained Cecil, patient, now that he had won the higher ground, he continued in a less strict tone, now the elucidating barrister convincing a sceptical court.

"They always have!" complained Markham.

"They are now our greatest threat, strangely, although they are of the same persuasion. They stir up trouble and sow dissent amongst the people, never a good thing. James is spending too much on buildings and functions; we need to protect the State; we are like a boat surrounded by ice floes in the Baltic Sea. We are fending off floes in too many directions our boat will be crushed."

"Why not go for Bacon?" Markham asked.

This time he caught Cecil's arm and forced him to stop walking,

"Dear Francis, my cousin, what are you thinking?"
Cecil smiled at him, removing the arm and continuing as if nothing had happened, Markham was again forced to catch up with him. "Does he present a problem, I am unaware of such."

"Everyone knows he walks in your shadow waiting to take over the mantle once you show any weakness or should you lose favour with the King."

Markham stared seriously into Cecil's eyes, challenging him, trying to wipe away the smile that was visible from the corner of Cecil's mouth.

"Go for Bacon?"

Cecil laughed aloud.

"Why not?" Markham sighed.

"And end up with egg on my face? He is far too clever and sly, never fear your Bacon will fry, my status after the plot will be sky high, and then, like Icarus, without wings, he will see that he cannot fly; if he tries to fly too close to the sun, his fat will fry!"

"So you bide your time?" Markham added.

"Yes, I will, unless, he deigns to show his hand, first, which I doubt. He will need just cause to clash with me and I give him none. He knows it is so."

Markham could not defeat this elfin goblin and his machinations; he valued his life too much, loved his family, who would inevitably suffer, too, dearly; he had cheated death often enough to value his life above all else. He was defeated before battle commenced. He was like a chess player who in his first three moves has seen that checkmate was inevitable. He was no match for Cecil intellect or for his convoluted schemes; all he had to do was flip his king onto its side and show that he had resigned, a victim to 'fool's mate'.

"Where are we going?" he asked as if in a trance, he was the subject and Cecil was his king, absolute.

"To Hoxton, it's such a charming place," breathed Cecil in his habitual arrogant manner.

"A little late for archery practice; it will be too dark to see the arrow's fletch let alone the target," Markham jested, the gallows humour, a mark of troubled times.

"Not to archer but to an arch enemy. William Parker, Lord Monteagle, a familiar face to you, being involved with your friends in the Babington Plot was he not?" Cecil asked, a smile playing on his lips.

He was an expert at finding the weak spot in a man's armour, at discovering the Achilles' heel of those in his circle. Bacon might have said: "Knowledge is power," but it was Cecil who knew *what* knowledge would give him power. The men walked in silence from that point, Cecil was deep in thought, rehearsing how he would act and considering exactly what he would say on arrival at Parker's house. Markham, on the other hand, began to wonder whether he would survive the machinations that Cecil had set in motion.

Cecil was about to recruit the first of the necessary nobles who would help him hatch his plot. It was a true piece of genius and it needed careful planning. It would be two years or thereabouts until Monteagle would be called upon again to do his service, but like any successful gardener, Cecil knew the ground had to be prepared before the seed could be planted and then only careful nurturing would produce the perfect plant and with even greater care and attention, the plant would bear the desired fruit.

Cecil did not mind, it was the preparation, he knew, that reaped the rewards. He planned the work and worked the plan, sowed the seed and reaped the harvest and that was the key to his success; he was a consistent and constant gardener and his plots bore much fruit.

Chapter 11 – The letter – 26th October 1605

Almost two years after Cecil's first visit, he returned to Monteagle's house.

Hoxton in the light was a wonderful part of the outskirts of London. The residence of William Parker, Lord Monteagle was large and comfortable. It was to this door that one of Cecil's boy runners delivered a letter and received a whole penny for his efforts from Parker and the sum matched by Cecil, as promised, on his return. The messenger had lied when he had told Parker that he did not know the identity of either the scribe or the sender.

When the messenger gave his report, he confessed to Cecil proudly, that he had left Parker scratching his head at such a strange anonymous missive. He was evidently puzzled by this highly unusual delivery and Cecil had smiled, at the time, to think how Parker would feel once he had read the warning letter that he had written. Normally, messengers were given the name of the sender often to gain entry to the recipient's house. No one wanted boys claiming to be delivering messages trooping through the houses.

The letter, as Cecil intended, was cryptic but not too cryptic; its meaning would be easily understood by a king who feared being stabbed, and was wary of being blown up by gunpowder. James had been brought up on stories of people being murdered using both stabbing and explosion; he was fearful almost to the state of distraction, having been almost assassinated already in Scotland.

Parker stood in his parlour overlooking the other fine houses; he was standing as straight as string on a plumb-line and was just as thin. He wore a wonderful peacock green doublet and black silk hose as black as tar, his suede shoes were moleskin black, too. He was a fashionable dresser, buying only the finest clothes, as all nobles should, in his view.

Parker read aloud the sentence that warned him to stay away from the opening of Parliament. He thought he could decipher the meaning but his mind kept saying that it was impossible for a blow to be struck at Parliament; he reread the salient section again to make sure. No matter how he read the letter, he could not be sure exactly what it might refer to in this case.

The only possible blow that he could think of was blow up, yet that could not be right. An explosion, yet unseen only a canon could provide such a blow or gunpowder, perhaps. He decided to read the letter again. It all seemed impossible.

"Yet I say they shall receive a terrible blow, the Parliament, and yet they shall not see who hurts them," he read aloud several times in the hope that repetition would make the meaning clearer and that he could puzzle out the strange riddle. Parker liked clarity and order not subterfuge and confusion. He looked out at the moats of the manor houses that housed ambassadors and Courtiers like him.

"A blow," he said to himself, "blow, wind; blow up, explode; a blow, a punch!"

None of them made sense but those were the only blows that came to mind. Was there to be a great storm? That could not be predicted so far hence; blow up, how could anyone blow up the Houses of Parliament? No cannon could be concealed, there was no high ground where a canon could be placed; bombardiers would be seen and would soon be dispatched by soldiers; no gunpowder could be left there in the Palace of Westminster, it was too well defended. The ground thereabouts and the precincts were patrolled and guarded.

That left blow as in 'struck'. Was a revolution planned? Were the Lords to be struck by terrible blows, beaten by the mob? Again, there were guards, seasoned soldiers, all fully armed, they would provide protection but the mob would be visible. Perhaps it was apocryphal; maybe metaphorical, the only danger he perceived was that the Puritans were going to take over.

"That would be a blow but not a surprise, everyone seemed to be promoting the Puritan cause; it was as fashionable as a Scottish accent at Court!" he complained aloud.

The more he spoke to himself about it, the more mystifying it became. That morning he had celebrated mass in the chapel of the Portuguese Ambassador who lived nearby and he seemed not to have a care in the world until the letter arrived. Taking his dog for a walk, to clear his mind, seemed the best course of action, along the fields to the north used for archery practice and where several duels had been fought.

He wanted to talk to his friend Ben Jonson but he was performing a play in town. Jonson would know what to do; he would soothe Parker's fears as only old friends could. They had both been in trouble together before, after fighting in Ireland alongside the Earl of Essex, Parker had taken part in the Earl's unsuccessful march of protest through London in 1601 and for his pains he had been punished by imprisonment plus a fine of £8,000.

Jonson had been equally roundly abused; his satires like The Poetaster, poking fun at Dekker and Marston, fellow playwrights, might have passed unnoticed if it had not also attacked lawyers and soldiers and his play *Sejanus* had been censored and criticised by the authorities as 'seditious and full of Popery'. Not satisfied with attracting attention of censors and Cecil, he had spent part of 1604 in prison for his criticism of King James's policy in Scotland.

William Parker, 4th Baron Monteagle, was tall thin and thirty years of age, an experienced soldier quite wise enough for his years but he wondered what the explanation for the strange note might be. Just as he slipped the letter into the draw of his escritoire and closed the lid, someone outside pulled on the bell. The sound startled him. One of his servants knocked on the door and entered.

"A gentleman, John Johnson to see you," he announced.

"Show him in, thank you," instructed Parker, straightening and smiling at his loyal servant despite the fear that gripped him.

Even after two years, more or less, he recognised the coded word, which announced the arrival of the harbinger of mischief and subterfuge. Robert Cecil, now Viscount Cranbourne, strode into the room, gave the servant his hat and gloves, and then untied the knot that held his cape in place. The servant placed the hat and gloves on the side table and lifted the heavy cloak off Cecil's shoulders before making a display of, carefully, gathering up Cecil's belongings, draping the cloak on one arm, picking up the gloves and laying them neatly on top of the cloak and finally placing the hat at the top of the pile. He pretended not to notice Cecil's small stature and his deformity. In return, Cecil thanked him; the servant bowed to both men and left the room, closing the door tightly behind him. His job as a servant of a prominent Catholic in uncertain times was to be discreet at all times and to leave his master to discuss matters in private.

Cecil peered around Monteagle's front room, noticing the dark stained wood panelling that reached from the floor to the ceiling, a wonderful work of wainscoting; the mouldings on the white plaster ceiling overhead; the dark black wooden floors of thick ship's planks, polished to a dull sheen not buffed to a shine, which would have made the surface slippery; it was a pleasing room of substantial size. Cecil seemed to be lingering over the detail in order to establish the fact that losing all this would be a terrible thing. He seemed to admire and treasure everything he saw, encouraging Monteagle to do the same. Further, he observed the brown, tiled bricks that surrounded the fireplace; the mantelpiece with a small shelf for the bell; and a metal fireguard before the steel grate to stop smuts and embers falling into the room.

There were four fashionable, Jacobean, high backed chairs with scrolled legs with a cane spine running up through them; a cushioned seat, covered in brown leather, held in place by studs on the frame; a scroll-legged table, which was more square than rectangular. In the grate was a fresh fire, flames flickered over burning kindling with thick logs just catching, even though it was so small, it warmed the room, taking the chill from the morning.

There were wicker baskets on either side of the mantelpiece, one with coal, one with wood. To burn both fuels meant wealth; coal was abundant but difficult to transport, shipped from Newcastle; firewood precious and expensive because it was used for building materials. One fuel was harvested from the forests beyond the fields; the other dug out from open cast mines in the northeast, hence its expense. Cecil sniffed the air approvingly; the room had been sprayed with a subtle scent to mask any odours, a sign of good taste and of noble husbandry. He cleared his throat before speaking.

"Good morning, Lord Monteagle."

"Good morning, sir," replied Parker unsure whether to call Cecil by his title or by his pseudonym. Without realising, Monteagle's mind went back to the November night in 1603; it was the fifteenth, almost two years ago.

"Who is the letter from?" asked Cecil obsequiously as a friend might. He was a diplomat first.

He knew that Parker would not deny receiving it; he would assume that Cecil's spies were watching his house and those of all the other leading Catholics. They would have seen the letter delivered.

"I have no idea," replied Parker uneasily.

This was an uncomfortable situation, an unexpected letter followed by a visit from one of the most powerful men in the Privy Council, if not the land. Cecil was the Secretary of State and could sign his death warrant immediately, then fabricate a case against him. Parker knew that, his face became flushed; he had done nothing wrong, except for, perhaps, attending the mass, having Catholic friends and having an obviously incriminating letter of such importance that it would merit the arrival of Cecil himself. It was like the arrival of King James himself, provide the right answers or he might hear the cry: 'Off with his head'. He was so attached to his head, his home, and his family, very much in that order. Cecil would receive the best attention.

"Perhaps from Francis Tresham?" Cecil ventured helpfully.

"Perhaps," agreed Monteagle pretending to consider the suggestion but in reality worrying for the fate of poor Francis but not enough to detract from his concern about himself.

"Perhaps from me; to save your life," suggested Cecil casually; he raised an eyebrow quizzically to complete the look.

"What would you have me do?" he asked immediately, realising in vivid detail the enormity of his task and the complexity of the scheme that a clever mind had devised, credible lies woven into half-truths.

What a web Cecil had weaved; suddenly it occurred to him, in all its horrific glory, that Cecil had hatched a plan of such enormity and cunning that the world might never see such superb subterfuge again. Then, he realised with a shock that robbed his face of all colour that he was a vital link in the chain. Caught in a snare, he could not escape, he had no choice but to agree to Cecil's terms or lose his head. He was reminded of Shakespeare: 'what a web we weave when we first practise to deceive'.

"Read the letter at your supper tonight; make sure you invite Ben Jonson," Cecil commanded imperiously; he found that such a tone had surprising results and wondered why so few people practised addressing people in such a manner. All those Caesars had got their way.

"He is town rehearsing his play," complained Monteagle nervously, Cecil's demands were quite ridiculous and unreasonable at times, he checked himself from asking: 'who does he think he is?'

As everyone knew, he was the most powerful man in England.

"Not tonight," Cecil assured him confidently.

"You have influence over him," gasped Monteagle, the colour draining from his face.

He was pleased they were not drinking or eating, as Cecil would have seen his hands tremble.

"I am Robert Cecil, protégé of Walsingham and Lord Burghley," Cecil announced defiantly, before asking Monteagle clearly: "What did you expect?"

"I had no idea your influence spread so wide and so deep," Monteagle admitted.

The fact that Cecil controlled even dissidents amazed him; so, he further conjectured that there could be truth in the rumour of Cecil's involvement in Philip Marlowe's death, the man was incredible, literally. His thoughts were disturbed by Cecil's next chilling announcement.

"Of course, he has been in trouble with the Crown over his plays; some of the dialogue is treasonable. The Privy Council questioned him over his play Sejanus; remember the play about corruption in the Roman Empire."

"I saw the play, but I had no idea he was a confidante of yours."

"Who do you think got him such a lenient sentence for murdering Spenser?"

"It was a duel and Spenser had a longer sword than Jonson; surely it was self-defence."

"Who do you think gave Spenser that advantage? I supplied the longer sword to give Spenser the upper hand, a longer thrust, he was my man."

"I see, Jonson was producing seditious plays and you sent Spenser to dispense with him and thus silence the troublesome playwright."

"It is you who makes that assumption."

Both men stared at each other coldly.

"When Spenser was dispensed with, you replaced him with Jonson and, now, you use his surname as your pseudonym."

Cecil smiled.

"As I say you make connections with consummate ease. I can neither admit nor deny your allegations but I do admire your train of thought. However, you can make any connections for yourself if you wish."

"So, you admit that you tried to have Jonson murdered, the plan backfired and so you turned him into your own spy. You offered him his life for his fealty."

"You catch on quickly; just like a fletch snagging on a bow string, excellent work but such seditious slander would not pass beyond these four walls."

Parker felt faint, the enormity of his task and the ramifications of his actions weighed heavily on his shoulders. It was also clear that Cecil's influence pervaded every corner of the court and every strata of society, he really was impossible to defy, he was the master spy of master spies.

"You make yourself abundantly clear; I am far too fond of my neck and my innards to risk them in that hazard. What are my instructions?" he asked, knowing that he had no choice but to acquiesce; he had to think of his family, his wife, his daughter; his three sons and, of course, his survival.

"You will have Jonson over for supper and you will read the letter aloud to your guests, you will inform them that you have only just received the letter and it baffles you. Further, you will advise them to avoid the opening of Parliament."

"Your will be done."

"Jonson will report to me, I need him seated close to you at supper, is that clear?"

"Of course, I will obey your instructions; you know I have no choice. Nothing has changed since our agreement that November night two years ago."

"I am glad to hear it and I assume you remember the caveats we put in place," said Cecil, a nod of affirmation allowed him to feel reassured.

"Of course," Monteagle replied, he had no choice but to agree. Cecil reflected on how well his plan was playing out, splendidly, in his view.

"Tomorrow, bring the letter to me, at Whitehall. Together we will visit the King; we will let him decipher it. He should have no difficulty interpreting it after the explosions at Kirk O'Field."

"Two barrels of gun powder placed in the room under Lord Darnley's sleeping quarters," Parker added, he was familiar with the history.

"The mystery was why he and his valet, Taylour, were found outside of the estate," said Cecil, smiling, he wondered how much Parker really knew.

"And beside them were a cloak, a dagger, a chair, and a coat," Parker continued. That had been part of the official reports that were distributed freely at that time; both far and wide.

"How curious, what could it mean?" wondered Cecil.

"But before your time!" argued Parker. "It was Walsingham in charge of State chicanery."

"Very cloak and dagger," agreed Cecil, stroking his chin.

"A mystery?" announced Parker, seemingly defeated by events beyond his capability of reasoning.

"Surely, Walsingham's influence," Cecil suggested knowing-full-well that he was right; he had read the transcripts in the official records.

Cecil always found that time was never wasted in research.

"Why so?" asked Parker.

He folded his arms.

"You do not know?"

"I assure you, I do not, please explain."

"By all means."

Cecil was always happy to have the floor.

"Thank you," his host said politely.

"It is obvious."

"Not to me."

"His signature is all over the occasion; the cloak and the dagger, a sign of his secretive measures, the chair, representing the seat of power and the coat the symbol for a turncoat, obviously he did not follow Walsingham's wishes," recited Cecil from memory. He had read those documents so many times.

"Very grim work," decided Parker, shivering noticeably. "It was a warning to us all, perhaps!"

"Perhaps, but secrets are secrets, your actions tonight and tomorrow will ensure your safety and that of your family," explained Cecil reassuringly.

"You guarantee it, on your word," challenged Parker; he needed Cecil's assurance because Cecil was renowned for his word being his bond.

Parker really had no choice but to put himself in the hands of the man who had so far guaranteed his freedom, despite that, he still wanted Cecil's word to seal their deal, he knew Cecil would keep his word once it was given.

"That action will save your life; I will protect you and your family. Your wife Elizabeth and all your children will be safe. You have my word and you know that once given, I keep my word."

"Thank you."

"You are loyal to King James."

"I have paid for my mistake in backing Essex. You told the exact payment last time we met. "

"Yes imprisonment and an £8,000 fine, I seem to recall; I take it that, now, your family is thriving and you do not wish to be re-imprisoned."

"All is well and I will do what you ask."

"I am relieved and take my leave, remember: 'trouble comes not in single spies but in battalions'."

"Indeed, 'sorrows come that way'; I appreciate what you say. Mark you I am familiar too with the 'tide in the affairs of men, which, taken at the flood, leads on to fortune; omitted, all the voyage of their life is bound in shallows and in miseries'."

"Wise words from *the Bard* but remember: 'this above all: to thine own self, be true, and it must follow, as the night the day, thou canst not then be false to any man'."

"Farewell, 'my blessings season this in thee! That is how it ends'."

"We understand each other perfectly, Shakespeare and each other, we understand him and ourselves, how fortunate we are, we happy few, we band of brothers."

"You are a cunning man, rather an ally than an adversary. These are times of adversity, 'troubled times, scarce a day goes by when a king does not lose his crown'. If life is a game of tennis, I would rather be on your side of the net."

"You are far too kind," Cecil breathed dramatically, leaving the troubled Lord Monteagle puzzled as to whether he was being genuine or ironic in his remarks. The phrase had not sounded sarcastic and yet he was not sure.

"I will send for your cape, wish you good day and see you tomorrow."

"All three, lucky me," said Cecil, a smile playing at his lips. He was pleased with himself and more so when Monteagle rewarded him with a grim-faced half smile.

Both men knew that their *die was cast* and they were bound by the actions that were required of them. Cecil watched Monteagle pick up a small bell and ring for his servant; Cecil wondered whether he could adopt the Latin for the phrase as his motto, 'iacta alea est', 'the die is cast'. As he considered this, his cape was brought in and placed gently on his shoulders and his hat and gloves handed to him; he wished both men a good day and followed the servant as he led him to the front door where he put on his hat and gloves. The die was cast, the plot was hatched; there was no going back.

Chapter 12 - The Priest – April 1604

The drawing room in John Cage's house was warm, due, in the most part, to a roaring fire and a brazier full of hot coals. It was similar to the parlour at Parker's house, wainscoting in dark wood, plaster ceiling painted white and floorboards made of ship's timber. It was the way fashionable houses of fashionable people were furnished. The only difference was it was much warmer. Cage hated the cold and he had terrible pain in his joints when it was damp. The stranger, who stood near the door, waited for the servant to leave and then listened to the sound of the servant's footsteps passing through the hall; his guest seemed reticent.

Cage admired the stranger's garb, he was dressed in fine clothes, and he had the bearing of a gentleman. It was unusual for someone to call so early after breakfast but the host knew his guest would explain his presence. Perhaps an invitation to hunt at Knightsbridge or on the Heath at Hampstead, there was also good hunting to be had in Clapham; though he preferred Sussex to Surrey, less woods more downs. He would want something in return of course, patronage was the way the world worked, Cage reflected dispassionately. He wryly supposed something for something was better than something for nothing. After introductions, they sat and talked, they drank *sack* served with fresh *native* oysters. Cage could always eat more oysters, they were so juicy, and without bread, hardly filling at all; his guest looked hungry.

He was pleasant enough and they had discussed the latest plays and traded a few hunting stories. The bread with which the oysters were served disappeared with surprising alacrity, his guest was the only one eating it, but he wolfed it down as if he had not eaten for days. Cage admired a man with appetite but his guest was devouring oyster and bread as fast as they could be served. Cage had only managed a few oysters himself before the dozen were demolished.

Twice he had to ring the bell for his butler and moved it from the mantelpiece to the table beside him. It was not good for Cage's digestion to be leaping up every time the stranger ate half a dozen oysters. Again, his guest waited until he was satisfied that the servant was not listening before continuing their conversation. He could have been more subtle thought Cage, just wanting his uninvited guest to say what his business was as it was obvious that there was something confidential the visitor needed to share with him, it certainly was not the oysters.

Cage wondered whether Robert Cecil or Francis Bacon had sent him. Everyone was wary of Cecil, wary of his power and influence. He would only send the finest of gentlemen as an ambassador, of that he was sure. The man chewed his last mouthful as Cage watched, and then he swallowed hard, moved to the edge of his chair and leaning forward, he spoke.

"I am from the Society of Jesus help me," pleaded the priest, sitting further forward still and placing his hands together in prayer. It looked like he was going to slip off the chair and onto to his knees to beg for mercy or pray for deliverance. He was yet another naive cleric from the seminary in Douai.

"We cannot give you the refuge you seek; I have a family," he asserted firmly. He was not going to harbour a priest again; he had done enough. It was someone else's turn.

"May I remind you that your duty is to God above all men and I am his representative on earth?" the priest stated, steel in his voice, if he could not appeal to this man's pity, he would bully him.

"No wonder the Protestants want to have a direct connection with God through the bible and cut you out of their worship," complained Cage looking down at the highly polished dark wood table, black and shiny; the almost empty pewter plate on the edge like the priest.

"That is bordering on blasphemy!" cried the priest accusingly.

He had never been spoken to in such a way.

"Better blasphemy than penury; I have my family to think of," argued Cage. "The fines for harbouring a priest will ruin me; I have hidden dozens of priests already, I must think of my wife and children."

"I know that but I have my flock," countered the priest, hoping that this would appease him.
"Without being disrespectful how could you know what having a family is like; sheep go to slaughter that is not the destiny that I wish for my sons and daughters. Why did you come here? Why didn't you stay in France?"

"The Pope commands us to go into the community and preach."

"Yes, but why here? Why not Russia or China, for pity's sake?" Cage demanded. "We have the French and Spanish wanting our Kingdom and you compound our problems."

"That is not the attitude to have when talking to the man of the cloth."

"Cloth you say? Cloth made from wool, they will have our hair and the skin off our backs if you stay. Have you seen a man flogged? I have; I wept to see his skin flayed."

"I take that very risk, plus the risk of being hung drawn and quartered. I do not baulk from my duty, I do not flinch from my calling, and I am in the service of God and not man."

"And I share that risk with you, the prospect of being hanged as a traitor, as you well know, anyone hiding a priest will be tried for treason, that's a merry legacy to leave my family."

"You must give me shelter."

"You must have mercy, it is in your power, have you any idea how many seminary and secular priests we have hidden and how many inspections we have had. Are you aware of the edict of 22nd of February 1604, after the Hampton Court Conference?"

"You are the lawyer!"

"King James ordered all Roman Catholic clergy whether Jesuits, or seminaries or any other priests, to leave his kingdom by 19th March, you are a month late. The Edict is very specific."

"I cannot leave."

"I hope you are not planning any plots."

"I need to tend my flock."

"Please, promise me you have no ideas of causing mischief, there have been too many unsettling events. James drafted the edict in July last year on the discovery of the Main and Bye plots. Please, assure me creating mischief is not your intent."

"I have my duty to do!"

"You realise that we are marked by the authorities! You ask too much!"

"And you give too little."

"You want my life; have it."

"God will protect you."

"He has done; for that reason, alone you can stay."

Cage slumped back into his chair and absently reached out to the pewter plate of oysters on the table, picked up the last one and, in one swift movement, upturned the shell and let one of the bi-valve molluscs slip into his mouth, chewing it hungrily as if it would be his last.

Part Two

Chapter 13 - i - Thomas Wintour and Guido Forcanessi

February 1605

The time of day was dawn, the sky was grey; the mood was glum. The weather was miserable and so were the two men waiting on the harbour wall, to see if the boatmen were going to risk a voyage. Storms had racked the coastline, damaged boats, and seriously affected the income of fishermen and the ferrymen who plied their trade across the channel in their small *doggers*. Drizzle and a north wind made being beyond the warmth of a fire a trial but Guido's money was running out, there was no prospect of finding work in Amsterdam, he had given up his work, the injured man had returned early and he had ensured Rosa had a decent burial. He had to get away from where she had died.

Guido knew he could find work amongst his friends in the London docks and he needed friendship above all else while he grieved and rebuilt his life. The plague was over and London by all reports had returned to normality more quickly than expected. The Dutch sailors told him that there was a shortage of workers due to the terrible toll the disease had taken. All his plans of peace and happiness of a family and security were dashed. In a storm, he had to head for a familiar harbour and London was that refuge.

"Waiting for the boat home?" the stranger asked kindly, wishing to start up a conversation, they had left the warmth of the harbour inn, showing their willingness to be passengers even in this awful storm. It just needed a fool to take them. Wintour had left the refuge because he was frustrated waiting around for a break in the weather. Noticing Guido, he had approached him; he admired a man who was abroad in such inclement weather.

"Yes," Guido replied guardedly, not wanting to surface from wallowing in his self-pity and remorse; he was intent on grieving over his lost love; he was entitled to do so.

"Ah, I thought you might have found the inn too stuffy and had come out to get some bracing air!" Wintour quipped.

Despite himself, Guido laughed; it felt good.

He had not laughed since he had kissed good-bye to Rosa.

She had made him laugh even up to their parting.

"Thomas Wintour, of Droitwitch and who are you friend?" the stranger asked in a kindly manner. Guido could not possibly resist Wintour's confidence and friendliness; it was impossible.

"Guido Forcanessi, sire, at your service," he replied confidently but will a tone of obsequiousness as was befitting his station.

When a man of noble birth or a member of the landed gentry addressed you, you spoke with reverence. There was always a chance that some gainful employment could be had from such a gentleman. His experience in Italy, in the Lowlands and struggling in London had taught him that much. A little deference and respect never went amiss.

"An Italian name, have you been fighting for the Spanish or the English?"

"For the English," Guido announced proudly. It was true, Guido had worked as much on the side of the rebels, destroying dykes and carrying munitions as he had for the Spanish nobles who administered Antwerp Bruges and Ghent.

"You were fighting against fellow Catholics?" Thomas asked askance, he could not fathom the reason. "For the Protestant cause?"

"For freedom for the Northern Provinces, fighting against the Spanish interlopers who invaded Italy and forced my family to flee their homeland and who tax all of their provinces to feed and pay for their army; I fought to defeat an enemy who lives off others and rules where they are not wanted; I cannot wait until Spain is defeated and retreats from my Italian home so that I can return and build a better future." fumed Guido with feeling.

It was clear that he despised the Spanish and whatever they had done. They were unstoppable in their empire building. Not only had Spain invaded his homeland, they had enormous wealth, due to the gold brought in from the Americas. They suffered from extreme arrogance also, because they thought they deserved all they had due to their piousness; it was God's reward for their devout worship and faith. That was how he saw them but he could not express such in his limited English, as it was he had relied on overheard phrases used by his fellow workers back in the London docks.

"Indeed, it is difficult is it not?" agreed Thomas, seeming to work out his thoughts as he spoke, it was part of his charm. "Do we put our faith first or the country of our birth? My father George always said we should put the country of our birth first."

"You are a Catholic?" Guido asked; he was surprised; he assumed all men in England were Protestants; he had never met a Catholic Englishman as far as he aware but he also knew that they usually kept their faith secret. He had never met a gentleman who was so open about his faith.

"Of course, though, I only admit it to fellow adventurers such as your good self," Thomas lied charmingly. In reality, he wore his faith as proudly as a pilgrim wore his shell.

"My English is not so good."

"I speak Latin, French and Spanish and a little Italian. Shall we try a mixture of the language we know; we'll try to establish a lingua franca between us?"

"I would prefer that."

"Good."

"You have been fighting against the Spanish?" asked Guido.

"I have, the Spanish wish to make England part of their dominion, my brother Robert has a small hop farm and salt pans, I do not wish to give them up to some Spanish nobleman, why would I?" Thomas asserted proudly.

"Of course," Guido replied.

Thomas was firstly an Englishman, secondly a Catholic.

"I have even been to Spain to beg the Spanish to stop the war and allow us to live in peace," he continued. "I plan to sell my hops once war is truly over; they fetch a good price here, English hops, the Flemish people love them in their beer. What do you plan to do now the war is all but over?"

"I survived the war; I intend to survive the peace!"

"Well said, I studied law but I find it hard, I have enjoyed being an adventurer more but waging war is no way to live, it is too harsh a life, cold, wet, beds, blood and gore, too little sleep and the money does not make up for it."

"Indeed, war is harsh."

"We need trade not war; I went to Spain with Christopher Wright to ask for such. Kit and I had our work cut out for us, he had been in trouble accused of helping the Earl of Essex to rebel two years before; we got no help from England. I only went myself because I know some Spanish, I have some experience of contracts and most of all Kit needed my help. "

"Were you successful?"

"Not as successful as our troops! All I succeeded in doing was tarnishing my name; the authorities thought I was asking for aid for a rebellion in England."

"Why would you do that?"

"Why indeed? I cannot imagine the Spanish succeeding in any attempt on our kingdom, the Armada proved our resilience; we are a sceptred isle; safe, and secure, but intelligent men who hold influence are a threat to the State. While I have been away many of my friends have been implicated in plots against the throne. The more the Catholics in Europe expand their territories, the more we are held in suspicion and contempt," Tom noted sadly, shaking his head. He thought it unjust.

"But you have been fighting for the crown in the Low Countries, does that not count."

"It would in an ideal world but not at present in England where the Protestants are fighting for domination, we are a distraction. The Puritans are more of an obstacle to a humanist state, Thomas More and Erasmus talked of toleration in a Utopian world; I am afraid England is no longer the place for toleration. Utopia has gone."

Although Guido did not understand everything and did not even know about Utopia, he got the gist.

"What can you do?"

"Run away and fight for my queen, my country and now my new king!"

"And when the fighting is over?"

"Return to England if I don't drown in a *dogger* first."

"I am bound for England, too."

"Come join me in ale, I speak a bit of Flemish and I will quickly ask the boatmen to call on us at the inn if they decide they want to risk the voyage. I trust them and their seamanship."

"I, too, have grown to trust these men but I still fear drowning more than most men."

"An honest admission and like men going to battle we all fear what is beyond the next crest of the wave. We must be brave if we are to set out into deeper water. We may well have to wait out the storm, better together than alone, we might yet establish ourselves as a band of brothers if others join us but I fear the weather has led to everyone but the two of us taking shelter wherever they can find it. Come Forcanessi, your name is a true mouthful, we shall shorten it if we can, Guido can be Guy, Forcanessi can be Forca; Guy Forca, yes why not? Forcan is too long and could be misunderstood!"

Forcanessi and Wintour swept into the inn, bringing with them the squall from outside. Wintour spoke in faultless Flemish and guided his new-found-friend to a table and bench close to the hearth. There was a roaring fire and china bowls of *juniper* were delivered to their table almost immediately. The warmth of the flames and the heat of the gin dispelled the chill that pervaded each and every bone of their bodies. Their clothes dried on them and the conversation broadened and flowed.

Wintour was a charming conversationalist and when Guido's conversation faltered, he helped oil the wheels of conversation by slipping into Spanish and Italian, on occasions Latin, when he was lost for words, and the two men grew to understand each other better. Unbeknownst to them, the two men were being watched, not by a trained spy, but by a regular informer to Robert Cecil; Cecil's tentacles spread far afield. He was the Secretary of State but his influence spread beyond the borders of the realm. His eyes and ears looked and listened at home and abroad.

Chapter 13 – ii - The Essex Rebellion Retold

Forcanessi and Wintour shared a *dogger* early that afternoon, and dined after dark at Dover; Guido was Thomas's guest that evening. It was late when they arrived at the coast, which meant the approach to the shore was relatively clear, boats generally only sailed in daylight, but winter nights came early. The current and tide were against them so it took them some time to get ashore. They could not make progress under sail the tide flowed more swiftly than the wind propelled the boat forward. Once the tide had turned, they could row ashore.

By seven o'clock, they were served their onion soup and that was followed by bread and local cheese. Wintour pressed his newfound friend to share a room at the inn where their teeth chattered even though they lay on straw fully clothed and wrapped in their cloaks.

Travelling up to London by cart took two days because Wintour willed it so. He was parsimonious when paying for a room for the night and for travel, yet he was generous with the money he spent on food and drink.

Eventually, two days later, they arrived in London at an inn where Wintour had assured Guido that he would have no trouble in finding new friends there and hinted broadly that he might find some employment, too. *The Duck and Drake* was where Wintour always stayed when in London. The pair strode in to the crowded room, Wintour led and Forcanessi followed trying to strut in the same carefree manner.

Smoke filled the parlour bar, candles on tables lit the room with the help of a roaring fire, small, dry logs, in two large baskets, were on either side of the hearth; the pot-boy tossed a log onto the flames every so often as he collected tankards; the landlord knew that a hot room encouraged people to drink more. The pipe smoke smarted in their eyes but they soon became used to it, relieved to be off the cold damp street and in the warmth.

Tom led Guido to a group hogging the fire.

"Guido Forcanessi, meet my two friends, Jack and Kit Wright."

"Christopher Wright, pleased to make your acquaintance, you may call me Kit."

"John Wright, good to meet you on the road of life, please; call me Jack."

"Guido Fawkes, I am, indeed, privileged to be in your company, Tom calls me Guy."

"So you have met the rebels!" someone cried.

"Rebels, we were acquitted," another shouted.

"Poor Essex paid the price for his vanity," a third voice added. Guido was not sure who was saying what, it was a series of calls from different people.

"What did he do?" he asked, mystified.

"He marched us up to the city to complain about his monopoly being taken away," Wintour explained.

"Monopoly, I am not familiar with this word."

"Queen Bess gave out monopolies to loyal subjects and he had the sole rights to sell sweet wines in London, but after his poor showing in the war in Ireland, they snatched the licence back off him," Wintour complained.

"How had he got such a wonderful gift?" Guido wondered.

"He was the Queen's favourite," Chris Wright exclaimed.

"What happened?" wondered Guido. Chris, patient Kit, explained clearly and succinctly how Essex had repeatedly pushed his luck with Queen Bess and, eventually, she had lost her patience and Cecil had removed Essex's monopoly. It was testament to his youth and his ability to simplify complicated stories that he was able to explain the complicated relationship between Elizabeth and her arrogant Earl.

"In August, we were visiting his house in the Strand and he gathered us all together, nobles and gentleman and we had to follow him to the gates of the city to protest against the removal of the monopoly," Catesby explained.

He was the leader of the group; the man all of them deferred to, he would be called a ringleader in later years.

"I think I understand," Guido said, not sure if he did but no one listened.

"It was a wonderful day and we marched along the Fleet past St Paul's to the Guildhall to demand support from the city to get an audience with the Queen," Catesby continued, "she was refusing to see our friend Bob; he hoped that his friends in the city would help him,"

"That snake in the grass, Cecil, had convinced everyone that he was bad and he had our friend Devereux arrested for treason, can you believe it?" Jack elaborated further.

He waited for Guido to respond but no response was forthcoming.

Someone in the crowd shouted, "Shame."

"He was accused of leading a rebellion, in the city of London? That Cecil, he makes night day," Tom said bitterly.

Guido tried to keep up with the conversation but the people talked so passionately and quickly that his limited English did not allow him to translate their words fully. All he could do was nod knowingly and sympathetically.

"Bob and Devereux are the same person, is that right?" asked Guido confused but not loud enough to be heard above the other voices around them.

"Poor old Essex, Robert Devereux, our friend Bob, how fortune's fickle wheel turned against him, his favour took a turn for the worse," sighed Jack trying to elaborate further for Guido's benefit.

"He started well, as you would expect, his great-grandmother was Mary Boleyn, sister to Anne Boleyn, making him the Queen's first cousin, twice removed," Kit explained.

"My friend Guido is glazing over, he cannot understand very well, just say that he was a relative of Queen Elizabeth, let's keep it simple!" Tom insisted.

"But it is not simple, there are wheels within wheels; his life is a complicated machine," Jack argued.

"Yes, but the mechanism might not be of interest," Tom replied testily, "He just needs to know the time, not how the works move!"

His friends were too wound up like springs in a timepiece to take into account their guests poor understanding. Their anger and passion obscured rather than clarified. Poor Guido desperately wanted to understand the situation regarding the poor Duke of Essex but he was unable.

Wintour was too exhausted to act as translator and Guido was too tired to think about translating every word. He merely heard snippets while he became thirstier and thirstier and yet his tankard seemed to be filled every time he took a gulp.

"Oh, but it will be of interest because you see, Bob Devereux was a ward of Lord Burghley, Bob Cecil's father," Jack said.

"Robert Cecil, we only call friends Bob!" Tom cried.

"They became bitter rivals especially as Cecil was a pen pusher and Devereux was the Queen's favourite," Jack added

"Cecil was not Elizabeth's favourite at this time, but he made himself useful and cut the legs from underneath others with his words and pen," elucidated Catesby.

"Queen Bess was upset at Bob *Devers* marrying Frances Walsingham, but Cecil was even more upset as that meant Francis Walsingham, his mentor, was now related to his enemy," explained Kit.

"Bob Devereux could do no wrong at court, especially after glory at the Battle of Zutphen; he was a soldier, handsome and strong," added Jack.

"He was eloquent and witty, too!" Tom said.

"His reward was Master of Horse and the tax revenues on sweet wine, not a bad reward!" Catesby said.

"He got too proud; the Queen cuffed him for his insolence once, a sight Robert Cecil enjoyed. He was never comfortable with our friend Bob being in the Privy Council," Tom said.

"Then the rot set in, he failed to capture Lisbon when Drake sailed to Spain a year after the Armada," Kit said, starting to sound excited.

"You forget the capture of Cadiz in '96!" Tom said, determined to support the memory of his friend and mentor.

"A small triumph, his undoing with the Queen came once he was made Lord Lieutenant of Ireland," Catesby continued. It was testament to his standing in the group that no one argued with his summation of the situation.

"He had too little money to take on the rebel O'Neil." Tom said. "He never had enough money for any of his campaigns."

"By the end of his time in Ireland, more than half the knights in England owed their rank to Essex," Kit said.

"They say the rebels joked about Bob and his generosity in knighting his troops: 'he never drew sword but to make knights'; I think it may have been true," Jack joked.

"You are not thinking like him, he was at Court, he was a skilful politician. He was shrewd, trying to build support against Cecil, his generosity allowed him to challenge the powerful men at Cecil's command," Catesby said, admiring his friend's guile.

"Are you still with us Guy?" Tom asked.

"The ale has not helped," Guido said.

"Have another," suggested Kit, mischievously.

"Relying on his general warrant to return to England, given under the great seal, Essex sailed from Ireland on the twenty-fourth September 1599, and reached London four days later," Catesby said.

"The Queen had expressly forbidden his return and was surprised by him when he presented himself in her bedchamber one morning at Nonsuch Palace before she was properly wigged or gowned," Tom said.

"On that day, the Privy Council met three times, and it seemed his disobedience might go unpunished," Catesby added.

"Although, the Queen did confine him to his rooms with the comment that 'an unruly beast must be stopped of his provender'. He was still her favourite," Tom said sadly.

They continued the story, Wintour translating, elaborating, or explaining where necessary. They explained that Essex had been confined to his house in London where he became ill with melancholy.

The Queen, they told him, sent broth and doctors. She had stripped him of his titles, Master of the Ordinance, Master of the Queen's Horse and Earl Marshall of England.

It took time to explain the patronage system but eventually Guido understood that it basically meant payments made to rich and influential people in return for favours and jobs that they could bestow.

The Italian seemed genuinely shocked by the practice, which had been at the centre of court life for so long.

"The Queen then went further and removed the *Farm of Sweet Wines,* a tax, which made Essex a good deal of money. The group insisted that she had been encouraged by Robert Cecil to do so and her need for parsimony in times where her revenues were falling forced her hand. In fact it was parliament, on Cecil's insistence, that robbed Essex of his *'Farm'*."

"He knew only Elizabeth would get them back and he would have to garner support from those in the city, too. Elizabeth leased land to various people from the Archbishop of Winchester in Southwark to the Archbishop of London and to Knyvett who built a house on the land that he leased in Whitehall opposite the palace. Leasing lands and granting monopolies raised money for the exchequer."

"She progressed through her kingdom to save money on running her court and she sold licences to sell diverse goods, which were called *'farms'* and became known as monopolies. He wrote a letter begging the Queen to reinstate his *Farm*."

"The monopoly brought in a sizeable amount of money but despite saying that he would be ruined and friends pleading on his behalf, he could not persuade her to relent. Cecil persuaded her to keep the *Farm* from Essex as parliament had removed it."

"There were many who detested Cecil and loved our Earl Essex; he was therefore rewarded with the greatest support from many wise and wealthy men who petitioned for the *Farm* to be returned."

That is what they told him.

They went on to describe the events of the following days. Scrambling over each other conversationally to voice an opinion, expand an idea, or colour in a grey area, they told him about their march, which Cecil called a rebellion.

On the evening when the friends met, the Chamberlain's Men including William Shakespeare performed *Richard II* to the gathered men at Essex's house in the Strand. There were murmurs of shock but mostly the company enjoyed the performance of the seditious play, it was a sign of Essex's humour and of his anger.

The Queen had taken away his income. Without realising what was happening to them, Essex had his very own servants wake the guests and they were encouraged to breakfast on ale and boiled bacon. Once they were fortified, he gathered them in the hall and stood on the stairs.

A man who was so well respected and adored by his followers, he seemed diminished by his treatment by the Queen. His eyes told of his secret suffering, the sadness of a friendship spoilt. The Earl of Essex, Robert Devereux spoke eloquently and passionately: "My monopoly has been removed; the taste of bitterness cannot be removed by sweet wine. Come with me friends and we will go to the city and petition for the return of the trade that is rightfully mine and was bestowed on me by the Queen."

They all agreed and cheered, or at least, any dissenters' protests were drowned out by the roar of the crowd.

"Here, here," echoed around the chamber.

"My gift, which was stolen by unscrupulous curs; they inhabit the corridors of Her Majesty's palace at Nonsuch Park and in the halls of Westminster."

"All who were gathered cheered; they were fond of their host and had benefitted from Devereux's generosity and favour. The throng, for it was a throng with so many of those who had benefitted from the Earl's generosity, moved out of the house in a great crowd," Tom added.

"It was a fine day," a voice asserted from somewhere deep within the crowd.

"We walked east along the strand to Ludgate Hill, heading onwards towards the city of London. As we processed through the streets, windows opened to see such an expedition," Catesby exclaimed, feeling proud at the remembrance of such a worthy crusade for justice.

"It seemed that we were part of an honourable crusade and all of London was on our hero's side. He was loved and had been treated shoddily, the Queen would surely restore his monopoly," Tom added.

"The crowds were on his side: 'We march to save the honour of Essex!' cried one."

"One man cried above the noise: 'Essex must have his sweet wine licence returned', the crowds were quite indignant, they loved Essex and they were, every one of them, on his side, it was an adventure, a day out," added Catesby nostalgically.

"Yet another added loudly, for all to hear: 'Jealous nobles at court have robbed him of his liberty and now they take his livelihood'. It was what most people felt," revealed Tom happily, he recalled the event as if it were yesterday, he had grown up on the story.

"The crowds were with us; the streets we passed were not; windows closed, nobody cared about our hero, the fine soldier, and the hero of yore was yesterday's man," Catesby complained.

All the men gathered at the inn nodded their agreement, a few cried: 'Amen'.

"They were frightened of Cecil and the Walsingham Web that had pervaded the streets of London for decades," Catesby explained.

"We cannot move in London without a spy following us; we should not speak freely even here in this tavern, but men cannot live their lives cowered in fear," Wintour said.

"The spy network was so powerful that many feared to speak out even in private, let alone in public; it was not their business, they did not care that a noble had lost his income, they did fear repercussions from the state," Catesby complained bitterly.

"Those city gents were worried about their hides," Tom added.

"We shouted but our appeals fell on deaf ears, the doors of their counting houses remained closed," Catesby grumbled. "Instead of convincing the city of the veracity of our demands, we had lunch."

"The lack of support took the wind out of our sails, no one was interested in our friend's shoddy treatment," Tom added.

"We thronged the pie shops and *'ordinaries'*, mourned our friend's misfortune, and complained of fortune's fickle wheel. Then, we all went home; Essex with his retinue, the crowd to their homes; our cause was lost."

"Afterwards, the Earl felt remorse, but it was not the time to repent and Elizabeth would not give our friend absolution. Cecil saw it as a chance to charge our Devereux with treason," explained Tom, "We, too, were implicated by association. We were threatened with execution!"

"Poor Bob, he was a fine man, a great adventurer and a loyal friend, we were lucky to escape with our entrails intact!" Kit cried bitterly, biting his fist in an overly dramatic display of sorrow.

"Devereux was hung?" Guido asked

"No he was a noble so he was beheaded," replied Kit with too much relish. "He was spared a public execution.

"And you survived, why?" he asked

"God's grace and luck!" Kit declared boldly.

The atmosphere changed as the gathered party reflected on his words. It was not for the first time that the gathered party had collectively, or individually, considered this strange occurrence. No one knew why Cecil had decided some would die and some would live. Those who would buy their lives did so by paying the onerous fines, which Cecil had levied on them for their disobedience to the crown.

"On 19th February 1601, the Earl of Essex was taken to court," Tom disclosed miserably. Each time the story was told, he felt sad. "He stood trial, was condemned and executed six days later."

Chapter 13 – iii - The Essex Trial, 19th February 1601.

Essex was tried, not at the Inns of Court, or elsewhere, but at the Palace of Westminster by a group of his peers, as befitted an Earl; that was the Privy Chamber, the Privy Council and some other lords.

A spacious Court was made in Westminster Hall, where the Lord Treasurer Buckhurst sat as High Steward of England, under a Canopy of State, where sat also, about the table, were the Earls, Barons, and Judges of the land according to their degree.

The judges were Lord Chief Justice Popham, Lord Chief Justice Anderson and Lord Chief Baron Justice Warburton, Justice Fenner, Justice Gawdie, Justice Kingsmill, Justice Walmesley and Mr. Baron Clarke; nine 'good men' in total.

These judges sat in the court, next to the *Bar*, before the High Steward. Seven Sergeants at Arms came in with maces before the High Steward, and laid them down before him in the Court.

The 'King at Arms' stood on one side of the High Steward by his chair of Estate and one of Her Majesty's Gentlemen Ushers with his white rod in his hand on the other side.

The Clerk of the Crown and his assistant sat before him to read the Common Indictments and Examinations. The Captain of the Guard, Sir Walter Raleigh, and forty of the Queen's Guard were there to attend the trial.

Then the Sergeant at Arms cried: "Oh, Yes!" It was an appeal for everyone to stop talking, but it only succeeded in turning the din into a whispered murmur.

The Lord High Steward of England commanded: "Silence, we will hear the Commission read, upon pain of imprisonment."

The charges against the Earl of Essex and the Earl of Southampton were read: "At Westminster, on the nineteenth of February, and in the forty third year of the Reign of Queen Elizabeth: For rebelliously conspiring and Endeavouring the Subversion of the Government by Confederacy with Tyronne that Popish Traitor and his accomplices, these following, Sir Christopher Blount, Henry Cuffe, Sir Charles Danvers and Sir Gillie Merrick."

"Are they all in custody?" asked Popham.

"Yes, my lord and the Counsel for the Queen will be assisting you. Pray silence for the Queen's Counsel: Sir Henry Yelverton, the Queen's Serjean, Sir Edward Coke, the Queen's Attorney General; and Mr. Francis Bacon."

A trinity of vipers as far as the Earl of Essex was concerned; Bacon and Coke, Devereux feared the most. He was disturbed to see how Cecil had picked peers who loathed him.

A Privy Councillor introduced the proceedings: "You will, as befits a noble, be tried before your peers on charges of treason, Robert Devereux, Earl of Essex. Part of our evidence will show that not only are you in favour of toleration and religious dissent, that given free rein would unsettle, nay topple the state and that you dealt with Catholics in an attempt to unseat Her Majesty, Queen Elizabeth."

Another continued: "In August 1600, your freedom was granted, the Queen gave you pardon for returning from Ireland without permission but, as a punishment, the source of your income, the '*sweet wines*' monopoly, was suspended. Your situation was desperate, and you shifted from sorrow and repentance to rage and rebellion. The '*Fruits of Sweet Wines*' were removed and your bitterness broke through, a sour end to a warm relationship, how sad. You were given sweetness and light and you repaid it with a sour face and dark deeds!"

Yet, another added: "In early 1601, you began to fortify Essex House, your town mansion and gathered your followers."

Essex objected to this, there was no evidence for that assertion.

He was ignored and his objection was not recorded because it was an outburst during the reading of the charges and we therefore inadmissible in the court.

Then, the first: "On the morning of 8th February, you marched out of Essex House with a party of nobles and gentlemen and entered the city of London in an attempt to force an audience with the Queen."

The second: "Robert Cecil, the Lord Privy Seal, had you proclaimed a traitor."

The third: "Finding no support among the Londoners, you retreated from the city, and surrendered after the Crown forces besieged Essex House. You were forced to give up your arms and submit yourself to custody."

"We were going home!" complained Essex angrily. It did not take much for him to lose his temper. Injustice especially irked him.

The First announced: "You are charged with dealing with Catholic conspirators."

"That is not true, I swear it; this is a popish plot; papists have been hired and suborned to witness against me. I am more sinned against than sinning!" objected Essex vehemently, frustration causing him to tremble with indignation at the unfairness of the accusation.

There was some sympathy for Essex; he was popular amongst his peers and the Peers. He was a dashing hero who had suffered from fortune's fickle wheel turning full circle. Once he had been the man who distinguished himself at Cadiz, the Queen's favourite, but his campaign in Ireland had failed and the relationship had soured.

The second continued; they took it religiously in turn: "As you say, yet all those who you claim will vouch for you have disappeared into thin air. You are the villain yet you see villains everywhere including our Lord Privy Seal, the very same hero who has protected us from subversion and rebellion for so many years. With his father the great Lord Burghley and Lord Walsingham, he has shielded us from the designs of foes on our shores and those who greedily eye the crown or kingdom from abroad."

"The Lord Privy Seal told me that none in the world but the Infanta of Spain had right to the Crown of England," the Earl of Essex, Robert Devereux argued.

Unknown to the Earl, Cecil was not at Hatfield House as everyone had been told, a rumour he had spread himself, but had been present in the courtroom all along. On that day, he had been following the trial at a doorway, cleverly concealed behind a fine tapestry, a French hunting scene, provided by his household.

Stepping out from behind the arras, like Polonius, he moved forward to enact a dramatic denial of the charge. Stooped and bent, he fell to his knees to praise the Lord and to thank God for the opportunity to clear his name.

"This is a lie," Cecil cried indignantly, pointing an accusing finger at Essex, "it is you who would wish the crown to go to the popish punk from Spain. You have played fast and loose with the Queen's favour and with the truth."

"I call a witness who will confirm the allegation, my uncle William Knollys," Essex announced defiantly.

"Call William Knollys!" the usher cried across the great hall. His voice was echoed by the call of other ushers calling for William Knollys.

Moments later a figure rushed into the hall.

"I am here my Lord," Knollys replied breathlessly.

"What say you?" The third inquisitor asked.

"I can say that *A Conference about the Next Succession to the Crown of England* was read before Cecil. It is true that the author, Robert Persons, did, amongst other proposals, suggest that a Catholic successor friendly to Spain would remove the threat of Spanish invasion. However, I never did hear Robert Cecil say the same such thing," Knollys testified, never once looking at poor Robert Devereux.

Essex almost fainted with the shock; Cecil had bought his own flesh and blood. Those who money should not buy had been bought. Essex wondered what Cecil had done or how much he had paid in order to buy such perjury from a person that he considered a friend.

"Thank God, there are honest men in this realm, but here we have before us a peer who has forgotten the merits of honesty and integrity. Robert Devereux, Earl of Essex, has been exposed as a traitor and through this honest witness; I am again proven to be an honest man," Cecil crowed triumphantly.

Announcing his innocence to the hall, he remained on his knees.

"You are nothing but a green-eyed monster, jealous of my place in the Queen's affections and my place at court. The court is being hoodwinked, I insist on fair play," parried Essex desperately, his response showing his growing anger.

His frustration was understandable.

"Insist away, from this day, in every way but mark my words: the Queen saw you as her tower of strength, but you found yourself in a pickle and how did you react? I will tell you how! You responded with your usual wrath and impatience," replied Cecil, baiting Essex. "Your temper is well known as is the way in which you have disabused the Queen, your contemptuous ways have been noted by the court and complaints recorded."

"Here, here," chorused the Privy Councillors that had been primed by Cecil to cheer him on.

"Let him speak!" cried Essex.

"The Queen has had enough," complained Cecil, "the State has had enough, you rebel against the Queen, you are a rebel against the State, and it is a bitter pill, knit your brow as you will, but the man who sold sweet wine has turned sour on his friends and on the State. Treason is your mistress, mischief is you mission, and sedition is your direction."

"It is well-known that your father William Cecil, his friends Robert Dudley, Francis Walsingham, and Nicholas Bacon would vouch for me this day; they knew the loyalty I have for the Queen, if they were here, they would recognise my fealty," Essex argued. His face was flushed with fury.

"I am sure they will not!" Cecil exclaimed dramatically, he enjoyed a bit of drama in the courtroom.

"You all know Henry Wriothesley, Earl Southampton; he will remind you all present that he and I were wards of Lord Burghley the father of Robert Cecil, the Lord Privy Seal, and that we all, Robert and his brother Thomas, grew up at Cecil House, all four boys together," Essex added.

"Are we talking of the same Southampton who with Lord Mountjoy was in secret correspondence with James VI of Scotland urging him to the throne?" asked Cecil rhetorically, "the same Southampton who's father was the patron of Shakespeare, the same man who encouraged the performance of the play *Richard II*, a seditious call to revolt. Is that the same Catholic Earl who helped in this Catholic plot? Yes, he was adopted like you were by my father; you were all in our home, but sadly a good home does not a good person make." Cecil goaded, knowing that the more he riled Essex, the more the peers would see him as a tempremental and untrustworthy fellow.

"Will you not call him?" asked Essex, ignoring the jibes. He would not be

"It is best you call another witness, perhaps your friends John and Owen Salisbury who went to Cadiz with you?"

"Why so, I call Southampton, not John and Owen?"

Essex was suspicious.

"I think I am correct in saying that Owen was barred from the Middle Temple when his brother was implicated in the Babington Plot. Each and every one of your witnesses has shown disloyalty to the Crown! Southampton on so many occasions."

"I am loyal and so are my friends; we are all loyal to the Queen, all those gathered here know that," asserted Essex.

At this Cecil sneered, he would have made a perfect barrister, he has researched his quarry and he knew where to strike. Essex was losing the battle and he knew it; he also knew that Cecil had not started to properly destroy him. Cecil was like a cat with a mouse he was toying with him.

"Loyal, indeed! Let me tell you that Lord Monteagle and Lord Percy did take a barge to the Globe theatre from *Bankside* on the very eve of your rebellion, Saturday, the seventh day of February, and were observed to pay for the Lord Chamberlain's Company to perform the old and tired, half-forgotten *Richard II*."

"A favourite of mine," argued Essex.

"Did you see yourself as Bolingbroke, replacing the Queen herself? Your friends clearly did! They commissioned a play for all to see. A play where the reigning monarch is deposed!"

"Indeed, the play was performed that afternoon and evening, and I say to you 'I live with bread, like you feel want, taste grief, need friends, I should not be subjected thus. How can you say to me that I wanted to be a king? My role has always been to serve the Queen."

"By taking up arms and parading through the city? Let me list those fine men who helped you."

"They are my friends!"

"Let me list them anyway: the Earls of Southampton, Rutland, Sussex and Bedford, Lords Monteagle, Cromwell and Sandys, fine men or malcontents?"

"Fine friends."

"You say so, I differ."

"Fine men all present know."

"Fine men or fickle friends, loyal subjects or traitors, deluded fools or diabolical dissenters? Those are the questions that need answering, answer me or answer me not, this seems likely a most unholy plot?"

"No religion but that of the Queen. I have no religion but the Queen's, she is the Supreme Leader of the Church of England; I worship her and serve her faithfully!" objected Essex passionately.

"Is that so? What of the Cromwell? You must know, as everyone else does, he is of the Puritan persuasion, a religion you have, in secret, shown sympathy for, worse still, Southampton, Lord Monteagle, Francis Gresham and Robert Catesby, all known Catholics, were also there. These 'gentlemen, I wager, would welcome a popish monarch."

"Their religion bars them not from my friendship."

"Yes but the London mob unsettled by bad harvest joined you, shouting: 'to the Court to the Court'! What was the good in that?"

There was a silence in the court, all the nobles felt uneasy when they heard of the mob or any protest, they lived in fear of an uprising and Essex's involvement in one did not bode well. They were all petrified that the poor would rise and remove the wealth they had amassed.

"If treason was my name then why did I not march for Whitehall and claim the Royal Seal? The Lord Mayor of London had himself promised to support my plea to have the *Farm of Sweet Wines* reinstated to my name."

Cecil hoped that Essex would become riled.

He was famous for losing his temper, he had become heated, he had let down his guard, and now he was running off at the mouth. Cecil would strike at his *Achilles heel*.

"A petition you say, twelve hours of mayhem, I say. That mayhem led to fighting in the streets, which led to deaths, the cavalry had to block the Strand from Essex House to the river."

"For what reason?"

"Why, because of your army gathered in the streets of London, ready to strike?"

"We were a band of friends going to complain."

"As you wish."

"As it was so!"

"The equestrian mounted soldiers showed great restraint," Cecil paused waiting to make sure all were listening intently, a few dozing clerks looked up at the sound of silence; it was not like Cecil to stop in mid-flow. "They were commanded by your peers: the Earl of Cumberland; joined by my own brother, Lord Burghley, who you are familiar with having, as you say, lived in our house; Thomas Cecil was assisted by Lord Thomas Howard and Lord Compton."

"You did not need to hound us with such armed men; we were going home!" complained Essex vehemently. "A footman of Southampton's household was shot by one of those who blocked the strand. No doubt due to over-eagerness for a fight. Lord Southampton himself came out onto his roof to protest that we meant no harm, particularly to the Queen, the use of troops of horse was out of character with our protest."

"Yes, I know, you were merely taking up arms to protect the Queen from the *'atheists'* and *'caterpillars'*, to quote your beloved *'Richard II',* who had gathered about the throne; is that not so?" Cecil spat venomously, showing his disgust for the play and Essex's arrogance. "Is that how you see me, see these peers gathered around you in this room?"

He seemed to be asking the court the question: 'what makes Essex so special that he can look down upon us as garden grubs? How dare he judge us as 'non-believers'? It was not designed to make Essex popular with his peers.

"You will twist my words, if I answer yes or no!" complained Essex angrily, he was well known for his short fuse; the Queen had put up with many of his tantrums.

He was vain and arrogant but he was also kind and considerate, he had a generous heart and was a loyal friend to many inside and outside court. Those friends seemed to be the fair-weather kind. Essex was being quite spectacularly rained upon and not one of them offered him any protection from the storm.

"You dissemble all truth!" complained Essex, almost apoplectic with rage; Cecil was being outrageous in his assertions and yet all the peers in the room were allowing him to get away with the most mendacious testimony.

"Why say you so, you know I am an honest man?" asked Cecil calmly. "Am I an *'atheist'*, a *'caterpillar'*, or the Secretary of State? Were the other *atheists* and *caterpillars* in fact the Privy Council that serves the Queen and carries out her wishes and follows her every command?"

A hush fell on the hall as Cecil's words hit home like a slap on Essex's face; he was stunned by the way words were manipulated.

"You twist the facts and make a mountain of a mole hill, we were but few men, yet, you produce five hundred soldiers at Charing Cross, four hundred men on the north bank and three hundred men on the south side of the river at Southwark, a total of almost twelve-hundred men to subdue a crowd of thirty! Here you summon, I am told, some twenty-five peers of the realm!"

"How will you do with those twenty-five? Will they save and serve you or condemn you?" Cecil asked menacingly, sweeping his arms left and right to indicate the gathered peers of the realm.

"You have appointed nine judges; will they be nine who tow your line? Is this trial all for show, will the truth be told this time? Will you listen to what I say, or am I doomed, yay or nay?" asked Essex, his voice rising as he spoke.

His indignation was reaching new heights, too. He hoped to appeal to his supporters and challenge the judges to oppose Cecil. It was an ambitious strategy. Cecil waited, silence greeted Essex's outbursts, and neither cheers of support, nor jeers of condemnation. Cecil waited a full minute, allowing the rant to ring in everyone's ears; Essex was beginning to sound like King Lear.

Then, he simply said: "You are entitled to a fair hearing."

He seemed to be saying that although Essex was entitled to a fair hearing he would not receive one.

"Yet you list at least three judges that are known to be displeased with me and would call me foe," complained Essex, his voice booming, he realised that he might be entitled to a fair hearing but he was not going to get one from that particular panel of judges.

"They are your peers, as is Lord Grey de Wilton," Cecil argued, knowing how de Wilton despised Essex.

"Ha, the scoundrel would eat my innards as good offal if he could; he hates my guts and would love to see my entrails pulled out; have them cooked before him; and eat them there and then as my dead eyes looked on."

"Awful as it may seem, he has been chosen for a reason and his role in this sorry drama is to prove your fiery temper and unreliability; did you not openly quarrel in Ireland, from whence you returned having failed to carry out the Queen's command?"

This remark was designed to sting Devereux; he was a brave soldier and loyal subject of the Queen despite his tantrums. His adventure in Ireland had turned out badly for many different reasons, some of his own making, others not. The main reason of course was lack of funds to launch an effective campaign and it was a strong possibility that Cecil had a hand in restricting the amount of money allocated to the campaign. He had been punished for returning from Ireland early by arrest. Essex was indignant; Cecil had succeeded in biasing the court against him. Essex had only one ace up his sleeve:

"I'll say no more of that rascal till I laugh in his face and call him a rogue, but what say you of Judge Coke's assertion that the witness statements that you have put before the court do not dissemble their brother, but more their affidavits resemble one another."

Even though Devereux had a point in what he said, too many of the statements were similar; it did look as if the witness reports had been manufactured to undermine Essex's cause, however, his peers did not receive this news with the cheers he had foreseen. He was quite correct that those who claimed to have been witnesses told the same story. So many of the accounts varied little and therefore suggested they had been manufactured.

"Coke is a cynical fellow, those confessions in the tower do not resemble each other; rather they echo one another," Cecil cleverly countered, smiling in a self-satisfied way at the row of judges who sat behind the long table at the end of the hall. The table had scrolled legs and would seat twelve for supper, the sight of the dining table made Cecil suddenly think about how hungry he was. He wondered how long it would be before the court clerk announced that it was time for a recess.

"How can you be so sure?" Essex argued.

He was trying to sow the seed of doubt in the courtroom.

"Those witness statements are similar because they all tell the truth."

"My friends all say the same, then!" cried Essex triumphantly. He knew that people were talking about the similarities of the three testimonies; it was his main defence. "How odd that they talk alike, use the same words, the same turn of phrase, in short they manufacture their speech!"

The silence that followed underlined the thoughts of all those present; Essex seemed friendless. Even though it seemed evidence had been falsified, he still would not be acquitted.

"We will hear the testimony of Sir Charles Danvers, Sir Christopher Blount," responded Cecil, delighting in name-dropping, he was enjoying humbling the proud Earl, "I will call the Earls of Bedford and Rutland to this court, too, and they have roundly condemned you as their confessions will reveal."

"And what of Lord Sandys and Lord Mountjoy?" asked Essex, hoping that they would provide some support.

"They similarly condemn you," announced Cecil accusingly. He was leaning on the law books spread before him, as if their advocacy emanated from their pages to his hands and from there to his mouth.

"Not too similarly" Essex suggested artfully, "as Coke says, 'the witness statement were too similar to have been written by more than one hand'. Coke told the court and told me the testimony seemed to have been given by the same person in four different cases."

"That would be fraud!" baulked Cecil.

"Yes, I agree," Essex said.

"What are you saying, tell the court!"

"Only that there is truth in what Coke says."

"That is for the court to decide."

"I merely note such," Essex declared, hoping that the court would be influenced in his favour.

He knew the Government could manufacture guilt or innocence: he had read about Cardinal Wolsey's fall from grace; the destruction of Thomas More who had right on his side; and the execution of Thomas Cromwell who had, after all, been the first Earl of Essex and whose head was on a spike on London Bridge. "Fraud it would be!"

"The statements may be in a similar vein, yet in a similar vein they may reason that you should be executed for treason."

"Perhaps they may vouch for me."

"Their testimony comes from the Tower but they are ensconced. Before you can complain, there is more. Most damning of all is the testimony of Francis Bacon, your erstwhile friend. He might say he is a friend but he has no loyalty to you."

"Bacon, your greatest rival at court, he would not testify against me," replied Essex scornfully. "He will side with the right and not with the might."

"Such loyalty befits a friend," Cecil suggested

"Francis Bacon will not desert me," asserted Essex.

"Not just he, but both Bacons. They already have testified, both brothers, Francis and Anthony. All that work to make Francis a rival to me was completely wasted."

"What rival could I make?"

"Oh, you have no rival; I can safely tell you that!" Cecil sneered feigning anger. "You tried to make Francis Bacon the Attorney General when Coke was the rightful heir to the title."

"You say that," Essex responded tersely.

"I am surprised he talks to you, when you tried to promote so raw a youth to so great a place. Coke is a man of great mettle, he does not condemn you as others would and should," Cecil argued.

"Perhaps Coke just wants justice," Essex asserted softly, he felt quite deflated by all the tribulations of the day.

"He wants justice," Cecil cried, "justice would have been Coke rising to Attorney General unopposed by Bacon, and you should have supported Coke not Bacon!"

"I have made no such search for precedents of young men who have filled the office of Attorney General, but I could name to you, Sir Robert, a man younger than Francis, less learned and equally inexperienced, who was striving with all his might for an office of far greater weight, no less than Secretary of State."

Essex had struck a nerve and Cecil could not help but reply in a hissing warning tone, vehemently delivered:

"Be careful what accusations you make against me; it is you who is on trial here; I merely speak for those who would prosecute you. I am a servant of the Queen who has been roundly abused by you over many years; and I have defended you at all times!"

Chapter 13 – iv - The Trial

During the break in proceedings, Robert Cecil and his lawyer, John Cage scurried to Cecil's chambers at Westminster Hall. Cecil slammed the door. He was furious that Essex had gained some knowledge that might sway the Peers. He tried to calm himself, he reminded himself that he was on top of the situation and he would succeed in making Devereux impeach himself.

"How did Devereux find out about my vying for the Secretary's post?" he whispered, trying to control his voice, it sounded like he was quietly gasping.

"Do not fret, you have shown that he has no friends and no excuse for his boorish behaviour, we have him beaten," the lawyer said soothingly.

"You think I have gone far enough to isolate him?"

"How much further could you go?" asked his lawyer, "he's trying to put you off balance, ignore him; of course, you will surely be appointed Secretary of State someday soon. However, it is your due, not something you would pursue. Everyone feels you deserve the post in return for your faithful service."

"I think my men can put that rumour around so that when they return from their midday meal, they will be able to see me as the faithful servant portrayed as scheming striver. Essex, I shall ensure, will be seen as a truculent child who has dangerous fits of anger."

"You have Essex all but condemned a traitor."

"You think so?" asked Cecil, needing to be as sure as possible about the efficacy of his prosecution.

"Of course," the lawyer assured him; he knew when one side was beaten.

Cage had canvassed opinion before the trial and during it, he was also aware of Cecil's influence, he knew of the power that he had over the other peers, the favours he could call in, the bullying and bribery that went on. By cajoling and controlling, he would destroy Essex, in yet another conflict he would prevail.

"What about the confessions?"

"The confessions?" the lawyer asked, startled.

"That fool Coke has interfered too much; noticing the confessions were too similar; I should have watched for that!"

"All is well."

"Essex has too much support."

"Why are you worried; you have mine?"

"Really, how kind you are, A recusant Catholic lawyer, who needs me, how lucky I am," Cecil hissed sarcastically; he felt no need to hide his contempt and so he did not.

"You can find another attorney of law to assist you if you wish."

"No, we know the Inns of Court is a viper's nest of Catholics, some twenty five in every hundred at a distant reckoning, closer inspection would reveal more. No, you are my man, loyal to me, needs must, the devil drives."

"We will win the case and you can release me from my bond to you."

"If we lose you will be bound in more than just fealty to me!"

"We will not lose!"

"It is a strange state of affairs, is it not? We have Robert Devereux who became the Earl of Essex, the 'Queen's Champion', who has, now, become traitor. The Queen is ill and when I do become Secretary of State, I will be forced to invite James of Scotland to take the Crown. My dear father, William, Lord Burghley once saw him as the most powerful threat to Bessie's throne and, now, he offers the stability that our country needs to thrive. Fortune makes strange bedfellows."

"I does indeed," Cage sighed.

"You and I, who would have thought that we would be working together in concert? In addition, there is the sizzling Bacon whose rise was all Devereux's doing; yet he turns on his patron like a mad dog upon his master. I almost feel sorry for Essex. These are indeed troubled times."

"Scarce a day goes by!"

"Indeed, you are right."

"Bacon is the son of an innkeeper, will he be trusted by the good nobles, and will Devereux make much of his humble birth and the lack of the chivalric code of a gentleman?"

"We are safe there, Devereux was adopted and brought up by my father, William, at Cecil House, his providence is not known, we can suggest he is the son of a punk or a flower seller, it matters naught, and it troubles me not."

"Bacon will testify."

"He is like a dog who bites the hand that feeds him."

"Have you read his *Essais*?" the lawyer asked emphasising the old way of pronunciation, which mirrored the way the word had been spelt, it was a Cambridge affectation.

"The *Essays* he wrote in Bordeaux he had published in '97 are talked of much but I have not been able to get a copy, mores the pity."

Cecil pronounced the word in the more modern manner.

"When we win, I shall lend you mine, it is a philosophical work looking at art and nature as two distinct areas; it is fascinating," the lawyer offered.

"Thank you," Cecil replied genuinely, he never took an offer of a book lightly. "I would like to read more of Francis's work."

"I hear he is the only man you fear."

"It is brave of you to say that particularly in your position. I fear no man, Bacon is a brain, not a man, he cannot bend his intellect to protect the State and save the Sovereign, and he will always be thus disadvantaged, always remember that. I merely wish to know my enemies thoughts, his strengths and weaknesses is that not true of you and your opponent?"

When they returned to court, Cecil brought out his most controversial witness, his cousin and Devereux's friend.

"We call Francis Bacon."

The courtroom buzzed with mumbled comments as Bacon sat in the witness chair to the left of Essex, to the right of the Privy Council who were at their table and in front of the prosecuting lawyer who scrutinised the witness as if he were a stranger. Bacon was a wild card, Cecil could not rely on him for support yet it seemed Essex could because of his generous patronage and their friendship. Both disliked Cecil, too. That was the way it looked at first glance.

"I know my Lord Essex did conspire to make himself king," asserted the prosecution lawyer, who had naturally been rehearsed by Cecil in what to say, "why choose '*Richard II*' to be performed on the day before the rebellion?"

"Will everyone stop calling it a rebellion?" Essex fumed.

"My Lord, please curtail your boorish ways in court, I am addressing the witness. Yet '*Richard II*' is all about rebellion."

"I was not leading a rebellion."

"Bolingbroke takes the Crown from Richard you intended to be Bolingbroke and you intended to take the Crown," the lawyer continued patiently. Essex turned slowly to face Bacon.

"But it was your choice Francis, not mine, you recommended the play, although it was out of fashion," Essex asserted skilfully.

"I cannot remember," Bacon answered mendaciously.

"I know you will vouch for the fact that I prefer the newer plays and the lighter entertainments, you know that, everyone does," Essex complained feebly.

He knew it did not look good. He knew his position was weak and a play about deposing a king made it weaker still.

"All I know is that you took a mob of armed men through the streets of London," Bacon replied coldly, he would not be drawn on the fact that he had chosen the play; he did not want to be tried for treason, too.

"I feel that you are not helping to acquit me, in fact you are persuading the honourable judges and my peers to condemn me," Essex sighed disbelievingly.

He was shocked by Bacon's bald-faced betrayal. His enemies seemed to relish his discomfort. There appeared to be very few looks of sympathy amongst his peers. He became increasingly concerned that they all seemed to fear Cecil more than they wanted justice and it was clear that they only wanted to save their own skins.

'Even 'Good Thomas' will not save me,' he thought.

He was right, the Queen's 'Good Thomas', Thomas Howard, Duke of Suffolk kept his face blank, neither encouraging, nor discouraging poor Essex. All his friends seemed to be deserting him though there were not many friends present at the trial. Cecil and Howard were definitely not on his side; they had already gained by his removal from court. He had to hope that his protégé Bacon would stand up for him in some way and help to save his life.

Thomas Howard had to wait until James's reign before he became Lord Chamberlain but already he had done well, being summoned to parliament as Baron Howard de Walden, he had become Lord Lieutenant of Cambridgeshire and the Isle of Ely on 8th April 1598, and he had become an admiral of a small fleet on 10th August 1599. In February 1601, he was Marshal of the Forces, which besieged the Earl of Essex at his house in London, and on the 19th he was sitting at the trials of Earls of Essex and Southampton, in his role as a peer and as Constable of the Tower of London where the accused were being held.

His implacable face did not reveal his pleasure at seeing Essex on trial, he found him arrogant and over-bearing. Also, his features did not reveal the fact that he was also rather hungry and wished the proceeding could be speeded up. His rise was like Essex's fall, as Thomas rose through the ranks of power, Essex fell from grace.

The court was adjourned, then, for the midday meal. Thomas Howard rose, motioned for the prisoners to be taken elsewhere and patted his rumbling stomach as he searched out Cecil to collect the good lunch he had been promised. Tudor politics was sophisticated enough for people to attach themselves to a rising star and drop those on their way down. That was how it had been, an early start at eight, evidence and witnesses read and called; a break about eleven, then more courtroom conversation, which depressed Essex more and added to Cecil's pleasure. Cecil knew that he just needed the heavy weight of evidence to submerge Devereux's puny defence. Later that afternoon, after lunch, the other evidence was read and Essex was asked to provide his own plea.

"I repeat, in my defence that the Lord Privy Seal, Robert Cecil, did dispute the succession plans of the Privy Council and did say to me that he would want to see the Spanish Infanta as the Queen of England when our fair 'Fairie Queen' had shifted off this mortal coil," Essex argued.

It was he who had encouraged James to the throne, if word of Cecil's disloyalty reached James's ears and James was to support Essex, he might be allowed a prison sentence at the Tower of London rather than execution, there might be a chance he would be pardoned by James once he came to the throne. If Devereux could convince his peers that there was doubt about Cecil's loyalty, he might escape conviction.

"No one would believe that," Cecil chided.

"And it was you who wanted to depose the Queen and replace her with King James of Scotland."

"I refute your accusation and say that it has already been proven as a counterfeit claim," Cecil countered calmly.

"It is known by all assembled that you have smarted under the perceived slights I provided when I had favour with the Queen. This is base revenge, the worst type of revenge, jealousy of the friendship the Queen had for me, you know my loyalty is not in question, I had the love of the Queen and the Queen had my love and loyalty, too," Essex argued emotively.

"Had, had, had, so you say; that was then, this is now; I had a meal yesterday, I am hungry today, a nobleman who looks to the past, is but a past master."

"Words, the court wants facts!" Essex interrupted impatiently.

"You had the Queen's friendship and you rewarded her thus with rebellion, you assuredly do not have her friendship, now!" Cecil cried, his voice booming through the hall.

"It seems so!"

"May I remind you, it is her court you stand in and her servants you try to besmirch. Your arrogance knows no bounds."

"Your father, Lord William Burghley, favoured me in Cecil House, and, now, I have been given the bill for his kindness, we grew up together and now you strike me when I am down, disavow me and besmirch my honour!" Essex bitterly replied.

He looked into Cecil's eyes, his own blazing with fury, but Cecil was unfazed. He returned the glare and spoke in clear and measured tones.

"For wit, I give you pre-eminence, you have it abundantly. For your nobility, I give you place. I am not a noble but a gentleman, which is no disgrace, I am no swordsman; there you have the odds, my body was not fashioned by the gods; but what I do have is innocence and with that conscience; truth and honesty are my true companions, so dear, to defend me against scandal. I have no fear; and the sting of slanderous tongues, wound me not, from those who truth and friendship has forgot. When all evidence is shown and all the many voices spent, I stand an upright man and your lordship a delinquent."

With those words Robert Cecil, left the hall.

Westminster erupted in calamitous uproar. Then the judges gave their verdict, and delivered the sentence too, Devereux's sphere of influence had waned and Cecil's only grew.

Chapter 13 – v - The End of Essex

The end was straightforward after the verdict. The Earls Essex and Southampton were taken in procession from Westminster Hall to the Tower of London for all of London to see. Axe blades were pointed towards them as they were marched along the Strand to Blackfriars and then further east to Tower Hill.

Essex was granted one last request from the exasperated Queen. He would be beheaded in privacy; it would not be a public execution.

Aged thirty-four, the brave, charming, hot headed, ill tempered, impatient, and irascible Essex was beheaded.

Southampton remained in the tower with a black cat for company while Essex prayed with his chaplain Mr. Ashton. Many were surprised by this pious repentance but it did not save him from the executioner's blade on 25th February 1601.

When James came to the throne, Southampton was released from the Tower, a repentant Catholic who changed his religion and was wary of Cecil from that time onwards.

Chapter 14 - The Priest Guest- April 1604

The priest sat with John Cage in the comfort of his front room, he had been a perfect guest, disappearing around the town to give communion to nobles far and wide. After, the first day, he seemed to eat like a sparrow but that had much to do with the fact that grateful householders always fed him after he heard confession followed by communion. Receiving two sacraments merited a meal; giving out penance for contrition and the consecration of the hosts proved hungry work.

"Tell me what you know of the Bye Plot," the priest politely asked, nestling himself into his usual chair.

"The conspiracy was hatched by Roman Catholic and Puritan nobles hoping to bring religious toleration for all religions. Anthony Copley was one of the Catholics involved," explained Cage wearily, rubbing his cheeks with his hands to accentuate his tiredness in the hope that his guest might take pity on him and allow him to go to bed.

"I know the name, what happened to him?" enthused the priest, deliberately ignoring Cage's *ennui*. He thought he could offer his tiredness up to God.

"The authorities had marked him as a *'bravo'* and when he returned without permission; he was put in the Tower."

"A *'bravo'*?"

"A bravo is someone who is an object of suspicion."

"Was he not loyal to the Crown?"

"Well however loyal or disloyal he was to Elizabeth, Copley was implicated in the Bye Plot. Copley and the other conspirators were tried and condemned to death; but Copley was pardoned on eighteenth, having made a confession relating the history of the plot."

"I know it is your job, but please spare me the details around the matter, this is not a lecture in law; what was the nub?"

"The nub of the plan was to kidnap the King and try to put Lady Arbella Stuart on the throne."

"It's laughable; did he think he would get away with it?"

"It was a desperate plan made by desperate people."

"What did Copley hope to gain from such rashness?"

"We have all been rash, look at the Earl of Essex and his march on the city; it has now been recorded as a rebellion, no less. The plotters hoped for religious toleration of course!"

"They hoped that the fines for not attending the Church of England services would stop; the recusant fines would end. Surely it would be easier to go to the service on Sunday and refuse the bread, which was possible; in actual fact the Pope made it permissible many years ago."

"Indeed it would have been easier."

"I can see that the Puritans would gain from such action but what did the Catholics hope to achieve? Those who wanted to worship would have their priest at home, they could take the host before or after the service by the State, but there was really no need to attract attention by staying away from church and no need to be needlessly fined."

"And many of the Catholics in London did exactly that and just as many became lapsed. Few were staunch and few were religious enough to make a stand, they wanted to continue in their professions or trades, I myself wanted to continue at law and so I attended the state services, signing the book and then stealing aboard a Spanish. Defying the state would jeopardise my work, I am sure others took the same pragmatic approach; why risk your work and risk arrest when you can sign the book and find a service to suit you. People have to sign the book, attend the services, they are used to worshipping in private."

"How many were recusants were there; was it a substantial number?" he asked, needing to know for his report when he returned to the Abbott.

The Jesuits needed to know how many of their flock needed succour. Their ethos was to educate and support fellow Catholics. Their methods were extremely sophisticated. They both stared into the fire wondering why they had to hide their religion and hide from the state. After a while, the priest looked across at the exhausted Cage wondering if it was his presence that contributed to Cage's inability to sleep.

Cage noticed his stare and immediately came back into the present and answered, "Not in our area, London, Cecil's spies are too thick on the ground, but, allegedly, elsewhere across the country, so we are told; no, in fact, we were warned; the state claimed that there were thousands of recusants but I fear their figures have been greatly exaggerated to discredit Catholics further."

"So it could have been a rumour spread by Cecil; he always gives information that is designed to frighten and intimidate. Could it have been a subterfuge to stir up trouble for the Catholics?"

"Perhaps," admitted Cage, "it seems the State is keen to undermine anyone who professes their faith to be Roman Catholic."

"It sounds like his hallmark do you not think?"

"You could be right," admitted Cage grudgingly, he knew the Jesuits enjoyed producing their own propaganda as much as the state enjoyed producing their propaganda.

"Go on," the priest added encouragingly.

"These recusants, or should I say for your benefit, faithful Catholics, were rumoured to have priests at home and were allegedly rich enough to refuse to go to services and were more than able to pay the fine."

"Were they fined every time?"

"It depended on the local sheriffs. Some ambivalent sheriffs allowed the practice to continue unpunished, others persecuted transgressors severely. No one knows the figures. It was possible for sheriffs to persecute a family and it was also possible for families to ignore the demand for them to attend church services."

"They could have indeed done so," agreed the priest but his agreement signalled that he did not agree, "but that would have been highly dangerous because, as we know, the State has spies everywhere. Cecil might have one of your servants in his employ."

"You are right, Cecil has everyone working for him."

"Including one of your servants?"

"Quite possibly, there is nothing I can do, I just go about my business as a model citizen in the hope that I will avoid arrest and execution."

"You are right, it is far better for us to appear to be following the rules by going to church and receiving the host even if it was not blessed, to us it is just bread, nothing more. We could with clear conscience attend their masses."

"There were those who realised that it was not incompatible to worship in church and receive communion at home."

"Our records show that many did, we do know, after all, it is we who administer the true sacrament."

"You say so, but many did not, from the reports of the bishops and from the list of attendances at masses in London. No one can be sure, some bishops exaggerated the recusancy problem in order to stir up agitation in the breast of those who hated Catholics especially those who were Puritan in mind and spirit; yet just as many of the bishops had good relations with the nobles; they had known each other for years, only new bishops and sheriffs would be prepared to jeopardise relations between the church and the nobility by introducing fines."

"So the new bishops told you of the recusants?" the priest enquired further, a barrister might say that he was leading the witness. Jesuit priests were masters at gleaning information and experts in producing their own propaganda. They were always on the look out for both.

"There were rumours; we knew which families were Catholic and who did not attend. Do not forget that many bishops in rural areas would have turned a blind eye to recusancy and would be joined by the sheriffs."

"They would disobey the law?"

"Getting on in a small community is more important than law and religion."

"Perhaps the stubborn recusants were told by their Jesuit priests to stay away from church, they might have been influenced by their Spanish allies?"

"When there is trouble outside the State, wise men avoid trouble within that State. This is sensible if you want to survive in this humanist hell-hole."

"I know it is difficult in these times."

"We are watched constantly, betrayal is around each corner. If we do not conform to the requirements of the state, we will be accused of some heinous crime, treachery to the crown or harbouring a priest, which you know is, now, illegal."

"You make your point well," replied the priest, unmoved but shifting in his chair and placing his palms together as if in prayer in order to focus more fully on what Cage said. He was naive in many ways but he had been taught enough about argument and rhetoric to understand complex problems. He wanted to win Cage over but he needed to ascertain the dangers for himself and others who might follow him.

"Very possibly, we have not had a happy time of late, people's memories of horrors are long, Queen Mary's reputation still haunts the streets: the Puritan presses extolling the suffering of Protestant martyrs: and the horrors committed by Catholics in Europe, have done little to help. At the time of the Bye Plot, the war with Spain had been going on for twenty years in the Netherlands, in the North Sea and in Ireland. It was the State's wish to sue for peace."

"The State claims that the Catholics have friends in all their enemies," the priest noted wryly.

"True enough, the State sees mischief in every corner and would have us fear our very shadow. The new regime provided hope for English Catholics, they protested their loyalty to the Crown when James ascended to the throne."

"As did the Puritans, both the Catholics and Puritans were constrained in their religion. My reports tell me that Catholics were ministered to by priests in secret."

"Really?" Cage had decided to play with him.

"That was what we were told."

Cage decided to put his priest's misconceptions to bed.

"We were quite happy if we could worship even if it had to be behind closed doors, it allowed us to continue working."

"Perhaps the Puritans felt they should have more from the King, they wanted to change too many of the old practices," Cage suggested. "The King is conservative and does not like to broach the subject of change. He needs to maintain his power through the bishops as well as through his espions."

King James had arrived in England pretending to want toleration for all religions and in reality, wanting toleration for none.

"They wanted the removal of what they call popish practices that the felt the church in the time of Elizabeth had allowed to remain or return to the mass. They wanted to read only the canonical gospels of Mathew, Mark, Luke, and John."

"So why the clumsy plot, these were intelligent people who were aware of the dangers. Knowing the risks, why would they be so careless?"

"Perhaps, as people say, it was just talk and Cecil acted on the rumours; perhaps the plotters realised the dangers but went ahead anyway; perhaps Cecil prepared a trap for them that they could not avoid; whatever the case, they paid for their rashness," explained Cage.

He was beginning to tire of explaining every detail and nuance to his guest. The priest had picked on him because of his knowledge, but there was a limit.

"That Cecil is a cunning fox, he needs to be watched," complained the priest talking metaphorically.

"The gaoled becoming the gaoler, the watched the watcher, he has too many eyes and ears, we could never compete with him, I would rather box in Southwark with bare knuckles, on one leg and a hand tied behind my back."

"We must pray for perseverance, then."

Chapter 15 – The Fisheries

Walking alongside and in the shadow of the Augustine priory of St. Mary Overy, Southwark's chief church, the two men seemed incongruous companions, one tall and upright; one short and stooped. The two men wore the fashionable *capotain* hat, with its tall conical crown rounded at the top and a narrow brim, but that was the only similarity.

Markham was wearing bright clothes and therefore his fashionable hat was dyed a light brown, almost beige, with a peacock feather in its bright crimson satin band, Cecil's hat was black with a bronze satin band but he wore a dark grey cloak and black hose making him look more like a crow or mendicant monk than an omnipotent Privy Councillor. It was bright but brisk and the narrow street funnelled the wind through the channel they negotiated between Thames-side taverns and warehouses and the old thirteenth century Minster.

Although it was July, there was a distinct nip in the air, the north wind winning over more gentle Gulf Streams and Continental warm fronts. The summer sun shone over the Thames but Clink Street around the religious buildings and warehouses was in shadow. The Bishop of Winchester, Archbishop Thomas Bilson, held what remained of the priory property after the dissolution.

"Bishop Bilson is a bald buffoon," complained Cecil delighting in his alliteration.

"But a useful one, does he not pay rent for his fishery?" asked Markham.

"I could list his credentials, a relative of the Duke of Bavaria, educated at Winchester and New College, Bishop of Worcester and he paid us £400 as an annuity for his appointment to the 'see' of Winchester."

"That is a princely sum for an impoverished priest."

"Indeed, but these men of the cloth are businessmen; they pay us rent for their properties and others pay them more to lease those properties."

"I heard he is a poet."

"Really, there is nothing poetic in his actions: he supports all the perfidious practices such as prostitution, drinking dens, bear-baiting and bare-knuckle rings. Everyone fancies themselves as playwright, or poet or wordsmith thanks to Bill Shakespeare!" grumbled Cecil. "He shares none of the rhythm and rhyme of the Bard and cannot match the product of the quill held by our great writer, the unequalled, Will."

"Why are we going to visit Winchester Palace, not to view the thirteen foot rose window, surely?" asked Markham, ignoring Cecil's attack on Bishop Bilson, he rather liked the affable bishop.

"No we are off to Clink Street to meet Catesby; I am going to give him a tour of the Bishop's estate!" announced Cecil, stopping to address Markham and wrong-footing him. Markham almost tripped over his master, such was his desire to let him lead, he knew that 'dogs follow their masters' or at least match their pace.

"Surely, you do not intend to show him the whole 700 acres!" Markham objected, thinking not of poor Catesby but of his aching feet once he had crossed one section of the vast estate. The Bishop did indeed lease a vast estate with sheep and cows, a pike garden, for fresh fish, a brewery, and a granary for storing corn and other grain and a mill to turn grain into flour.

"Do you realise how long it would take to walk; no, we're going to the fishery."

"Why do you loathe the Bishop so much?"

"Perhaps it is his Bishopric I loathe!"

"Not all."

"Like any man, I enjoy visiting the Rose, the Swan and the Globe."

"Really."

"The lessees are friends of mine, you know Francis and Philip; I introduced you!"

"I know Bill and James, too!"

"Everyone knows them, or claims to; everyone would like to have Shakespeare's wit and Burbage's money!"

"So you do not disprove of the theatre like our Puritan cousins?"

"No, nor do I want the graveyard where the punks are laid to rest to become consecrated ground and their bodies dug up and tossed into the Thames, as some would want!"

"So what is it?"

"The way Bilson has drawn up rules for stews and how he runs his own doll-tear-sheets strutting in the theatres! I find the whole business abhorrent."

"There was need for rule and regulation and the '*Winchester Angels*' are the prettiest girls even if they are far more expensive than all the rest."

"Spoken like a true Catholic! You obviously speak from experience! He is a bishop, a man of God; he should not be running brothels and making his money from whores! I thought they were called the '*Winchester Geese*'. Don't tell me, I know, the only ones you have met are the ones who look like angels!"

"I thought Henslowe had leased some brothels, inns and lodging houses from Bilson; isn't he part of the theatre, too?" Markham asked. "If theatre owners turn pimp, shouldn't anyone? Why should such a lucrative source of revenue be denied the bishops, they spend their money on the poor."

"Perhaps but he is not a man of God, Henslowe is one of us, a mere mortal."

"Surely, not. He is much wealthier than a mere mortal."

"You are right though; Henslowe has his hand in everything; you name it dye-ing, starch making and wood selling, pawn-broking, money lending, all manner of vices and usury."

"A priest without religion, then."

"Ha, well said! He helps me, he once said of his actors 'should these *fellowes* come out of my debt I should have no rule over them', he is a wise man."

"He is one of yours; that is your expression for the recusants, no, for everyone! The Bishop is not one of yours and that is why you despise him! You can get your cut from everyone else but not from him."

"He still pays the annuity, we get our money, I admit, but not as much control as we would like; James needs the Bishops not only for their wealth but for their power in parliament."

"So why not get one of your people to take over the '*Epicopo Wintonensi*'?" asked Markham, he had received a classical education and he was intelligent, and 'well read', but that did not mean that he was considered to be an equal by others there. As a Catholic, it was expected that he would know Latin and refer to the Winchester Episcopal body in such terms. Those in the Court, the Privy Council, and in the Church, felt themselves superior to others in every way. Markham was not a member of any of those three institutions.

"I like the way you think, my own bishop within the viper's nest of the Lord Bishops. A good idea but the other bishops would smell a rat. All in good time! Besides he has brought order to the 'bad lands' around here and he helps us with our records, he is a good ally but not a good friend. I grant him one thing and that is he keeps our lists up to date."

"Do they really help? Surely, the churchwardens' lists of mass attendance are not accurate, are they? They hardly provide a clear picture; surely there is too much leeway for error. Are they really of any use?"

"They are and they are not, they tell us who is not here and who was, who has arrived and who has left, we can see at a glance what is going on should we be pursuing an individual. I know the feast days around Easter allow for people to travel home and that would have explained why people did not take compulsory communion in London but we can act if they are not recorded at their other church."

"You know everything and from such a discreet source."

"We can trace others; you are in my service already so I need not look for you! Besides, you are in the tower under lock and key. Others will be led to believe that you have been let out for good behaviour should they spot you and that is what I shall tell them. Very few know your role as my protector. As for the attendance registers at church, they show habits and we need to see habits are kept up. It is useful for us to keep track of those in the guilds and in trade for tax purposes, too; my clerks work hard; I have to raise the money to pay for my '*spione*' entourage."

"Your *espions* are everywhere!"

They walked hurriedly along Clink Street.

"I need eyes and espies everywhere in these strange times. My office grows in need and influence but each clerk and snitch and punk earns every penny I pay them. They all work for me!"

"Are we not arrived at the palace? I can see the rose windows," he announced quickly.

He was anxious to answer before Cecil caught his breath for another detailed explanation about statecraft and the need to be aware of everything. Markham had seen the portrait of Elizabeth wearing a dress that had a pattern, which looked like it had eyes dotted all over the material, suggesting that she had eyes everywhere and the state saw everything. He was relieved the lecture had been brought to a close. He was well aware of why they kept lists of those taking communion at various churches around the capital and of Cecil's need to be involved in the minutiae of statecraft. That did not make it interesting listening.

Arriving at the great wooden double doors, they lapsed into silence; Markham could not resist looking at the famous rose window in all its stained-glass glory, while Cecil affected their entry. It truly was a wonderful sight, all the colours and detail, Markham marvelled. Standing in the shadow of the doorway reminded him of his first visit to the Palace of Westminster; the bishop's palace had the same oak-panelled, greyish stained, door, the same wrought iron handles with a protuberance like the tooth that a chick uses to peck its way out of its eggshell; but this was on the underside. The handles were the circumference of a large Spanish watermelon.

Cecil grabbed one bringing it to the horizontal and slammed the knocker against the thick oak three times. An iron plate, nailed to the door, where the iron tooth struck, protected the oak from damage from the tooth in the knocker. The great iron ring resonated as the tooth struck the square metal plate three times.

Markham watched for signs of life and he was rewarded a few minutes later by the wrought iron ring moving in a clockwise direction and the two halves of the door splitting from their married state. One of the Bishop's men, looking suspiciously like an old Henrician church monk, opened the door slightly so that he could peer out.

He was dressed in the simple brown robes of a medieval monk; he could have been Friar Tuck. The confident rapping on the door convinced him it was either someone very important, or a beggar with bravado, perhaps a *bravo*. A quick glance at the apparel of the gentlemen assured him that they were the former type and he opened the door wide to admit them.

"Good afternoon, my sons," the priest said meekly as he assuredly pushed the door closed, so it married with its other half, and he tugged the corresponding iron ring on the inside, just to check the catch of the lock had fully engaged. Once he had regained his rightful place in front of his guests, he bowed solemnly. The guests, in turn, inclined their heads to acknowledge the gesture.

It was quiet and still, the noise of the street did not penetrate the walls and the priest seemed to want them to appreciate that fact. He seemed to want them to understand the serenity of the place.

They found themselves in a rectangular hall with two rose windows on the front and back walls, an arched doorway between each and at the ends of the hall, two smaller rectangular doors made out of the same sturdy wood. Above them was a vaulted ceiling, a *cruck* frame supported by oak beams joined through tongue and groove and secured by wooden pegs.

"Good afternoon, Father, I am Robert Cecil, come to meet the venerable Bishop Bilson," Cecil explained with no hint of impatience and every sign of respect. Cecil and Markham both returned the bow.

"Indeed, we were expecting you, 'My Lord', we are honoured to receive you; it is not often that we receive a visit from the Secretary of State, himself! Shall I show you the way to the gardens and orchard?" asked the priest.

"No need kind friar, I know the way," replied Cecil bowing to him for a second time, but with fewer flourishes.

"Then, bless you both, I hope you enjoy the sunshine out there," the priest answered, showing not the slightest concern over Cecil's companion's silence.

"Thank you, Father," Cecil said before leading Markham to an identical door on the opposite wall.

Turning the wrought iron ring to his left, he pulled one of the double oak doors towards him. The great arch of the door was split and sunlight flooded into the dim hall as one half of the arch was drawn into the hall, creaking on its great iron cardinals.

Without speaking, he led the way into the courtyard, being south-facing, it benefitted from the sun all day.

Markham did not need to be told to close the door behind him and the large clunk as the mortise lock bit broke the silence. The other two would not wait for him, he knew that.

Fortunately being taller than both, he was able to catch up easily in a few strides. There was not another noise in that space until Cecil started to stroll on the flagstones, his leather shoes making a slapping sound. There was an echo and then that echo was joined by Markham's stride to keep up with Cecil and the echo of that, too.

"Was he a Catholic priest?" Markham whispered incredulously.

"No doubt a convert," Cecil replied in hushed tones, "people expect someone in a habit to greet them at a religious house."

"I thought you said..."

"What I said is not relevant here, it was outside the walls."

"Of course, I beg your forgiveness, but I am still curious about the Father you called friar."

"Many monks converted to avoid being thrown onto the streets, some were kept on by the new bishops because of their expertise, in writing contracts."

"We have lay lawyers, now."

"The church prefers its traditions and few lawyers are experts on canon law, some monks will have been studying law since they were eleven years of age, such knowledge cannot be dispensed with easily," the priest continued unabashed by the interruption.

"Indeed." agreed Markham.

"Further, others, amongst these brothers, are skilled in medicinal matters or simply good scribes; such skills are all rare and there is a good life for those prepared to change faiths. It would be madness to throw these brothers onto the streets."

"Here comes Bishop Bilson," warned Markham quickly, tugging on Cecil's cape to encourage him to turn to face the approaching bulk of the bishop.

"Ah, Thomas, 'Your Grace', Bishop of Winchester," Cecil greeted Bilson as if he were a long lost friend, bowing with a flourish.

"Dear Robert, it is I!"

"It is an honour to meet with you again after our time at Hampton Court. You are looking fuller of figure and wealthier and healthier than ever."

"Well met, Lord Privy Seal of all England, it is an honour your Lordship, to receive the chief Privy Councillor and devoted, loyal servant of the crown, the Secretary of State and your bodyguard, Markham!" responded Bilson with an equally friendly tone but his words, not his manner, said everything he wanted to say. Bilson bowed feebly, leaning forward at the waist and inclining his chin slightly, like a half-hearted nod. Moreover, he heaped praise on Cecil without mentioning his fine intellect and he teased him about having Markham for protection. Cecil bridled as Bilson knew he would.

"He is more like a puppy," Cecil explained. "A loyal and faithful servant."

"I am, it is true and I hope I may prove myself as loyal to you," Markham announced hoping to ingratiate himself with Bilson; a man of the Archbishop's influence would be a useful ally to Markham.

"I hope not, a dog with two masters;" counted Bilson slyly, a smile playing on his flabby face, "but I appreciate your sentiments and should Cecil let you go, I would be honoured to have such a distinguished *'fellowe'* in my service; your reputation as a swordsman of finesse and daring precedes you."

"Your Grace is too kind," replied Markham courteously.

"You're not a Jesuit, are you?" asked Bilson.

"Far from it!" cried Markham in alarm.

"My good friend Markham is a friend of the Church," Cecil announced, "I can vouch for him; like all good Protestants he has a direct relationship with God and does not require popish priests to intercede on his behalf."

"It is true." Markham felt the need to support Cecil's claims.

"However, he is friends with Catholics and is an obedient servant of both God and His Majesty."

"Thank you," breathed Markham, it was awkward to admit he was a lapsed Catholic.

"Furthermore, he has renounced his recusancy and his Catholic faith. It is a marvel how the Lord works in his mysterious ways."

Bilson nodded with satisfaction, he was not entirely convinced of Markham's conversion, but had established beyond reasonable doubt that he was not some Jesuit spy. They walked on through the courtyard; the chapel was to their left and the lodgings to their right, Markham could smell the horses' excrement and the smell of their urine on straw as they approached the stables.

"Good, Cecil has read my book *The True Difference Betweene Christian Subjection and Unchristian Rebellion*, as have many in the Lowlands when they challenged Philip of Spain and they took succour from it," continued Bilson. Cecil had read the book and it was as needlessly wordy as Bilson's present pontificating. They walked past the stable building and through an archway that provided a bridge between the courtyard and the garden, the echo of feet on stone ringing off the walls and resounding in their ears. The noise disappeared suddenly, followed by the thrum of a myriad of insects basking in the sun shining on the wall and distant birdsong. The feel of soft grass beneath their feet made an imperceptible change in their rhythm and bearing, they slowed their pace unconsciously and allowed nature to surreptitiously envelop them.

"King James was not fond of your idea that kings might forfeit their Crown," Cecil insisted provocatively, enjoying the feel of soft grass under his feet.

"Only corrupt kings!" countered Bilson defensively. He worried that Cecil might yet trap him into treason, such was the Privy Councillor's reputation, and Bilson could not afford to risk that. "I am sure the King realised that!"

"And what of corrupt bishops?" Cecil asked wistfully.

"Let us not bore Markham," Bilson suggested quickly, "he is a man of action, not a thinker."

"Indeed but as Socrates said: 'the unexamined life is not worth living!' do you not find it so?" Markham exclaimed haughtily, hoping to be treated as an equal amongst these fine thinkers.

There would never be a chance of that, Bilson and Cecil knew it; Markham did not, he was too naive and too hopeful to even countenance being seen as an inferior, after all he was well educated and intelligent.

Neither man felt Markham's wit matched theirs not that it ever would. They saw themselves as totally superior to him.

"I enjoy Saint Thomas Aquinas more than Socrates but I know that Cecil is keen to see my fisheries, are you both fond of pike and brown trout?"

With that Bilson dismissed any chance for philosophical or theological discussions and steered the increasingly impatient Cecil to his goal. They progressed slowly, Bilson's bulk slowed them down and Cecil's gait was always slow, poor Markham had to halve his normal stride and force his legs to move more slowly as Cecil and Bilson continued their dialogue.

"How are you and the other scholars faring with the new Bible and prayer book?" Cecil asked, trying his best to get Bilson on his side despite his burning desire to get to his meeting with Catesby.

They had passed into the garden and the smell of flowers was incredible, Cecil and Markham found themselves taking deeper breaths; outside in Clink Street it was wiser to take shorter breaths while trying to ignore the stench and filth from the gutters.

"It is a long endeavour, we hope to be finished within five years," Bilson replied optimistically.

He was determined that the new version would be the best that is was possible to produce and he hoped it would last for decades if not for centuries to come. It was important to get the details correct and with that in mind he had put his best scholars on to the task.

"I would have thought it would have taken you ten," Cecil ventured.

"With God's help, we might be able to finish sooner, I have many other duties and distractions."

"Talking of distractions, your gardens look wonderful, so well-tended and ordered."

"Order is a virtue."

"Indeed," replied Cecil.

For the first time Cecil turned to Markham, Markham panicked; he had not been listening intently to the conversation, but drinking in the fine gardens with their healing herbs, that smelt so sweet, such as lavender. The flowers like the roses would yield oils for the apothecary. He had been lost in a world of scent and the sound of birdsong.

"What do you think of the fisheries?"

"Pike, I like, I care '*nowt*' about trout," Markham announced to both, smiling to show he was joking, both men politely smiled at his remark though neither found it clever or funny.

"A good choice, pike or *Esox Lucius*, are ideal for my sweet water gardens!" Bilson said, "I keep trout as they are not so carnivorous and easier to clean when fished out, though I find the meatiness of the pike more rewarding, Friday is still fish day despite other popish rituals disappearing. We seem to have picked up that habit and cannot lose it."

The Bishop led the way towards a doorway in a high brick wall that led into the cloistered gardens.

"Fish can be better than fowl if prepared in the proper way," commented Cecil, pleased that they were finally being led to their destination.

"I have never seen pike before," confessed Markham.

"Just look in the water," seethed Cecil losing patience.

Markham, without the slightest acknowledgment of Cecil's ire, stared into the water and was charmed by the life he saw in the pool. He liked fish, it was his favourite dish; he looked forward to Fridays and tucking into the white flesh. It fascinated him to see his supper growing.

"They are pike shaped hence the name, they have pointed snouts, and we call the trout pike, too, because they are equally pointed."

"I see," said Markham with emphasis, nodding his head sagely to show he appreciated his education.

"The difference is in the colour; they are often olive green, shading from yellow to white along the belly. The flank is marked with short, light bar-like spots and there are dark spots on the fins. Sometimes the fins are reddish," Bilson explained in his annoying pontificating way. "They are a large fish though, sometimes they are twice the size of this."

"Fascinating," said Cecil unconvincingly, "are the pike generally larger?"

Bilson was not only a man who made his living from the most disgusting of practices but he was also boring, noted Cecil to himself. He, too, wished he could just listen to the chaffinches' song and not have to hear Bilson droning on.

"The trout can also be a goodly size, but you are right the pike do grow to a greater size; either would make a decent supper."

"I can see why you prefer the pike," said Cecil inferring that the Bishop would like more of a meal on his plate to feed his fat belly, he would want an extra helping of fish flesh. Cecil saw gluttony as a sin.

"How so?" challenged Bilson, feeling for the first time, slightly, peeved.

"As you said before, the pike has a meatier taste than the trout so naturally it would be more satisfying," Cecil replied, smiling politely, pleased at the way he had avoided causing offence.

Bilson, reassured, continued his lecture.

"The younger pike have yellow stripes along a green body, later these stripes divide into light spots, and the body turns from green to olive green, it is really quite remarkable. Obviously, we have to keep the pike separate from the trout," continued Bilson, warming to a subject he knew well.

"Fascinating," remarked Cecil, sounding as if he was not at all fascinated.

"Why do you have so many ponds?" Markham asked curiously.

"You ask many questions my dear Markham," complained Cecil good-naturedly.

"The full-grown fish spawn in spring; we need to have deep pools for the males and we have to make the pools deep to replicate the spawning grounds, we put the males in first and then add the full-grown females after."

"Hence the deep pool," Markham remarked. He was thoroughly enjoying his tour of the pools.

"The males follow the females around and the female flaps its tail frantically and releases up to sixty eggs. These we net and take to a smaller pond. Would you like to see?" Bilson offered enthusiastically.

He had no desire to go back to his study, scrolls, books, and clerical work on such a sunny day. He would be bothered by his clerics and would have to work hard, strolling with Cecil and Markham was infinitely preferable.

"You are kind my Lord Bishop but we are meeting a friend by the trout ponds and he will explain all, we have taken up much of your time, thank you for your care."

"It has been an honour, I never have had such gracious company and Markham's interest in pike is most gratifying, if you should require anything further, Brother Stephen will be accompanying you at a discreet distance, he is totally trustworthy; beckon to him and he will get a message to me."

"That is most kind; may we bid you farewell," Cecil replied.

"Farewell to thee and God be with you," said the Bishop.

He stopped himself from making the sign of the cross to bless them; such popish display might antagonise Cecil. It was a hard habit to break. There had been so many changes and yet Bilson was a creature of habit and giving out blessings had been drummed into him as a novice.

"Your Grace, I have one last question, how do they hunt?" Markham asked.

"Of course, such an apposite question from such a gallant gentleman," replied the Bishop kindly; he liked his pupil's candid nature and willingness to learn. It was endearing.

"You are too kind," Markham opined.

"The pike have their own way of hunting; they can remain still, yet they move their fins, flapping madly, but before striking they bend their body and dash out to the prey using their large fins to push them through the water."

"Clever creatures," sighed Markham admiringly.

"But most cunningly of all they catch their prey sideways on and with their sharp pointed teeth; they impale it before turning the prey headfirst in their mouths and swallowing it."

Markham felt that Cecil was very like those pike. He swallowed hard before asking the next question.

"What do they eat?"

"Pike eat anything but fish is their natural choice, though we have fed them with water voles, rats and frogs," answered Bilson assuredly.

The Bishop was, so it seemed, impressed by Markham's interest if not his intellect. Markham's throat tightened further, the pike *was* the water-based equivalent to Cecil. He attacked his prey from the side when they least expected and dug his teeth in hard, he cared not whether they were Calvin, Catholic, Jewish, Protestant or Puritan, if they were in his pond they were his prey and he swallowed them whole, head first before they knew what was happening.

"All I care about is how best to eat them, I have heard you have many recipes."

"They are not easy to cook, the flesh is bony and they have large epipleural bones," Bilson explained.

"'Y' shaped," Cecil interjected as he saw Markham about to ask yet another question. Markham opened and closed his mouth just like the fish in the pools below them.

"Exactly, but they are fairly easily filleted, especially the larger ones, there are receipts going back as far as Roman times; I will have my three favourites sent to you," Bilson promised, it was a trifle, a junior scribe would copy a few recipes from their records.

Bilson knew that it was the simple things that mattered most; such a kind gesture was guaranteed to please the recipients.

"You favour us greatly, adieu Lord Bishop and thank you once again for all you have done, Your Grace," Cecil spluttered, beaming from ear to ear, seldom did anyone give him a favour or a present.

He almost changed his mind about Bilson being a buffoon; almost but not quite.

"To do the King's will; I must do the King's servant's will. It is always a pleasure to serve Lord Cecil, Baron Cecil of Essendon and now Viscount Cranbourne," Bilson replied obsequiously, knowing that Cecil had the ear of King James and was extremely influential. Bilson wanted to work on King James's bible and to put his conservative values into the new prayer book.

"The announcement has not been officially made but your Lord Bishops are as well informed as ever," Cecil admitted coyly as befitted his position, he had to appear to be humble when new honours were lavished upon him, in truth, he felt it was high time his loyalty was rewarded and the work that he had undertaken deserved even more opportunities for patronage.

"Adieu to you," Bilson cried quickly, he did not want to let Cecil know how he knew about the appointment; a swift exit was required before he became mired in politics.

Just as Cecil had his spies, the Church and the Lord Bishops had their informers, their spies and a spectacularly good intelligence service of their own, not as good as Cecil's but not far behind it. Returning his adieu, Cecil and Markham and the incongruous pair made off between the pike ponds to the brown trout fishery to make their appointment.

Catesby stood in his cape a felt hat, on his head, it was not tall and fashionable like Markham's but flat like the style worn by Thomas More in earlier times, the hat had belonged to Catesby's father.

They spotted him as they came upon the first of the salmon pools. One of the fishery workers, a very old, surprisingly upright and tall lay brother, was talking to him about the salmon. Everyone seemed to dote on the fish.

The sun came out from behind a cumulus cloud and warmed the back of their necks. They were in a true haven, amongst the sights and smells and sounds of the country; a little bit of paradise right on the periphery of the sprawling mass of the South Bank of London.

The lay brother, Father Thomas, was trying to explain about the brown trout, "Our trout are purely freshwater, they are named '*salmo trutta morpha fario*' and they are fed on corn worms and wax worms which will become moths otherwise. Corn worms eat corn and millet and wax worms…"

"They are whitish caterpillars with black-tipped feet and small brown heads," cried Catesby enthusiastically, "we had them infest the hives last year, they ate the pollen and then ate the beeswax; they destroyed the honey comb!"

Father Thomas would not be distracted, not even when Markham and Cecil joined them even though that was an unusual occurrence to be sure, three well-dressed and obviously wealthy gentlemen visiting the fisheries was remarkable. Catesby's comments seemed to fall on deaf ears as Father Thomas continued: "The brown trout come in all manner of colours, from largely silver with relatively few spots and a white belly, to the colour of brass, fading to creamy white on the fish's belly, with larger spots surrounded by lighter halos."

"Well Saint Robin, you should be wearing a halo, your behaviour has been angelic of late, have you finally learnt your lesson?" asked Cecil, by way of a greeting, while the brother drew breath.

"I have, indeed, and now I am learning about trout, I hope to start my own fish farm soon," replied Catesby good-naturedly.

"Did they charge for giving you all this knowledge?" Cecil enquired innocently, though Catesby knew he was referring to the fine he had paid for his transgressions against the State.

"Everyone charges for everything these days; they made me pay," confessed Catesby earnestly. He showed Cecil that he knew to which knowledge he was referring and that he had paid dearly for the lesson he had learnt in Queen Elizabeth's reign. His fine had cost him the house he had been born in, had inherited and had hoped to pass on to his children.

The monk remained motionless.

"Carry on the lesson," Cecil commanded, nodding at the horrified lay brother, normally people who came to the ponds hung on his every word and certainly never conversed amongst themselves, "we will walk with you and tarry when you tarry. I must check that the Bishop of Winchester records such charges."

Now that Catesby had joined the two of them, they made an awkward three, a strange trinity. Cecil in the centre and the two tall men on either side; they were obliged to let the monk lead the way, as the pathways between the pools would not accommodate more than three people abreast. The monk was still mystified by their behaviour.

He led the group to a pond with clear shallow water and gravel at the bottom, at one end there was a waterfall, letting a trickle of water into the pond. The water appeared still on the surface yet a little spout at the other end stopped the pond from overflowing and ensured the flow of water was constant.

There was a fine net across the circumference of the spout to stop any spawn flowing through. The whole farm mirrored nature but had been manufactured by a team of workers, digging out pools and streams. It was a magnificent achievement.

"When she is ready to spawn, in the wild, in late autumn, the hen trout picks a site. It tends to be where the water flows steadily over clean gravel at the tail of a large pool," continued the lay brother, happily.

"We have recreated it here with that waterfall gently feeding this quite shallow pond, in which we have scattered gravel, the water flows quickly carrying away any silt; it is clear water that she likes. You should come back here in the autumn; early November would be the best time to see them spawn."

"I will indeed return in the first few days of November to see this miraculous feat," promised Catesby earnestly.

"At that juncture of time, the hen fish fashions a pit in the gravel; we call this pit a 'redd'; she does that using her tail to dig, it's amazing really," the lay brother insisted.

Neither of his listeners looked that convinced.

"Rather like the pit you have dug for yourself, hey Robin," Cecil added, laughing and nudging Markham at the same time.

Markham looked horrified. Robert Catesby was his friend and he knew that Robert only liked his friends to call him Robin and he did not consider Cecil a friend, a useful ally, at that moment in time, but definitely not a friend. Markham suspected Cecil knew this and merely wanted to irritate Catesby.

He enjoyed toying with people. Markham did not like this aspect of his master, he was toying with Catesby for sport and he knew that Catesby could not show any reaction to the jibe, it was a cruel game to play on a vulnerable person.

"I like my new pit, it serves me well. Since you dried up my pond and made me choose another, I find life more ordered and to your liking; indeed, you did me a service, I am happily living in my new surroundings and I have a new venture to keep me busy."

"So I have heard, pray continue, kind brother," Cecil said. Father Thomas and Catesby looked at one another, both of them wondering to whom the comment was addressed.

The monk decided it must be him.

"Once the 'redd' is dug, she is joined in the hole by the male. Hundreds of eggs and the male's milt are squirted into the base of the 'redd', her eggs take in water and sink into a nest. They are quickly covered up by the female," he continued.

"Look at me as the hen fish that protects my eggs, look how well Markham thrives under my auspices. He is in my nest," Cecil interjected, there was warmth in his voice but his eyes were cold.

"The female immediately creates another redd, upstream of the first, and the gravel, from the second hole, fills the first redd to cover the first clutch of eggs," their guide continued.

"Surely some eggs miss the 'redd' and drift downstream. Then, fish, including other trout, will eat them!" suggested Cecil; he had been on a trout farm tour before.

"Some will find their way into other cracks and crevices where they may well survive," argued the exasperated Father Thomas. It really was irksome.

He really was becoming quite perturbed by the constant interruptions and the conversations that were being held with their barbed comments and subtle secret meanings. He was even more taken aback as Catesby and Cecil ignored him entirely and verbally duelled in front of him. He was not sure if the fish would appreciate such animosity.

"That is possible but unlikely," Cecil decided, "the hen protects the little eggs. Without her protection, the other spawn will be lost, just like the State protects those that are in its redd. Those that are lost, perish."

"We are aware of how nature works, its cruelty and its comfort," Catesby replied. "I have seen the cruelty that lost eggs endure and I now come for the protection a hen can offer her spawn."

"So, you wish my protection in order that your shipping business will grow from an 'aelvin'; to a small fry; and thence to a parr."

"Precisely so; you know that we want to bring over sack and need a licence to do so; you can supply it through your influence."

"Yes," assented Cecil, as though he were about to consider something else, or wanted to put a caveat on what he was about to reveal. "I can arrange for that to be done and you will be beholden to me."

"Of course," replied Catesby guardedly.

The monk looked at them both. Cecil waved, rolling his hand, encouraging the Father Thomas to speak.

"You were at the part where the eggs miss the 'redd' and are eaten by prey," Cecil reminded him.

"But I suppose if they did miss the 'redd' and could not find succour in the rocks, then they would succumb to any number of creatures that would prey on them, not here of course, but in the wild, that could well be the fate that befell them," decided the monk.

He led them on to the next pond and because the path was so narrow, the three, stood shoulder to shoulder as they walked to yet another pool. Their progress was slow owing to the fact that they had to follow the footsteps of the priest who shuffled slowly across the grass. The monk, Father Thomas, had been kept on after the dissolution of the monasteries simply because he had an outstanding knowledge of fish. He was extremely old, now, more than seventy-five-years old, then, he had been a young novice of seven years old.

"In that previous pond, the eggs grow before hatching into tiny 'aelvins' in the spring. We leave them in the gravel pool until they have eaten all their yolk sack and become fry, we collect the fry and feed them all manner of insects in this deeper pond where the grow into 'parr'."

The three guests looked into another shallow pool, next to the others, which was teeming with life. There were small fry darting to and fro constantly, they were full of life.

The whole idea that nature could be copied in this way, and so effectively, fascinated them all, even cynical Cecil who had seen several fish farms.

"Do you sell the 'parr'?" asked Catesby.

"Some are sold, but dearly so, we keep most of them. If you want a cheaper fish, the pike fits that description, although its flesh tastes meatier, the trout are as dear as parr, like lamb is to mutton. As you know pork is cheaper than lamb so pike is cheaper than trout," explained Father Thomas patiently. He led them further on to the fourth pool, this was wilder still than the third, and looked more like a village pond than one constructed by man. The sheer scale of the operation was remarkable. There were other fish farms in England but not of this scale.

"I see," said Catesby.

"When the fish have reached a certain size, which takes between two and five years, they lose their parr markings and become smolts."

"So how long does this all take?" asked Cecil.

"If they are spawned in December they will hatch in March; it can take two years for the parr to turn into smolts; and it may be three or four years or more before the fish are taken to the table."

"Fascinating, thank you and this is where they live for that time?" added Cecil in the same tone as he had used for Bilson when he was being boring. He could not help using his supercilious tone.

"Fully grown brown trout are insect eaters and bottom feeders. They want to live in cover, even a weed bed will give them a feeling of safety."

"Cunning," said Markham.

"So we have several natural ponds in which we allow weeds and vegetation to grow freely over the banks. There the trout can lie, guarding one flank by resting it up against the bank wall; I have seen such behaviour many times," Father Thomas elucidated further.

"I, too, have seen such behaviour when I was in the country," Catesby added to verify the practice and to support Father Thomas; he had grown fond of him in their short time together.

"The trout will allow the currents to move food towards them and when the wind blows, they swim into the wind, looking for food trapped on the surface. They are clever creatures."

"I have heard it said that in Virginia, the new plantations, they have found a trout with all the colours of the rainbow on its scales, truly unbelievable but that is what I have been told," Cecil announced to all and sundry.

"Fascinating," said Father Thomas, sounding deceptively like Cecil did when he had said the same.

It seemed that any consideration beyond his fish and prayer was not worthy of his thought.

"Come Catesby, we will take our leave of our fish expert and we will become fishers of men; I intend no blasphemy with that remark, merely keeping the theme, God be with you, Father, thank you and adieu."

"And God be with you, too, my sons," said the monk with relief. Father Thomas smiled and waved as the other two thanked him and wished him a good day.

"I'm quite hungry after seeing all these fish," Markham said as they strolled around the grounds some more. Markham was always hungry; his tall frame craved fuel like a fire. The walled-garden provided a windbreak so there was little more than a breeze and the sun was beginning to warm their faces and raise the dew from the grass.

Markham felt that a smoke of tobacco would be in order at this time of the morning, it would dull his hunger, but Cecil had forced him to leave his pipe behind. Markham had reluctantly agreed to do so, after much protest, arguing that it soothed his humours. Unfortunately, he knew that the more he protested, the more Cecil would stubbornly refuse. If he were not so fond of his habit of smoking his pipe, he would have given up tobacco, first James and, latterly, Cecil seemed to be conspiring against him. Markham could not see the harm in a pipe and all his friends had enjoyed a smoke but he was not at liberty to mix with friends. "Ah, the trout pond," sighed Cecil, "so like the affairs of State, large trout hiding in the shallows and reed beds, amongst the pond weed and in the shelter of an underwater root; Catesby, I have you on my side do I not?"

"You have arranged to have me pardoned, like Markham, and he will not disagree, we owe you our liberty!"

"I agree with Catesby, we owe you our liberty and a debt of fealty, you have been merciful and kind, allowing us to leave our past behind," Markham added immediately without being asked.

Markham knew that his service could be terminated at any time and his freedom replaced by a visit to the Tower; officially, Markham was still there. In fact, their liberty was at Cecil's discretion and all three men knew it.

"Well, said," Cecil cried; he tried to clap Markham on the shoulder but the stretch proved too much as he was not standing close enough, he patted Catesby's flank instead. "I cannot get you a monopoly on 'sherries'; you realise that. Parliament took away the Queen's grants. That fool Essex did not realise it was not Bess that took his monopoly of sweet wines, it was the Houses, mark you, both the Commons and the Lords. I will introduce you to a man who imports wine and has storage space in his warehouses; Edmund Doubleday who is a brave and burly fellow with a good legal mind, a tavern and, more importantly for you, experience in importing victuals from overseas."

"Thank you My Lord," Catesby said with genuine appreciation, he could now start to rebuild his fortune and provide security for his family without relying solely on his wife's fortune. He felt his spirits lift.

"Congratulations Robin," Markham said, patting his old friend on the back.

"Isn't it marvellous news, Griffin?"

They smiled at each other while Cecil looked on but his smile was one of satisfaction, he knew the plot he was hatching was developing nicely.

Chapter 16 –

Catesby & Cecil -The mortar pounded by the pestle.

The sun shone brightly despite it being winter, Catesby, on his first visit to Hampton Court, wondered whether it was always summer sunshine in that magical palace.

"How gracious of you to grant me an audience, in private, Your Lordship," Catesby exclaimed respectfully, he walked beside Cecil, in the gardens, on the path leading from the palace to the real-tennis courts where King Henry VIII used to play.

It was a beautiful day, chilly but not cold, the sun shone in a pale blue sky; puffs of cloud as white as bleached linen hung in the air above them. They were both warmly dressed and there was no wind to speak of, nevertheless, Cecil had learnt his lesson and he was wearing a warm burgundy red felt cap. Doublets covered wool undergarments, capes protected the neck and body; large buckskin gloves kept their hands warm.

"Pragmatism has always ruled in my domain, rashness in yours; it seems it is an inherited trait, which makes me wonder how your family has lasted so long," Cecil commented frankly, he noticed that the taller Catesby had modified his pace to allow him to keep up, he felt as if he were an ancient mother being taken for a walk by a dutiful son on Sunday.

"Things have changed."

"Indeed so, but not for your family, your father fined and almost imprisoned, you fined and a spell at the Tower, as I say, inherited rashness. For you matters have changed but surely not for the best, your fines cost you your family home!"

"Matters are altered, the Queen is gone, God rest her soul, the king is a Scot, I no longer dream of what might have been; I am happy with my lot."

"There are those a lot worse off than you in this realm."

"My only crime was to be in the wrong place at the wrong time with a very dear friend of mine," Catesby responded pithily.

"I admire your rhyme but cannot forgive the crime, I like the way you defend yourself and I can safely say, I know, for a fact, what you say is true."

"How so?"

"Your servants give a very accurate account of you and I know what you say is true because I know you for an honest man, my spies have informed me that it is so; you have made amends by making a good marriage, your wife's fortune has improved your fortune; you fell down and she has lifted you back up. I think you have learnt your lesson; you are remorseful. Please, do not look so downhearted at my words; everybody knows it is true. Come let us be friends for this short interview."

"I agree to your terms and bow to your magnanimity," Catesby acquiesced; he had been broken before by Cecil, it had cost him dear. Though his blood boiled at Cecil's glib words, his new venture was the only option if he was ever going to adequately provide for his children.

"Excellent, so I know your family are well, or so my latest reports tell me," Cecil said.

"Your influence is well-known and I, for one, recognise your mastery of events. I have ended up suspecting all my servants of spying for you; I cannot dismiss them all; I have even begun to suspect my old nursemaid who was ill tempered when I was young and age has not tempered her rage. She has little patience with my own children and despised me for being a colic baby and later prone to tantrums."

"You grew out of that, I see your charm; we are not enemies, I admire the way you defended your friend Essex," Cecil conciliatorily explained.

"He was a good man."

"He was a fool and you know it, you were loyal to him but you were aware of his flaws."

"I forgave him his virtues and loved him for his faults," Catesby admitted sheepishly, knowing Cecil would be annoyed.

"And for that you became as big a fool as he!" Cecil spat; he could not believe how anyone could support the Earl of Essex.

"I paid the price."

"Indeed you did, monetarily, a hefty fine indeed, added to which was your sentence, it could not have been easy for your children only to see you with a guard present."

"You know my Achilles heel."

"Yes, it is my role! It was prudent to baptise them in the religion of the estate. Was that on Essex's advice?"

"Essex was a good friend but I baptised my children because their mother wished it so; Catholicism is being expunged from the realm, we are excluded from much and it looks as if King James will not improve matters for us. I want my children to have all the opportunities available to them, not to be treated like lepers."

"I heard Essex advised it."

"He was not my priest, he was just a friend."

Catesby and Cecil would never agree about Essex, Cecil had grown up with him, Catesby knew him as a generous friend.

"A friend and a fool, only a foolish man would bait the Queen the way he did. He behaved disgracefully towards her after all the favours she had granted him. He behaved like an ungrateful cur to Her Majesty and to my father who took him in."

"I could not agree with you more, in hindsight, you are right, we used to think Devereux and the Queen were playing tennis themselves, but he took it too far, beyond the game."

"There are penalties for overstepping the mark!"

"You need not remind me, I have abundant experience of that. You made a fine example of Devereux. He was once the fine Earl of Essex, the next a criminal to be executed, from favoured favourite to the block. It was all your handiwork."

"I had no time for people who were intent on fermenting trouble, he was a nuisance."

"I have neither wish to join him at Westminster Hall nor on the scaffold hung for my beliefs, I am not a Lord, I would not be lucky enough to have the executioner's axe, nor do I wish to join my old friend on a spike on London Bridge!"

"Good, then let us talk of happier things; as you say times have changed. He escaped a hanging, Elizabeth allowed him a noble's execution, she was too kind to him, he was executed in private, and you would not be so lucky."

"It is not something I would want my children to witness, I assure you. There is no danger of my starting any insurrection, if I did your spies would hear of it, that I know. Enough talk of the past; let us talk of the future. You wish to talk to me about my sherry monopoly."

"About granting it, yes indeed, but, as I said, you will need a good Protestant partner, Edmund Doubleday is your man; he owns the lease on the *Saracen's Head* in King Street. He was one the High Constables of Westminster and he is built for enforcing the law; he has been described in *Anglorum Speculumas* as 'a man of great stature, valour, gravity and activity'; he has recently been given a position at the Mint Office; and with Andrew Bright, he has been granted the offices of distilling herbs and sweet waters at the Palace of Whitehall and keeping the library there."

"Will they be able to help?"

"It is a much better choice than a courtier who needs my patronage, they are at the Palace already, so they will hold the reins in England; You will still hold the reins in Spain. You can trust Andrew and Edmund."

"Fair enough," Catesby agreed, but he had little choice, they both knew that.

"You negotiated that part of the deal, it should be yours."

"So we can unload the shipment we have from Sandeman and deliver it to the palace?"

"Of course, it will save you smuggling it in from the Continent!"

"Your influence does spread wide."

"The State is fragile and there is a need for eyes everywhere," Cecil cautioned.

His voice was hard; it sounded like a warning to Catesby's ears.

"Spies in the shires, informers in the towns, nothing gets past you!"

"I have to look everywhere."

"A watch that I am aware about every day."

"So sell me the *sack* for the opening of parliament," insisted Cecil warmly. He stared at Catesby with his cold grey-blue eyes. "That will be your first firm order: Bring your shipment from Flushings, immediately."

"You will not need much it is very strong. Surely, you do not need the whole amount, it is a significant shipment."

"It is not just the Lords and Members of the Commons, all the Court will be there, too. You have not seen how the Court drinks! I may have to order more than you have shipped. How much do you have ready to be delivered onto the hard?"

"Thirty-six barrels!" Catesby declared.

"That might just do!" Cecil smiled as he spoke. Catesby gulped. It was a large order. An order that size would launch their company; put him on the first rung of the ladder and it would also help him climb out of his debts. His wife had not yet paid back all the various monies he owed.

"It should handsomely suffice, how many Lords are you expecting?"

"You have not seen the way the new Court drinks to inebriation; how they pick at delicate dishes of food, take one of a dozen that they are offered and then throw the other eleven away, I have never seen such terrible waste," Cecil complained.

"What a scandalous shame when we have so many paupers in the realm," Catesby angrily asserted, he had a keen sense of justice and high regard for those who worked hard, not for those who lived off others and did not generate wealth.

"They are profligate and wasteful, they rejoice in the fact that they can afford to waste food and are proud to drink like the debauched. They make a drunken docker look like a sober Puritan. Queen Elizabeth would never have stood for such profligacy and debauchery!"

"Indeed, I have not seen, nor heard of such behaviour, though ignorance does not deny existence, especially as you tell me so, so few know how the court works these days. If you want my whole shipment, I cannot refuse you."

"You cannot refuse me; so let us see what we have agreed so far; the sherry monopoly will be awarded to Edmund Doubleday and contracts with Sandeman will have his name added as a codicil. Your ownership of the goods will remain until they are landed in England, from thence my friend will distribute them with your help in the Midlands where your influence is great and in London where he is well -connected. We will of course pay you and your investors a reasonable rate."

"Agreed, if it will allow me to build up a healthy trade for me to hand down to my children."

"We are all aware of the care you have for your children, you make a much better father than yours and for that matter mine. Although mine trained me up where yours destroyed your inheritance."

"I cannot argue with that but, now, I merely want to do my best and for their mother and my family," Catesby confessed openly, knowing he was throwing himself at Cecil's mercy.

"Your dynasty is of little concern of mine while I am charged with the dynasty of the House of Stuart, but I am touched by your pragmatism you are beginning to think like me and no longer liked that fool Essex, the big *pazzo*."

"He blinded us all with his charm and good looks."

"I can only impress with my intellect."

"A far more worthy and worthwhile quality."

"You would not think so by the way good looks and charm rule the Court, now. It was bad enough in the reign of Queen Bess, with her favourites, but James falls in love with any pretty boy that he espies. I have a job to persuade him to follow the advice of the Privy Council, rather than acquiesce to the whim of a boy at Court who has caught his fancy. Trying to get an answer can be like one of his hunting trips. The quarry eludes me."

"He cannot help himself perhaps, Elizabeth favoured good-looking men, too."

Cecil looked steely.

"At least, she awarded favours based on merit, Raleigh and Drake deserved to have her favour; all you need, now, is good looks and a silver tongue to flatter him and he will love you more than his children. The wasters become more important than his wife or his Chief Minister."

Cecil looked disgusted, he wore the mask of an actor all the time.

Cecil was appalled by James's lack of sober reflection; he came up with grand schemes and then abandoned them, he seemed to listen to reason then favoured one of his inner circle and their view.

"A disgraceful turn of affairs, a minister ignored for a handsome rogue. I grant you people cannot judge on looks alone, too much emphasis is on how people look, nowadays, it should be on what they can achieve. It is the fashion but this fashion will not last, James will see sense."

"Well spoken, but you need not flatter me, and you flatter James; you have sold your goods, ingratiating yourself will win no reward. Sell and hold your peace, there is no need for you to butter me up even more; although wait, I have wounded you. I can tell by the stunned expression on your face. Perhaps I am being unfair, maybe you half-believe some of what you say."

"Oh, indeed, I do!" protested Catesby.

"So we are agreed on that, talent and statecraft are being replaced by beauty and debauchery; ill will come of it," Cecil surmised neatly, ever the lawyer.

"We are indeed agreed on that!"

The Stuart Court was filled with people who flattered or looked beautiful. James did not want advice; he wanted to be surrounded by pretty boys and those who said the right things to him. His palace was a place of pleasure and those who gave it were rewarded with power. James could be swayed by something as insignificant as a pretty face on a young man or the smile of an innocent girl. Rumours of his court, and the behaviour of his courtiers, made his fiefdom seem like a hedonistic hotbed full of debauchery of all kinds; it was full of the sort of behaviour, of which the Puritans would never have approved. That was well understood. Catesby and Cecil knew that the excesses of the Court were becoming an embarrassment to those who knew the way of life at the Elizabethan court and it was becoming even wider knowledge amongst the members of parliament that James was spending beyond his means and yet he did not seem to care.

"Good, now comes the third part of our agreement; the King is profligate and is a spendthrift, all I save he spends; revenues are low; expenditure by the Exchequer is high, so I have to ask you what discount you can offer?"

"A discount, I had never thought of a discount; a commodity so rare and sought after would not require it."

"I can get hold of it easily."

"You were in London, were you not, when Drake delivered his first batch of sherry, it commanded a premium."

"I ate yesterday, I am hungry today, what is past is past, it is the present I am interested in," Cecil growled impatiently.

It was all part of his negotiation strategy.

"Sherry is still popular and rare."

"Yes, yes, rare and expensive, desired by those at Court, but I could go direct to those who deal with *sherries* for the Spanish in the Lowlands, I would barter cloth for *sack* but why would I when I have barrels on board a boat that will be in Southwark in a few days, why risk the voyage, down to Spain to collect the wine and back again, through the Bay of Biscay twice, why takes such risks when you can take all the risks for me?"

"It seems we need to pay a landing fee!"

"Let's just say it is a discount to the Crown; the Crown, your best customer as of today."

"What did you have in mind?" asked Catesby.

He realised the potential of having the Crown as a customer, particularly if they drank as much as Cecil purported.

"A firkin free for every barrel delivered!"

"If I was dealing with anyone else, I would say I would have to do my sums to see if that was acceptable to me and my investors, however as it is you and I value my life and my business, I agree readily and shake on it now."

They shook hands like kindred spirits, their eyes met in friendship. Cecil's thoughts did not match his actions, Catesby's did.

"So in thirty-six gallons, you give me nine you make full price on eighteen gallons and half on the next eighteen, we pay for twenty-seven and you deliver thirty-six!"

"Agreed, I will make you a bill of sale."

Cecil smiled knowingly the last thing he wanted was documentary evidence of their agreement and he knew that Catesby was not in position to argue.

Cecil did not like paper trails that might lead to him.

"No need, we are friends, are we not?" Cecil replied.

"If you say it, I believe it," Catesby concluded. The trusting gentleman had to agree to everything. Cecil had removed the need for paperwork, the one piece of evidence that would prove the barrels were *sack*.

"Let the bygone days be bygone and the future be ours. We will settle this on a handshake and the state will pay in its usual terms, cash on delivery."

"Agreed, I will be able to pay back the original investors, which will be a relief and have money for another order."

"What are you going to call your new venture?" Cecil asked.

"Quercus."

"The oak, a good pun, the *sack* is shipped in oak."

"And from little acorns, oak trees grow," Catesby added.

It seemed like he was encouraging him; what a web he wove.

"You must make haste to open the trade to the whole of the land, Oxford and beyond," Cecil suggested in the hope that he would draw more Catholic gentlemen and nobles into his net.

His goal was to trawl for all the influential Catholics and encourage their involvement in the import business. Then, he would arrange for them to meet at Holbeche House and in one fell swoop, he would destroy the top echelon of the Catholic power brokers, sending the rest into disarray and panic.

"I already have arrangements for trading posts and horses have been promised. They will be at my disposal for disbursing the *sack* on my say so!"

"Your business will grow."

"I will ensure sack is available from here to my home town! Our second shipment will be distributed in the Midlands, I have the orders confirmed and the bills of lading pending."

Cecil knew all this; he had set up the whole scenario.

"I will be able to keep the drunken sots at Court in clover whilst allowing the Lords, and the Members of Parliament, a chance to raise one glass, at least, to the crown and to the King when the toast comes."

"A mutually satisfactory agreement has been reached."

"We are both relieved, and, for this relief much thanks, when parliament opens we need to convince the King to balance his receipts and his expenditure, too long it has been that horrible refrain: 'Spend, spend and God will send', I loathe it."

"I agree," Catesby added and he meant it, he found waste distasteful and gluttony disgusting.

"Good, I have made arrangements for you to house the *sherries* when you have landed them; the cellars are close to the Parliament building. I will discuss the rental with Thomas Percy."

"I will land the *sack* at Lambeth or Southwark."

"I can rely on you to transport the goods."

"Of course, once landed we can store the barrels in my house in Lambeth and thence to Westminster."

"You will need a bellman to watch over the barrels, unarmed in the palace precincts of course, but able to raise an alarm if any theft is tried."

"I have someone in mind, Guido Forcanessi."

Cecil was stunned by the coincidence, but his face was a mask, as ever, he showed no hint of surprise or shock. Life was strange; an opportunity snatched away and then returned; how fortune's fickle wheel turned to aid and abet, or hinder and hurt; it smiled on Cecil as he had already created a provenance for Guy Fawkes. Matters could not have worked out better even if he had planned them he reflected, then he remembered that in fact he had.

That was the man who his continental spies had mentioned returning to England with Wintour, and who, his London spies told him, frequented the *Duck and Drake*. He had been wondering who it was and how he could put someone at the heart of the Catholics that he wanted to destroy to good use. Then, it turned out to be Guido Forcanessi after all.

He knew Rosa had been carried off by the plague, her landlady and the prostitute who shared her lodgings confirmed that, Guido had felt it necessary to inform them both on his return to London. They were suitably moved but offered him no more than cursory sympathy as they too had suffered from loss through all manner of misfortunes, plague being only one of them and Mary, the prostitute who pretended to be an actress, thought she had a dose of the pox herself. They had their own problems.

It was uncanny that his pazzo, his Guy, should return and end up as the watchman. It was maybe not such a coincidence, far stranger events happened in London every day.

"So as not to upset the guard you best call him John Johnson, a servant of Percy."

"Very well, it is just but a trifle."

"I knew you would see it my way."

"A pleasure."

"You are far too kind," Cecil breathed dramatically, leaving Catesby puzzled as to whether he was being genuine or ironic in his remarks. The phrase had not sounded sarcastic and yet he was not sure.

Chapter 17 – The Conversation between Cecil and Ramsay

"Everyone finds James difficult; he will go down in history as the wisest fool in Christendom!" Cecil soothed obsequiously, it was his first private meeting with James's favourite. "He upsets all men and all religions without a care."

"Who said he was the wisest fool in Christendom?" asked the Ramsay, he was far more handsome, but not as bright as Cecil. He was, however, the King's favourite.

"No one has yet, but by the time I suggest it is true, and let it be known to those in influence, it will form a part of various ambassadors' correspondence. I should think that it will be the current thinking perhaps by next year," Cecil suggested mischievously.

"You are so very witty, Cecil," Ramsay responded admiringly.

"You are far too kind," Cecil breathed dramatically, leaving Ramsay, the King's favourite, puzzled as to whether he was being genuine or ironic in his remarks. The phrase had not sounded sarcastic and yet he was not sure.

"I thought James wanted to prevent quarrels over religion," he complained wondering how much of what Cecil said he should take at face value.

"As you know, he needs the bishops to assuage the power of the parliament but he does not want the Puritans with their simple services and their lack of hierarchy, King James likes pomp and ceremony and the bishops do a good job in keeping order with their leases to publicans and theatre owners and their prisons, not forgetting the monies they pay the state for their own leases. The Puritans want to destroy all that and, then, we will have the sort of mayhem we had after the final dissolution of the monasteries. The bishops will be dispossessed and the nobles will buy their land and palaces, enriching themselves further."

"The greedy beggars," sighed Ramsay, he had not been awarded any land as yet, titles yes, assets, no.

"You would not believe the amount of monastic lands that moved into nobles' hands. The Crown will not benefit from the break up financially and a layer of the legal system will be removed in one fell swoop, resulting in mayhem. As things stand, the bishops are the bulwarks for the Crown."

"There you are right, already many Puritans are considering Virginia as a place to settle, they see it as a new promised land; they will have to cross the ocean not just the Red Sea, in this case!" announced Ramsay, after which, he laughed haughtily.

Cecil smiled warmly, he was warming to the Scotsman and perhaps he could see his merits. He seemed to have James's interests at heart from all reports and if he was a pretty, self-aggrandising, violent groundling in Cecil's theatre so be it. Cecil had enough enemies to deal with without adding another.

"The bishops hold the key to balance in Parliament, you must see that, without them there would be havoc, and there is no advantage in keeping the Puritans happy; they disapprove of James and his extravagance and love of music and entertainment. They would wish our banquets consisted of bread and water not quail and partridge, sermons would provide the music and sitting on hard chairs for hours would replace the dancing," Cecil warned.

"They are far too serious for me," admitted Ramsay openly. He enjoyed good food and good wine.

"Have no fear, your treats are safe. James feels under threat from those political simpletons, he feels that if they get rid of the bishops, he will be next!"

"He has told me he will make the Puritans do as he says or he will harry them from the land," Ramsay confided.

"Indeed he will, if he can."

"So we are safe?"

"Not quite, as we are both under threat of Catholics; they have a propensity to become favoured by Queens and kings!" cautioned Cecil cunningly; he was sowing his seeds again, the constant gardener.

"I will persuade him of the danger of the papists," Ramsay offered openly. He did not care for *Sassenach* Catholics or their attempts to gain favour at Court. Cecil was a big enough threat.

"I have encouraged him to reinstate the fines and declare the religion illegal, starting with outlawing priests and those sheltering them."

"He wanted the Catholics to be free to worship in their own churches, did he not?"

"He did but I told him the Parliament would never agree. So he has turned against them, he needs to call a parliament because he needs the money. The less disputes that need settling, I have argued, the less time that it will take for the money to be awarded to him; the money, that he so desperately needs will."

"You are like James when he hunts, if the king fancies a particular stag among the herd, he lets the keepers know; they mark the spot where the stag stood. There they lead the dogs, which are trained to follow one animal only. Away they run straight upon its tail."

"Yes, I get what I want."

"Without stop, the King hurries after the dogs until they have got the game. Then, he thrusts his arms into the stag's guts and smears all the courtiers' faces and their hands with blood. I have been stained with the blood, by you," Ramsay explained.

"Indeed, everyone succumbs, the webs we weave stretch far and wide," Cecil breathed menacingly, "you cannot escape the web, you cannot remain untarnished by the stain of my influence, but it is not blood but the mark of State, the red of the cross of Saint George."

"I have sworn allegiance to James whether that be the James the sixth of Scotland or James the first of England."

"That you must hold dear in all you do as much as you revere the cross of Saint Andrew. Now that the lion and unicorn are joined, England and Scotland are united under one monarch. They have become one state under one king. The King himself wills it and although it has not passed through parliament, as yet, it will. You work for the State and its benefit then you are a patriot or you are against us and you will be branded a traitor."

Chapter 18 – the Duck and Drake

Guido had found sporadic shifts in the docks on his return from Amsterdam; there were also commissions from his new Catholic brotherhood, mainly moving goods or furniture. He found lodgings with a widow in St. Clément's, which was a short walk to the Strand and therefore not far from the *Duck and Drake* where he found his new found friends. Rather than look for even more work on the docks, he wanted them to give him errands to do and small tasks. His work at the docks paid his rent and paid for food. The errands allowed him extra luxuries like a pint of ale, which he was beginning to get a true taste for and for the odd treat of cooked food from a stall.

He did not know that soon he would be asked to transport and guard the *sack* that would be served at the King's opening of the new parliament.

It was bitterly cold beyond the doors of the Inn. He shivered as he entered; a wave of warmth hit him as he strode towards the gathering of men who habitually drank by the fire. The heat from all the bodies and the crush of men made him feel uncomfortable but all the drinking places of London were the same, it was a place to keep warm and wash away the drudgery of the day, rinse the dust from the throat and slake the thirst.

"Guido," called Wintour as he noticed his approach or rather he noticed the movement in the corner of his eye as a group of revellers parted to let him through, "Come and join us!"

It was that night that he was formerly introduced to Robert Catesby; he could not miss him. He was a tall handsome man, Guido judged him to be almost six foot and he was stout without being fat, he held himself like a noble that was for sure. Guido forced himself towards the stranger by the fire and bowed, Catesby bowed a nobles' bow, a perfunctory dipping of the chin, and an inclination of the head.

"Let me introduce you soberly and properly to Robert Catesby, the finest, most dashing and courageous horsemen in the country, your new employer," insisted Wintour.

He was fond of Guido, the sad stranger he had met on the hard that day. There was something of the lost sheep about him.

"And you are Guido Forcanessi, a far too complicated name we shall have to call you Tom Thompson or John Johnson for simplicity sake. And for simplicity all round you can call me Robin," Catesby cheerfully announced.

He had already decided to make Guido his 'bellman' in the cellars; he had been encouraged by Cecil to offer him the job.

"I am most pleased to see you again, sir," replied Guido, never for once forgetting his place despite the affable nature of his new acquaintance. He realised that he was in the presence of gentry and would have to behave as such. Kit dispensed a jug of potent winter ale into pewter tankards while everyone shook hands and dispensed with social niceties.

"Raise your tumblers to better times to come; the toast is: 'confusion to our enemies'," Wintour exclaimed, raising both hands, in one he carried his drinking vessel.

Despite his new found comrades plying him with drink, on every occasion that they met, and making him feel welcome, he knew that they were being friendly and were not wanting him to be their friend. They drained their tumblers, Guido found he liked the taste of the barely wine, the strong winter ale, which balanced sweetness with bitterness, warmth with strength.

"Robert is well connected and his ancestors were King's councillors," Kit confided in Guido.

"I think my friend exaggerates, too much!" Catesby responded, not wanting to make himself the centre of attention that night, it was a time of celebration for all.

"Guido won't know it but you certainly do, the rhyme written by Colyngbourne: *'The Cat, the Rat and Lovel our Dog, Rule all England under a Hog'*. Remember?"

"Yes but since then, things have changed, I am now a model citizen wishing to influence no one."

"Come Catesby!" shouted Kit.

"I saw my father imprisoned several times for disobeying the law of the land, for helping Father Edmund Campion and for his recusancy. I, on the other hand, have kept pace with change and have had my son baptised an Anglican. This is a time for a new world order," Catesby eulogised in the hope that once he had spoken; they could talk of lighter affairs and meeker matters. Wintour seized the opportunity.

"Ah, mention of the New World! What say you about all this? Guido, have you been following; are you aware of the Americas?" Wintour asked.

"Not really, my English is not so good, I just drink and listen," Guido confessed candidly.

"Guido understands well enough, me thinks but he prefers to listen; his speech does not match his comprehension. I noticed on the boat how he likes songs and rhymes," Wintour explained to the group.

"Raise your tankard to the New World and new opportunities while I'll give him a song to remind him of the old, remember this lament: *'Catesby has gained Chastleton but lost his daughter and son'*, it was very hard for us both growing up without a father, you take having a father for granted. My father missed the time he could have spent with us. I am determined that will not happen to me!" Catesby announced, he could not help but reflect on the cruel past. They drained their tin tankards.

"To Father Edward," announced Kit.

"Dear Father Edward, a great man, may he rest in peace," Catesby reflected sorrowfully, looking into his tankard for answers.

"Indeed," sighed Kit, drinking from his.

"Too dark a thought for a day like today," Catesby insisted. "We are friends united at their favourite tavern; let us spend time together, let us spend, copper and silver, drink ale and then, spend, spend and God will send!"

The group laughed at this command and drained their tankards afterwards, slamming the pewter bases on to the wooden tabletops with a loud bang.

"No, we must go slowly," Guido complained nervously, he was already feeling woozy, he could feel the heat from the fire and the more he drank the thirstier he felt; already they had filled his tankard twice since his first drink of strong winter ale.

He could not normally afford such expensive and strong drink. The winter ale was three times the strength of normal ale and it was taking its toll on all the gathered party.

"You'll find Catesby a generous host and he has married well, he is a sober man in general, if slightly tipsy now," Tom announced, clapping a hand on Catesby's shoulder.

"You should have seen him in the old days, he was as wild as a bobcat, I mean very wild and he would scatter money around as if he were a farmer sowing seed," Kit added.

"It is true that in his youth he was very wild and spent much above his rate," Jack agreed.

"What do you mean by 'above his rate'?" Guido mumbled, mystified; he did not understand most of the words that they said and many of them spoke too quickly to decipher what they were saying but he had picked up on the words 'spent money'.

"We mean he had an income and he spent more than he received, he was allowed to have credit beyond his means," explained Wintour whose own intake of ale had clouded his ability to explain clearly.

"Credit!" Guido cried, nodding sagely, he had been refused credit so often; he understood that word.

More drinks came, ale in a large earthenware jug; impotently, Guido covered the top of his tankard with his left hand.

Physically but gently, Catesby removed the hand and cupped Guido's right elbow pushing it upwards, guiding his hand to his mouth. He smiled so charmingly, Guido allowed the pewter to touch his lips and drank. He drained his drinking vessel and Wintour filled it again from the jug.

"We all laugh, dine and drink together," remarked Catesby, looking around at his companions in an affable way. They all seemed to adore him and he seemed to adore them all.

"To good times," Guido said nervously, he did not yet feel at ease with his newfound friends.

Guido wondered when they were going to eat, if at all. The alcohol had gone into an empty stomach, he had been working all day; he had only eaten a chunk of bread, less than a closed handful, and a small lump of cheese.

He was feeling light headed, hungry and thirsty but the more he drank, the thirstier he became, the merrier he was; the more muddled his mind became.

"See how well he regards you, like Hal, he has the common touch, all men are his equals," Thomas Wintour announced.

"Indeed," cried Kit.

"He is like Henry from the history plays, leading his men to Agincourt. Who could not admire this man who makes all men his friend?" Wintour added for good measure.

The entire group were smiling at each other or at him; he felt that this was his new family.

"He is a gentleman!" Guido cried enthusiastically, sounding slightly slurred; already this man charmed him.

"Thank you Guido, praise indeed," teased Catesby.

His physical appearance, his physique, all was admirable, he was like a Caesar; more importantly, he was the king of that band of men, and he treated Guido as though he were the only person in the room.

"To Catesby, the finest gentleman to hand, or in this tavern grand, the greatest in the Duck and Drake make no mistake, or perhaps this sceptred land," Kit announced affably. They all laughed at his joke

"I'll drink to that!" Catesby agreed readily, calling for more beer, which was delivered by a willing *pot-man* who knew Catesby's generosity.

For the first time since Rosa's death, Guido felt special. These men were kind and giving, like true Christians should be, they were all so loving to one another; kind to each other. That was the message of Christ, wasn't it? 'Love one another' no matter how humble, no matter where they have come from.

"He is a fine gentleman," Guido mumbled as he was handed a new tankard and sipped thirstily from it. The fire was making him thirsty or was it the ale, he no longer cared; he was drunk.

A few more draughts of the strong barely wine and he would have difficulty walking.

"He is a worthy swordsman, too," Thomas Wintour enjoined before clapping Guido on the shoulder.

"A true gentleman," Guido agreed, in turn, he was glad that everyone admired Catesby as much as he did. The room was becoming unsteady in his eyes and Guido felt as if he were back at sea, swaying in a storm. The movement of the room alarmed him while he was sitting quite still. "I can use a sword!"

Guido was exaggerating slightly, he had worn one once in a ceremony and parried with his shadow but in the wars in the Lowlands he had been a sapper and a reserve pike-man, he had only marched with his pike for protection, never using it in battle.

"Yes but are you a worthy swordsman?" asked Kit, teasing him, too. Guido looked puzzled; he was not sure what worthy meant. Wintour normally spoke in *dog Latin,* or in true Latin, the *lingua franca* of the Roman Catholic Church, to help Guido but on this occasion, he had forgotten to translate.

"Wordy?" he repeated, puzzled, before looking into his half empty tankard, He noticed with horror that he had almost finished his drink and he had made room for the *pot man* to fill it.
"I am not that worthy; I have spent time in the Tower," Catesby confessed sheepishly, a smile playing on his lips. He liked to shock.

"The Tower of London!" Guido slurred incredulously yet admiringly. He knew that place; it was a foreboding building on the north shore, visible from most of the docks east of London Bridge. He knew it as a place of punishment, poor people went to *'the Clink'* and rich gentlemen went to *'the Tower'*. "You were sent to *'the Tower'* and you came out, I thought people died in there!"

"Yes, I was imprisoned."

"You were?" cried Guido sceptically.

"Along with Jack and I," added Kit, smiling, "I'll vouch for that. Cecil was worried we might rebel when the Queen had a sickness so they locked us up with Francis Tresham!"

"Francis Tresham, who is he?" Guido asked out of pure curiosity, generally he asked in the hope that they might have a few hours of work for him. He wanted to be busy every hour of the day so he could bear his loneliness better, idle hours allowed him to think of Rosa and what might have been. He wanted to bury her memory in his own activity so that he could quash his pain.

"Francis joined Bob Devereux's household and we all met up with his cousin by marriage, the fine fellow, William Parker, Lord Monteagle."

"I will never remember these names," complained Guido.

"Don't worry, you will meet all except for dear Bob, Bob, he went to the Tower!" Wintour explained.

"Bob died?" Guido complained.

"He was executed," explained Kit.

"Hanged?" gulped Guido.

"They beheaded him," Wintour whispered to ease the shock.

Guido seemed to mumble something about 'losing his head' while looking into his empty tumbler.

"He was the Earl of Essex, a favourite of Queen Elizabeth," Kit added.

"When Essex returned from his commission in Ireland without permission, in order to see the Queen, he fell from royal favour; the Queen he often fought but this time he was exiled from court and his monopoly taken away!" Catesby explained. "I spoke to him about it and he said his downfall was due to the influence of Robert Cecil. He warned me to be on my guard evermore."

All these names and the spinning room left Guido flummoxed and he decided to put on his most erudite face and wear that as a mask for the rest of the evening. All that he succeeded in doing was to give the impression that something or someone had upset him and he was wearing the countenance of a sulking child.

"Cecil is the Secretary of State, the King's right hand man; they were always vying for the Queen's attention," Wintour elucidated further, seeing Guido's pained expression.

"Yes," agreed Guido, nodding sagely, yet he understood little.

"Glad you follow," Catesby lisped drunkenly.

The names were strange, his thinking was muddled, the alcohol in his blood and the warmth of the fire made him think of bed. Guido sat smiling, pursuing his lips and nodding helpfully, all dependent on the tone of voice, happy, indignant and questioning.

"Lord Thomas Howard did not help!" added Catesby bitterly.

"He led the forces that attacked us; he would not listen to our protestation that we were no threat," elucidated Wintour still further, hoping Guido would understand the word protestation. Guido understood the word it was similar to '*protesta*', but his face showed him looking even more bad-tempered when in fact he was falling deeper into a stupor.

"He wanted glory," Catesby announced bitterly, sounding as aggrieved as Guido looked. "He has blood on his hands, the blood of innocent men, yet he walks free, a murderer unpunished, it was he who gave the orders to send soldiers to the Strand. Everything got out of hand."

The alcohol had left Guido in a complete stupor and he suddenly realised that they were not in fact explaining things to him but reliving the memory of a dear friend under the guise of chronicling the event for the benefit of Guido alone.

It was clear to him that the man, Bob Devereux, Earl of Essex, was obviously sorely missed and it would not have surprised Guido if he had been unjustly treated from what everyone said. They seemed very passionate about the whole event. It sounded to him as if Cecil was a man to be feared, he hoped he would never meet him.

"Dear Essex thought he had everyone's backing so he marched to the city to gather more supporters who would help him to regain his sweet wine monopoly."

"I have heard of Essex and his rebellion from a Flemish man in the Lowlands, he was a brave man, he told me; was it a revolution? I have been told it was a Catholic plot!"

"Essex was a Protestant!" Catesby spat indignantly; he was fed up with every plot being seen as an attempt to put a Spanish king on the throne. "It was not a revolution, it was a protest. He was letting the Queen know his support against her unfair decision."

"He might even have been a Puritan; he had enough Puritan friends, that much was true," Wintour added.

"The main thing is he bore no malice towards any religion at all, Catholics, Calvinists, Lutherans, Puritans, even those Anabaptists who Cecil has seen fit to persecute," Catesby argued.

"That is no word of a lie; we all know many of his closest friends were of the Catholic persuasion," Wintour agreed. "He actively drew Catholics and Puritans to his cause."

"The flame to draw the moths was the promise of more religious toleration. In return for which, we would ensure that he was returned to favour and that Cecil was removed from the Privy Council," Catesby continued, "all he did was get us into as much trouble as he was in!"

"Robert Catesby almost lost his life thanks to Devereux and his devilment!" Wintour bitterly complained.

"I cannot forget that day Sunday, 8th February 1601," announced Catesby proudly, a glint came into his eye as he fondly remembered the feelings he had at that time, he was supporting a just cause for a brave man who had won more battles for his queen than he had lost, "it was a great march; we, his friends, and several other gentry, and many influential peers, were involved in our progress towards the city."

"There was no support; no one had the stomach for causing trouble for Queen Elizabeth," Wintour moaned.

"I think everyone realised how foolish we had been trying to oust Cecil when the Queen was so displeased with Essex," Catesby added as realising for the first time the extreme folly of their adventure.

"Our way was blocked attempting to return to Bob's house!" Wintour continued.

"They were too late to stop our march so they wanted to punish us for taking part!" Catesby bemoaned, "They swooped on us from the other side of the strand."

"Catesby fought valiantly in spite of an injury," Wintour said proudly, looking at his companion with true devotion, "what was it that was said at the time? I quote, and cherish the quote as I cherish dear Catesby, 'Mr. Catesby did show such valour and fought so long and stoutly as divers afterwards of those swordsmen did exceedingly esteem him and follow him in regard thereof'. See!"

"Our entire attempt failed," Catesby admitted sadly, "after a siege at Essex House, we surrendered to the authorities."

The mood in the room, momentarily, turned morbid like a funeral procession that had arrived at the graveside. They stared into the fire as if it were the grave itself.

"Lucky Catesby, due to his minor role in the affair, escaped a conviction for treason and possible execution, but was fined the crippling sum of 4,000 mark," added Wintour.

"A sum even I cannot entertain!" cried Catesby.

"4,000?" Guido exclaimed, he knew a thousand meant *'mille'*; it seemed a huge sum and he was shocked, sipping from his tankard as if it might be the last drink he would be bought that night.

These men were extraordinary; they could lose thousands and still drink like demons. They were an extraordinary group of people and the seemed to like him. Guido's spirits soared.

"I had to sell my manor at Chastleton, but I was still left with my life and an income from my other estates. Now, I spend most of my time between my wife's houses at Morecrofts and Lambeth," admitted Catesby sheepishly.

He did not want to admit it but losing the house where he had grown up had affected him deeply. Above all, he had wanted to share the happiness of growing up in such a wonderful *'Arcadia'* with his children. He had wanted to show them the beautiful house's wonderful woodwork, clever joinery, casement windows, plastered walls, ornate ceilings, wainscoting, heavy wooden doors, solid furniture and generous fireplaces.

He had dreamed of showing them the superb grounds where they would have learnt about the wonders of nature, fish in the lake there, the honeybees in the hives, the seasons changes and mysteries It had been his dream to share with them experiences that he had never been able to share with his father. He was thinking of those halcyon days back in Chastleton and the fact that his children would not grow up playing in its corridors as he had. It saddened him, but he was determined to rebuild his life and improve the lot of his children.

"Christopher Wright and I went to Spain," Wintour boasted, we wanted the heat to die down and Catesby sent us to negotiate with Jerez."

"Why?" Guido had drunk more than he could handle by this stage and he was reduced to asking obvious questions.

"Ah, this will all be clear."

"What is Jerez famous for?"

"What?" Guido knew, everyone knew, he had just not heard, he had almost nodded off.

His new companions were charming company but their stories were very long-winded and difficult to follow; long and boring Rosa would have said. He thought of her, then when his friends talked of war. He missed her more than ever. He felt like crying but managed to control himself. He wanted to sleep, go home and wallow in his grief.

"*Jerez*, sack; we enjoy it thanks to Francis Drake; he raided Cadiz. Cadiz was one of the most important Spanish seaports, and Spain was preparing '*The Armada*' in order to invade England," said Catesby.

"Guido surely knows the history!" cried Wintour exasperatedly. He knew that Guido might not understand English fully but he was not ignorant and should not be treated in that way, he felt strongly that the others were making too many assumptions and it was not fair. He was foreign not stupid. They could not see that.

"Drake daringly raided the port," Catesby continued, oblivious to the interruption, it was his story and he would tell it his way.

"Drake!" cheered Guido, "a fine gentleman like Catesby!" He wanted to show his love for this band of brothers and his hatred of the Spanish, too.

"Thank you, again, Guido, but back to Drake," insisted Catesby gently. "Sir Francis went on to destroy the Spanish fleet, and amongst the spoils that he brought back were 2,900 barrels of Sherry! They were waiting on the hard to be loaded aboard Spanish ships! We just helped ourselves."

Guido smiled. These men were adventurers, brave and strong, stories of these *'privateers'* had greeted him wherever he went on the Continent.

"Amazing, that was seventeen years ago and now *sack* is one of the most popular drinks that can be found, if you can get hold of it, it disappears as quickly as it arrives." Wintour added.

"So why did Catesby send you to Spain?" Guido asked perplexed as usual. The group spoke far too fast, too closely after one another, interrupted and changed subjects too readily for Guido to follow especially with the intoxicating effect of the triple strength winter ale.

"Pay attention, this is where you come in," Wintour warned him.

"Me?" Guido asked wishing he had not let them fill his tankard so many times already, he was no longer capable of paying any attention to anything.

"Yes, you!" cried Wintour good-naturedly.

"What do I have to do?" Guido wondered, hoping it did not involve leaving his chair or his drink. Just in case he took another draught of his ale.

"Don't worry, it's easy; where was I? Yes, we went to Cadiz and then onto Jerez de Frontera," Wintour continued, taking a sip of his ale too, in order to wet his throat.

"To fight the Spanish, good, I hate the Spanish!" Guido spat drunkenly.

"Spoken like a true Catholic Englishman," Wintour said encouragingly.

"Yes," interrupted Catesby, "Our friend Essex, had the licence for sweet wines and lots his monopoly. I therefore negotiated the licence for *Jerez sack*. Not only that but I have also negotiated the disbursement of the goods throughout the Midlands and in London with the help of Edmund Doubleday of the Saracen's Head on King Street."

"You have done well," Wintour agreed, feeling slightly drunk himself, Catesby, seemed to be slurring his words, too.

"Marvellous," Guido said, having heard someone else in the pub say it to someone else behind him.

"I can, now, not only bring *'sack'* in to the port of London but I can distribute it throughout the land! What do you think about that?"

"He doesn't understand," Wintour exclaimed.

"The distribution of *sack* is my monopoly," Catesby explained, exaggerating hugely, he had in fact only a single order and permission to sell in the Midlands. He was known for his hyperbole and optimistic view of everything. The ale had clouded his thought too. He stood by the heat of the fire and that made him thirstier still.

"Yes," Guido growled, he had almost fallen asleep because he was incapable of any other sound at that stage of the evening after so much drink.

"So, that is agreed, we will talk on your involvement tomorrow," Catesby said. He quaffed some ale satisfied that soon his family fortunes would be restored

"Agreed!" enthused Guido amicably. Catesby placed his left hand on the back of Guido's chair while he put his face in front of Guido's so their eyes met.

"You are a most trusted man," insisted Catesby.

"Good! You are a gentleman!" cried Guido meeting Catesby's gaze while smelling his beery breath. The hairs on their beards almost touched. "A true gentleman!"

"A gentleman earns his own money and pays his debts, remember that," Catesby said, bringing his right arm up so he could sup from his tankard.

"I will remember," promised Guido.

He brought his tankard to his lips, they both had to move their heads back to accommodate the two tankards. They clashed the pewter pots together in a show of solidarity.

"Yes, and I know these vagabonds have said my wife is wealthy but a gentleman needs his own money. Fines have almost ruined my family, my father before me and me too as a result of my loyalty to Devereux, but I will make a living through the *sack*, I will change the family fortunes, I will see my children, all the time unlike my poor father. Then, I will gain back my manor at Chastleton!"

With that declaration, he fell back into one of the wicker and wood chairs arranged around the hearth and sat staring drunkenly into the bottom of his tankard.

The group kept talking but Guido and Catesby, who had drunk more quickly than most, snored through until they were both woken, the next day, by the landlord.

Wintour was sound asleep upstairs in his room. Guido had drunk because of nerves being surrounded by so many important individuals and to forget the loss of Rosa; Catesby had drunk to forget his misfortune and the loss of his beloved Chastleton.

Chapter 19 – Catesby, Cecil, Doubleday and Sitwell.

Catesby was ecstatic, explaining to his business partners, Thomas Sitwell and Edmund Doubleday, and his sleeping partner Robert Cecil, the merits of *sack*. The four men sat around a dining table in Catesby's Lambeth house. In front of them was a large bowl of cracked hazelnuts, cobs and filberts fresh from Kent, salt in a pewter bowls and glasses of *sack* in Catesby's best *Cristallo* glasses, from Bohemia. The clear yellowish tinge to the clear glass was not the same quality as Venetian *Murano* but Catesby had lost those when Chastleton was sold. The nut shells lay in clusters near each man's glass.

"Fino En Rama is unfiltered and unclarified, taken from the middle of the cask during spring when the flor growth is at its thickest," he exclaimed.

"It must be made in limited quantities," Cecil remarked.

"Yes, indeed, and is best drunk within three months of delivery," Catesby continued unabated.

"What does '*En rama*' mean?" Doubleday asked.

"I am told it means in an unrefined and most delicate state, prior to the normal stabilisation, clarification and filtering processes that *sack* goes through," Catesby answered, he had become quite an expert on the commodity, which would restore his family's fortunes. Catesby was pleased to answer, as Cecil asked a series of questions.

"How else can we encourage the King to favour this wine?" asked Cecil conscious of the need to please the King. "We should extoll its rarity."

"The *sack* is produced from *Palomino Fino* grapes which are grown in the chalky '*albariza*' soil of Jerez, a rare grape indeed," replied Catesby confidently.

He had learnt much from the Sandeman family. They were the experts.

"Good; what else?" Cecil asked encouraging his pupil like any good mentor; Catesby needed to sell the wine to Cecil so that he, in turn, could sell its merits to King James.

The more rarefied, the greater the value, the more it would appeal to the King.

"The 'Solera' system, in which the wines from different years are blended, contributes to its remarkably consistent quality," Catesby continued.

"Quality, good, good, yes," Cecil enthused.

"It is aged under a covering of fresh, naturally occurring yeast, which the men of Jerez call *'flor'*, for a minimum of five years," Catesby confirmed.

"So is this what makes the *sherris sack* from Jerez de la Frontera so special?" added Cecil.

"Yes, it is not the common sweet *sack* matured in wood for a limited time; this is no common *Oloroso Sherris*."

"The Spanish call it *sacar*," Sitwell interrupted, taking another approving sip of wine. "We have been bringing in barrels with little disruption since 1590, my father tells me, we cannot get enough; it sells four times as much as the *juniper* even though it is more expensive than the Dutch spirit. This is far superior, it complements the nuts perfectly."

"I serve the *sacar* at the *Saracen's Head*, what does *sacar* mean in English?" asked Doubleday not in the least embarrassed by his ignorance, nor bashful about asking questions.

"It means to draw out," Catesby added.

"I speak a little Spanish," Cecil said.

"Of course, forgive my enthusiasm," Catesby apologised.

"Sir John Falstaff was fond of *sack*, especially *sherris sack*," Sitwell added jovially, taking a swig of wine.

He held the wine in his cheeks and swilled it in his mouth, then, opening his lips slightly to let a little air into his mouth, he swilled it one more time before he swallowed it with a satisfied smile spreading over his face. He was enjoying the tasting.

Cecil looked peeved that he had been beaten to the quip; it was normally he who mentioned '*The Bard*' and quoted from his plays; everyone knew it. Instead, he rattled off some facts he had been told by another importer.

"We all know the history. The Duke of Medina Sidonia abolished taxes on export of wine from Sanlucar de Barrameda a year before Columbus set sail, English merchants were given preferential treatment in 1517."

Cecil reeled off the facts with such rapidity, scarcely hiding his boredom; the others had to strain their ears to understand. He could barely sip his drink, he had too much paperwork to do and *sack* robbed him of his energy; the others were becoming more animated the more they drank. Cecil would have liked to relax and ease into a lunchtime snack, followed by a good dinner, a little later, like these gentleman.

"You know your history of Spanish wines," Catesby responded, impressed by Cecil's depth of knowledge.

"The wine was very popular in England after that time and continues to be much appreciated," Cecil added.

"Then, war came," Catesby said soberly.

"Those dark days meant we were never sure if the wine we shipped was second-rate wines, '*Bastards*', or first-rate wines, like '*Rumneys*' and '*Sacks*', we just put the barrels on the boat and hoped for the best," Sitwell admitted.

Doubleday opened his mouth to speak, Cecil rolled his eyes and Sitwell and Catesby pretended not to notice. It was going to be a very long and involved tasting session.

Chapter 20 - Guido's Task

The March morning provided bright sunlight; there were no drapes or curtains on the windows in Guido's humble lodgings so the spring sunshine flooded through the dusty leaded windows that looked out onto the fetid yard at the back of his lodgings. At eleven o'clock, he breakfasted like a gentleman at an inn; he would have been two hours away from his midday break if he had still been working on the docks.

The nobles led a different life and kept different hours, Guido was beginning to get a taste for it. Thomas Percy showed his contempt for the King and his broken promises, Thomas Wintour and his friend; John Wright agreed with Catesby that they should make the most of their good fortune at winning the supply of wines to the parliament banquet and plan the distribution of another shipment into the Midlands.

Guido was shown the house near the parliament buildings where the wine would be stored. It was not large enough for all the barrels but the owner, Mrs Bright, had agreed to allow them to excavate a small portion of the floor so that they could fit them all in. Guido was to supervise the dig and to work out how far the proposed hole should go; he had worked on fortifications in the Low Countries and understood about making embankments, digging trenches, excavating tunnels and building embrasures.

The floor was earth as was common in many warehouses, it was basically a brick shed with no windows but light leaked through the eaves, it was a dim place but it was dry and cool, ideal for storing barrels, their wine would be safe and moving it across the road to the palace of Westminster would not cause too much work or movement, which would in turn help the sediment settle more quickly once the barrels were set up. The barrels needed to be rolled regularly so that the lees did not form a crust but just before settling the wine for the final time in order to serve, it was helpful to limit the amount of rolling so that the sediment would fall more quickly.

Cecil watched their work through his agents; he had an idea, for he knew a man who owned a house next to the palace, which would be a better size. Cecil would ensure the cellar was free to rent in May before the July opening of parliament. It had a cellar which ran right under the parliament building, it was much more suitable and no one would believe that the destruction of the current warehouse, so far away, would cause damage to the either Westminster Hall or Westminster Palace. Thomas Bates helped Guido with his work to extend the cellar to accommodate the barrels. They had to use shovels and pick-axes to gouge out more room in the confined space, it was hard work, tunnelling was never a pleasant task.

That March morning, they had been summoned to meet at Catesby's house in Lambeth to meet Everard Digby so Guido was allowed a much needed lie in; working at the docks and preparing the cellar for warehousing the '*sack*' was becoming onerous to say the least. He worked too hard, he ate too little and slept too infrequently.

"So Guido, we're to call you John Johnson, I actually knew a Thom Thomson, he was a small man and kind to me, but he died a year after I joined the Catesby family," Bates remarked as he opened the door to the tardy 'bellman'.

"When was that?" asked Guido slipping through the door and embracing Bates one he had closed the door, the stood apart and shook hands like old friends.

"I joined the family over ten years ago, 1594, what were you doing then?"

"I was at Antwerp, trying to make a living."

"So," said Catesby as he arrived from the kitchens, having supervised the organisation of lunch, "what have we here, two men chatting like washer women?"

"We're getting to know each other as those who work together should!"

"There's little you need to know about Guido except that he's a big Italian, a gentle man as much as you and I; he has a broad back and can drink like an Englishman."

"You know all about me," complained Guido, "but what do I know about Thomas, Robin?"

"He is a reliable retainer and his loyalty is beyond question," Catesby explained.

He did not mind Guido using Robin instead of Robert. It was the name that Wintour used to address him and that was good enough for him, he was not going to insist of formality. Theirs was an easy relationship. A friendship based on a shared endeavour.

"A good worker, like me," Guido quipped.

"He is an efficient messenger, remembering all the details of any message and his ability to drive a wagon will help us in the transfer of the sack to my house and thence to the river."

"I'm always happy to help Robert," Bates said, "I always call him Robin, on account of his handsomeness and good singing voice."

"Now you know why we have retained such a loyal servant, flattery! It's utter nonsense of course!" Catesby replied jovially without embarrassment.

"I have not yet mentioned your reputation amongst men for having a noble character and amongst women for being a dashing escort and a fellow of impressive dignity," Bates continued.

"He is also known to be a courageous horseman and a supreme swordfighter," announced Everard Digby from the open doorway, which he seemed to fill. "He is generous and affable."

They all turned to see who had spoken; a man seemed to be blocking up the entrance to the room. His voice was deep and booming as befitted such an enormous vessel.

"As you are shy and withdrawn," Catesby replied laughing heartily.

Digby guffawed as he stepped through the doorway and down the stone steps at the doorway and onto the floorboards.

"Edmund!" cried Catesby happily. He was glad to see his old friend and confidant.

"We can all praise him to the rafters but I can tell you he has won many of his acquaintances over to Catholicism, I number myself as one of those converts, born Anglican and converted to the Roman faith but keep it quiet," Digby announced proudly to all those present, his eyes met theirs in turn as he spoke. His presence was like a warm caress. His laughter was infectious and his manner warm.

"While I convert to Protestantism and keep it quiet," parried Catesby.

"For your family, Catesby, we all know that, but the fact remains you have had great success in converting Protestants to the Church of Rome."

"It is you who say it," protested Catesby, always on his guard.

"Who could be a better Catholic, then, bless me, doesn't he baptise his children into the Church of England. This is a man who adjusts his gallop to the firmness of the ground."

"I want them to be safe."

"And so they shall be! So Catesby, this house in Lambeth is to be the first headquarters of our new sack importers!"

"Indeed it is and here is the workforce."

"I know the venerable Mr. Bates, I recognise his face from many encounters and from when it was less wrinkled, but this new man, John Johnson I have yet to have the pleasure," Digby announced, smiling broadly at Guido.

Digby bowed expansively, bending low at the waist, using a flourish of the hands one of which held his fashionable buckled beige suede hat. Guido bobbed his head and bowed as low as he could in reply. Everard Digby had been born in Leicestershire and he looked like a countryman with a ruddy complexion and a well-developed mid-riff bulge, formed by pints of Leicestershire ale that was delivered to his large house in Rutland. He was almost thirty but looked much older with his beard and his large beer belly. Drink had aged him by at least ten years.

"Dear Sir Everard Digby, our staunch ally and wealthy Catholic convert," Catesby sighed happily, "Digby owns large estates in Rutland, he is a very popular character, being warm and friendly beyond measure as well as being an excellent horseman, swordsman and musician!"

"Bring me a clavichord or lute and I will play '*Greensleeves*' as Henry intended."

"He plays so well, even the birds stop singing in order to hear him play!"

"You flatter me! The birds stop singing because they have flown away in fear!"

"Do not listen to him, he is adept at all he does; I have seen him play field sports with a passion!"

"If only my ability could match my passion, I feel I am not as good at anything at Catesby says, that's why everyone likes him; he's charming and over-fulsome in his praise."

"I keep my investors happy!"

"I have invested the considerable sum of £1,500," Everard boasted, "and have brought this scheme under my management skills and who is the new man."

"Not a nobleman and adventurer like us," Catesby explained.

"Did you say he was a nobleman and adventurer like us? Did he fight at Cadiz?"

"No, he is not quite like us, but he is a noble man and up for adventure; if adventure means importing sack then he is an adventurer!"

Robert Keyes arrived, a Jesuit convert, a tall man with a red beard. He was the next man to join the company.

"Welcome Robert"

"Good morrow, Robin."

"Tell Guido where you fit in."

"Ah, another investor in our company," remarked Keyes helpfully, smiling at all and sundry. "Since October last year my main function has been to tend to Robert Catesby's home in Lambeth, which we have used as a storage facility for the *sack* and all the necessary tools to set it up and serve it."

"I see," Guido pretended he understood. It was best to let these nobles talk and then in the quiet moments ask Bates what to do.

"We cannot just have *sherries* arriving, we need corks and bungs and taps and spiles." There were quizzical looks.

"Spiles?" asked Guido

"I will explain all," replied Keyes. "Let me give you a watch, a watch for a watch, we will let you know the full tides so that you can land at high tide. It will make it easier for you and Bates to plan the loading, and unloading, of the barrels if you know the times of the tide and can tell the time, Bates will teach you, if you do not know"

"Thank you," Guido replied, pleased that he was being trusted with the timepiece and the tide tables, he was also glad that he would have the support of the more experienced Bates.

"You want to load and unload at high tide, make it easier on the arms and legs, less steps to walk up and down, the steps at low tide are very high and slippery, at high tide the stones are dry and but a few, just a hop, skip and jump from boat to hard."

"High tide will be best," Bates agreed.

"You will want to check the time of high tide from the tide tables and time things accordingly, it might be best to confirm the tides with a merchantman, too. You would be wise to set your time from a church clock so you know your timepiece is accurate. Keep it well wound but do not wind it too tight or you will break the spring and that will be the end of it."

Tall and well built, another visitor arrived, announcing himself as Tom Percy; he was forty-one but looked younger, he wore a serious expression but he addressed the group in a polite manner, he appeared to be a man of serious nature and not as at ease as the other members of the group.

Guido noticed his eyes were large and lively and he liked him immediately. Their first meeting at the *Duck and Drake* hardly counted as Guido was just a mere bystander and he had not absorbed the characters fully nor engaged meaningfully with them.

"Ah, Guido, I recognise you," Percy cried, "You were at the tavern looking on as our group enjoyed themselves, next time we will show you some drinking games and you will not be allowed to sit by like an audience at *the Swan*!"

"Ducks, drakes and swans, it sounds as if he will get wet the next time you both meet," Guido remarked mischievously, falteringly only slightly.

They all laughed and Guido beamed, not only had he cracked his first English joke, he had finally found new friends and perhaps with their help he might forget that Rosa was no longer beside him.

Chapter 21 - Cecil and a conversation with Markham 1604

They ate lunch together, after visiting Monteagle's house, at the Cheshire Cheese in a little alleyway off Fleet Bridge Street. Markham chose the venue and explained there had been a tavern there since 1538 after the 13th-century Carmelite Monastery was closed down. The vaulted cellars acted as a wonderful larder and kept wines and ales cool all year around.

An open fireplace kept them warm, they were some of the first diners there that day and Cecil ordered soup and venison pie for them. Markham did not mention that this was one of Devereux's favourite haunts; he did not want to antagonise his master.

"We had hoped for improvement under James," Markham complained bitterly. "There was every chance that he would be tolerant of other religions."

"James, being the snake in the grass he is, supported the Earl of Essex against me!" chortled Cecil gamely. The matter had been dealt with efficiently and therefore a little levity was allowed. "That was before he came to the throne, afterwards I could not allow him to show his followers such favour!"

"We were, indeed, shown great favour as Essex's supporters and prominent Catholics at the beginning of the reign. So that was what was worrying you! Did you fear James would favour the Catholics above you?" he asked mischievously, he could tell when Cecil was in the mood to jest a little.

"James claimed his utter detestation of papists," Cecil argued, sipping some soup that he found too hot, so he put his spoon down on the table, folding his arms, in a defiant action signalling to the soup that he was prepared to let it cool.

The soup steamed sullenly, waiting for Cecil to attack it with a spoon. Next, to the soup was a cold veal pie, which Cecil looked forward to eating after the soup.

He could not resist picking pastry from it and nibbling at the crumbs so that he had something to taste. It was a rare treat to have a midday repast.

"That's what you tell us!" complained Markham, watching as Cecil smiled with satisfaction, his protégé was really getting to know the mechanism of statecraft.

" Maybe but so what? Besides, if we allowed the Catholics tolerance we would have to allow the same to the Puritans. James was never fond of the Puritans and grew to despise the Catholics as well."

"Only once you poisoned him," Markham sneered dismissively; he drank some soup, too, but finding it equally hot, determined to show how tough he was by drinking it anyway. It burnt his tongue but he made sure that he blew on the spoon as he raised the steaming spoon to his mouth when he was sure that Cecil was not looking.

"In February last year he told the bishops that they must 'see to the severe and exact punishment of every Catholic', a pretty full increase in my fortunes would you not say. There was a time when Essex thought he could usurp me," Cecil boasted, looking into the fire, allowing Markham to blow twice on the hot soup nearing his open lips.

"All Catholics are aware of that; you publicised it so well. That proclamation of February twenty-second ordering all priests out of the realm, reversing the repeal of recusancy fines and making the fines payable immediately, with arrears. Did you want to ruin us, lull us into recusancy and then find out who was recusant?" he ranted, knowing that the more he spoke before shovelling the soup into his mouth the more it would cool.

"Of course, you are right, by asking for the arrears, I was pleasing James, he desperately needs money and what easier ways are there to collect funds?"

"Tax the Puritans?"

"You are all wealthy landowners with plenty of money to spare, I see your wealth made by the toil of workingmen, and I see that it is spent by the profligates at court. We make the money, they spend it, it is unjust; it is a disgrace. The Scots are taking over parliament itself and celebrating royally while they are about it."

"You are wrong about our wealth!" seethed Markham, "many of us are farmers and you know that recent years have not been kind to us and the harvests have been poor."

"Poor you, I want to destroy you not pity you!" Cecil smiled, he almost felt sorry for Markham; he was such a poor player. "Drink your soup!"

Cecil held all the cards and the winning hand, yet Markham insisted on asking for another deal. The soup on the wooden spoon was quite warm by the time he slurped it. Both men stared at each other as if truly communicating, not just talking, for the first time in their lives.

"So you were behind the move last April to excommunicate Catholics making us exiles or outlaws. Catholics have become enemies of the State, it is worse than during the Armada. We are nothing. Everyone fears us, yet our religion preaches tolerance and love. You make everyone feel we are murderers or plotters, all guilty of treason," complained Markham, rapidly losing his appetite for both soup and pie.

"Worse, I have ensured that you will never trouble me again by seeing that King James decreed your rents need not be paid and that you be put beyond the protection of the law," Cecil admitted.

Markham, for the first time in his adult life, was speechless.

Chapter - 22 - Catesby, Wintour and the *Sack*

Catesby stood by the fire in the withdrawing room of his Lambeth house.

"Well met cousin," he cried happily when Wintour entered through the door announced by Catesby's wife's servant.

"I've brought our watchman, John Johnson, with me," Wintour announced, leading Guido into the room.

"He has met Thomas Bates, who has helped him with his work, good old Bates is a good teacher, he has been working for the Catesby family for all the years that I can remember," Catesby announced affably.

"I seem to remember Thom from time in memorial," Wintour added for good measure.

"He is a reliable retainer and his loyalty is beyond question, he is an efficient messenger, remembering all the details of any message, his ability to drive a wagon stands him in good stead against other men of ordinary condition," parroted Guido, copying, verbatim, Catesby's earlier description of the family retainer, whilst he clamped his hand gently onto Wintour's shoulder.

"Very good," Catesby laughed, Guido learnt quickly, he was an excellent parrot. His memory would serve him well. Catesby felt sure he would follow all instructions fully.

"He has been a great help to me."

Guido's confidence had grown amongst these men, they had encouraged it and enjoyed the way he adopted their easy and fun-loving nature.

"Ah very well, I met Markham last night. Cecil's persecution is getting worse; it is becoming unsafe for us all," Catesby warned.

"I have felt the anti-Catholic sentiments growing since Cecil convinced parliament to treat us like lepers."

"We must have a plan to fly from London when the fire gets too hot!"

"It is not that bad, is it?" Wintour asked. "Besides which we have a consignment to watch in London and one to deliver in the Midlands."

"Should it get so, I will send for you and Jack Wright, I will tell you, and he can warn Kit and anyone else, agreed?" Catesby replied. "Things are not so bad as to affect our delivery of the *sack* but I know that we need to move to the Midlands quickly after the Westminster delivery is made in order to oversee the distribution of the order Doubleday has organised. That was part of my deal with him."

"Indeed," replied Wintour and Guido nodded his head to show he acquiesced, although he felt he would not be fleeing if things got too hot nor would he be included amongst those moving up to the Midlands. He felt sure he would be left high and dry working in the docks until their next shipment. He did not mind, they paid well and he could wait for their return by working in the docks. Since the recent plagues, and the expansion of trade due to the Spanish treaty and peace in most of Europe, he had found even more work.

"How much do you remember from the other night?" asked Catesby already knowing what the answer might be.

"Not much!" Guido admitted sheepishly.

"Sit and I will explain," Catesby commanded though there was gentleness in his voice.

"Thank you."

Guido sat while Catesby and Wintour paced the room, they were both impatient for their hard work to pay off. They had invested time, money and emotion into bringing about a business that would help them escape from their pasts.

Cecil might finally leave them alone and forget that they had been on the side of the Earl of Essex.

When Catesby was ready to explain he stopped and stood still, Wintour mirrored his action and waited for Catesby to speak.

"We will keep it short but you should know the background. I had seen how much Essex, our friend Bob Devereux, had made from his sweet wine monopoly. To buy back my house and to ensure my money is my own and not my wife's inheritance; I thought we could negotiate with the Spanish to import *Jerez* on a regular basis since hostilities were ceased. *Jerez* came into the country every now and then but there was no regular supply."

Wintour took up the rest of the narrative after an encouraging nod from Catesby.

"To this end, I was sent to Flanders to meet with the Constable of Spain, who was on his way to England to conclude the peace negotiations between Spain and England. He was a personal friend of some of the owners of leading *bodegas*. At the same time, just in case others might get wind of our plans, I was to inform the Constable of the condition of the Catholics in England."

Guido felt he should speak at this point, "A noble endeavour."

"I was hoping he might intercede for us when meeting King James to discuss the terms of their treaties," continued Wintour, unable to disguise the disappointment in his voice.

"A cry for fairness?" Guido suggested.

"I entreated him to solicit his Majesty at his coming hither that the penal laws may be recalled, and we be admitted into the ranks of his other subjects," Wintour added.

"You have to understand that although I have obeyed all the laws, Cecil has gone too far in his censure of the Catholics, especially when he has decreed, through the King, that no one need pay us rent," interrupted Catesby.

"Of course our tenants continue to pay us; the ways of the country are not the ways of this great port," explained Wintour.

Catesby again confounded and complicated the problem by trying to make Guido understand the complexities of English politics, power and influence, "The Privy Council's influence reaches only as far as the great cities and town of this commonwealth, not to the villages and shires; that would be too much even for Cecil to achieve. He is happy if he can influence the city folk, they are the ones who pay the majority of his taxes on tobacco, monopolies and traded goods."

Wintour seemed to be annoyed by Catesby's digression and firmly brought the conversation back to his mission in Flanders, he said, "I was not impressed by the interview with the Constable to intercede for us during peace negotiations, but he did give me the name of a man who owns a *bodega* in *Jerez* who might sell to us; I was further discouraged on behalf of the Catholics when I met Hugh Owen and William Stanley."

"You best explain who they are to Guido, he might not know," Catesby offered helpfully.

"They are the heads of the English Catholics in exile, unofficially of course," Wintour said conspiratorially, waiting for Guido's nod of understanding.

"I see," he added in order to fill the silence that had resulted from his lack of response. Guido looked down at his feet. He really was lost; they spoke far too quickly about complicated matters of which he had no idea. Pride meant that he could not ask for explanation.

Satisfied, the narrator, Wintour, continued, "They told me that Spain was too financially wanting and that they were too eager to conclude a peace to be of any assistance. So I carried on my journey to Spain to negotiate with the Sandeman family on Jerez de la Frontera. I passed Santiago de Compostela on the way and prayed for success and all the Catholics in this kingdom."

"Prayer is always good," noted Guido encouragingly.

Prayer was the only word he had really understood apart from the place names.

"Whether it was my prayers being answered or Senor Sandeman needing our business, I will never really know but things are dire in Spain after the costly wars they have waged and they need to trade with us. Many Spaniards are reduced to penury."

"That is too bad," Guido added.

"We lost all hope then, Catholics have become exiles in our own country, we are broken and the King and Cecil have removed all our influence at Court, Cecil is keen for the Scots to be the King's favourites, above us," Catesby exclaimed bitterly

"I returned to Catesby in Lambeth to tell him the disappointing news that I had learnt in the Lowlands and the lack of support form our Catholics friends both in exile and from Spain but also I was full of joy at my negotiations with Senor Sandeman, I had secured, in principle, our first shipment of thirty-six barrels of their finest '*sherris sack*'; life is bittersweet and there's the rub; it was on that voyage that I met you," Wintour continued, making sense to Guido, finally.

"Your scepticism was warranted," Catesby expanded, "for the treaty between Spain and England was pronounced on August 19th, with no provisions for the English Catholics,"

Guido understood the word 'provisions'; he was Italian, not stupid.

"That is a tragedy," said Guido forcefully.

"So we carry on, along the road, more friendless than befriended, 'mores the pity'," Catesby complained.

"That is a tragedy," Guido repeated, hoping he sounded sufficiently upset. He needed a job that would keep him under the protection of these influential men. They were nobles and could offer more than mere money alone. He was grateful for the wages he received but they could open so many doors for him if he did his job well, which he was determined to do.

"However, we did manage to write to a Senor Sandeman and he confirmed that he was prepared to send us as much *sack* as we would need and together with some friends, we set up a business with one of the Anglican godfathers to my son and one or two others," Catesby proclaimed happily. This was a white lie, the business had been set up with Cecil's man and later the godfather had been persuaded by all three that he should invest in the firm and become one of its leading lights; he did not want to refuse Catesby, he dared not refuse Cecil.

He was plotting a delicate course through shoals. He seemed to cheer up at the change in their fortunes.

"How noble you are," Guido announced admiringly. Catesby was good man, unfortunately, destined for infamy.

"Thank you, you are a good man," noted Catesby. He was, of course, right. Guido was a good sort but fate had prepared for him a place in history that might last for eternity.

"Your friends help you," Guido added. He wished that he had friends like that, not the fair-weather ones.

"Yes, indeed, they do. We make money through these friends who own the monopoly for the *sack*, we ship the wine from the Sandeman family and bring the wine to England and we have won the contract for Westminster, for the various houses of our parliament and their numerous functions. That is where you come in."

"We have a shipment docking at Southwark, which we will have to transport to my house and from thence we need someone to guard the load on its journey from Lambeth to the cellars at Westminster and thereafter until the whole is taken up for a banquet."

Guido's English was improving only slightly but he could understand more than he could speak and he had picked up some phrases from his friends, which made his English sound better.

"Upon my word all you want me to do is load and unload these barrels of sack and guard them?" asked Guido incredulously, it seemed a mean task and all simple work seemed to pay simple wages. Mean work would pay mean wages but Guido wanted to impress his new friends, it might lead to further commissions.

"You have no idea the value of this commodity; this wine is rare and special. Storing it properly and looking after it will take great care. The barrels will need to be rolled frequently and that is why you have Bates to help you when he can be spared. We have purchased the lease to the room, which belongs to John Whyneard. It is unused and might need cleaning up first."
"I can do that and you say that Bates will help me, too. We will make the room fit for storing fined wine."

"You will have help to clear the room and transport the barrels, yes, but there may not be room for all thirty six barrels, we have the owner's agreement that we can dig out the cellar to make more room and that is where your expertise comes in, you were an engineer in the lowlands were you not?"

"Indeed, I was, and I made ramparts and embrasures above the ground and excavations and tunnels below the ground. We should be able to dig out the cellar easily."

Guido liked the sound of 'expertise' he knew that experts were paid well and, indeed, his group of sappers had been paid well for breaking dykes and building fortifications. The further they needed to expand the cellar to accommodate the number of barrels, the more he would get paid. At the very least, he would be paid as a night watchman, at best, as chief engineer. He desperately needed the work and might be able to sleep at some stage during his vigil. If it was such important work, he might be able to persuade Catesby to pay his rent and then all he would need was money for food for his lunch during the week, which he could earn from a day or so on the dockside. It seemed he would not be working as hard as he had done so and with more pay.

Things were improving for him finally maybe fortune's wheel was turning in his favour.

"There will be a mixture of firkins and kilderkin," Catesby continued. "They will be too heavy to lift on your own; I will make sure some of my servants are on hand to help you and they will be under the direction of Bates and he will be under your direction. Of course, he will report to me but the scheme is in your charge unless Bates sees that you are not coping and you need help."

"Thank you."

"We should have everything stored and ready for His Majesty's 'Grand Opening of Parliament'."

"When is that day?"

"Thirty six barrels need to be in place by 20th July to let them settle, Parliament opens on 28th July, so we can tap and spile the barrels once we take them upstairs to the hall."

"That sounds sensible."

"Your English has improved in leaps and bounds Guido. What say you to taking the post of guard of the *sack*?"

"Aye, I will guard your *Jerez sack*, though it will be cold and lonely work."

"A summer opening will be preferable to a winter one, imagine if you had to be watchman in winter. Imagine the misery it would bring if the Parliament opened in December or February, you would be miserable in those cold cellars. Winter nights are the worst."

"The summer heat never penetrates the old walls of large buildings, hence the cool of a church on a summer's day, it will not be too cold and I will wrap up well, the cool airs will be helpful to the spirit stored in the barrels. Yes, I will do this willing for my friends."

"We will reward you handsomely, the King enjoys his *sack* already, he will become our best customer, but the '*Opening of Parliament*' promises to be one of the biggest gatherings we have seen since the Queen's death."

"I will guard the wine well"

"I know you will," Catesby said with real feeling. "We will have to call you John Johnson, we cannot have a foreigner working for us, just speak little; otherwise they'll think it some Catholic plot to bring in workers from Italy and Spain to undermine the Commonwealth."

"I, John Johnson, accept your commission."

"To success, to our venture, and confusion to our enemies." Catesby cried to the group, he had three glasses of *Sherris sack* standing on the sideboard by the window.

He left the fire and brought two glasses back, one for Guido Forcanessi, and one for Thomas Wintour. Handing them over, he returned to the sideboard and raised the third glass.

"Health gentlemen," Wintour toasted.

"To Johnson and his commission," added Catesby.

"To *sack* and *Jerez* success," cheered Wintour.

"That's easy for you to say," teased Catesby.

"To our venture," Guido cried, not sure how much the venture was theirs and how much it was his.

Wintour spoke next.

"I have a Spanish toast: *'Salut, denario, y amor'*, health, money and love!"

Guido needed all three in his life, more than ever before.

Chapter – 23 – Bacon and Cecil, Baking and Cooking, after the conclusion of The Treaty of London signed at Somerset House, 18th August 1604.

Cecil knew how long Bacon had been at law; he took up his residence in law at Gray's Inn in 1579; he had written *'Temporis Partus Maximus'*. He had worryingly, for Cecil, shown signs of sympathy towards Puritanism, attending the sermons of the Puritan chaplain of Gray's Inn and accompanying his mother to the Temple Church to hear Walter Travers.

He became a Bencher in 1586, and he was elected a reader in 1587, delivering his first set of lectures in Lent the following year. In 1589, he received the valuable appointment of reversion to the Clerkship of the Star Chamber. For twenty-six years, he had been snapping at Cecil's heels.

"I am worried about your criticism of the English church's suppression of the Puritan clergy."

"I have three goals in life."

"A trinity of devices to live by," Cecil noted dryly.

"If you like!" Bacon agreed peevishly, he intensely disliked being interrupted and he knew his cousin was aware of that. He was even more annoyed, having that knowledge and knowing that Cecil detested it, too; he was sure that Cecil was being deliberately provocative as usual.

"What are they, number them?" Cecil added.

"One to uncover truth," Bacon boasted.

"That is my goal, too!"

"Two, to serve my country," Bacon bragged.

"There we are united."

"Thirdly, to serve my Church." Bacon boomed.

"You should support the State's Church and the Lord Bishops alone, you should not support the Puritans one iota; I need you to serve the Crown and that means, over church matters, at least, keep your silence."

"Silence is the virtue of fools," Bacon replied impatiently.

Cecil was always trying to make him do what he did not wish to do; all he wanted was to continue writing, preferably in favour of the Puritan church. Instead, he was embroiled in politics. At one time, competing with Cecil might have interested him but he was aware that Cecil had shored up the political world and he was wise enough to know there was little point in trying to compete with the man who had the ears and eyes of all.

"It is not something I would consider, even if you could make an argument that I accepted; I have always wanted to have my say!"

"Our nation's security relies on your silence, I am trying to make peace with Spain and I cannot afford to let them think we are going even further from the Church," argued Cecil, "I have persuaded Spain that we will not support the Lutherans and Calvinists that lay at their doorstep; they cannot see England move further towards Protestantism! I give not a Spanish fig for the French Huguenots and the Calvinist rebels in the Lowlands. What England needs is peace; England is my only concern, the others compete with us for trade and the world's wealth, we need to snatch it."

"There be three things, which make a nation great and prosperous," regaled Bacon, "they are: a fertile soil for growth of crops; busy workshops for making goods; and easy conveyance for men and goods from place to place."

"Yes, yes, all in good time," Cecil agreed soothingly, "let us first have peace and unity as a base to build from; we need these at the cornerstones; you speak of cardinals when the foundations have not yet been laid."

"You sound like you are an architect!" complained Bacon; he valued thought and theology above mathematics.

"I have several books on the subject," responded Cecil dryly.

"Some books are to be tasted, others to be swallowed, and some few to be chewed and digested: that is, some books are to be read only in parts."

"Indeed, that is so," Cecil agreed.

"Others should be read, but not curiously, and some few to be read wholly, and with diligence and attention," Bacon pronounced, desperately trying not to sound pompous.

He liked his words. They still rang true. Bacon reflected on his verbose announcement with some satisfaction, it was his favoured treatise on the written word and had won him many plaudits.

Only Cecil had criticised it, out of spite, Bacon thought.

"How many times have I heard that?" asked Cecil rhetorically and dismissively in the same breath. "You rehearse it every time you are abroad and I am sure in your mirror at home, while you use your hair comb."

"You vex me with your indulgent criticism," Bacon complained, his face flushing. He wondered why Cecil always annoyed him and why he could not just leave him to reflect.

"You cause vexation to me with your incessant quotes," replied Cecil with a smile playing on his lips.

"Better than you and your third rate rhyming, pretending you have half the ability of Shakespeare," Bacon parried viciously.

"You lawyers twist words and twist truths and twist backs," Cecil whispered menacingly.

Even Bacon raised his eyebrows at such an audacious comment.

Cecil was the one who was known, throughout the land, as a twister of words, truths and the odd back, beheading nobles and granting them their lives; he was the 'Master of Deceit'.

"I have been a Member of Parliament for Liverpool and Middlesex, I have tried to simplify the law and stop persecution on religious grounds," Bacon argued, trying to gain the moral high ground, he was not just any lawyer.

"You have also been acquainted with Devereux. From 1591, you acted as the Earl's confidential adviser."

"I remember a year later, in 1592, I was commissioned to write a tract in response to, the Jesuit, Robert Parson's tract, it was called 'Certain Observations Made upon a Libel', showing England as Athens standing against belligerent Spain," Bacon replied.

"Yes, for two years you worked with the traitor, then, in February, Queen Elizabeth summoned Parliament to investigate the Roman Catholic plot against her. When the post of Attorney General fell vacant, in 1594, even Devereux's influence was not enough to secure you that office. He was not be pleased when you thanked him by sending him to Tower Hill to lose his head!"

"I, also, failed to secure the lesser office of Solicitor General, in 1595, but, to console me for those disappointments; Essex presented me with a property at Twickenham."

"It must be worth £1,500."

"The following year, I became Queen's Counsel," Bacon said, deciding it was prudent to ignore Cecil's remark.

"And two years later you were arrested for debt. You should have married Lady Hatton."

"I would have married her without the interference of Coke!" spat Bacon vehemently.

"Dear old Edward Coke, didn't he help me to prosecute your old friend and the man who bought you your home, Bob Devereux, Earl of Essex."

"My relationship with Bess was improved nonetheless, when I severed those ties, as you yourself just testified."

Both men chortled despite themselves, Cecil saw Bacon's ribbing.

"Are you trying to make a rhyme, to make your speech like mine, that's a waste of your time."

Both men howled with laughter, each other's hilarity encouraged the other to laugh even more.

They saw the ridiculousness of the situation and it made the atmosphere less tense.

Bacon and Cecil both thought that after this interlude, they might well agree on the best course of action to take after all. Cecil further felt that he might convince Bacon of the merits of destroying the Catholic nobles *'in one fell swoop'*. He adored that expression, so neat and tidy and so final.

Chapter 24 - James and the letter -
The Monteagle letter in the last days of October 1605

On 7 July 1604, James had angrily prorogued Parliament after failing to win its support for either full union of England and Scotland. It also failed to grant the financial subsidies James needed to pay for his court. James was less than pleased and complained in no uncertain terms.

"I will not thank where I feel no thanks due," he had remarked in his closing speech. "... I am not of such a stock as to praise fools ... You see how many things you did not well ... I wish you would make use of your liberty with more modesty in time to come."

As James's reign had progressed, his Government had faced growing financial pressures, due partly to creeping inflation but also to the profligacy and financial incompetence of James's Court. However, necessity, that is lack of money, had forced him to recall parliament. The recall was to be in July 1605 but had been delayed by yet another plague.

Cecil was keen to avoid 'a plague on all your houses' so agreed with James that November would make a better month to have the 'Grand Opening of Parliament'. James was keen to move forward, he had told parliament what he thought of them over a year ago and was keen to see them change their ways. He hoped he would achieve full union and that they would become more generous with their award of finance to him, he desperately needed money. He might well have kept Parliament prorogued if he did not. James was in fighting mood and, then, the letter arrived.

James stood in his bedchamber reading aloud the letter Cecil had just given him. The King stood by the fire; the draperies were open and the mirror above the mantle shelf provided him with more light.

Gathered in the room, with the King, were Cecil, Whyneard and a servant. The morning sunshine lit the room, enabling James to read without the aid of a candle.

"Therefore I advise you as you value your life, to find some excuse not to attend this Parliament and retire yourself into your country. For though there is no sign of any trouble, yet I say, they shall receive a terrible blow at this Parliament, yet they shall not see who hurts them," James read aloud for all to hear.

"A blow, what could that mean?" asked the King's favourite of favourites, John Ramsay, 1st Earl of Holderness, now Gentleman of the Bedchamber, an influential post. It was one of the few that Cecil could not influence.

"We cannot risk idle rumours," Cecil warned emphatically. He was such a consummate actor.

"Agreed but we should search the Palace of Westminster," the King proclaimed.

"We should put off the search until the afternoon before parliament is due to sit," Cecil suggested. "Thus, we can be sure any plotters will be discovered.

"Monday, then," Whyneard added.

"In the meantime, the Keeper of the Wardrobe, Whyneard should report to us," the King insisted.

Cecil had to agree with the recent summary given by Owen, in his daily reports, that the King had grown larger around the girth due to too much drinking and feasting and not enough hunting or other sport. Cecil himself noted that James looked fatter that day and that it was not due to his clothes, he was in his bedchamber, and he had noticed that James was becoming tubby, he assumed this was due to his heavy drinking and the eating bouts that heavy drinking inevitably brought on. Even without Owen's report; James's medium build made him seem fatter still and his clothes did little to dispel the image of a corpulent King. Cecil, on the other hand, dressed fashionably, a jag in the sleeves of his doublet; King James wore his plainer clothes loosely.

They were clearly too big for him, hiding his corpulence and the bulk of the quilted doublet that would prevent injury should he be attacked by a stiletto made him seem even larger. The King sprayed himself with perfume, as was the fashion, but Cecil thought that he should apply it more liberally; a stench pervaded the room.

"I will send word to my sources that a plot has been discovered but I will do it discreetly. Would Your Majesty agree to our increasing the guard around you?" Cecil asked.

"Indeed, it is my wish, my Lord Cecil, this is a most puzzling event and we will need to have this resolved," James demanded, his large eyes rolled towards a sideboard where some *sack* was decanted into a crystal decanter. He scratched his thin beard, "Care for a drink?"

"Your Majesty is too kind," Cecil answered, Cecil breathed dramatically; leaving James puzzled as to whether he was being genuine or ironic in his remarks. The phrase had not sounded sarcastic and yet he was not sure.

Cecil abhorred James's dress sense and the fact that he never changed his clothes until they were worn out but he equally hated watching James eat and drink but on that occasion he had no choice. The stammering brought on by his tongue being too big for his mouth, also resulted in clumsy eating and drinking.

The servant poured the King a drink and all prepared for the ensuing spitting, sloshing and spraying that would follow. Whyneard had built up immunity. Ramsay seemed immune to it all. Cecil had learnt to keep a diplomatic distance.

James drank heartily and most of the liquid poured down his throat, some leaked from the sides of his mouth but mercifully found its way back into the cup. Elegantly, he dabbed the sides of his mouth with a white silk napkin, which had been stained with sherry. Cecil had suggested red silk; he used them at his home, the stains of gravy and wine hardly showed. His suggestion had been ignored.

Cecil looked at the King's hands that people said were as soft as wool cloth; they were white, not because he washed them, he never did. Washing hands or bathing were things the King never considered. Cecil remembered that Queen Elizabeth religiously took a bath at least once, if not twice a year, whether she needed it or not. James needed to wash more, but he never bathed, he merely sprayed.

He was extravagant in the use of perfume, which stifled the smell of his lack of hygiene. Instead of washing his hands, he would rub his fingers slightly with a wet napkin. James leant against the sideboard, his legs were weak, and he always needed to prop himself up with the aid of someone or something. Cecil realised that James was drinking out of habit rather than for enjoyment and wondered how it affected him.

Cecil did admire James's wit, he delivered witty comments in a grave and serious manner, which Cecil enjoyed, he also admired that fact that his diet was simple and his habits were regular, unlike the rest of the Court. He disliked his extravagance, the lavish parties with too much drink and too much food. He also abhorred the bloodying of James's courtiers with stag's blood at the hunt. Cecil was an urban fox. However badly James ran the Court, he left Cecil to run the country and that suited Robert Cecil perfectly.

In a perfect world, Cecil would have maintained his control of Court that he had achieved in the latter part of Elizabeth's reign; the control he had so cunningly wrested from Queen Bess's favourites, through plotting and, in part, through convincing parliament to remove the lucrative monopolies that she had awarded her favourites. Cecil had wrested power from the old guard, those who had achieved glorious things in their youth and had lived off their reputations. He had introduced a new order to Elizabethan Government. Slowly, but surely, he was moulding James's State to his model. This plot was part of that plan.

"A blow by cannon ball do you think?" asked James.

"We will ensure your troops are posted on high parts that have a view of Westminster," Cecil assured him. "There will be no cannonade on the day Parliament opens. The militia and my men will see to that."

"A wise precaution, an explosion by means I cannot fathom, yet," James announced, taking another sip of sherry to steady his nerves. "What say you Whyneard?"

"There are only two ways gunpowder can be exploded, Your Majesty," Whyneard replied, "the blow would have to be from an attack; a blow that they shall receive suggests many people, a barrel perhaps exploded as they have done to the dykes across the Channel."

"A consideration," Cecil admitted, whilst dissembling, he knew the conclusion he wanted them both to draw and wondered why it was taking so long.

"Aye, when I was a babe, in arms, gunpowder was used to destroy the house in which I slept," James remembered dreamily, trying to imagine himself back to Scotland and back to that time. He took a swig from his glass. Cecil decided to speak before James sprayed them all with his words.

"Your Majesty, might I suggest a thorough search of the palace precincts, the hall and the palace in the knowledge that we can make Westminster secure!"

"I will order it now, Whyneard will you do me that service?" the King asked plaintively.

"Of course Your Majesty," replied Whyneard.

"I want every back room searched for any evidence of powder and I want all closets and chests cleared from thence and placed in storage in Whitehall, but only once they, and their contents, have been thoroughly checked," insisted James pragmatically.

"Your wish is my command, Your Majesty."

Epilogue – Mid-December 1605

Markham and Cecil moved easily through the crowd at the 'Frost Fair' on the Strand. Markham was good at clearing a space. His tall stature, and the sword by his side, allowed him to make his own path. He made an excellent bodyguard and a resplendent plough.

Cecil had sent him to the Lowlands shortly after their visit to the house and he had awaited the summons, which had come when winter's bite had a firm hold on the city and he had seen ice off the eastern shore of England as the merchant boat had brought him across the North Sea. They found a spot by a brazier roasting chestnuts and warmed their chilled bones before moving on, watching a boy as he broke the burnt shells with a nut-cracker and laid them out on an iron frame for people to pick up and peel.

Cecil enjoyed all sorts of nuts, especially the sweet chestnut but he could not be bothered to struggle with the thick leather gloves that he wore. Determining to send one of his servants out to buy some, at a later date, he followed Markham as he left the Strand and walked down to the river. Waiting for them were Cecil's boatmen and his boat; it was damp and frosty and Cecil willingly accepted the proffered gloved hand of the port side oarsman.

Markham had led the way through the crowd but he demurred at the boat, he knew he was a crowd-clearer and he immediately reverted to faithful servant on the riverbank, following his master. Allowing Cecil to settle into his seat, Markham waved away the helpful hand and stumbled clumsily into the boat, standing upright instead of crouching. The boat lurched alarmingly from side to side; the boatman could not swim and wondered if he would be able to hang on to the oar to keep him afloat if they all toppled in; he wondered how long he would survive in the freezing water. At the last minute when, both boatmen and Cecil felt that the boat's rocking would spill them into the Thames, and their impending doom. Markham sat down. He was oblivious to the mayhem, which he had almost caused.

The boat had rocked back and forth, and then settled. The boatmen and Cecil looked alarmed; none of them had been in the Thames yet and it was icy cold that night. Markham seemed undisturbed by the rocking; he had boarded larger vessels, ships to war, a narrow gangplank was not a problem, but confined spaces could not cope with his large frame so he had avoided *wherries* wherever he could. It was true, he dreaded falling in, one or two of his friends had fallen into the Thames, over time, and their clothes had buoyed them up for a few minutes before their boots, swords and cloaks had dragged them down into the currents and from there into the depths of the river, never to be seen again. They were never found again. Consequently, London Bridge was his favoured crossing.

Characteristically, Markham covered his fear by brash yet unfounded confidence. Settling himself into the cushioned seat next to Cecil, he stared out at the lanterns of other boats. The sight was breath-taking in the dark night, so many *wherries* lit up on the sides of the river, the reflection of their lanterns on the water made the water gold, the Thames looked like a black velvet cloak speckled with gold stars.

"You have been back for a few days, tell me, what is the news on the street, my dear Markham?" asked Cecil settling further back in his seat, wrapping his cloak more tightly around his body and breathing a cloud of condensation towards the oarsman who took up position.

They knew where they were going, Hampton. It was a trip that they had taken many times; it was not too cold on this particular occasion. The Company of Watermen rented the boat to Cecil. It was Cecil's own personal transport service.

The Company had been established in 1555 by Act of Parliament to regulate the Watermen plying their trade on the River Thames. Under this Act the Company introduced apprenticeships for those wishing to learn the skills of the Watermen, Markham would have benefitted from attending their instruction regarding moving around in a boat, Cecil ruefully decided.

Markham was feeling the cold but he pretended not to notice it, he would not give Cecil the satisfaction.

"The news is that Robert Catesby died at the Sherriff's raid on Holbeche House on 8th November," replied Markham.

"Catesby, rest in peace, 1572 to 1605, he used up his lease, loved dead and alive," Cecil declared solemnly and unconvincingly.

"You're always looking for rhymes to give the ballad singers. You give them the words to put to music. Perhaps you can make a rhyme of the fact that they say Thomas Percy and Catesby were both shot with a single bullet," suggested Markham scornfully, he did not like Cecil revelling in his friends' misfortune.

"I put that rumour about, but I thought that it might be pushing the cart too far to say they were shot in the gullet, but I could think of no other word to rhyme with bullet," admitted Cecil candidly.

"I wondered where they got their weapons from?" asked Markham archly.

"Any idea?" Cecil replied mischievously.

"None at all, my Lord Privy Seal, Secretary of State," replied Markham slowly and conspiratorially, "as I have no idea where they got the gun powder to blow up their own refuge."

"I agreed with Monteagle that we would spare them the ritual of public execution; better the Sherriff's bullet then long and painful torture, then hanging, which would be followed by being drawn and quartered. It was a trade, a quick death for his help."

"He escaped death after the Essex rebellion," Markham noted coldly, he wanted to survive himself.

"I swore he would eventually pay and he did," Cecil commented absently.

"Did he pay for favouring Essex over you, is that what it was?"

"He rebelled against the state," Cecil snapped. He would not have his reasons questioned by anyone.

"Driven by you?"

"I merely removed a preening extrovert whose own interests always superseded those of the Queen and her commonwealth. I grew up with Devereux; I saw how selfish and self-serving he was. You have no idea how vexed he made the Queen!"

"He was kind to me!" Markham protested.

"Look at his record, cantering around Cadiz, galloping off on expeditions where he was not wanted and, finally, sloping off with his tail between his legs, it was disgraceful the way he ran home from Ireland to find succour from the Queen."

"I admit he was a nuisance but no more than that, he was a decent man who loved the Queen," complained Markham bitterly.

"Spare me the false feelings; that is old news, we are interested in our future not in people past, I mourn the Queen but must live in the present, what else do they say?" Cecil demanded impatiently.

"They say the Sheriff's men arrived to ambush them well ahead of the hunted men."

"In that case there must have been some form of intelligence sent ahead, I suppose," Cecil cunningly concluded. It was he who had ordered the ambush.

"You sent word for the Sherriff's men to lie in wait for the fugitives, when did you manage to do that?"

"I sent word on 5th November; our messengers had my letter delivered by 6th."

"Impressive!" Markham sighed. "Timed to perfection, you had instructed them where to go, they walked into your trap on the 8th, you are truly a magician."

"Thank you."

"Pleasure."

"Monteagle and I had agreed that they should be ambushed by the sheriff's men who were ordered to shoot on sight in order to kill. We insisted on no survivors but even sheriff's men can have soft hearts when they have seen others fall. We had to bring back some wounded. The main thing was the chief ringleader perished. Their testimony could have finished my story prematurely. All's well that ends well."

"How did you get them to the house so quickly?" asked Markham beginning to feel uncomfortable, Cecil had a cool head and a cold heart.

"The secret is fresh horses along the route. I was surprised it took Catesby so long to reach the house, but I suppose they knew that I would be pursuing them; they must have hidden in various places along the way."

"You are testing the story on me," accused Markham.

"They might have travelled when light faded to avoid detection," continued Cecil, ignoring the remark. "Catesby and his men could hear the hounds bark, to avoid their pursuers they travelled in the dark', what do you think? It needs work but I think it has a ring to it."

"A definite echo of Shakespeare," Markham declared facetiously, he smiled when he said it to let Cecil know he was teasing.

"I fear you have adopted my humour," Cecil responded kindly, Cecil barely suppressed a smile. There was a slight upturn of his lips, which Markham only just caught before his master adopted his usual inscrutable look.

"I have become more Cecil than Cecil?" Markham protested, feigning being horrified.

"I fear so!" agreed Cecil affably.

"And what do you have in mind for me now, Lord Salisbury?" he asked, his voice quaking slightly.

"You have survived thanks to my intervention, history has implicated you in the Bye Plot and Main Plot, you should be dead; you owe your life to me. My reprieve delivered you from certain death."

"For which I have served you loyally and you promised to spare me and my family. So what is my role now the Catholics at court no longer threaten your supremacy? I will willing serve you, just tell me what you would have me do and I will gladly do it," Markham insisted, he really was worried.

"You must disappear," Cecil decided with finality, his eyes, which had met Markham's up to now, suddenly espied a distraction on the shore and looked away. Markham was left looking stunned.

"Sent to the Tower?" asked Markham aghast, his voice trembling.

"No, what reward would that be?"

"What then?"

"A time in the Low Countries with the English regiment," Cecil said.

"My property and my wife Anne?"

"Who would you like to benefit from your lands?"

"I trust my cousin Sir John," said Markham bravely.

"Leave your lands to Sir John Harrington by all means," Cecil allowed kindly, "bid your wife follow you or bid her farewell, whatever suits, but I need a reliable man to keep an eye on the situation and in particular Sir Edmund Baynham."

"That rogue, the last time I heard of him, he was one of the *Cursed Crew,* he took on the *night-watch*," Markham spat derisively.

He dreaded serving with such an oaf, he was a bully and a brigand to say the least.

"You are correct, he was part of the *Cursed* or *Damned Crew* who left the Mermaid tavern at midnight and set off apparently looking for trouble on 8th March, 1600. They 'cast off their cloaks and upper garments, drew rapiers and daggers, marched through the streets' and when challenged by the watch they attacked. After a scuffle they were overpowered, disarmed and marched to the Counter prison."

"I remember it was reported that Baynham was heard shouting that he 'cared not a fart for the lord mayor or any magistrate in London'," Markham remarked.

"Instead of being tried by the ordinary London authorities however they were remitted to Star Chamber on the personal intervention of the Queen, 'for the more exemplar punishment of so great and outrageous disorder'," Cecil added.

"Having at first denied the charges they changed their plea to guilty, confessed their faults and submitted themselves to the court, and proved that all was done in drink and heat. They were fined £200 and imprisoned."

It was a terrible punishment being sent to serve Baynham but he knew that under the circumstances his fate could have been even worse than that. The consequences were dire not deadly. He would prefer banishment to death. He had faced the prospect from the executioner's hands.

"Straight from the *Mermaid Tavern* to *Star Chamber,* only because your friend Essex knighted him on the sands in Ireland. Yet, he was imprisoned and fined for his behaviour but all was forgiven. A shame really, he might have made a good lawyer if he had not left *the Middle Temple*, a waste," Cecil reflected dreamily.

"Life might have been different for us it is true; he was not the only member of the *Cursed Crew*," quipped Markham.

"We few, we cursed crew, we band of brothers," replied Cecil, smiling.

"I will miss your buffoonery," sighed Markham.

"I will miss your handsome face and protection, but needs must..."

"The devil drives."

"Precisely, you have learnt well," allowed Cecil, an unusual event for Cecil to praise Markham's intelligence, he looked upon him as a competent swordsman with more brawn than brain.

"I have learnt from the *maestro*." Cecil smiled at that. Markham had been a good pupil and at last he was learning.

"You'll dine at Hampton with some friends of mine tonight, then in the morning you will leave from thence and you will be escorted onto a ship bound for the Low Countries. Sir Edmund will be expecting you. He's a fellow *'Papist'*, a *'Lord of the Realm'* and *'a good soldier',* so you both have more than one thing in common."

"I should thank you for my life."

"You are far too kind," Cecil breathed dramatically, leaving Markham puzzled as to whether he was being genuine or ironic in his remarks. The phrase had not sounded sarcastic and yet he was not sure.

Afterword

Cecil was a consummate plotter who undermined enemies and helped his supporters, he himself wrote:

"I spend my time in sowing so much seed as my poor wretched fingers can scatter, in such a season as may bring forth a plentiful harvest. I dare boldly say no shower or storm shall mar our harvest except it should come from beyond the middle region."

This was written just a fortnight before the discovery of poor Guy Fawkes. What does it mean? It is ambiguous, which is probably what Cecil wanted. I think it is a coded message proclaiming that nothing could stop his plot from succeeding except if those in his service, in the Midlands bungled their part; that is failed to kill all the Catholics hiding in the house.

This must surely be the assassination of all those Catholic nobles who fled London. If they were dead, they could not protest their innocence. The sheriff's men from the 'middle region' did not 'mar' his plan. They ambushed and destroyed anyone who might have told the truth. Might those 'plotters' have set the record straight if they had been allowed to survive?

Another curious incident was that Thomas Bates, Robert Catesby's servant, while on his deathbed, claimed that Catesby had visited Cecil three times in the months leading up to November 5th 1605. To be fair, there is no recorded evidence yet found that Cecil and Catesby ever met. Equally, there is no evidence that they did not. Perhaps we will never know the whole truth of the plot.

Other Books

We hope you have enjoyed the story of Robert Cecil and the Gunpowder, Treason and Plot. You might like to consider the following books by the same author:

Switch, a dark thriller, Chandler meets 'Fifty Shades of Grey'; a nightmare comes true!

Waterwitch, a sailing adventure: two brothers sailing a boat around the Mediterranean during the Falklands War, resulting in disastrous consequences.

Major Bruton's Safari or Uganda Palaver, a witty account of a coronation and safari in Uganda. As a guest of the Ugandan people, a group of disparate people experience Africa with a caustic commentator, critical of his own friends and family.

Innocent Proven Guilty, a thriller on the lines of 39 Steps. A teacher discovers his brother dead in a pool of blood, he wants to find the murderer but he has left his footprints behind.

Seveny Seven, 'Punk Portrait' The story of growing up in London during the punk era, a whimsical autobiography that explodes the myth that 'Punk' was an angry working class movement.

Carom, this is a thriller about an art theft and drug smuggling. Finn McHugh, and his team pursue Didier Pourchaire, a vicious art thief. The action moves between London, Paris, Helsinki and St. Petersburg. Everyone wants to catch the villain resulting in a messy bagatelle. Carom is an Indian board game.

Ad Bec is a dish best eaten cold; a schoolboy takes revenge on a bully. The story is set in a seventies progressive preparatory school. Stephen is a late arrival at a prep school in the depths of Shropshire. He is challenged to do a 'tunnel dare' by the school bully. When the tunnel collapses on the bully, Stephen has to solve the dilemma, tell no one and be free or rescue the bully.

Karoly's Hungarian Tragedy is Michael's first departure into historical biography. This is the story of Karoly Ellenbacher taken into captivity and used as a human shield by Romanian soldiers during the war, arrested during the communist era and sent down a coal mine, he escaped to England in 1956. His story of survival is barely credible.

Michael Fitzalan has written four plays:

Veni, Vidi, Vicky, - a story of a failed love affair.

George and the Dragon, a painter discovers a cache of bonds and sovereigns in a cellar, not knowing that it belongs to a vicious gang. Thankfully his niece's friend is a star lawyer and can help him return the money before it is too late, or can she?

Symposium for Severine is a modern version of Plato's Symposium but with women being the philosophers instead of men.

Superstar is play that sees Thomas Dowting meeting Jesus in the Temple, travelling to Angel to meet his girlfriend Gabrielle. They convince Thomas to volunteer for work abroad. Three weeks later J C Goodman takes over Thomas's job and moves in with Gabrielle.

Switch and Major Bruton's Safari have been turned into scripts.

Michael is working on a script, which he may turn into a novel; *M.O.D, Mark O'Dwyer, Master of Disguise*, a private detective agency, Francis Barber Investigators, is retained to find out why a model was defenestrated from a Bond Street building.